When should I travel to get the best airfare?
Where do I go for answers to my travel questions?
What's the best and easiest way to plan and book my trip?

frommers.travelocity.com

Frommer's, the travel guide leader, has teamed up with **Travelocity.com**, the leader in online travel, to bring you an in-depth, easy-to-use resource designed to help you plan and book your trip online.

At **frommers.travelocity.com**, you'll find free online updates about your destination from the experts at Frommer's plus the outstanding travel planning and purchasing features of Travelocity.com. Travelocity.com provides reservations capabilities for 95 percent of all airline seats sold, more than 47,000 hotels, and over 50 car rental companies. In addition, Travelocity.com offers more than 2,000 exciting vacation and cruise packages. Travelocity.com puts you in complete control of your travel planning with these and other great features:

Expert travel guidance from Frommer's - over 150 writers reporting from around the world!

Best Fare Finder - an interactive calendar tells you when to travel to get the best airfare

Fare Watcher - we'll track airfare changes to your favorite destinations

Dream Maps - a mapping feature that suggests travel opportunities based on your budget

Shop Safe Guarantee - 24 hours a day / 7 days a week live customer service, and more!

Whether traveling on a tight budget, looking for a quick weekend getaway, or planning the trip of a lifetime, Frommer's guides and Travelocity.com will make your travel dreams a reality. You've bought the book, now book the trip!

Travelocity.com
A Sabre Company

Frommer's®

Other Great Guides for Your Trip:

Frommer's Colorado

Frommer's National Parks of the American West

Frommer's Rocky Mountain National Park

Frommer's Arizona

Frommer's New Mexico

Frommer's Utah

Here's what the critics say about Frommer's:

"Amazingly easy to use. Very portable, very complete."
—*Booklist*

♦

"The only mainstream guide to list specific prices. The Walter Cronkite of guidebooks—with all that implies."
—*Travel & Leisure*

♦

"Complete, concise, and filled with useful information."
—*New York Daily News*

♦

"Hotel information is close to encyclopedic."
—*Des Moines Sunday Register*

Denver, Boulder & Colorado Springs

6th Edition

by Don & Barbara Laine
and Eric Peterson

IDG Books Worldwide, Inc.
An International Data Group Company
Foster City, CA • Chicago, IL • Indianapolis, IN • New York, NY

ABOUT THE AUTHORS

Residents of northern New Mexico since 1970, **Don and Barbara Laine** have traveled extensively throughout the Rocky Mountains and the Southwest, spending as much time as possible in the outdoors, and especially in the region's national parks and monuments. In addition to this book they have authored or contributed to a number of other travel guides, including *Frommer's Colorado, Frommer's Utah, Frommer's Rocky Mountain National Park, Frommer's Zion & Bryce Canyon National Parks,* and *Frommer's National Parks of the American West.*

Eric Peterson is a Denver-based freelance writer who has contributed to numerous travel publications, including *Frommer's National Parks of the American West.* He also writes for several Colorado-based business and entertainment periodicals, makes a mean chicken chili, and takes as many weekend treks into the Rockies as possible.

IDG BOOKS WORLDWIDE, INC.

An International Data Group Company
909 Third Avenue
New York, NY 10022

Find us online at **www.frommers.com**

ISBN 0-7645-6209-6
ISSN 1042-8763

Editor: Christine Ryan
Production Editor: M. Faunette Johnston
Photo Editor: Richard Fox
Design by Michele Laseau
Cartographer: Roberta Stockwell
Production by IDG Books Indianapolis Production Department

SPECIAL SALES

For general information on IDG Books Worldwide's books in the U.S., please call our Consumer Customer Service department at 1-800-762-2974. For reseller information, including discounts, bulk sales, customized editions, and premium sales, please call our Reseller Customer Service department at 1-800-434-3422.

Manufactured in the United States of America

5 4 3 2 1

Contents

v

List of Maps

Acknowledgments

The authors wish to thank for their help Rich Grant and Jill Strunk with the Denver Metro Convention & Visitors Bureau, Melissa Schiff with the Boulder Convention and Visitors Bureau, Elizabeth Youngquist with the Colorado Springs Convention & Visitors Bureau, Suzy Blackhurst at Market Reach in Estes Park, and Dick Putney at Rocky Mountain National Park.

An Invitation to the Reader

In researching this book, we discovered many wonderful places—hotels, restaurants, shops, and more. We're sure you'll find others. Please tell us about them, so we can share the information with your fellow travelers in upcoming editions. If you were disappointed with a recommendation, we'd love to know that, too. Please write to:

Frommer's Denver, Boulder & Colorado Springs, 6th Edition
IDG Books Worldwide, Inc.
909 Third Avenue
New York, NY 10022

An Additional Note

Please be advised that travel information is subject to change at any time—and this is especially true of prices. We therefore suggest that you write or call ahead for confirmation when making your travel plans. The authors, editors, and publisher cannot be held responsible for the experiences of readers while traveling. Your safety is important to us, however, so we encourage you to stay alert and be aware of your surroundings. Keep a close eye on cameras, purses, and wallets, all favorite targets of thieves and pickpockets.

What the Symbols Mean

✪Frommer's Favorites

Our favorite places and experiences—outstanding for quality, value, or both.

The following abbreviations are used for credit cards:

AE	American Express	EC	Eurocard
CB	Carte Blanche	JCB	Japan Credit Bank
DC	Diners Club	MC	MasterCard
DISC	Discover	V	Visa
ER	EnRoute		

Find Frommer's Online

www.frommers.com offers up-to-the-minute listings on almost 200 cities around the globe—including the latest bargains and candid, personal articles updated daily by Arthur Frommer himself. No other Web site offers such comprehensive and timely coverage of the world of travel.

The Best of Denver, Boulder & Colorado Springs

The old and the new, rustic and sophisticated, urban and rural—you'll find all these elements practically side by side in and immediately adjacent to the cities of Denver, Boulder, and Colorado Springs.

Founded in the mid–19th century by both East Coast gold-seekers and European and Asian immigrants in search of a better life, these cities on the Front Range of the majestic Rocky Mountains weren't as wild as Colorado's mountain towns such as Telluride and Creede, but they did have their day. According to historian Thomas Noel, in 1890 Denver had more saloons per capita than Kansas City, St. Louis, New Orleans, or Philadelphia. But these Colorado cities soon became home to a more sophisticated westerner—the mine owner instead of the prospector, the business owner rather than the gambler.

Today, these thoroughly modern cities have virtually all the amenities you'd expect to find in New York or Los Angeles: opera, theater, modern dance, art, excellent restaurants, and sophisticated hotels and convention centers. You'll also find historic Victorian mansions, working steam trains, and old gold mines. You can go horseback riding, hiking, skiing, or shopping; do the Texas two-step to a live country band; or spend hours browsing through a huge four-story bookstore, a gigantic model-train shop, or the world's largest hardware store. You might also join the locals at what many of them enjoy most—being outdoors under the warm Colorado sun—so don't forget your hiking boots, mountain bike, skis, sunscreen, and sunglasses.

Although Denver is certainly a city, bustling and growing, it's still comfortable and relatively easy to explore. Boulder and Colorado Springs call themselves cities, but we like to think of them more as big western towns, where the buildings aren't very tall and there's lots of open space. In all three, the residents are friendly, relaxed, and casual.

In this book, we'll be putting Denver, Boulder, and Colorado Springs under a magnifying glass, but that's not all. We'll also be taking a look at some of the nearby attractions where the locals spend their weekends, including the state's premier natural wonder: Rocky Mountain National Park.

1 Frommer's Favorite Denver, Boulder & Colorado Springs Experiences

- **United States Mint (Denver):** This is where all that money comes from—at least the coins. If you've ever wondered just how those heavy chunks of metal actually become legal tender, this is your opportunity to find out as you watch the stamping of some of the five billion coins produced here each year. But let's be honest—the real reason to visit the mint is simply to be surrounded by all that cold, hard cash. See chapter 5.

- **Molly Brown House Museum (Denver):** Restored to its 1910 appearance, this handsome home was built in 1889 of Colorado lava stone with sandstone trim, and from 1894 to 1932 it was the residence of James and Margaret (Molly) Brown. The "unsinkable" Molly Brown became a national heroine in 1912 when the Titanic sank and she took charge of a group of immigrant women in a lifeboat and later raised money for their benefit. See chapter 5.

- **Butterfly Pavilion & Insect Center (Denver):** A walk through this butterfly conservatory is an excursion into a world of grace and beauty. The constant mist creates a hazy habitat to support the lush green plants that are both food and home to the colorful butterflies that inhabit this oasis. A separate insect room includes exotic insects from around the world, and has a "touch cart" that allows you to get up close to a cockroach or tarantula—that is, if this is something you really want to do. See chapter 5.

---

❷   Did You Know?

- Denver has more days of sunshine each year than San Diego or Miami Beach.
- More beer is brewed in metropolitan Denver than in any other city in the United States.
- According to a federal study, Denver has the highest proportion of thin people of any city in the country.
- The patriotic song "America the Beautiful" was written by teacher Katharine Lee Bates (1859–1929) after an 1895 wagon trip to the top of Pikes Peak, near Colorado Springs.
- At an elevation of 6,035 feet, Colorado Springs has two-thirds the amount of oxygen found at sea level; and Pikes Peak, at 14,110 feet, has only one-half the oxygen.
- In 1984, art students at Cheyenne Mountain High School in Colorado Springs staged the world's highest art exhibit by hauling their various creations to the top of Pikes Peak.
- When millionaire Cripple Creek miner Scott Stratton, a bachelor, died in the early 1900s, 13 women claimed to be his widow.
- Talented folk singer Judy Collins, who achieved fame in the 1960s and continues to perform today, studied music in Denver.
- The world's highest automobile tunnel, the Eisenhower Tunnel, crosses the Continental Divide 65 miles west of Denver, at an elevation of 11,000 feet.
- The key collection at the Baldpate Inn near Rocky Mountain National Park could unlock Hitler's desk, Mozart's wine cellar, Fort Knox, and Westminster Abbey.
- Of all the land in the continental United States above 10,000 feet in elevation, 75% of it is in Colorado.
- The National Trust for Historic Preservation in 2000 named Boulder as one of the nation's top cities for preserving historic sites, managing growth, and maintaining a vibrant downtown.

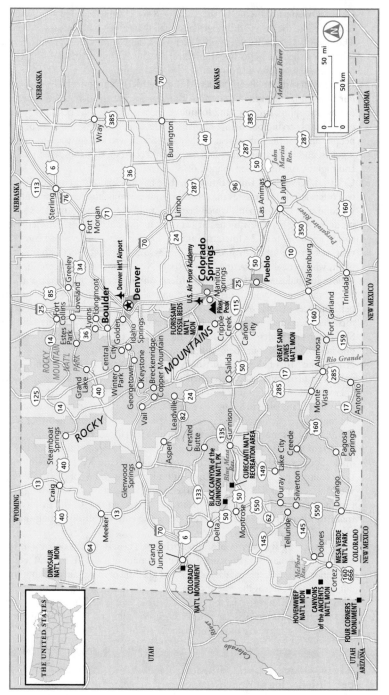

- **Country-western dancing at the Grizzly Rose (Denver):** Known to locals as "the Griz" or "the Rose," this huge dance hall draws such national acts as George Thorogood, Garth Brooks, Willie Nelson, Leann Rimes, Tanya Tucker, and Johnny Paycheck. There's live music every night of the week, Sunday is family night, and dance lessons are available. See chapter 5.
- **People-watching on Pearl Street Mall (Boulder):** This four-block-long tree-lined pedestrian mall marks at once Boulder's downtown core and its center for dining, shopping, strolling, and loafing in the sun. It's also the best spot in Colorado for observing our fellow humans. Here you'll see students, local business people, and a variety of tourists as they sit back to watch the musicians, mimes, jugglers, and other street entertainers that hold court on the landscaped mall day and night, year-round. See chapter 6.
- **Celestial Seasonings Tour (Boulder):** The nation's leading producer of herbal teas offers a tour that excites the senses as it takes you behind the scenes into the world of tea. The company, which began in a Boulder garage in the 1970s, now produces more than 50 varieties of tea from more than 100 different herbs and spices, imported from 35 foreign countries. Guided tours move from a consumer taste test in the lobby to marketing displays, and finally into the production plant, where the overpowering "Mint Room" is a highlight. See chapter 6.
- **Colorado Shakespeare Festival (Boulder):** Among the top Shakespearean festivals in the United States, this 2-month annual event offers more than a dozen performances of each of four Shakespearean plays each summer. Actors, directors, designers, and everyone associated with the productions are fully schooled Shakespearean professionals. During the festival, company members conduct one-hour backstage tours before each show. See chapter 6.
- **Hiking the Mills Lake Trail in Rocky Mountain National Park:** Although it's packed at first, this moderately rated trail usually becomes much less crowded after you've logged a few miles. At trail's end (elevation 10,000 feet), there's a gorgeous mountain lake ringed by towering peaks. This lake is an excellent spot for photographing dramatic Longs Peak, especially in late afternoon or early evening, and it's the perfect place for a picnic. See chapter 6.
- **Garden of the Gods:** There's nothing like sunrise at Garden of the Gods in Colorado Springs, with its fantastic and sometimes fanciful red-sandstone formations sculpted by wind and water over hundreds of thousands of years. Although you can see a great deal from the marked view points, it's worth spending some time and foot-power to get away from the crowds on one of the park's many trails, to listen to the wind, and to imagine the gods cavorting among the formations. See chapter 7.
- **Pikes Peak Cog Railway (Colorado Springs):** There is perhaps no view in Colorado to equal the 360° panorama from the summit of Pikes Peak, and for those who enjoy rail travel, spectacular scenery, and the thrill of mountain climbing without all the work, this is the trip to take. The 9-mile route, with grades up to 25%, takes 75 minutes to reach the top of 14,110-foot Pikes Peak. The journey is exciting from the start, but passengers really begin to "ooh" and "aah" when the track leaves the forest, creeping above timberline at about 11,500 feet. See chapter 7.

2 Best Hotel Bets

- **Best Historic Hotels:** From its spacious, well-appointed lobby to the richly polished wood of its elegant Victorian and almost whimsical art-deco rooms, the **Brown Palace Hotel,** 321 17th St., Denver (☎ **303/297-3111**), has an air of sophistication, refinement, and class. The Brown has operated continuously since it opened in August 1892.

A handsome downtown hotel, the **Hotel Boulderado,** 2115 13th St., Boulder (☎ **303/442-4344**), has been skillfully renovated and restored, while retaining its original Otis elevator, lovely leaded-glass ceiling, and spectacular cherry-wood staircase, which caused quite a stir when the hotel opened in 1909.

Designed by New York City architects in the Italian Renaissance style, **The Broadmoor,** Lake Circle, at Lake Avenue, Colorado Springs (☎ **719/ 634-7711**), opened in 1918. Colorado's most elegant and best-preserved hotel of the era, it's filled with objets d'art from around the world, including Oriental art from the Ming and Tsin dynasties and a huge carved wooden bar from an 1800s British pub.

- **Best for Business Travelers:** All rooms at **Loews Giorgio Hotel,** 4150 E. Mississippi Ave., Denver (☎ **303/782-9300**), are spacious and provide at least three phones. Furthermore, two floors are designed for business travelers: All rooms are equipped with phones with modem hookups and in-room fax, and receive complimentary newspapers.

- **Best for a Romantic Getaway:** Housed in a magnificent and historic stone mansion, the **Castle Marne Bed and Breakfast,** 1572 Race St., Denver (☎ **303/ 331-0621**), is furnished with antiques and reproductions. Three suites feature whirlpool tubs for two, and three rooms offer private balconies equipped with delightful outdoor hot tubs for two.

  The Alps, 38619 Boulder Canyon Dr., Boulder (☎ **303/444-5445**), is nestled among trees on a hillside outside town; you won't find a TV in your room here, but you will have a cozy fireplace, and there might be a whirlpool tub for two or a private porch.

  The **Two Sisters Inn,** 10 Otoe Place, Manitou Springs (☎ **719/685-9684**), offers a cozy honeymoon cottage where you'll find fresh flowers, a big feather bed, a gas log fireplace, and lots of privacy. What more could you ask for?

- **Best Hotel Lobby for Pretending You're Rich:** The lobby of the **Brown Palace Hotel** (Denver, see address and telephone, above) features walls of Mexican onyx and a floor of white marble. The elaborate cast-iron grillwork surrounding the six tiers of balconies draws your eye to the stained-glass ceiling high above. Luncheon and afternoon tea are served in the lobby nearly every day.

  Considering that the first guests at **The Broadmoor** (Colorado Springs, see address and telephone, above) when it opened in 1918 were millionaire John D. Rockefeller Jr. and his party, it would be easy to imagine yourself here mingling among the wealthy, reading the financial news, and sipping a cognac by the hotel's elegant marble staircase, surrounded by priceless 17th-century art.

- **Best Moderately Priced Hotels:** As a member of a well-respected hotel chain, the **Hampton Inn,** 4685 Quebec St., Denver (☎ **800/HAMPTON** or 303/ 388-8100), offers reliably clean and comfortable rooms at a reasonable price.

  At **Days Inn Boulder,** 5397 S. Boulder Rd. (☎ **800/325-2525** or 303/ 499-4422), everything is tops except the prices, which are surprisingly affordable for the quality. You can enjoy the best of two worlds at the **Hearthstone Inn,** 506 N. Cascade Ave., Colorado Springs (☎ **719/473-4413**): the intimacy and personal attention of a bed-and-breakfast plus the privacy and services of a small hotel, all at a very affordable rate.

- **Best Inexpensive Motel:** For those who appreciate small mom-and-pop establishments, the **Cameron Motel,** 4500 E. Evans Ave., Denver (☎ **303/757- 2100**), offers a clean, quiet alternative to budget chains.

- **Best Service:** Dedicated to providing guests with the best possible service, the **Brown Palace Hotel** (Denver, see address and telephone, above) succeeds extremely well, yet without pretension. Among other things, it offers 24-hour room service, concierge, and in-room massage.

  Taking good care of its guests is a point of pride for **The Broadmoor** (Colorado Springs, see address and telephone, above): It offers 24-hour room service, full concierge, in-room massage, valet laundry, shuttle bus between buildings, and a multitude of recreational activities, as well as almost anything else you might ask for.

- **Best Bed-and-Breakfast:** A lovely garden surrounds the **Briar Rose,** 2151 Arapahoe Ave. (☎ **303/442-3007**), a brick home in downtown Boulder. It's furnished with antiques and gracefully enhanced with fresh flowers; coffee and tea are always available here.

  At **Holden House 1902 Bed & Breakfast Inn,** 1102 W. Pikes Peak Ave., Colorado Springs (☎ **888/565-3980** or 719/471-3980) no two rooms are alike, but all are delightfully and individually decorated with antiques and family heirlooms. This B&B also prides itself on personal service.

- **Best Views:** Although the **Regal Harvest House,** 1345 28th St., Boulder (☎ **303/443-3850**), is on a main thoroughfare, the rooms at the back look out over a lovely park that leads to the Boulder Creek Path, beyond which are the magnificent Rockies.

- **Best for Families:** Two swimming pools, shuffleboard, and a separate kids' play area at the **Sheraton Colorado Springs Hotel,** 2886 S. Circle Dr., Colorado Springs (☎ **719/576-5900**), should help keep the kids busy while the parents enjoy the putting green and billiards room.

- **Best Location:** Right next door to the U.S. Air Force Academy, Colorado Springs' most popular attraction, the **Radisson Inn North,** 8110 N. Academy Blvd. (☎ **800/333-3333** or 719/598-5770), is also close to a major shopping mall.

3 Best Dining Bets

- **Best Spots for a Romantic Dinner: Little Russian Cafe,** 1424H Larimer St., Denver (☎ **303/595-8600**), a quiet, charming cafe with old-world atmosphere and dim lighting, is perfect for an intimate dinner, with or without the chilled vodka.

  John's Restaurant, 2328 Pearl St., Boulder (☎ **303/444-5232**), is a small, charming chef-owned restaurant with a simple elegance that soothes and never intrudes.

  The place where locals celebrate anniversaries and other special events, **La Petite Maison,** 1015 W. Colorado Ave., Colorado Springs (☎ **719/632-4887**), is cozy, intimate, and casually elegant, with soothing chamber music played in the background.

- **Best Spots for a Celebration:** Denver's most elegant restaurant is the **Palace Arms,** in the Brown Palace Hotel, 321 17th St. (☎ **303/297-3111**)—it also serves some of the most elegant food. Try a regional dish, such as roasted rack of Colorado lamb or seared breast of pheasant, or go for one of the more innovative dishes, like fresh lobster enchilada or Scottish smoked salmon.

  When they're not celebrating at La Petite Maison (see above), Colorado Springs locals splurge on a night out at **The Tavern,** located in The Broadmoor, Lake Circle (☎ **719/634-7711**), with splendid service and some of the best food in town.

- **Best Decor:** Occupying the same premises as when it opened in 1893, the **Buck-horn Exchange,** 1000 Osage St., Denver (☎ 303/534-9505), still has the magnificent 138-year-old hand-carved oak bar in the upstairs Victorian parlor and saloon. The downstairs features an amazing collection of taxidermy, a menagerie that includes everything from leopard to buffalo.

  A fun place to dine, **Antica Roma,** 1308 Pearl St., Boulder (☎ 303/442-0378), is a slice of a Roman piazza, with a central fountain, brick walls, and balconies boasting flowers and the occasional drying laundry.

  In the shadow of Pikes Peak in the majestic Rocky Mountains, **Briarhurst Manor,** 404 Manitou Ave., Manitou Springs (☎ 719/685-1864), is a magnificent 1876 stone Tudor mansion, complete with a rich wood interior and Gothic oak staircase.

- **Best Values:** You'll find much more than rabbit food here! **Healthy Habits,** 865 S. Colorado Blvd. (☎ 303/733-2105), is a cafeteria-style restaurant with a 70-item salad bar plus a pasta bar with fresh sauces and pizza; the all-you-can-eat price includes fresh-baked desserts.

  You'll get fine food at reasonable prices in a casual atmosphere at the **Corner Bar** in the Hotel Boulderado, 2115 13th St., Boulder (☎ 303/442-4560).

  It's amazing to find a restaurant that prepares so many different dishes well—candy, ice cream, Southwestern, Greek, basic American—and for such low prices. Perhaps that's why Colorado Springs residents have been coming to **Michelle's,** 122 N. Tejon St. (☎ 719/633-5089), since it opened in 1952.

- **Best for Kids:** More a theme park than a restaurant, **Casa Bonita,** in the JCRS Shopping Center, 6715 W. Colfax Ave., Lakewood (☎ 303/232-5115), has practically nonstop action, with divers plummeting into a pool beside a 30-foot waterfall, puppet shows, a video arcade, and fun house. Yes, there's food, too: tacos and other standard Mexican fare, country-fried steak, and fried chicken, served cafeteria style.

  There's something about trains that brings out the kid in all of us, and at **Giuseppe's Old Depot Restaurant,** 10 S. Sierra Madre St., Colorado Springs (☎ 719/635-3111), you've got one parked outside the door and plenty more rolling by just outside the large windows.

- **Best Burgers & Beer:** A full one-third pound of good ground beef is the foundation of a great burger at **Tom's Tavern,** 1047 Pearl St., Boulder (☎ 303/443-3893); choose from a variety of beers to wash it all down.

  It's a great combination: fresh ground beef, molded into huge half-pound hamburgers, charbroiled just the way you want them, and served with an assertive hand-crafted ale. This is what awaits you at **Judge Baldwin's Brewing Co.,** in the Antlers Adam's Mark Hotel, 4 S. Cascade Ave., Colorado Springs (☎ 719/473-5600).

- **Best People Watching:** With outdoor seating on the 16th Street Mall in downtown Denver, **Marlowe's,** 511 16th St. (☎ 303/595-3700), is the place to sit and watch the world stroll by.

  Sitting inside or outside, you'll get a great view of the Pearl Street Mall at **14th Street Bar & Grill,** 1400 Pearl St., Boulder (☎ 303/444-5854). You'll see all kinds of people passing by—students and families, the old and the young, and even street entertainers from musicians to mimes.

- **Best Pre-theater Dinner:** The Denver in-crowd heads to **Strings,** 1700 Humboldt St. (☎ 303/831-7310), before going out on the town, both for the fresh seafood and pastas, and to make sure they rub elbows with all the right people.

- **Best View:** Perched on the side of a mountain above Boulder, with a wall of windows framing the city below and plains beyond, **Flagstaff House Restaurant,** 1138 Flagstaff Rd. (☎ **303/442-4640**), offers extraordinary views, especially as the sun sets or the city gradually disappears in a swirling snowstorm.

  Large picture windows at **Charles Court,** in The Broadmoor, Lake Circle, Colorado Springs (☎ **719/634-7711**), afford diners a splendid vista out over The Broadmoor's personal lake. Shouldn't everyone have one?

- **Best Wine List:** With more than 2,000 choices, **Flagstaff House Restaurant** (Boulder, see address and telephone, above) boasts an award-winning wine cellar.

- **Best Desserts:** Homemade desserts at **John's Restaurant** (Boulder, see address and telephone, above) include two house specialties: Chocolate Intensity and strongly flavored Italian ice cream.

  With all the fine restaurants that seem to specialize in desserts, the **Craftwood Inn,** 404 El Paso Blvd., Colorado Springs (☎ **719/685-9000**) stands out, particularly for the way it combines raspberries and chocolate.

- **Best Fast Food:** At **Illegal Pete's,** 1447 Pearl St., Boulder (☎ **303/440-3955**), you'll get a choice of unique burritos that are both mouthwatering and massive, as well as salads, chile fish, chicken, and vegetarian tacos.

- **Best Natural Foods:** Fresh and healthy are the key words at **Adam's Mountain Cafe,** 110 Cañon Ave., Manitou Springs (☎ **719/685-1430**), which serves interesting dishes that have a decidedly Mediterranean style.

- **Best Chinese Cuisine:** Ask any Denver resident: **The Imperial Chinese Restaurant,** 431 S. Broadway (☎ **303/698-2800**), is the place to go for Chinese food. Choose from classic and innovative Szechuan, Hunan, Mandarin, and Cantonese dishes. Items such as Nanking pork loin, seafood bird's nest, and sesame chicken are the specials of the house.

- **Best Italian Cuisine:** The Roman piazza–like atmosphere in **Bravo! Ristorante,** in the Adam's Mark, 1550 Court Place, Denver (☎ **303/626-2581,** or ext. 3164 from within the hotel), is a fitting setting for the fine cuisine. Flavorful yet light sauces complement the al dente pasta, producing such taste treats as lasagna with fennel sausage, eggplant, and sweet peppers; and fettuccine with diced tomatoes, roasted garlic, and red chiles.

  At **Antica Roma** (Boulder, see address and telephone, above), you can enjoy real homemade pasta with authentic sauces such as marinara and pesto, fresh crusty Italian bread, and an excellent selection of Italian wines.

- **Best Seafood:** The atmosphere at **McCormick's Fish House & Bar,** in the Oxford Hotel, 1659 Wazee St., Denver (☎ **303/825-1107**), may be 100 years old, but the seafood is flown in fresh daily. Choices often include salmon from Alaska, mussels from Maine and Florida, and fresh yellowfin tuna from Hawaii.

- **Best Vietnamese Cuisine:** Denver's first Vietnamese restaurant, **T-Wa Inn,** 555 S. Federal Blvd. (☎ **303/922-4584**), is also its best; here you can get shrimp and crabmeat wrapped in rice paper, hearty meat-and-noodle soups, and other choice offerings.

- **Best American Cuisine:** The specifics change daily at **Flagstaff House Restaurant** (Boulder, see address and telephone, above), but Rocky Mountain game highlights many of the dishes, each individually and creatively prepared with the freshest ingredients.

  It certainly isn't cheap, but the creative and exquisitely prepared American cuisine served at **Charles Court** (Colorado Springs, see address and telephone, above) can't be beat.

- **Best Continental Cuisine:** Roast Rack of Lamb Chilindron (a contemporary version of a spicy Spanish dish) and a Basque concoction of salmon, mussels, shrimp, scallops, and Chilean sea bass are just two examples of the fine dishes created by chef John Bizzarro at **John's Restaurant** (Boulder, see address and telephone, above).
- **Best Mexican Cuisine:** In addition to enjoying delicious standard Mexican fare such as burritos, enchiladas, tamales, and tostadas at **La Estrellita,** 2037 13th St., Boulder (☎ **303/939-8822**), you can order unusual variations such as stuffed sopaipillas and Mexican-style ribs.
- **Best Regional Cuisine:** For carefully prepared Colorado game and other western cuisine (such as venison, pheasant, and trout), come to **Craftwood Inn** (Colorado Springs, see address and telephone, above).

2

Planning a Trip to Denver, Boulder & Colorado Springs

It's important to spend some time preparing for any trip, including one to Colorado's major cities. This chapter offers a variety of planning tools—information on when to go, how to get there, how to get around, and other tips.

1 Visitor Information & Money

VISITOR INFORMATION

Start by contacting **Colorado Travel and Tourism Authority,** 1127 Pennsylvania St., Denver, CO 80203 (☎ **800/COLORADO** or 303/ 832-6171), for a free copy of the official state vacation guide, which includes a state map and describes attractions, activities, and lodgings throughout Colorado. On the Internet, information is available at **www.Colorado.com.** Another good Internet source for Colorado information is the Web site of the *Denver Post,* the state's major daily newspaper, at **www.denverpost.com.**

The **Colorado Hotel and Lodging Association,** 999 18th St., Suite 1240, Denver, CO 80202 (☎ **303/297-8335;** www.coloradolodging. com), offers a free guide to lodging across the state. The **Colorado Reservation Service** (☎ **800/777-6880**) will make reservations for lodging statewide, air and ground transportation, and ski and golf packages. The nonprofit **Bed and Breakfast Innkeepers of Colorado** has prepared a directory describing the group's more than 170 member B&Bs across the state, including a number of historic inns in Denver, Boulder, and Colorado Springs. Directories can be obtained from the association at P.O. Box 38416, Colorado Springs, CO 80937-8416 (☎ **800/265-7696;** www.innsofcolorado.org). Another source of information for those seeking unique lodging is **Historic Hotels of the Rockies** (☎ **303/546-9040;** www.historic-hotels.com). The association's free brochure describes more than a dozen historic hotels in Colorado and other Rocky Mountain states.

Hostelling International–American Youth Hostels, 733 15th St. NW, Washington, DC 20005 (☎ **202/783-6161;** www.hiayh.org), has a computerized system for making reservations in hostels worldwide. The organization also publishes a directory of all U.S. hostels, free to members and $3 for nonmembers. In Colorado, you can contact **Hostelling International–American Youth Hostels Rocky Mountain Council** at P.O. Box 2370, Boulder, CO 80306 (☎ **303/ 442-1166;** www.hostelweb.com).

A free copy of *Colorado State Parks,* which contains details on the state's 40 parks, is available from state park offices at 1313 Sherman St., Suite 618, Denver, CO 80203 (☎ 303/866-3437; www.coloradoparks.org). State park offices can also provide information on boating and snowmobiling.

MONEY

Generally, Colorado is not particularly expensive, especially compared to destinations on the East and West coasts. In Denver, Boulder, and Colorado Springs, you'll find a wide range of prices for lodging and dining; admission to most attractions is less than $10 (it's sometimes free, especially in Boulder). Those traveling away from the major cities will discover prices in small towns usually quite reasonable, but ski resorts such as Vail and Aspen can be rather pricey, especially during winter holidays. Traveler's checks and credit cards are accepted at almost all hotels, restaurants, shops, and attractions, plus many grocery stores; and automated-teller machines for all the major national networks are practically everywhere.

2 When to Go

Colorado has essentially two tourist seasons: warm and cold. Those who want to see the state's parks and other scenic wonders, hike, mountain bike, or raft will usually visit from May through October; those who prefer skiing, snowboarding, and snow-mobiling will obviously have to wait for winter, usually from late November through March or April, depending on snow levels. Although you can visit most major museums year-round, some, especially those in smaller communities, close in winter. The best way to avoid crowds at the more popular destinations is to try to visit from March through May and October through mid-December.

To hear Coloradans tell it, the state has perfect weather all the time. Although they may be exaggerating just a bit, the weather here is usually quite pleasant, with an abundance of sun and relatively mild temperatures in most places—just avoid those winter snowstorms that come sweeping out of the mountains.

Along the Front Range, including Denver, Boulder, and Colorado Springs, summers are hot and dry, with pleasantly mild evenings and cool nights. The relative humidity is low, and temperatures seldom rise above the 90s. Evenings start to get cooler by mid-September, but even as late as November the days are often sunny and warm. Surprisingly, winters are milder and less snowy than those in the Great Lakes or New England regions; many golf courses remain open year-round.

Average Monthly High/Low Temperatures (°F) and Precipitation (inches):

		Jan	Feb	Mar	Apr	May	June	July	Aug	Sept	Oct	Nov	Dec
Denver	Temp. (°F)	43/16	47/20	52/26	62/35	71/44	81/52	88/59	86/57	77/48	66/36	53/25	45/17
	Precip. (in.)	0.5	0.6	1.3	1.7	2.4	1.8	1.9	1.5	1.2	1.0	0.9	0.6
Elev. 5,280'													
Col.	Temp. (°F)	41/16	45/20	49/24	60/33	69/43	80/52	85/57	82/56	75/47	66/37	50/25	44/19
Springs	Precip. (in.)	0.3	0.4	0.9	1.2	2.2	2.3	2.9	3.0	1.3	0.8	0.5	0.5
Elev. 6.035'													

Most of Colorado is considered semiarid, and overall the state has almost 300 sunny days a year—more sunshine than San Diego or Miami Beach. The prairies average about 16 inches of precipitation annually; the Front Range, 14 inches; the western slope, only 8 inches. Rain, when it falls, is commonly a short deluge—a summer afternoon thunderstorm. However, if you want to see snow, simply head to the mountains, where snowfall is measured in feet instead of inches, and mountain peaks may still be white in July. Mountain temperatures can be bitterly cold, especially if it's windy, but even at the higher elevations of Colorado's top ski resorts you'll find plenty of sunshine.

Calendar of Events

Below are some of the major annual events in Denver, Boulder, Colorado Springs, and the surrounding area. You'll find additional events on the Internet at **www.colorado.com,** as well as on each city's individual Web site. We strongly recommend, however, that if a particular event is especially important to your visit you confirm the date by telephone before you leave home.

January

- **Great Fruitcake Toss,** Colorado Springs. This zany event, where contestants compete to see who can throw a fruitcake the farthest, has been covered by national media and is among the most outlandish and festive spectacles of the year. It is held in Manitou Springs' Memorial Park, five miles west of downtown Colorado Springs. Call ☎ **800/642-2567** or 719/685-5089 for more information. Early January.
- ✪ **National Western Stock Show and Rodeo,** Denver. World's largest livestock show and indoor rodeo, with about two dozen rodeo performances, a trade exposition, western food and crafts booths, and livestock auctions. Call ☎ **303/297-1166** for details. Second and third weeks in January.
- ✪ **Boulder Bach Festival,** Boulder. Music of the master baroque composer. Call ☎ **303/494-3159** or see www.boulderbachfest.org for details. Last weekend in January.

February

- **Loveland Valentine Remailing Program,** Loveland. More than 200,000 valentines are remailed annually from Loveland. Call ☎ **970/667-6311** for details. Before February 14.
- **Buffalo Bill's Birthday Celebration,** Golden. Ceremonies and live entertainment that commemorate the life of the legendary scout and entertainer take place at the Buffalo Bill Memorial Museum. Call ☎ **303/526-0744** for further information. Late February.

March

- **Colorado Springs Dance Theatre Wine Festival,** Colorado Springs. This annual 3-day benefit for the Colorado Springs Dance Theatre is held at the Broadmoor Hotel. Call ☎ **719/630-7434** for further information. Early March.
- ✪ **Pow Wow,** Denver. More than 1,500 Native Americans (as well as 60 drum groups), representing some 85 tribes from 32 states, perform traditional music and dances. Arts and crafts are also sold. Call ☎ **303/934-8045** for details. Mid-March.
- **Saint Patrick's Day,** Denver. Among the largest Irish holiday parades in the United States, with floats, marching bands, and more than 5,000 horses. Call ☎ **303/892-1112** for further information. March 17.

April

- **Easter Sunrise Service,** Colorado Springs and Denver. Worshippers watch the rising sun light red sandstone formations in the Garden of the Gods in Colorado

Springs. For details call ☎ **719/634-6666.** Denver's Easter Sunrise Service takes place at Red Rocks Amphitheatre, also in the midst of stunning geological formations. Call ☎ **303/295-4444** for further information. Easter Sunday.

May

- **Cinco de Mayo,** Denver. More than 250,000 people from around the Denver metro area celebrate this annual Hispanic event with mariachi bands, dancers, Mexican food, and other activities. Call ☎ **303/534-8342** for information. Early May.
- **Plant and Book Sale,** Denver. The largest volunteer-run plant and book sale in the nation, this event at Denver Botanic Gardens offers more than 250,000 plants and thousands of new and used books. Experts are on hand to give gardening advice. Call ☎ **303/370-8187** for details. Early May.
- ✪ **Boulder Kinetic Fest,** Boulder. A wacky event that's a real crowd pleaser. Most years an average of 70 teams race over land and water at Boulder Reservoir in a variety of imaginative human-powered conveyances. Activities include the kinetic parade, kinetic concerts, the kinetic ball, and a hot-air balloon launch. Call ☎ **303/444-5600** for details. Early May.
- **Bolder Boulder,** Boulder. This footrace attracts some 40,000 entrants each year, plus numerous spectators. Participants walk, jog, or run the 10K course. Call ☎ **303/444-RACE** or see www.bolderboulder.com for details. Memorial Day.

June

- **Capitol Hill People's Fair,** Denver. Among Denver's most vibrant street festivals, with hundreds of booths at Civic Center Park where both locals and visitors view arts and crafts and sample food from local restaurants. There's also live entertainment on six stages. Call ☎ **303/830-1651** for further information. First weekend in June.
- **Greek Marketplace,** Denver. Greek food, music, dancing, and dance lessons are highlights of this festival, which also includes a children's carnival. Call ☎ **303/388-9314** for details. Mid-June.
- ✪ **Colorado Shakespeare Festival,** Boulder. Considered among the top Shakespeare festivals in the country, primarily performed in an outdoor theater. Call ☎ **303/492-0554** for details. Late June through late August.
- **Garden Concerts,** Denver. Jazz, blues, and folk music concerts are presented in the outdoor amphitheater at **Denver Botanic Gardens.** Call ☎ **303/370-8187** for information. June through August.

July

- **Pikes Peak Auto Hill Climb,** Colorado Springs. This "race to the clouds," held annually since 1916, takes drivers to the top of 14,110-foot Pikes Peak. Call ☎ **719/685-4400** for additional information. July 4.
- **Cherry Creek Arts Festival,** Denver. Some 200 artists personally display their work and give demonstrations in what is considered one of the country's top arts festivals. Call ☎ **303/355-2787** for further information. July 4th weekend.
- **Denver Black Arts Festival,** Denver. Features the work of black artists and entertainers, plus a parade. Call ☎ **303/329-3976** for further information. Mid-July.
- **Pearl Street Art Fair,** Boulder. Annually, 150 local and regional artists display their works on the pedestrian Pearl Street Mall. Offering "fine art to fun art" as well as live musical performances, this festival has been held every year since 1979. Call ☎ **303/449-3774** for more information. Third weekend in July.

✪ **Pikes Peak Highland Games and Celtic Festival,** Colorado Springs. This festival is sponsored by the Scottish Society of the Pikes Peak Region, and features the caber toss and other traditional games, Celtic music, a Highland dance competition, and Scottish foods. Call ☎ **719/481-4597** or 719/487-1383 for details. Third Saturday in July.

August

• **Pikes Peak or Bust Rodeo,** Colorado Springs. This is the largest outdoor rodeo in the state and a popular stop on the professional rodeo circuit. Call ☎ **719/ 635-3547** for details. Early August.

• **Colorado State Fair,** Pueblo. National professional rodeo, carnival rides, food booths, industrial displays, horse shows, animal exhibits, and entertainment by top-name performers. Call ☎ **800/876-4567** for additional information. Mid-August through Labor Day.

• **Rocky Mountain Wine and Food Festival,** Winter Park. Colorado's finest chefs and many of America's best-known vintners offer their creations to benefit the National Sports Center for the Disabled. Call ☎ **970/726-1548** or 303/376-1548 for further information. Third weekend in August.

September

• **Colorado Springs Balloon Classic,** Colorado Springs. Every Labor Day weekend, more than 100 colorful hot air balloons launch from Memorial Park, making this one of the five largest balloon rallies in the country. Call ☎ **719/ 471-4833** or visit www.balloonclassic.com for more information. Labor Day weekend.

• **A Taste of Colorado,** Denver. Billed as "a festival of mountain and plain," this is Denver's largest celebration, with an annual attendance of about 400,000. Local restaurants serve house specialties; there are also crafts exhibits and free concerts. Call ☎ **303/295-6330** for details. Labor Day weekend.

• **Central City Vintage Car Show,** Central City. This outdoor display along Central City's Main Street includes more than 100 collector cars, with awards for the best. Call ☎ **303/582-5251 ext. 302.** Mid-September.

• **Fall Festival,** Boulder. An Oktoberfest celebration in downtown Boulder, this festival includes polka bands, food, children's carnival rides, and arts-and-crafts sales and demonstrations. Call ☎ **303/449-3774** for information. Late September or early October.

October

✪ **Great American Beer Festival,** Denver. Hundreds of American beers are available for sampling, and seminars are presented at what is considered the largest and most prestigious beer event in the United States. Call ☎ **303/447-0816** for further information. Early October.

• **Colorado Performing Arts Festival,** Denver. This celebration of performing arts, which takes place at the Denver Performing Arts Complex, includes dance, music, theater, and storytelling. Call ☎ **303/640-2678** for information. Early October.

• **Pumpkin Festival,** Denver. This family event, sponsored by Denver Botanic Gardens and held at Chatfield Arboretum southwest of town, includes pumpkin picking, food, crafts, hayrides, and other activities. Call ☎ **303/973-3705** for details. Mid-October.

November

• **Colorado Ski Expo,** Denver. Skiers and snowboarders get together at Currigan Hall to check out the newest equipment and get information on the state's resorts, accommodations, and discount packages. Call ☎ **303/837-0793** for details. Early November.

- **Holiday Sale,** Denver. Handmade Christmas ornaments, gifts, dried-flower arrangements, and food items are among the unique items available at this annual sale at Denver Botanic Gardens. Call ☎ **303/370-8187** for information. Mid-November.

December

- **World's Largest Christmas Lighting Display,** Denver. The Denver City and County Building is illuminated by some 40,000 colored floodlights. All month.
- ✪ **Parade of Lights,** Denver. A holiday parade winds its way through downtown Denver, with floats, balloons, and marching bands. Call ☎ **303/534-6161** for additional information. Early December.
- **Holiday Home Tour,** Colorado Springs. A tour of bed-and-breakfast inns, decorated for the holidays, with proceeds to benefit the Old Colorado City Historical Society. Call ☎ **719/632-9194** for more information. Early December.

3 Health, Safety & Insurance

HEALTH

About two-thirds of Colorado is more than a mile above sea level, which means there is less oxygen and lower humidity than many travelers are accustomed to. This creates a unique set of problems for short-term visitors, such as the possibility of shortness of breath, tiredness, and other physical concerns.

Those not used to higher elevations should get sufficient rest, avoid large meals, and drink plenty of nonalcoholic fluids, especially water. Individuals with heart or respiratory problems should consult their personal physicians before planning a trip to the Colorado mountains. Those in generally good health need not take any special precautions, but it is best to ease the transition to high elevations by changing altitude gradually. For instance, spend a night or two in Denver (elevation 5,280 feet) or Colorado Springs (elevation 6,035 feet) before driving or taking the cog railway to the top of Pikes Peak (elevation 14,110 feet).

Lowlanders can also help their bodies adjust to higher elevations by taking it easy for their first few days in the mountains, cutting down on cigarettes and alcohol, and avoiding sleeping pills and other drugs. The drug Diamox can be taken to help prevent and relieve symptoms of altitude sickness. It is available by prescription only; consult a medical professional about its use.

Because the sun's rays are more direct in the thinner atmosphere, they cause sunburn more quickly. The potential for skin damage increases when the sun is reflected off snow or water. A good sunblock is strongly recommended, as are good-quality ultraviolet-blocking sunglasses.

SAFETY

While there are many reasons to visit Colorado, the two cited most often are its historic sites and magnificent outdoor activities. However, visiting historic sites and participating in outdoor activities can lead to accidents.

When visiting such historic sites as ghost towns, gold mines, and railroads, keep in mind that they were probably built more than 100 years ago, at a time when safety standards were extremely lax, if they existed at all. Never enter abandoned buildings, mines, or railroad equipment on your own. When you're visiting commercially operated historic tourist attractions, use common sense and don't be afraid to ask questions.

Walkways in mines are often uneven and poorly lit, and are sometimes slippery due to seeping groundwater that can also stain your clothing with its high iron content. When entering old buildings, be prepared for steep, narrow stairways, creaky floors, and low ceilings and doorways. Steam trains are a wonderful experience as long as you remember that steam is very hot, and that oil and grease can ruin your clothing.

When heading into the great outdoors, keep in mind that injuries often occur when people fail to follow instructions. Pay attention when the experts tell you to stay on established ski trails, hike only in designated areas and carry rain gear, and wear a life jacket when rafting. Mountain weather can be fickle, and many of the most beautiful spots are in remote areas. Be prepared for extreme changes in temperature at any time of year, and watch out for those sudden summer afternoon thunderstorms that can leave you drenched and shivering in a matter of minutes.

State health officials have lately been warning outdoor enthusiasts to take precautions against the Hantavirus, a rare but often fatal respiratory disease first recognized in 1993. About half of the country's confirmed cases have been reported in the Four Corners states of Colorado, New Mexico, Arizona, and Utah. The disease is usually spread by the urine and droppings of deer mice and other rodents, and health officials recommend that campers avoid areas with signs of rodent droppings. Symptoms of Hantavirus are similar to flu and lead to breathing difficulties and shock.

INSURANCE

Before starting out, check your medical insurance policy to be certain you're covered away from home; if you're not, purchase a special traveler's policy, available from travel agents, insurance agents, and travel clubs. It's useful to carry a medical insurance identification card or other proof with you at all times. Besides being prepared for medical emergencies, it's wise to carry insurance to cover you in case of an accident, loss of personal possessions such as luggage and cameras (this may be included in your homeowner's or renter's policy), or trip cancellation. If you are a motorist, be sure to carry proof of automobile liability insurance, and be certain that your policy includes protection from uninsured motorists. If you're renting a car, check your credit cards to see if any of them include a collision damage waiver (CDW) when you rent with their card; it may save you as much as $12 a day on the cost of your rental.

4　Tips for Travelers with Special Needs

FOR TRAVELERS WITH DISABILITIES

Travelers with disabilities will find the cities of Colorado fairly accessible, although some historic buildings are not wheelchair accessible, so you should check before going.

If you're planning to visit Colorado's national parks and monuments, you can get the National Park Service's **Golden Access Passport,** available free at all the parks. This lifetime pass is issued to any U.S. citizen or permanent resident who is medically certified as disabled or blind. The pass permits free entry and gives a 50% discount on park service campgrounds and activities, although not on those offered by private concessionaires.

Amtrak will, with 24 hours' notice, provide porter service, special seating, and a discount (☎ **800/USA-RAIL**). If you're traveling with a companion, **Greyhound** will carry you both for a single fare (☎ **800/231-2222**).

FOR GAY & LESBIAN TRAVELERS

In general, gay and lesbian travelers will find they are treated just like any other travelers in Colorado. Even cities such as Colorado Springs, home of Focus on the Family and other conservative groups, have become somewhat more open-minded about alternative lifestyles recently. Those with specific concerns can contact **Gay, Lesbian, and Bisexual Community Services Center of Colorado** (☎ **303/733-7743**) in Denver; the organization can also provide information on events and venues of interest to gay and lesbian visitors.

FOR SENIORS

Many Colorado hotels and motels offer special rates to senior citizens, and an increasing number of restaurants, attractions, and public transportation systems are now offering discounts as well. **Train travelers** 62 and older receive a 15% discount on most Amtrak fares. You can save sightseeing dollars if you are 62 or over by picking up a **Golden Age Passport** from any federally operated park, recreation area, or monument. There is a one-time fee of $10 that entitles holders to free admission to parks and other federally managed fee areas plus a 50% savings on camping fees.

Membership in the **American Association of Retired Persons (AARP),** 601 E St. NW, Washington, DC 20049 (☎ **800/424-3410** or 202/434-2277; www.aarp.org), entitles you to discounts at numerous places; the organization can help with specifics on motels, airfares, and car rentals.

FOR TRAVELERS WITH PETS

Many of us wouldn't dream of going on vacation without our pets. Under the right circumstances, it can be a wonderful experience for both you and your animals. Dogs and cats are accepted at many motels around the state, but not as universally in resorts and at the more expensive hotels. Throughout this book, we've tried to consistently note those lodgings that take pets. Some properties require you to pay a fee or damage deposit in advance, and most insist they be notified at check-in that you have a pet.

Be aware, however, that national parks and monuments and other federal lands administered by the National Park Service are not pet-friendly. Dogs are usually prohibited on all hiking trails, must always be leashed, and in some cases cannot be taken more than 100 feet from established roads. On the other hand, U.S. Forest Service, Bureau of Land Management areas, and most state parks are pro-pet, allowing dogs on trails and just about everywhere except inside buildings. State parks require that dogs be leashed; regulations in national forests and BLM lands are generally looser.

Aside from regulations, though, you need to be concerned with your pet's well-being. Just as people need extra water in Colorado's dry climate, so do pets. We especially like those clever spill-resistant travel water bowls sold in pet shops. And keep in mind that many trails are rough, and jagged rocks can cut the pads on your dog's feet.

One final note on pets: There is no punishment too severe for the human who leaves a dog or cat inside a closed car parked in the sun. The car heats up more quickly than you'd think—so don't do it, even for a minute.

FOR STUDENTS

For inexpensive accommodations, as well as the opportunity to meet other traveling students, join **Hostelling International–American Youth Hostels,** Box 37613, Washington, DC 20013-7613 (☎ **202/783-6161;** fax 202/783-6171; www.hiayh. org; E-mail: hiayhserv@hiayh.org); they'll send a directory of all U.S. hostels for $3, or free with membership. Twelve-month membership is free for those under 18, costs $25 for those ages 18 to 54, and is $15 for those 55 and older.

5 Getting There

BY CAR

An excellent road system, connecting to interstate highways heading in all directions, makes driving both a good and an economical choice. This is especially true for those planning excursions out of the Denver, Boulder, or Colorado Springs city limits. Although these cities have good public transportation within their boundaries, a car, either your own or a rental, is practically mandatory for those intent on getting out into the country.

Some 1,000 miles of interstate highways form a star on the map of Colorado, with its center at Denver. (See state map in chapter 1.) **I-25** crosses the state from south to north, extending from New Mexico to Wyoming; over its 300 miles, it goes through nearly every major city of the Front Range, including Pueblo, Colorado Springs, Denver, and Fort Collins. **I-70** crosses from west to east, extending from Utah to Baltimore, Maryland. It enters Colorado near Grand Junction, passes through Glenwood Springs, Vail, and Denver, and exits just east of Burlington, a distance of about 450 miles. **I-76** is an additional 190-mile spur that begins in Denver and extends northeast to Nebraska, joining I-80 just beyond Julesburg.

Denver is about 1,025 miles from Los Angeles, 780 miles from Dallas, 600 miles from Kansas City, 510 miles from Salt Lake City, 440 miles from Albuquerque, 750 miles from Las Vegas, 820 miles from Phoenix, 1,010 miles from Chicago, and 1,800 miles from New York.

BY PLANE

Those flying to Colorado will probably land at Denver International Airport or Colorado Springs Airport. Both offer car rentals and shuttle services to their city's hotels.

Denver International Airport, opened in 1995, is 23 miles northeast of downtown Denver, about a 35- to 45-minute drive. It has five runways and averages 1,300 flights each day. An information line (☎ **800/AIR-2-DEN**) provides data on flight schedules and connections, parking, ground transportation, current weather conditions, and local accommodations. The local airport information and paging number is ☎ **303/342-2000**. Airlines serving Denver include **Air Canada** (☎ 888/ 247-2262; www.aircanada.ca), **American** (☎ 800/433-7300; www.aa.com), **America West** (☎ 800/235-9292; www.americawest.com), **Continental** (☎ 800/525-0280; www.flycontinental.com), **Delta** (☎ 800/221-1212; www.delta.com), **Frontier** (☎ 800/432-1359; www.frontierairlines.com), **Korean Air** (☎ 800/438-5000; www.koreanair.com), **Martinair** (☎ 800/366-4655; www.martinair.com), **Mexicana** (☎ 800/531-7921; www.mexicana.com), **Midwest Express** (☎ 800/452-2022; www.midwestexpress.com), **Northwest** (☎ 800/225-2525; www.nwa.com), **Sun Country** (☎ 800/359-6786; www.suncountry.com), **TWA** (☎ 800/221-2000; www.twa.com), **United and United Express** (☎ 800/241-6522; www.ual.com), **US Airways** (☎ 800/428-4322; www.usair.com), and **Vanguard** (☎ 800/826-4827; www.flyvanguard.com).

Colorado Springs Airport, which in 1994 completed an extensive expansion, has more than 100 flights each day, with connections to most major U.S. cities. The airport is located in the southeast corner of Colorado Springs, and its main phone is ☎ **719/550-1900**. The airport is served by **American** (☎ 800/433-7300;

www. aa.com), **America West** (☎ 800/235-9292; www.americawest.com), **Continental** (☎ 800/525-0280; www.flycontinental.com), **Delta** (☎ 800/221-1212; www. delta. com), **Mesa** (☎ 800/637-2247; www.mesa-air.com), **Northwest** (☎ 800/225-2525 domestic, or 800/447-4747 international; www.nwa.com), **TWA** (☎ 800/221-2000; www.twa.com), and **United** (☎ 800/241-6522; www.ual.com).

FLIGHTS FROM THE UNITED KINGDOM

British Airways (☎ 800/247-9297, 0845/773-3377 in London; www.british-airways.com) offers one daily nonstop flight between London and Denver. Travelers from the United Kingdom can take British Airways flights to such cities as Philadelphia or Chicago and make connecting flights to either Denver or Colorado Springs.

BY TRAIN

Amtrak (☎ 800/USA-RAIL; www.amtrak.com) has two routes through Colorado. One, which links San Francisco and Chicago, passes through Grand Junction, Glenwood Springs, Granby, Winter Park, Denver, and Fort Morgan en route to Omaha, Nebraska. Another, which runs between Los Angeles and Chicago, travels from Albuquerque, New Mexico, via Trinidad, La Junta, and Lamar before crossing the southeastern Colorado border into Kansas.

BY BUS

Greyhound (☎ 800/231-2222; www.greyhound.com) has an extensive network that reaches nearly every corner of the state, with daily connections to just about everywhere.

PACKAGE TOURS

Travelers who want to avoid the hassles of planning, making reservations, renting cars, and all the rest have some good package tours available to them, including a few unique choices. Below are some of the better companies that offer tours to the Denver, Boulder, and Colorado Springs areas.

Discover Colorado Tours, 11930 W. 62nd Pl., Arvada, CO 80004 (☎ 800/641-0129 or 303/425-3586), offers personalized individual and group tours lasting a half day, full day, or several days throughout Colorado, including trips to gold-mining areas, ghost towns, Rocky Mountain National Park, Pikes Peak, and the U.S. Air Force Academy.

Gray Line, 5855 E. 56th Ave. (P.O. Box 646), Denver, CO 80217 (☎ 303/289-2841), provides traditional bus and van tours to the U.S. Air Force Academy, Pikes Peak, Rocky Mountain National Park, and historic sites of Denver.

Maupintour, 1515 St. Andrews Dr., Lawrence, KS 66047 (☎ 800/255-4266), offers well-planned multiday tours of Rocky Mountain National Park and other scenic and historic areas.

Sample Colorado Tour Company and Travel Club, P.O. Box 621906, Littleton, CO 80162-1906 (☎ 303/904-2376), offers scheduled and custom tours with a historic theme throughout the state—both day trips from Denver and multiday excursions.

For those who enjoy train travel, **American Orient Express Railway Company,** 2025 First Ave., Suite 830, Seattle, WA 98121 (☎ 888/759-3944 or 206/441-2725; fax 206/727-7309), has vintage rail cars outfitted in polished mahogany and brass, dining cars decked out with china, silver, crystal, and linen, and a cuisine to match. One of its offerings is a trip from Denver to Salt Lake City with a stopover in Yellowstone National Park.

6 Getting Around

BY CAR

Cars are not really necessary for those visiting Denver, but they're handy in Boulder and Colorado Springs, and practically essential for those planning excursions into the nearby mountains and other parts of the state. From Denver, it takes a little over an hour to drive the 70 miles to Colorado Springs and about 35 minutes for the 27-mile drive to Boulder.

Colorado law requires all drivers to carry proof of insurance, as well as a valid driver's license. Safety belts are required for drivers and all front-seat passengers; all children up to age 16 must wear safety belts or be in approved child seats, regardless of where they're seated in the vehicle. The minimum age for drivers is 16; teenagers under 16 with valid licenses from their home states are not allowed to drive. Motorcyclists are not required to wear helmets, and radar detectors are permitted.

The maximum speed limit is 75 mph on interstate highways and 65 mph on non-interstates, unless otherwise posted. A driver will be considered intoxicated with a minimum blood-alcohol content of 0.10%. Colorado law allows drivers to make a right turn at a red signal after coming to a complete stop, unless otherwise posted.

A state highway map can be obtained from visitor centers or by mail (see "Visitor Information & Money," above). Otherwise, maps can be purchased at bookstores, gas stations, and most supermarkets and discount stores. Maps are available free to members of the American Automobile Association. An excellent source for all kinds of maps and road atlases is **Mapsco Map and Travel Center,** 800 Lincoln St., Denver, CO 80203 (☎ **800/456-8703** or 303/623-4299).

ROAD CONDITIONS

A recorded 24-hour hotline (☎ **303/639-1111**) provides information on road conditions statewide, and information on possible delays due to road construction is available at ☎ **303/575-ROAD** (7623). Some of Colorado's roads and highways are closed during winter months. One is U.S. 34, the Trail Ridge Road through Rocky Mountain National Park. It's the highest continuous highway in the world, crossing the Continental Divide at 12,183 feet. Also, Colo. 82, over Independence Pass (elevation 12,095 feet) east of Aspen, is the main route between Denver and Aspen in the summer months, but is closed in winter. In addition, the Mount Evans Road (Colo. 103 and Colo. 5) is open June to September only. It stretches from Idaho Springs (35 miles west of Denver) to the 14,264-foot summit of Mount Evans and is the highest paved road in North America. Among the world's highest tunnels at 11,000 feet, Eisenhower Tunnel carries I-70 beneath Loveland Pass, west of Denver, year-round, though this stretch of interstate is sometimes closed by winter storms. Snow tires or chains are often required when roads are snow-covered or icy.

ROAD EMERGENCIES

In case of an accident or road emergency, call 911. American Automobile Association members can get free emergency road service wherever they are, 24 hours a day, by calling AAA's emergency number (☎ **800/AAA-HELP**). In Colorado, AAA headquarters is located at 4100 E. Arkansas Ave., Denver, CO 80222-3491, just off South Colorado Boulevard (☎ **800/283-5222** or 303/753-8800). The AAA Web site is www.aaa.com.

RENTAL CARS

National rental agencies readily available in Colorado include **Advantage** (☎ 800/777-5500; www.arac.com), **Alamo** (☎ 800/462-5266; www.goalamo.com), **Avis**

(☎ 800/331-1212; www.avis.com), **Budget** (☎ 800/527-0700; www.budgetrentacar.com), **Dollar** (☎ 800/800-4000; www.dollarcar.com), **Enterprise** (☎ 800/325-8007; www.pickenterprise.com), **Hertz** (☎ 800/654-3131; www.hertz.com), **Kemwel Holiday Auto (KHA)** (☎ 800/576-1590; www.kemwel.com), **National** (☎ 888/227-7368; www.nationalcar.com), and **Thrifty** (☎ 800/ 847-4389; www.thrifty.com). Campers, travel trailers, and motor homes are available in Denver from **Cruise America** (☎ 800/327-7799; www.cruiseamerica.com); Harley-Davidson motorcycles can be rented in the Denver area at **Park Meadows Hog Rental** (☎ 303/799-0600; www.denverharleyrentals.com).

BY PLANE

Commuter airlines connect many of the state's major cities and resorts. See "Getting There," above.

BY TRAIN

Amtrak (☎ **800/872-7245;** www.amtrak.com) runs several train routes through the state. See "Getting There," above. On winter weekends, the **Rio Grande Ski Train** (☎ **303/296-I-SKI**) runs to Winter Park Ski Resort, leaving Denver early in the morning and returning after the lifts close.

BY BUS

Most large towns in the state are accessible by **Greyhound** bus lines (☎ **800/ 231-2222;** www.greyhound.com).

Fast Facts: Colorado

American Express   American Express is located at 555 17th St., Qwest Tower, Denver (☎ **303/383-5050**). To report a lost card, call ☎ **800/528-4800.** To report lost traveler's checks, call ☎ **800/221-7282.**

Banks   Colorado National Bank is the state's oldest, with numerous branches. Other major banks include Bank One, Chase Manhattan, First Federal, and Norwest. Automated-teller machines are practically everywhere. If you can't find one in a shopping center or in front of a bank, call ☎ **800/THE-PLUS.**

Business Hours   Banks are typically open weekdays from 9am to 5pm, occasionally a little later on Friday, and sometimes for several hours on Saturday. Most branches have automated-teller machines that are available 24 hours a day. Generally, stores are open 6 days a week, with many open on Sunday, too; department stores usually stay open until 9pm at least one evening a week. Discount stores and supermarkets are usually open later than other stores, and some supermarkets in major cities are open 24 hours a day.

Car Rentals   See "Getting Around," above.

Climate   See "When to Go," above.

Driving Rules   See "Getting Around," above.

Drugstores   You'll find 24-hour prescription services at selected Walgreens Drug Stores throughout the state. For locations, call ☎ **800/WALGREENS.** Many supermarkets and discount stores also have pharmacies.

Embassies/Consulates   See "Fast Facts: For the Foreign Traveler" in chapter 3.

Emergencies   Throughout most of Colorado, the number to dial for any emergency is ☎ **911;** coins are not required at pay phones. In a few rural areas, it is necessary to dial 0 (zero) for the operator.

Information   See "Visitor Information & Money," above.

Liquor Laws   The legal drinking age is 21. Except for 3.2% beer (sold in supermarkets and convenience stores 7 days a week from 5am to midnight), alcoholic beverages must be purchased in liquor stores. These are open Monday through Saturday from 8am to midnight. Beverages may be served in licensed restaurants, lounges, and bars Monday through Saturday from 7am to 2am, Sunday from 8am to 2am, and Christmas Day from 8am to midnight, with the proper licenses. Incidentally, 3.2% beer, which is sold only in Colorado, Utah, Oklahoma, and Kansas, does have less alcohol than beer sold elsewhere despite what some storekeepers may tell you. According to the Budweiser people, 3.2% beer has about 4% alcohol by volume (which is equivalent to 3.2% alcohol by weight), while full-strength American beers have about 5% alcohol by volume. Some microbrews and specialty beers and ales have higher alcohol content.

Maps   See "Getting Around," above.

Newspapers/Magazines   The state's largest daily newspaper is the ***Denver Post,*** which is published in Denver and distributed statewide. Other cities and large towns, especially regional hubs, have daily newspapers, and many smaller towns publish weeklies. National newspapers such as *USA Today* and the *Wall Street Journal* can be purchased in cities and major hotels, and you can find practically any newspaper or magazine you want (at least the Sunday edition) at **Tattered Cover Bookstore,** 2955 E. 1st Ave., Denver (☎ **800/833-9327** or 303/ 322-7727).

Taxes   Colorado state sales tax is 3%, but each county and city tacks an additional local tax on top of that, and many also charge a hotel tax. Therefore, sales taxes in the state vary, but usually total from 6% to 9% for purchases and 9% to 13% on lodging.

Telephone/Fax   Colorado uses four telephone area codes. In the immediate Denver and Boulder area, they are **303** and **720.** To make local calls here, you will have to dial all ten digits, starting with 303 or 720. The south-central and southeastern parts of the state, including Colorado Springs, use area code **719;** and the rest (west and north) use **970.** In 719 and 970 areas, local calls are reached by using only the seven-digit number. Long distance calls in all areas of the state require dialing 1 plus the area code plus the seven-digit number.

Pay phones are owned by different companies and may have different policies and fees. Most charge 25¢ to 35¢ for local calls, and emergency 911 calls are free. Calls from Denver to Boulder are considered local. For local directory assistance, dial 1-411. For long-distance directory assistance, dial 1 + the area code + 555-1212. Phone books have lists and maps defining the local area and listing area codes for the United States and Canada.

Because some local phone companies add high service fees to the cost of long-distance calls, it may be best to access the long-distance service you use at home and charge your call to a phone company credit card or, with some companies, to a bank card or your home phone. Each long-distance company has a different access number. For instance, to get into the AT&T system from any phone, dial ☎ **1-800/CALL-ATT.**

Many hotels, motels, and even small bed-and-breakfasts can provide fax service for a small fee, and 24-hour fax services are provided by Kinko's Copies outlets in the Denver, Boulder, and Colorado Springs areas. Among Kinko's in Denver are the outlet at 1555 S. Colorado Blvd. (☎ **303/757-1122**) and one in nearby Lakewood at 96 Wadsworth Blvd. (☎ **303/232-3994**).

Time   Colorado is on Mountain Standard Time (7 hours behind Greenwich Mean Time), 1 hour ahead of the West Coast and 2 hours behind the East Coast. Daylight saving time is in effect from early April to late October.

Weather   Call ☎ **303/337-2500** for a Denver and Boulder area forecast.

3 For Foreign Visitors

American fads and fashions have spread across other parts of the world to such a degree that the United States may seem like familiar territory before your arrival. But there are still many peculiarities and uniquely American situations that any foreign visitor may find confusing or perplexing. This chapter will provide some specifics about getting to the United States as economically and effortlessly as possible, plus some helpful information about how things are done in Colorado—from receiving mail to making a local or long-distance telephone call.

1 Preparing for Your Trip

ENTRY REQUIREMENTS

Immigration laws are a hot political issue in the United States these days, and the following requirements may have changed somewhat by the time you plan your trip. Check at any U.S. embassy or consulate for current information and requirements. You can also plug into the **U.S. State Department's** Internet site at **http://state.gov.**

Visas The U.S. State Department has a **Visa Waiver Pilot Program** allowing citizens of certain countries to enter the United States without a visa for stays of up to 90 days. At press time these included Andorra, Argentina, Australia, Austria, Belgium, Brunei, Denmark, Finland, France, Germany, Iceland, Ireland, Italy, Japan, Liechtenstein, Luxembourg, Monaco, the Netherlands, New Zealand, Norway, San Marino, Slovenia, Spain, Sweden, Switzerland, and the United Kingdom. Citizens of these countries need only a valid passport and a round-trip air or cruise ticket in their possession upon arrival. If they first enter the United States, they may also visit Mexico, Canada, Bermuda, and/or the Caribbean islands and return to the United States without a visa. Further information is available from any U.S. embassy or consulate. Canadian citizens may enter the United States without visas; they need only proof of residence.

Citizens of all other countries must have (1) a valid passport that expires at least 6 months later than the scheduled end of their visit to the United States, and (2) a tourist visa, which may be obtained without charge from any U.S. consulate.

Obtaining a Visa To obtain a visa, the traveler must submit a completed application form (either in person or by mail) with a 1½-inch-square photo, and must demonstrate binding ties to a residence abroad. Usually, you can obtain a visa at once or within 24 hours, but it may take longer during the summer rush from June through August. If you cannot go in person, contact the nearest U.S. embassy or consulate for directions on applying by mail. Your travel agent or airline office may also be able to provide you with visa applications and instructions. The U.S. consulate or embassy that issues your visa will determine whether you will be issued a multiple- or single-entry visa and any restrictions regarding the length of your stay.

British subjects can obtain up-to-date passport and visa information by calling the **U.S. Embassy Visa Information Line** (☎ **0891/200-290**) or the **London Passport Office** (☎ **0990/210-410** for recorded information).

Immigration Questions   Telephone operators will answer your inquiries regarding U.S. immigration policies or laws at the **Immigration and Naturalization Service's Customer Information Center** (☎ **800/375-5283**). Representatives are available from 9am to 3pm, Monday through Friday. The INS also runs a 24-hour automated information service, for commonly asked questions, at ☎ **800/755-0777.**

MEDICAL REQUIREMENTS   Unless you're arriving from an area known to be suffering from an epidemic (particularly cholera or yellow fever), inoculations or vaccinations are not required for entry into the United States. If you have a disease that requires treatment with narcotics or syringe-administered medications, carry a valid signed prescription from your physician to allay any suspicions that you may be smuggling narcotics (a serious offense that carries severe penalties in the U.S.).

For HIV-positive visitors, requirements for entering the United States are somewhat vague and change frequently. According to the latest publication of *HIV and Immigrants: A Manual for AIDS Service Providers,* "although INS doesn't require a medical exam for everyone trying to come into the United States, INS officials may keep out people who they suspect are HIV positive. INS may stop people because they look sick or because they are carrying AIDS/HIV medicine."

If an HIV-positive non-citizen applying for a non-immigrant visa knows that HIV is a communicable disease of public health significance but checks "no" on the question about communicable diseases, INS may deny the visa because it thinks the applicant committed fraud. If a non-immigrant visa applicant checks "yes," or if INS suspects the person is HIV positive, it will deny the visa unless the applicant asks for a special waiver for visitors. This waiver is for people visiting the United States for a short time, to attend a conference, for instance, to visit close relatives, or to receive medical treatment. For up-to-the-minute information concerning HIV-positive travelers, contact the Center for Disease Control's **National Center for HIV** (☎ **404/332-4559;** www.hivatis.org) or the **Gay Men's Health Crisis** (☎ **800/AIDS NYC** or 212/807-6655; www.gmhc.org).

DRIVER'S LICENSES   Most foreign driver's licenses are recognized in the U.S., but you may want to get an international driver's license if your home license is not written in English.

CUSTOMS REQUIREMENTS   Every visitor over 21 years of age may bring in, free of duty, the following: (1) 1 liter of wine or hard liquor; (2) 200 cigarettes, 100 cigars (but not from Cuba), or 3 pounds of smoking tobacco; and (3) $100 worth of gifts. These exemptions are offered to travelers who spend at least 72 hours in the United States and who have not claimed them within the preceding 6 months. It is altogether forbidden to bring into the country foodstuffs (particularly fruit, cooked meats, and canned goods) and plants (vegetables, seeds, tropical plants, and the like).

Foreign tourists may bring in or take out up to $10,000 in U.S. or foreign currency with no formalities; larger sums must be declared to U.S. Customs on entering or leaving, which includes filing form CM 4790. For more specific information regarding U.S. Customs, call your nearest U.S. embassy or consulate, or the **U.S. Customs** office at ☎ **202/927-1770** or www.customs.ustreas.gov.

INSURANCE

Although it's not required of travelers, health insurance is highly recommended. Unlike many European countries, the United States does not usually offer free or low-cost medical care to its citizens or visitors. Doctors and hospitals are expensive, and in most cases will require advance payment or proof of coverage before they render their services. Policies can cover everything from the loss or theft of your baggage and trip cancellation to the guarantee of bail in case you're arrested. Good policies will also cover the costs of an accident, repatriation, or death. See "Health & Insurance" in chapter 2 for more information. Packages such as **Europ Assistance** in Europe are sold by automobile clubs and travel agencies at attractive rates. **Worldwide Assistance Services, Inc. (☎ 800/821-2828)** is the agent for Europ Assistance in the United States.

Though lack of health insurance may prevent you from being admitted to a hospital in non-emergencies, don't worry about being left on a street corner to die: the American way is to fix you now and bill the living daylights out of you later.

MONEY

The U.S. monetary system has a decimal base: One American **dollar** ($1) = 100 **cents** (100¢). Dollar bills commonly come in $1 (a "buck"), $5, $10, $20, $50, and $100 denominations (the last two are not welcome when paying for small purchases and are usually not accepted in taxis or at subway ticket booths). Note that a newly redesigned $100 and $50 bill were introduced in 1996, and a redesigned $20 bill in 1998. Redesigned $10 and $5 notes entered circulation in the summer of 2000. Despite rumors to the contrary, the old-style bills are still legal tender.

There are six coin denominations: 1¢ (one cent or a "penny"); 5¢ (five cents or a "nickel"); 10¢ (ten cents or a "dime"); 25¢ (twenty-five cents or a "quarter"); 50¢ (fifty cents or a "half dollar"); and the $1 pieces (the older, large silver dollar, the small Susan B. Anthony coin, and new in 2000, the "golden dollar" coin).The "foreign-exchange bureaus" so common in Europe are rare even at airports in the United States, and nonexistent outside major cities. It's best not to change foreign money (or traveler's checks denominated in a currency other than U.S. dollars) at a small-town bank, or even a branch in a big city; in fact, leave any currency other than U.S. dollars at home (except the cash you need for the taxi or bus ride home when you return to your own country)—it may prove a greater nuisance to you than it's worth.

Traveler's checks in U.S. dollars are accepted at most hotels, motels, restaurants, and large stores. Sometimes picture identification is required. Visa, American Express, and Thomas Cook traveler's checks are readily accepted in the United States. Be sure to record the numbers of the checks, and keep that information separately in case they get lost or stolen.

Credit cards are the method of payment most widely used. Cards used in the United States are Visa (BarclayCard in Britain), MasterCard (EuroCard in Europe, Access in Britain, Diamond in Japan), American Express, Discover, Diners Club, enRoute, JCB, and Carte Blanche, in descending order of acceptance. You can save yourself trouble by using "plastic" rather than cash or traveler's checks in 95% of all hotels, motels, restaurants, and retail stores. A credit card can also serve as a deposit for renting a car, proof

---

Travel Tip

Be sure to keep a copy of all your travel papers (including your passport and visa) separate from your wallet or purse, and leave a copy with someone at home should you need it faxed in an emergency.

---

of identity, or a "cash card" for drawing money from automatic-teller machines (ATMs) that accept them. Expect to be charged up to $3 per transaction, however, if you're not using your own bank's ATM. One way around these fees is to ask for cash back at grocery stores that accept ATM cards and don't charge usage fees. Of course, you'll have to purchase something first.

If you plan to travel for several weeks or more in the United States, you may want to deposit enough money into your credit-card account to cover anticipated expenses and avoid finance charges in your absence. This also reduces the likelihood of your receiving an unwelcome big bill on your return.

You can telegraph money, or have it telegraphed to you very quickly, using the **Western Union** system (☎ **800/325-6000**).

SAFETY

While tourist areas are generally safe, crime is on the increase everywhere, and urban areas in the United States tend to be less safe than those in Europe or Japan. Visitors should always stay alert. This is particularly true of large U.S. cities such as Denver. It's wise to ask the city's or area's tourist office if you're in doubt about which neighborhoods are unsafe.

Remember also that hotels are open to the public, and in a large hotel, security may not be able to screen everyone entering. Always lock your room door—don't assume that once inside your hotel you are automatically safe and no longer need be aware of your surroundings.

DRIVING   Safety while driving is particularly important. Question your rental agency about personal safety and ask for a traveler-safety brochure when you pick up your car. Obtain written directions—or a map with the route clearly marked—from the agency showing how to get to your destination. (Many agencies now offer the option of renting a cellular phone for the duration of your car rental; check with the rental agent when you pick up the car.) And, if possible, arrive and depart during daylight hours.

Recently, more and more crime has involved cars and drivers. If you drive off a highway into a doubtful neighborhood, leave the area as quickly as possible. If you have an accident, even on the highway, stay in your car with the doors locked until you assess the situation or until the police arrive. If you're bumped from behind on the street or are involved in a minor accident with no injuries and the situation appears to be suspicious, motion to the other driver to follow you. Never get out of your car in such situations. Go directly to the nearest police precinct, well-lit service station, or 24-hour store.

Always try to park in well-lit and well-traveled areas if possible. If you leave your rental car unlocked and empty of your valuables, you're probably safer than locking your car with valuables in plain view. Never leave any packages or valuables in sight. If someone attempts to rob you or steal your car, don't resist the thief/carjacker—report the incident to the police department immediately by calling ☎ **911**.

2 Getting to the U.S.

The idea of traveling abroad on a budget is something of an oxymoron, but travelers can reduce the price of a plane ticket if they take the time to shop around. For example, overseas visitors can take advantage of the APEX (Advance Purchase Excursion) reductions offered by all major U.S. and European carriers. For the best rates, compare fares and be flexible with the dates and times of travel.

Most international visitors will fly to Denver International Airport. Airlines offering flights into Denver include **Air Canada** (☎ 888/247-2262; www.aircanada.ca), **American** (☎ 800/433-7300; www.aa.com), **America West** (☎ 800/235-9292; www.americawest.com), **Continental** (☎ 800/525-0280; www.flycontinental.com), **Delta** (☎ 800/221-1212; www.delta.com), **Frontier** (☎ 800/432-1359; www.frontierairlines.com), **Korean Air** (☎ 800/438-5000; www.koreanair.com), **Martinair** (☎ 800/366-4655; www.martinair.com), **Mexicana** (☎ 800/531-7921; www.mexicana.com), **Midwest Express** (☎ 800/452-2022; www.midwestexpress.com), **Northwest** (☎ 800/225-2525; www.nwa.com), **Sun Country** (☎ 800/359-6786; www.suncountry.com), **TWA** (☎ 800/221-2000; www.twa.com), **United and United Express** (☎ 800/241-6522; www.ual.com), **US Airways** (☎ 800/428-4322; www.usair.com), and **Vanguard** (☎ 800/826-4827; www.flyvanguard.com). International travelers can also take flights to O'Hare International Airport in Chicago, LAX in Los Angeles, and JFK International Airport in New York, and catch connecting flights to Denver from there.

British Airways (☎ 800/247-9297, 0845/773-3377 in London; www.british-airways.com) offers one daily nonstop flight between London and Denver. Travelers from the United Kingdom can also take British Airways flights to such cities as Philadelphia or Chicago and make connecting flights to Denver.

Visitors arriving by air, no matter what the port of entry, should cultivate patience and resignation before setting foot on U.S. soil. Getting through Immigration control may take as long as 2 hours on some days, especially summer weekends, so have your guidebook or other reading material handy. Add the time it takes to clear Customs and you'll see that you should allow extra time for delays when planning connections between international and domestic flights—an average of 2 to 3 hours at least.

In contrast, travelers arriving by car or by rail from Canada will find border-crossing formalities streamlined to the vanishing point. And air travelers from Canada, Bermuda, and some places in the Caribbean can sometimes go through Customs and Immigration at the point of departure, which is much quicker.

3 Getting Around the U.S.

BY PLANE Some large U.S. airlines offer travelers on their trans-Atlantic or trans-Pacific flights special discount tickets for any of their U.S. destinations (American Airlines' Visit USA program and Delta's Discover America program, for example). These tickets are not for sale in the United States, and must be purchased abroad in conjunction with your international ticket. These programs are the best, easiest, and fastest ways to see the United States at low cost. You should obtain information from your travel agent or the office of the airline concerned well in advance since the conditions attached to these discount tickets can be changed without advance notice.

BY RAIL Amtrak (☎ 800/USA-RAIL; www.amtrak.com) connects Denver to both the East and West Coasts. International visitors can buy a **USA Railpass,** good for 15 or 30 days of unlimited travel on Amtrak. The pass is available through many foreign travel agents. Prices for a 15-day pass are about $285 off-peak, $425 peak; a 30-day pass costs $375 off-peak, $535 peak. (With a foreign passport, you can also buy passes at some Amtrak offices in the United States, including locations in San Francisco, Los Angeles, Chicago, New York, Miami, Boston, and Washington, D.C.) Reservations are generally required and should be made for each part of your trip as early as possible.

Amtrak also offers low-cost passes available to anyone, covering certain regions of the country. Reservations are generally required for train travel and should be made for each part of your trip as early as possible.

Visitors should also be aware of the limitations of long-distance rail travel in the United States. With a few exceptions, service is rarely up to European standards: Delays are common, routes are limited and often infrequently served, and fares are rarely significantly lower than discount airfares. Thus, cross-country train travel should be approached with caution.

BY BUS   The cheapest way to travel the United States is by bus. **Greyhound/ Trailways** (☎ **800/231-2222;** www.greyhound.com), the sole nationwide bus line, offers an **Ameripass** (☎ **888/454-7277**) for unlimited nationwide travel for 7 days (for $199), 15 days (for $299), 30 days (for $409), and 60 days (for $599). Passes must be purchased at a Greyhound terminal. Special rates are available for senior citizens and students. Be aware that bus travel in the United States can be both slow and uncomfortable, so this option isn't for everyone. In addition, bus stations are often located in undesirable neighborhoods.

BY CAR   The most cost-effective, convenient, and comfortable way to travel around the United States is by car. Because much of Colorado outside Denver, Boulder, and Colorado Springs is rural, with limited or nonexistent public transportation, it is also the best way to explore this state. The Interstate highway system (high-speed, limited-access roadways) connects cities and towns all over the country; plus there's an extensive network of federal, state, and local highways and roads.

Some of the national car-rental companies include **Alamo** (☎ 800/327-9633), **Avis** (☎ 800/331-1212), **Budget** (☎ 800/527-0700), **Dollar** (☎ 800/800-4000), **Hertz** (☎ 800/654-3131), **National** (☎ 800/227-7368), and **Thrifty** (☎ 800/ 367-2277). See individual city listings for local rental agencies.

If you plan on renting a car in the United States, you probably won't need the services of an additional automobile organization (see "AAA," below), as some rental agencies provide the same services. Be sure to ask when you pick up your car. To rent a car, you need a major credit card and a valid driver's license. You usually need to be at least 25 years old. Some companies do rent to younger people, but add a daily surcharge. Be sure to return your car with the same amount of gas you started out with; rental companies charge excessive prices for gasoline.

Fast Facts: For the Foreign Traveler

Automobile Organizations   Auto clubs will supply maps, suggested routes, guidebooks, accident and bail-bond insurance, and emergency road service. The major auto club in the United States is the **American Automobile Association (AAA),** with close to 1,000 offices nationwide, including offices in Denver, Boulder, and Colorado Springs. Members of some foreign auto clubs have reciprocal arrangements with the AAA and enjoy its services at no charge. If you belong to an auto club, inquire about AAA reciprocity before you leave home. You may be able to join AAA even if you're not a member of a reciprocal club. AAA has a nationwide emergency road service telephone number (☎ **800/AAA-HELP**), and you can get information on-line at www.aaa.com.

Business Hours   Banks are usually open weekdays from 9am to 5pm, often until 6pm on Friday, and sometimes Saturday morning. There's 24-hour access to the automatic-teller machines (ATMs) at most banks, plus in many shopping centers, grocery stores, and other outlets.

Generally, business offices are open weekdays from 9am to 5pm. Stores are open 6 days a week, with some open on Sunday, too; department stores usually stay open until 9pm at least 1 day a week. Discount stores and supermarkets are often open later than other stores, and some supermarkets are open 24 hours a day.

Climate   See "When to Go," in chapter 2.

Currency & Currency Exchange   See "Money" in "Preparing for Your Trip," above.

Electricity   The United States uses 110-120 volts, 60 cycles, compared to 220-240 volts, 50 cycles, as in most of Europe, Australia, and New Zealand. In addition to a 100-volt converter, small appliances of non-American manufacture, such as hair dryers or shavers, will require a plug adapter, with two flat, parallel pins. Downward converters that change 220-240 volts to 110-120 volts are difficult to find in the United States, so bring one with you.

Embassies/Consulates   All embassies are located in the nation's capital, Washington, D.C.; some consulates are located in major cities, and most nations have a mission to the United Nations in New York City. If your country isn't listed below, call for directory information in Washington, D.C. (☎ **202/555-1212**) for the number of your national embassy.

The embassy of **Australia** is at 1601 Massachusetts Ave. NW, Washington, DC 20036 (☎ **202/797-3000;** www.austemb.org). There are consulates in New York, Honolulu, Houston, Los Angeles, and San Francisco.

The embassy of **Canada** is at 501 Pennsylvania Ave. NW, Washington, DC 20001 (☎ **202/682-1740;** www.canadianembassy.org). Other Canadian consulates are in Buffalo (NY), Detroit, Los Angeles, New York, and Seattle.

The embassy of **Ireland** is at 2234 Massachusetts Ave. NW, Washington, DC 20008 (☎ **202/462-3939**). Irish consulates are in Boston, Chicago, New York, and San Francisco.

The embassy of **Japan** is at 2520 Massachusetts Ave. NW, Washington, DC 20008 (☎ **202/238-6700;** www.embjapan.org). Japanese consulates are located in Atlanta, Kansas City, San Francisco, and Washington D.C.

The embassy of **New Zealand** is at 37 Observatory Circle NW, Washington, DC 20008 (☎ **202/328-4800;** www.nzemb.org). New Zealand consulates are in Los Angeles, Salt Lake City, San Francisco, and Seattle.

The embassy of the **United Kingdom** is at 3100 Massachusetts Ave. NW, Washington, DC 20008 (☎ **202/462-1340**). Other British consulates are in Atlanta, Boston, Chicago, Cleveland, Houston, Los Angeles, New York, San Francisco, and Seattle.

The following countries have consulates in the Denver area: **Australia,** 999 18th St. (☎ 303/297-1200); **Costa Rica,** 3356 S. Xenia (☎ 303/696-8211); **Denmark,** 5353 W. Dartmouth Ave., Lakewood (☎ **303/980-9100**); **France,** 1420 Ogden St. (☎ 303/831-8616); **Germany,** 350 Indiana St. (☎ 303/ 279-1551); **Italy,** 16613 W. Archer Ave., Golden (☎ 303/271-1429); **Japan,**

1225 17th St. (☎ 303/297-0027); **Korea,** 1600 Broadway, Suite 500 (☎ 303/830-0500); **Mexico,** 48 Steele St. (☎ 303/331-1110); **Netherlands,** 5560 S. Chester Court, Greenwood Village (☎ 303/770-7747); **Norway,** 370 17th St. (☎ **303/592-5930**); **Sweden** (☎ 303/758-0999); **Switzerland,** 2810 Iliff St., Boulder (☎ 303/499-5641); and **Thailand,** 717 17th St. (☎ 303/312-1934).

Emergencies   Call ☎ **911** to report a fire, call the police, or get an ambulance anywhere in the United States. This is a toll-free call (no coins are required at public telephones).

Gasoline (Petrol)   Petrol is known as gasoline (or simply "gas") in the United States, and petrol stations are known as both gas stations and service stations—an odd name since almost all the service stations you'll encounter in Colorado are self-serve. One U.S. gallon equals 3.75 liters, while 1.2 U.S. gallons equals 1 Imperial gallon. You'll notice there are several grades (and price levels) of gasoline available at most gas stations, and that their names change from company to company. Unleaded gasoline with the highest octane is the most expensive, but most rental cars will run fine with the less expensive "regular" unleaded. Prices fluctuate, but at press time the regular unleaded gas cost in Denver, Boulder, and Colorado Springs was about $1.65 per gallon. Be aware that gasoline prices are almost always higher—sometimes significantly so—in tourist areas such as the gateway towns to Rocky Mountain National Park.

Holidays   Banks, government offices, post offices, and many stores, restaurants, and museums are closed on the following legal national holidays: January 1 (New Year's Day), the third Monday in January (Martin Luther King, Jr. Day), the third Monday in February (Presidents' Day, Washington's Birthday), the last Monday in May (Memorial Day), July 4 (Independence Day), the first Monday in September (Labor Day), the second Monday in October (Columbus Day), November 11 (Veterans' Day/Armistice Day), the fourth Thursday in November (Thanksgiving Day), and December 25 (Christmas). Also, the Tuesday following the first Monday in November is Election Day and is a federal government holiday in presidential-election years (held every four years, and next in 2004).

Stores and some restaurants often close only for New Year's Day, Easter, and Christmas.

Legal Aid   The foreign tourist will probably never become involved with the American legal system. If you are "pulled over" for a minor infraction (for example, of the highway code, such as speeding), never attempt to pay the fine directly to a police officer; this could be construed as attempted bribery, a much more serious crime. Pay fines by mail, or directly into the hands of the clerk of the court. If accused of a more serious offense, say and do nothing before consulting a lawyer. Here the burden is on the state to prove a person's guilt beyond a reasonable doubt, and everyone has the right to remain silent, whether he or she is suspected of a crime or actually arrested. Once arrested, a person can make one telephone call to a party of his or her choice. Call your embassy or consulate.

Liquor Laws   See "Liquor Laws" under "Fast Facts: Colorado," in chapter 2.

Mail   If you want your mail to follow you on your vacation and you aren't sure of your address, your mail can be sent to you, in your name, c/o General Delivery at the main post office of the city or region where you expect to be (call ☎ **800/275-8777** for information on the nearest post office). The addressee must pick mail up in person and must produce proof of identity (driver's license, passport, etc.). Most post offices will hold your mail for up to 1 month, and are open Monday to Friday from 8am to 6pm, and Saturday from 9am to 3pm.

Mailboxes are blue with a blue-and-white eagle logo, and carry the inscription UNITED STATES POSTAL SERVICE. If your mail is addressed to a U.S. destination, don't forget to add the five-digit postal code, or ZIP (zone improvement plan) code, after the two-letter abbreviation of the state to which the mail is addressed (CO for Colorado, CA for California, NY for New York, and so on).

Within the United States, at press time, it cost 20¢ to mail a standard-size postcard and 33¢ for a letter, although a 1¢ increase in these rates was being considered for 2001. For international mail, a first-class letter of up to one-half ounce costs 60¢ (46¢ to Canada and 40¢ to Mexico); a first-class postcard costs 50¢ (40¢ to Canada and 35¢ Mexico); and a preprinted postal aerogramme costs 50¢.

Newspapers/Magazines   National newspapers generally available in Colorado include the *New York Times, USA Today,* and the *Wall Street Journal.* National news magazines include *Newsweek, Time,* and *U.S. News & World Report.* The state's major daily newspaper is the *Denver Post.*

Post   See "Mail," above.

Radio & Television   Six coast-to-coast networks—ABC, CBS, NBC, PBS (Public Broadcasting Service), Fox, and CNN (Cable Network News)—play a major part in American life. In Colorado, television viewers usually have a choice of at least a dozen channels via cable or satellite. PBS and the cable channel Arts and Entertainment (A&E) broadcast a number of British programs. You'll also find a wide choice of local radio stations, each broadcasting particular kinds of talk shows and/or music—classical, country, jazz, pop—punctuated by news broadcasts and frequent commercials. There is also a growing number of Spanish-language radio stations in Colorado's major cities.

Safety   See "Safety" in "Preparing for Your Trip," above.

Taxes   In the United States, there is no VAT (value-added tax) or other indirect tax at a national level. Every state, as well as each city and county, has the right to levy its own local tax on all purchases, including hotel and restaurant checks, airline tickets, and so on. Sales taxes in Colorado vary, but usually total about 7%. An exception is the tax on lodging, which often runs to 10%. Sales tax is not usually included in the price tags you'll see on merchandise or in the rates you're quoted for lodging. These taxes are not refundable.

Telephone, Telegraph, Telex, & Fax   The telephone system in the United States is run by private corporations, so rates, especially for long-distance service and operator-assisted calls, can vary widely. Before calling from a hotel room, always ask the hotel phone operator if there are any telephone surcharges. There almost always are—often as much as 75¢ or $1, even for a local call. These charges are best avoided by using a **public pay telephone,** which you'll find clearly marked in most public buildings and private establishments as well as on the street. Convenience grocery stores and gas stations always have them. Many convenience groceries and packaging services sell **prepaid calling cards** in denominations up to $50; these can be the least expensive way to call home. Many public phones at airports now accept American Express, MasterCard, and Visa credit cards. **Local calls** made from public pay phones in most locales cost either 25¢ or 35¢. Pay phones do not accept pennies, and few will take anything larger than a quarter.

Most long-distance and international calls can be dialed directly from any phone. **For calls within the United States and to Canada,** dial 1 followed by the area code and the seven-digit number. **For other international calls,** dial 011 followed by the country code, city code, and the telephone number of the person you are calling.

Calls to area codes **800, 888,** and **877** are toll-free. However, calls to numbers in area codes **700** and **900** (chat lines, bulletin boards, "dating" services, and so on) can be very expensive—usually a charge of 95¢ to $3 or more per minute, and they sometimes have minimum charges that can run as high as $15 or more.

For **reversed-charge** or **collect calls,** and for person-to-person calls, dial 0 (zero, not the letter O) followed by the area code and number you want; an operator will then come on the line, and you should specify that you are calling collect, or person-to-person, or both. If your operator-assisted call is international, ask for the overseas operator.

In the past few years, many American companies have installed voice-mail systems, so be prepared to deal with a machine instead of a receptionist if calling a business number.

For local **directory assistance** ("information"), dial ☎ **1-411;** for **long-distance information,** dial 1, then the appropriate area code and ☎ **555-1212.**

Telegraph and telex services are provided primarily by Western Union. You can bring your telegram into the nearest Western Union office (there are hundreds across the country) or dictate it over the phone (☎ **800/325-6000**). You can also telegraph money, or have it telegraphed to you, very quickly over the Western Union system, but this service can cost as much as 15-20 percent of the amount sent.

Most hotels have **fax machines** available for guest use (be sure to ask about the charge to use it), and many hotel rooms are even wired for guests' fax machines. A less expensive way to send and receive faxes may be at stores such as Mail Boxes Etc., a national chain of packing service shops (look in the Yellow Pages directory under "Packing Services").

There are two kinds of telephone directories in the United States. The so-called **White Pages** list private households and business subscribers in alphabetical order. The inside front cover lists emergency numbers for police, fire, ambulance, the Coast Guard, poison-control center, crime-victims hotline, and so on. The first few pages will tell you how to make long-distance and international calls, complete with country codes and area codes. Government numbers are usually printed on blue paper within the White Pages. Printed on yellow paper, the so-called **Yellow Pages** list all local services, businesses, industries, and houses of worship according to activity with an index at the front or back. (Drugstores/pharmacies and restaurants are also listed by geographic location.) The Yellow Pages also include city plans or detailed area maps, postal ZIP codes, and public transportation routes.

Time   The United States is divided into four **time zones** (six, including Alaska and Hawaii). From east to west, these are: eastern standard time (EST); central standard time (CST); mountain standard time (MST), which includes Colorado; Pacific standard time (PST); Alaska standard time (AST); and Hawaii standard time (HST). Always keep time zones in mind if you are traveling (or even telephoning) long distances in the United States. For example, noon in New York City (EST) is 11am in Chicago (CST), 10am in Denver (MST), 9am in Los Angeles (PST), 8am in Anchorage (AST), and 7am in Honolulu (HST).

Daylight saving time (DST) is in effect in Colorado and most of the country from the first Sunday in April through the last Saturday in October (actually, the change is made at 2am on Sunday). Daylight saving time moves the clock 1 hour ahead of standard time. Note that Arizona (except for the Navajo Nation), Hawaii, most of Indiana, and Puerto Rico do not observe DST.

Tipping   Tipping is so ingrained in the American way of life that the annual income tax of tip-earning service personnel is based on how much they should have received in light of their employers' gross revenues. Accordingly, they may have to pay tax on a tip you didn't actually give them.

Here are some rules of thumb:

In hotels, tip **bellhops** at least $1 per bag ($2 to $3 if you have a lot of luggage) and tip the **chamber staff** $1 per day. Tip the **doorman** or **concierge** only if he or she has provided you with some specific service (for example, calling a cab for you or obtaining difficult-to-get theater tickets). Tip the **valet parking attendant** $1 every time you get your car.

In restaurants, bars, and nightclubs, tip **service staff** 15% to 20% of the check, tip **bartenders** 10% to 15%, tip **checkroom attendants** $1 per garment, and tip **valet-parking attendants** $1 per vehicle. Tip the **doorman** only if he has provided you with some specific service (such as calling a cab for you). Tipping is not expected in cafeterias and fast-food restaurants.

Tip **cab drivers** 15% of the fare.

As for other service personnel, tip **skycaps** at airports at least $1 per bag ($2 to $3 if you have a lot of luggage) and tip **hairdressers** and **barbers** 15% to 20%. Tipping theater or movie ushers and gas-station attendants is not expected.

Toilets   Foreign visitors often complain that public toilets are hard to find in most U.S. cities. There are few on the streets, but you can usually find a clean one in a visitor information center, shopping mall, restaurant, hotel, museum, department or discount store, or service station (although service-station facilities often leave much to be desired). Note, however, a growing practice in some restaurants of displaying a sign: REST ROOMS ARE FOR PATRONS ONLY. You can just ignore this sign or, better yet, avoid arguments by paying for a cup of coffee or soft drink, which will qualify you as a patron.

Settling into Denver

4

It's no accident that Denver is called "the Mile High City." When you climb up to the State Capitol, you're precisely 5,280 feet above sea level when you reach the fifteenth step. The fact that Denver happens to be at this altitude was purely coincidental; Denver is one of the few cities that was not built on an ocean, lake, navigable river, or even on an existing road or railroad.

In the summer of 1858, a few flecks of gold were discovered by eager Georgia prospectors where Cherry Creek empties into the shallow South Platte River. A tent camp quickly sprang up on the site. (The first permanent structure was a saloon.) When militia Gen. William H. Larimer arrived in 1859, he claim-jumped the land on the east side of the Platte, laid out a city, and, hoping to gain political favors, named it after James Denver, governor of the Kansas Territory, which included this area. Larimer was not aware that Denver had recently resigned.

Larimer's was one of several settlements on the South Platte. Three others also sought recognition, but Larimer, a shrewd man, had a solution. For the price of a barrel of whisky, he bought out the other would-be town fathers, and the name *Denver* caught on.

Although the gold found in Denver was but a teaser for much larger strikes in the nearby mountains, the community grew as a shipping and trade center, in part because it had a milder climate than the mining towns it served. A devastating fire in 1863, a deadly flash flood in 1864, and American Indian tribal hostilities in the late 1860s created many hardships. But the establishment of rail links to the east and the influx of silver from the rich mines to the west kept Denver going. Silver from Leadville and gold from Cripple Creek made Denver a showcase city in the late 19th and early 20th centuries. The U.S. Mint, built in 1906, established Denver as a banking and financial center.

In the years following World War II, Denver mushroomed to become the largest city between the Great Plains and Pacific Coast, with about 500,000 residents within the city limits and more than 1.8 million in the metropolitan area. Today, it's a sprawling and growing city, extending from the Rocky Mountain foothills on the west far into the plains to the south and east. It's also a major destination for both tourists and business travelers. Denver is noted for its dozens of tree-lined boulevards; 200 city parks comprising more than 20,000 acres; and architecture ranging from Victorian to sleek contemporary.

1 Orientation

ARRIVING
BY PLANE
Denver International Airport (DIA) is 23 miles northeast of downtown, usually a 35- to 45-minute drive. Covering 53 square miles (twice the size of Manhattan), DIA boasts one of the tallest flight control towers in the world, at 327 feet.

The airport, which has 94 gates and 5 full-service runways, can handle around 33 million passengers annually.

Major national airlines serving Denver include American, America West, Continental, Delta, Frontier, Northwest, Sun Country, TWA, United, and US Airways. **International airlines** include Air Canada, British Airways, Korean Air, Martinair Holland, and Mexicana de Aviación.

Regional and **commuter airlines** connecting Denver with other points in the Rockies and Southwest include Aspen Air, Mountain Air Express, and three United Express airlines: Air Wisconsin, Great Lakes Aviation, and Mesa.

For airlines' national reservations phone numbers and Web sites, see "Getting There," in chapter 2. For other information, call the Denver International Airport **information line** (☎ **800/AIR-2-DEN,** TDD 800/688-1333; or ☎ 303/342-2000). Other important airport phone numbers include: **administration,** ☎ **303/342-2200; ground transportation,** ☎ **303/342-4059; vehicle assistance,** including emergency car start, ☎ **303/342-4650; paging,** ☎ **303/342-2300;** and **parking,** ☎ **303/342-4096.**

GETTING TO & FROM THE AIRPORT   Bus, taxi, and limousine services shuttle travelers between the airport and downtown, and most major car-rental companies have outlets at the airport. Because many major hotels are some distance from the airport, travelers should check on the availability and cost of hotel shuttle services when making reservations.

The cost of a **city bus** ride from the airport to downtown Denver is $6; from the airport to Boulder and suburban Park-n-Ride lots, it is about $8. The **SuperShuttle** (☎ **800/525-3177** or 303/370-1300) provides transportation to and from a number of hotels downtown and in the Denver Tech Center. The **SuperShuttle** has frequent scheduled service between the airport and downtown hotels for $17 one-way, $30 round-trip; door-to-door service is also available. **Taxi** companies (see "Getting Around," below) are another option, with fares generally in the $30 to $50 range, and you can often share a cab and split the fare by calling the cab company ahead of time. For instance, **Yellow Cab** (☎ **303/777-7777**) will take up to five people from DIA to most downtown hotels for a flat rate of $43.

Those who prefer a bit of luxury may prefer the ride provided by **Mile Hi City Limousine** (☎ **800/910-7433** or 303/355-5002; www.whitedovelimo.com). Rates to different parts of the Denver metro area vary, so call for prices. The company operates sedan and stretch limousines built to accommodate three to 12 people. Charter services are also available.

BY CAR
The principal highway routes into Denver are **I-25** from the north (Fort Collins, Cheyenne) and south (Colorado Springs, Albuquerque); **I-70** from the east (Burlington, Kansas City) and west (Grand Junction); and **I-76** from the northeast (Sterling). If you're driving into Denver from Boulder, take **U.S. 36;** from Salida and southwest, **U.S. 285.**

Metropolitan Denver & Environs

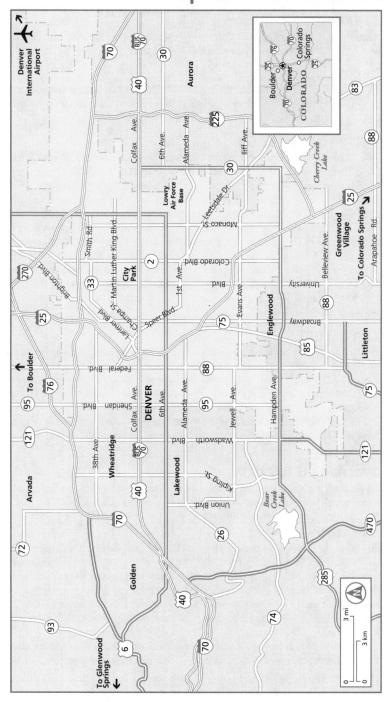

BY TRAIN

Amtrak serves Union Station, 17th and Wynkoop streets (☎ **800/USA-RAIL** or 303/825-2583), in the lower downtown historic district.

BY BUS

Greyhound, 19th and Arapahoe streets (☎ **800/231-2222**), is the major bus service in Colorado, with about 60 daily arrivals and departures to communities both in and out of the state.

VISITOR INFORMATION

The **Denver Metro Convention and Visitors Bureau** operates a visitor center at 1668 Larimer St. (☎ **303/892-1112**), just off the 16th Street Mall, that is open Monday through Friday from 8am to 5pm and Saturday from 9am to 1pm. Visitor information is also available in Tabor and Cherry Creek Shopping Centers, and at the Colorado State Capitol and Denver International Airport. Ask for the *Official Visitors Guide,* an impressive 150-plus-page full-color booklet with a comprehensive listing of accommodations, restaurants, and other visitor services in Denver and surrounding areas.

For advance information, contact the Denver Metro Convention and Visitors Bureau, 1555 California St., Suite 300, Denver, CO 80202-4264 (☎ **800/ 593-8559**). Their Web site is **www.denver.org.** Another good Internet resource is **www.denver.citysearch.com**.

CITY LAYOUT

You can never truly get lost in Denver, as long as you remember that the mountains, nearly always visible, are to the west. All the same, it can be perplexing to get around a city of half a million people. One element of confusion is that Denver has both an older grid system, which is oriented northeast–southwest to parallel the South Platte River, and a newer north–south grid system that surrounds the older one.

There's a good Denver map in the *Official Visitors Guide,* available free of charge from the Denver Metro Convention and Visitors Bureau (see "Visitor Information," above).

MAIN ARTERIES & STREETS

It's probably easiest to get your bearings from Civic Center Park. From here, Colfax Avenue (U.S. 40) extends east and west as far as the eye can see. The same is true for Broadway, which reaches north and south.

DOWNTOWN DENVER   North of Colfax and west of Broadway is the center of downtown Denver, where the streets follow the old grid pattern. A mile-long pedestrian mall, **16th Street,** cuts northwest off Broadway just above this intersection. (The numbered streets parallel 16th to the northeast, extending all the way to 44th; and to the southwest, as far as Fifth.) Intersecting the numbered streets at right angles are **Lawrence Street** (which runs one-way northeast) and **Larimer Street** (which runs one-way southwest), 12 and 13 blocks north, respectively, from the Colfax–Broadway intersection.

I-25 skirts downtown Denver to the west, with access from Colfax or **Speer Boulevard,** which winds diagonally along Cherry Creek past Larimer Square.

OUTSIDE DOWNTOWN   Outside the downtown sector, the pattern is a little less confusing. But keep in mind that the numbered *avenues* that parallel Colfax to the north and south (Colfax is equivalent to 15th Avenue) have nothing in common with the numbered *streets* of the downtown grid. In fact, any byway labeled an "avenue" runs east–west, never north–south.

FINDING AN ADDRESS

NORTH–SOUTH ARTERIES   The thoroughfare that divides avenues into "east" and "west" is **Broadway,** which runs one-way south between 19th Street and I-25. Each block east or west adds 100 to the avenue address; thus, if you wanted to find 2115 E. 17th Ave., it would be a little more than 21 blocks east of Broadway, just beyond Vine Street.

Main thoroughfares that parallel Broadway to the east include **Downing Street** (1200 block), **York Street** (2300 block; it becomes **University Boulevard** south of Sixth), **Colorado Boulevard** (4000 block), **Monaco Street Parkway** (6500 block), and **Quebec Street** (7300 block). Colorado Boulevard (Colo. 2) is the most significant artery, intersecting I-25 on the south and I-70 on the north. North–south streets that parallel Broadway to the west include **Santa Fe Drive** (U.S. 85; 1000 block); west of I-25 are **Federal Boulevard** (U.S. 287 North, site of several sports arenas; 3000 block), and **Sheridan Boulevard** (Colo. 95; 5200 block), the boundary between Denver and Lakewood.

EAST–WEST ARTERIES   Denver streets are divided into "north" and "south" at **Ellsworth Avenue,** about 1¹/₂ miles south of Colfax. Ellsworth is a relatively minor street, but it's a convenient dividing point because it's just a block south of **1st Avenue.** With building numbers increasing by 100 each block, that puts an address like 1710 Downing St. at the corner of East 17th Avenue. **First, Sixth, Colfax** (1500 block), and **26th** avenues, and **Martin Luther King Jr. Boulevard** (3200 block) are the principal east–west thoroughfares. There are no numbered avenues south of Ellsworth. Major east–west byways south of Ellsworth are **Alameda** (Colo. 26; 300 block), **Mississippi** (1100 block), **Florida** (1500 block), **Evans** (2100 block), **Yale** (2700 block), and **Hampden** avenues (U.S. 285; 3500 block).

Neighborhoods in Brief

Lower Downtown (LoDo)   A 25-block area surrounding Union Station, and encompassing **Wynkoop Street** southeast to **Market Street** and **20th Street** southwest to **Speer Boulevard,** this delightful and busy historic district was until recent years a somewhat seedy neighborhood of deteriorating Victorian houses and warehouses. But a major restoration effort has brought it back to life, so today it is home to chic shops, art galleries, nightclubs, and restaurants that are kept hopping by Denver's movers and shakers. Listed as both a city and county historic district, it boasts numerous National Historic Landmarks, and skyscrapers are prohibited by law. In addition, the 50,000-seat stadium, Coors Field, home of the Rockies baseball team, opened here in the spring of 1995.

Central Business District   This extends along **16th, 17th, and 18th streets between Lawrence Street and Broadway.** Here, the ban on skyscrapers certainly does not apply. Here is where you'll find the Brown Palace Hotel, the Westin Hotel at Tabor Center, and other upscale lodging properties; numerous restaurants and bars; plus the popular 16th Street Mall.

Far East Center   Denver's Asian community is concentrated along this strip of **Federal Boulevard,** between **West Alameda** and **West Mississippi** avenues, which burgeoned in the aftermath of the Vietnam War to accommodate throngs of Southeast

Asian refugees, especially Thai and Vietnamese. Look for authentic restaurants, bakeries, groceries, gift shops, and clothing stores. The Far East Center Building at Federal and Alameda is built in Japanese pagoda style.

Five Points   The "five points" actually meet at 23rd Street and Broadway, but the cultural and commercial hub of Denver's black community, from **23rd** to **38th** streets, northeast of downtown, covers a much larger area and incorporates four historic districts. Restaurants offer soul food, barbecued ribs, and Caribbean cuisine, while jazz and blues musicians and contemporary dance troupes perform in theaters and nightclubs. The Black American West Museum and Heritage Center is also in this area.

La Alma Lincoln Park/Auraria   Hispanic culture, art, food, and entertainment predominate along this strip of **Santa Fe Drive,** between **West Colfax** and **West Sixth** avenues, notable for its Southwestern character and architecture. This neighborhood is well worth a visit for its numerous restaurants, art galleries, and crafts shops. Denver's annual Cinco de Mayo celebration takes place here each May.

Uptown   Denver's oldest residential neighborhood, from **Broadway** east to **York Street** (City Park) and **23rd Avenue** south to **Colfax Avenue,** is best known today for two things: It's bisected by 17th Avenue's "Restaurant Row" (see "Dining," below), and several of its classic Victorian and Queen Anne–style homes have been converted to captivating bed-and-breakfasts (see "Accommodations," below).

Washington Park   A grand Victorian neighborhood centered on the lush park of its namesake, "Wash Park" is one of Denver's trendiest and most popular neighborhoods. Bounded by **Broadway** east to **University Boulevard** and **Alameda Avenue** south to **Evans Avenue,** it features a good deal of dining and recreational opportunities, but little in the way of lodging. It is a great place, however, for architecture and history buffs alike to take a drive or walk past the grand rows of houses.

Capitol Hill   One of Denver's most diverse and oldest neighborhoods just southeast of downtown, Capitol Hill is centered around the gold-domed Capitol Building, encompassing **Broadway** east to **York** and **Colfax Avenue** south to **6th Avenue.** The north edge is continuously improving after years of neglect and criminal activity, and now features such attractions as the Fillmore Auditorium and a lively restaurant and bar scene. There are also several commercial and retail districts in the area, nestled amidst Victorian houses and more modern lofts and apartments. Also located here are the Molly Brown House Museum (see Chapter 5) and several lodging options, ranging from B&Bs to luxury hotels (see "Accommodations," below). You'll notice that there are no old wooden buildings here. After a disastrous fire in 1863, the government forbade the construction of wooden structures until after World War II.

Cherry Creek   Home of the Cherry Creek Shopping Center and Denver Country Club, this area extends north from **East 1st Avenue** to **East 8th Avenue,** and from **Downing Street** east to **Steele Street.** You'll find huge, ostentatious stone mansions here, especially around Circle Drive (southwest of 6th and University), where many of Denver's wealthiest families have lived for generations.

Glendale   Denver fully surrounds Glendale, an incorporated city in its own right. The center of a lively entertainment district, Glendale straddles Cherry Creek on South Colorado Boulevard south of East Alameda Avenue.

Tech Center   At the southern end of the metropolitan area is the Denver Tech Center, along **I-25** between **Belleview Avenue** and **Arapahoe Road.** In this district, about a 25-minute drive from downtown, you will find the headquarters of several international and national companies, high-tech businesses, and a handful of upscale hotels heavily oriented toward business travelers.

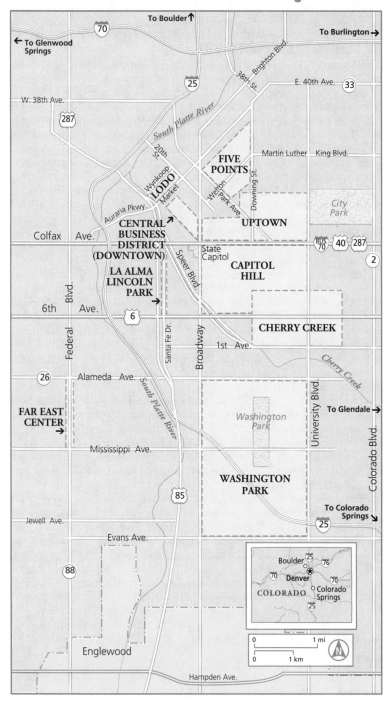

2 Getting Around

BY PUBLIC TRANSPORTATION

The **Regional Transportation District (RTD)** (☎ **800/366-7433** or 303/299-6000 or TDD 303/299-6089 for route and schedule information, 303/299-6700 for other business; www.rtd-denver.com) calls itself "The Ride" for its bus routes and light-rail system, with free transfer tickets available. It provides good service within Denver and its suburbs and outlying communities (including Boulder, Longmont, and Evergreen), as well as free parking at 50 Park-n-Ride locations throughout the Denver-Boulder metropolitan area. The light-rail service is designed to get buses and cars out of congested downtown Denver; many of the bus routes from outlying areas deliver passengers to light-rail stations rather than downtown.

The local fare is $1.25 during peak hours (Monday through Friday from 6 to 9am and 4 to 6pm) and 75¢ during off-peak hours. Seniors and passengers with disabilities pay only 25¢ off-peak, and children age 5 and under travel free. Regional fares vary (for example, it costs $2.50 between Denver and Boulder). Exact change is required for buses, and train tickets can be purchased at vending machines beneath light-rail station awnings.

Each route has its own schedule, including departure time of the last bus or train (which varies from 9pm to 1am). Maps for all routes are available at any time at the RTD **Civic Center Station,** 16th Street and Broadway; and the **Market Street Station,** at Market and 16th streets. RTD also provides special service to Colorado Rockies home baseball and Broncos home football games. All RTD buses and trains are completely wheelchair accessible.

Free buses run up and down the 16th Street Mall between the Civic Center and Market Street every 90 seconds during peak hours (less frequently at other times), daily from 6am to 1am.

Visitors particularly enjoy the **Cultural Connection Trolley** (☎ **303/299-6000**), which runs daily every 30 minutes between 9:30am and 7:30pm with stops at Denver's most popular tourist attractions, including the State Capitol, Denver Botanic Gardens, Denver Zoo, U.S. Mint, and most major downtown museums. A full-day pass costs $3 (children age 5 and younger ride free); detailed route information is available at the Denver Visitors Center on Larimer Street. The trolley ticket is also good on RTD buses and light rail.

From June through August you can ride the open-air **Platte Valley Trolley** (☎ **303/458-6255;** www.denvertrolley.org). Between 11am and 4pm daily there's a half-hour "Denver Sightseeing Route" ride ($2 adults, $1 seniors and children), which operates from 15th Street at Confluence Park, south to Decatur Street along the west bank of the Platte River. Another excursion leaves at noon Monday through Friday, and 2pm Saturday and Sunday ($4 adults, $3 seniors, $2 children). This 1-hour trip takes visitors west of Decatur Street, following a portion of a historic tram line that ran to Golden until 1950. During April, May, September, and October the trolley runs, weather permitting, Tuesday through Sunday between 11am and 3pm; and in winter, it operates only on weekends, 11am to 3pm, also weather permitting. Special charter trips can be arranged for off-hours; call for details.

BY TAXI

The main companies are **Yellow Cab** (☎ **303/777-7777**), **Zone Cab** (☎ **303/ 444-8888**), and **Metro Taxi** (☎ **303/333-3333**). Taxis can be hailed on the street, though it's preferable to telephone for a taxi or wait for one at a taxi stand outside a major hotel.

For the traveler seeking true luxury, Denver has several limousine services, including **Admiral Limousines,** 4400 Garfield St. (☎ **800/828-8680** or 303/296-2003); **Executive Transportation** in Denver (☎ **800/546-6120** or 303/755-5089), which covers the entire state, with Suburbans, 15-passenger vans, town cars and limos; and **Parker Suburban Limousine** in Commerce City (☎ **888/271-1305** or 303/ 288-1305), featuring four-wheel-drive Suburbans.

BY CAR

Because cars are not really necessary downtown, visitors can save rental costs and parking fees by arranging to stay downtown while in Denver and then renting a car when planning to leave the area.

The Denver office of the **American Automobile Association (AAA)** is at 4100 E. Arkansas Ave., Denver, CO 80222-3405 (☎ **800/222-4357** or 303/753-8800); there are several other locations in the Denver area.

CAR RENTALS   Most major car-rental agencies have outlets in or near downtown Denver, as well as at Denver International Airport. These include **Alamo,** 24530 E. 78th Ave. (☎ 800/327-9633 or 303/342-7373); **Avis,** 1900 Broadway (☎ 800/831-2847 or 303/839-1280; 303/342-5500 at DIA); **Budget,** 1980 Broadway (☎ 800/527-0700 or 303/341-2277; 303/342-9001 at DIA); **Dollar,** 7939 E. Arapahoe Rd., Denver Tech Center (☎ 800/800-4000 or 303/790-0970; 303/342-9099 at DIA); **Enterprise,** 5179 S. Broadway (☎ 800/736-8222 or 303/794-3333; 303/342-7350 at DIA); **Hertz,** 2001 Welton (☎ 800/654-3131 or 303/297-9400; 303/342-3800 at DIA); **National,** at Denver International Airport (☎ 800/227-7368 or 303/342-0717); and **Thrifty,** in the Sheraton Hotel in the Denver Tech Center (☎ 800/367-2277 or 303/985-7756; 303/342-9400 at DIA). You can rent campers, travel trailers, motor homes, and motorcycles from **Cruise America,** 8950 N. Federal Blvd. (☎ 800/327-7799 or 303/ 426-6699; www.cruiseamerica.com.).

Per-day rentals for midsize cars range from $30 to $50, although AAA and other discounts are often available, and weekend and multiday rates can also save money. Four-wheel-drive vehicles, trucks, and campers cost more.

PARKING   Downtown parking-lot rates vary from 75¢ per half hour to $10 per full day. Rates are higher in the vicinity of the 16th Street Mall, the central business district, and in hotel lots (some downtown hotels charge as much as $26 per night). Keep a handful of quarters if you plan to use on-street parking meters.

Fast Facts: Denver

American Express   The American Express Travel Agency is located at 555 17th St. (☎ **303/383-5050**); it's open Monday through Friday from 8:30am to 5pm. Full member services and currency exchange are offered. To report a lost card, call ☎ **800/528-4800;** to report lost traveler's checks, call ☎ **800/221-7282.**

Area Code   Area codes are **303** and **720,** and local calls require 10-digit dialing. See the "Telephone/Fax" section under "Fast Facts," in chapter 2.

Baby-sitters   Front desks at major hotels can often arrange baby-sitters for their guests.

Business Hours   Banks are usually open weekdays from 9am to 5pm, occasionally a bit later on Friday, and sometimes on Saturday. There's 24-hour access to the automatic teller machines (ATMs) at most banks, plus in many shopping centers and other outlets.

Generally, business offices are open weekdays from 9am to 5pm and govern-ment offices are open from 8am until 4:30 or 5pm. Stores are open 6 days a week, with many also open on Sunday, too; department stores usually stay open until 9pm at least 1 day a week. Discount stores and supermarkets are often open later than other stores, and some supermarkets are open 24 hours a day.

Car Rentals   See "Getting Around," earlier in this chapter.

Doctors/Dentists   Doctor and dentist referrals are available by calling ☎ **1-800-DOCTORS** (☎ 800/362-8677). **Centura Health Advisor** (☎ **800/ 327-6877** or 303/777-6877) provides free physician referrals and answers health questions; the **Parent Smart Line** (☎ **303/861-0123**) specializes in referrals to children's doctors and dentists, and also has staff on hand to provide advice.

Drugstores   Throughout the metropolitan area, you will find Walgreens and Payless pharmacies, as well as Safeway and King Soopers grocery stores (which also have drugstores). The **Walgreens** at 2000 E. Colfax Ave. is open 24 hours a day (☎ **303/331-0917**). For the locations of other Walgreens, call ☎ **800/ WALGREENS.** For an old-fashioned, family-owned drugstore, there is **Watson's,** 900 Lincoln St. (☎ **303/837-1366**), open Monday through Friday from 8am to midnight, Saturday from 10am to midnight, and Sunday from 10am to 8pm.

Emergencies   Call ☎ **911.** For the **Poison Control Center,** call ☎ **303/ 739-1123.** For the **Rape Crisis and Domestic Violence Hotline,** call ☎ **303/ 318-9989.**

Eyeglasses   One-hour replacements and repairs are usually available at **Pearle Vision,** 2720 S. Colorado Blvd. at Yale Avenue (☎ **303/758-1292**), and **Lenscrafters,** in Cherry Creek Shopping Center (☎ **303/321-8331**).

Hospitals   Among Denver-area hospitals are **St. Joseph's,** 1835 Franklin St. (☎ **303/837-7111**), just east of downtown, and **Children's Hospital,** 1056 E. 19th Ave. (☎ **303/861-8888**).

Maps   Denver's largest map store, **Mapsco Map and Travel Center,** 800 Lin-coln St., Denver, CO 80203 (☎ **800/456-8703** or 303/623-4299), offers USGS and recreation maps, state maps and travel guides, raised relief maps, and globes.

Newspapers/Magazines   The *Denver Post* (www.denverpost.com) is Colorado's largest daily newspaper. The *Rocky Mountain News* (www.rockymountainnews. com) also covers the metropolitan area. (The papers signed a joint operating agreement in 2000.) A widely read free weekly, *Westword* (www.westword.com), is known as much for its controversial jibes at local politicians as for its enter-tainment listings. National newspapers such as *USA Today* and the *Wall Street Journal* can be purchased at newsstands and at major hotels.

Photographic Needs   For photographic supplies, equipment, 1-hour photo processing, and repairs, visit **Wolf Camera** at one of its twenty Denver locations; its downtown branch, at 1545 California St.(☎ **303/623-1155** or 888/ 644-WOLF for other locations; www.wolfcamera.com), claims to be the biggest single-floor camera store in the world. Check Sunday's Denver Post for discount coupons for Wolf Camera's services. Another good source for photo supplies and film processing is **Mike's Camera,** 759 S. Colorado Blvd. (☎ **303/733-2121;** www.mikescamera.com), which has a repair and rental facility at 240 Broadway (☎ **303/744-3459**).

Post Office   The main downtown post office is at 951 20th St., open Monday through Friday from 7am to 6pm, Saturday from 9am to 1pm. For full 24-hour postal service, go to the General Mail Facility, 7500 E. 53rd Place. For other post office locations and hours, call the U.S. Postal Service (☎ **800/275-8777**).

Radio/TV   A large variety of music, news, sports, and entertainment is presented on some four dozen AM and FM radio stations in the Denver area, including KOA (850 AM) for news and talk, KKFN (950 AM) for all sports, KVOD (1280 AM) for classical music, KEZW (1430 AM) for big band and nostalgia, KWBI (91.1 FM) for Christian ministry and music, KIMN (100.3 FM) for adult hits, KRFX (103.5 FM) for classic rock, KXPK (96.5 FM) for rock alternative, KBCO (97.3 FM) for alternative music, KYGO (98.5 FM and 1600 AM) for new and classic country respectively, KUVO (89.3 FM) for Latin, jazz, and blues music and news, and KDJM (92.5 FM) for soul and '70s music.

Denver has 14 television stations, including KCNC (Channel 4), the CBS affiliate; KMGH (Channel 7), the ABC affiliate; KUSA (Channel 9), the NBC affiliate; and KDVR (Channel 31), the Fox affiliate. Other major stations include KWGN (Channel 2), the WB affiliate; and KRMA (Channel 6), the PBS affiliate. Cable or satellite service is available at most hotels.

Safety   Although Denver is a relatively safe city, it is not crime-free. Safety is seldom a problem on the 16th Street Mall, but even streetwise Denverites avoid late-night walks along certain sections of East Colfax Avenue, just a few blocks away. If you are unsure of the safety of a particular area you wish to visit, ask your hotel concierge or desk clerk.

Taxes   State and local sales tax in Denver is about 7% (it varies slightly in neighboring counties and suburbs). The hotel tax is about 5%, bringing the total tax on accommodations to about 12%.

Useful Telephone Numbers   For a weather report, time, and temperature, call ☎ **303/337-2500.** Statewide road condition reports are available by calling ☎ **303/639-1111.** For information on possible road construction delays in the Denver area and statewide, call ☎ **303/573-ROAD (7623).**

3 Accommodations

Although most hotels and motels in the Denver area do not have seasonal rates (as you'll find in many other parts of Colorado), hotels that cater to business travelers, such as the **Brown Palace** and the **Warwick** (see below), often offer substantial discounts on weekends, sometimes as much as 50% off the regular rates.

The lodging industry is still trying to catch up with the construction of Denver International Airport several years ago, and you'll find that many of the major chains and franchises have built or are in the process of constructing facilities near the new airport. Among those now open near the airport are **Courtyard by Marriott at DIA,** 6900 Tower Rd., Denver, CO 80249 (☎ **800/321-2211** or 303/371-0300), with a rate of $96 for two; **Fairfield Inn–DIA,** 6851 Tower Rd., Denver, CO 80249 (☎ **800/228-2800** or 303/576-9640), which charges $59 for a double; and **Hampton Inn DIA,** 6290 Tower Rd., Denver CO 80249 (☎ **800/426-7866** or 303/ 371-0200), with rates of $80 to $90 for two.

Chain hotels in the downtown area include: **Comfort Inn,** 401 17th St., Denver, CO 80202 (☎ **800/228-5150** or 303/296-0400), with a convenient location and rates of $129 to $175 double; **La Quinta Inn Downtown,** 3500 Park Ave. W. (at

Downtown Denver Accommodations

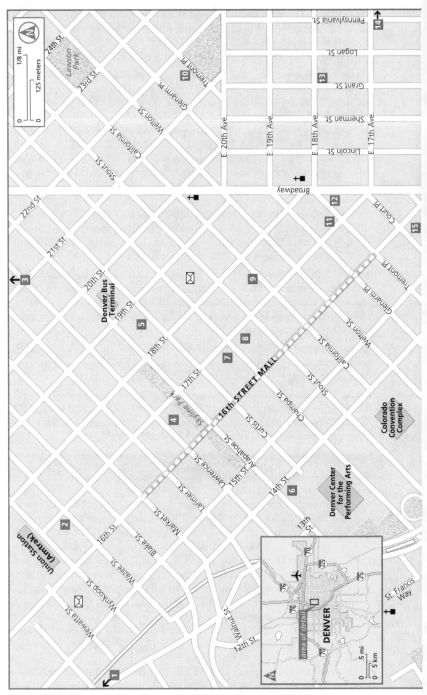

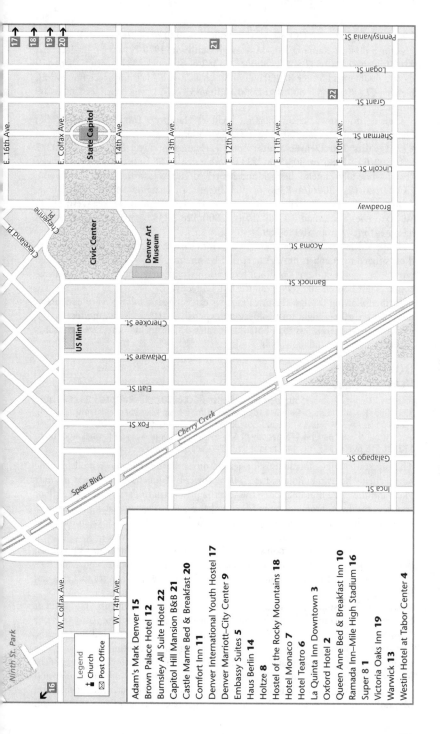

Legend
✝ Church
☒ Post Office

Adam's Mark Denver **15**
Brown Palace Hotel **12**
Burnsley All Suite Hotel **22**
Capitol Hill Mansion B&B **21**
Castle Marne Bed & Breakfast **20**
Comfort Inn **11**
Denver International Youth Hostel **17**
Denver Marriott–City Center **9**
Embassy Suites **5**
Haus Berlin **14**
Holtze **8**
Hostel of the Rocky Mountains **18**
Hotel Monaco **7**
Hotel Teatro **6**
La Quinta Inn Downtown **3**
Oxford Hotel **2**
Queen Anne Bed & Breakfast Inn **10**
Ramada Inn–Mile High Stadium **16**
Super 8 **1**
Victoria Oaks Inn **19**
Warwick **13**
Westin Hotel at Tabor Center **4**

I-25 exit 213), Denver, CO 80216 (☎ **800/531-5900** or 303/458-1222), charging $69 for a double; **Ramada Inn–Mile High Stadium,** 1975 Bryant St. (at I-25 exit 210B), Denver, CO 80204 (☎ **800/272-6232** or 303/433-8331), with rates of $79 to $89 double; and **Super 8,** 2601 Zuni St. (at I-25 exit 212B for Speer Boulevard), Denver, CO 80211 (☎ **800/800-8000** or 303/433-6677), which charges $59 to $69 double.

Outside downtown, chain lodgings include: **Hampton Inn,** 4685 Quebec St., Denver, CO 80216 (☎ **800/HAMPTON** or 303/388-8100), with a double rate of $59; **Quality Inn Denver South,** 6300 E. Hampden Ave., Denver, CO 80222 (☎ **800/647-1986** or 303/758-2211), with rates of $89 for a double room (see "Family-Friendly Hotels," below); and **Motel 6,** 480 Wadsworth Blvd., Lakewood, CO 80226 (☎ **800/466-8356** or 303/232-4924), charging $45 to $50 double. Among the four Best Westerns in the metro area is **Best Western Denver West,** 11595 W. Sixth Ave., Lakewood, CO 80215 (☎ **800/528-1234** or 303/238-7751), which has rates for two from $69 to $89.

These official, or "rack," rates do not take into consideration any discounts, such as those offered to members of AAA or AARP. Be sure to ask if you qualify for a reduced rate. Because a chain hotel's national reservation service may not be able to offer discounts, your best bet may be to call the hotel directly.

In the following listings, the price range is categorized as follows: **very expensive,** more than $150 per night for two persons; **expensive,** $100 to $150; **moderate,** $50 to $100; **inexpensive,** less than $50. These rates do not include the 12% tax that is added to all accommodations bills.

DOWNTOWN
VERY EXPENSIVE

Adam's Mark Denver. 1550 Court Place, Denver, CO 80202. ☎ **800/444-2326** or 303/ 893-3333. Fax 303/626-2543. www.adamsmark.com. E-mail: sales@denver.adamsmark.com. 1,225 units. A/C TV TEL. $179–$300 double; $375–$1,200 suite. AE, CB, DC, DISC, MC, V. Underground valet parking $15 per day or $19 overnight; self-parking $2 per half hour up to $12, or $15 overnight; 7 ft. 4 in. height limit. Pets accepted with a deposit.

The largest hotel in Colorado, this former Hilton has been completely remodeled. The hotel actually has two buildings: the 22-floor Tower Building on the east side of Court Place and the Plaza Building across the street (a pedestrian bridge on the second floor connects the two). From the upper floors of the Tower the west-facing rooms have marvelous views of the Front Range, and it's a real treat to relax and watch the lights of the city come on as the sun drops behind the curtain of mountains.

The decor of both guest rooms and public areas is classical, with an emphasis on brass, marble, and solid woods such as oak and mahogany. Colors are muted and restful. Terrific weekend packages are available starting at $79, and theater packages can be arranged.

Dining/Diversions: The hotel houses several dining establishments and bars. For fine Italian food complemented by singing wait staff, head for Bravo! Ristorante (see "Dining," below) on the ground floor of the Plaza Building. Just behind Bravo! is the Tiffany Rose, a lounge (open daily from 11am to midnight) offering light snacks, live piano music most evenings, and a jazz combo on Friday and Saturday nights. Opening off the lobby is Trattoria Colorado (see "Dining," below), offering buffet and menu dining at all three meals daily. The Capitol Bar, in the front corner of the Plaza overlooking the 16th Street Mall, is an elegant cigar bar, with light fare from 11:30am daily.

On the ground level of the Tower Building are Players, a sports bar with large-screen TVs that serves sandwiches and salads from 11am and coffee service between 6 and 10am daily; and the Supreme Court Cafe and Nightclub (see "Denver After Dark," in chapter 5), offering American food daily for lunch and dinner, with happy hour weekdays from 4 to 7pm and live music after 9pm Monday through Saturday.

Amenities: Laundry (including self-serve), dry cleaning, and shoe shine; health club with sauna, weight room, cardiovascular machines, and outdoor pool; business center; meeting space for up to 4,500; florist; gift shop; and executive level with concierge and business services, full breakfast, local and national newspapers, and happy hour with hors d'oeuvres, coffee and desserts.

✪ **Brown Palace Hotel.** 321 17th St., Denver, CO 80202. ☎ **800/228-2917** or 303/297-3111 in Colorado; 800/321-2599 elsewhere in North America. Fax 303/312-5900. www.brownpalace.com. E-mail: marketing@brownpalace.com. 241 units. A/C TV TEL. $210–$350 double; $350–$1245 suite. Weekend rates start at $169 double. AE, CB, DC, MC, V. Valet parking $18 overnight.

For more than 100 years, the Brown has been the place to stay for anyone who is anyone. A National Historic Landmark, the Brown Palace opened in August 1892 and has been operating continuously ever since. Designed with an odd triangular shape by the renowned architect Frank Edbrooke, it was built of Colorado red granite and Arizona sandstone. The lobby's walls are paneled with Mexican onyx, the floor is white marble, and elaborate cast-iron grillwork surrounds six tiers of balconies up to the stained-glass ceiling. During his presidency, Dwight Eisenhower (1953–1961) maintained the Western White House here. The Eisenhower Suite is richly decorated, and a dent in the fireplace trim is reported to have been made by an errant golf swing.

Guest rooms are uniquely decorated in either Victorian or art-deco style. Each has a desk, remote-control TV (with Spectravision), and its own heating and cooling control. The water's great here: The Brown Palace has its own artesian wells!

Dining/Diversions: Excellent meals are served in the Palace Arms (see "Dining," below). Ellyngton's (smoke-free) serves breakfast and lunch (light grills and pastas), and a champagne brunch on Sunday. The Ship Tavern, the hotel's oldest restaurant, is open daily for drinks and casual dining. The Churchill Bar (see "Denver After Dark" in chapter 5), a sophisticated cigar bar with a library atmosphere, occupies founder Henry C. Brown's office, next to the Palace Arms. Afternoon tea and cocktails are available in the lobby daily. Reservations are recommended for the English tea, which includes sandwiches and pastries from the Brown Palace bakery. The Brown Palace Club serves lunch for private members and hotel guests only.

Amenities: 24-hour room service, concierge, dual voice-modem lines and voice mail in all rooms, complimentary high-speed Internet access, turndown, robes, laundry, and in-room massage (available for an extra charge). Fitness center, business center, boutiques, beauty salon, meeting facilities for up to 750.

Denver Marriott–City Center. 1701 California St., Denver, CO 80202. ☎ **800/228-9290** or 303/297-1300. Fax 303/298-7474. www.marriotthotels.com/DENDT/. 613 units. A/C TV TEL. $159–$189 double; $375–$800 suite. Children under 18 stay free in parents' room. AE, MC, V. Parking $19 per day with in/out privileges. Small pets accepted with deposit.

Located in the heart of the financial district, the Denver Marriott–City Center's location makes it a great choice for both business and leisure travelers. It's just one block from the 16th Street Mall, and convenient to Larimer Square, the convention center, Mile High Stadium, Coors Field, Elitch Gardens amusement park, the U.S. Mint, and the Denver Art Museum. Rooms are equipped with one king-size or two double beds, desk, data port on phone, and TV with in-room movies.

Allie's American Grille offers casual breakfast, lunch, and dinner. The Great Divide Brew Pub serves light lunch fare. Amenities include room service, valet service, masseuse (available by appointment), concierge level, indoor pool, fitness center with Cybex equipment, health spa, wet/dry saunas, guest laundry, gift shop, and meeting facilities for up to 2,000 people.

Hotel Monaco. 1717 Champa St. at 17th St., Denver, CO 80202. ☎ **800/397-5380** or 303/296-1717. Fax 303/296-1818. www.monaco-denver.com. 189 units. A/C MINIBAR TV TEL. $170–$205 double; $215–$970 suites; call for weekend rates. AE, CB, DC, DISC, MC, V. Valet parking $19 per day. Pets accepted.

Billing itself as "Denver's hippest high-style luxury hotel," the Hotel Monaco opened in 1998, sporting eye-catching interiors inspired equally by Art Deco and French design. Located in a renovated building in the heart of the central business district, this is one of the few hotels in Downtown Denver that is 100% pet-friendly—they even deliver guests a named goldfish upon request. Another perk at the Monaco is the nightly "Altitude Adjustment Hour" in the lobby, where guests enjoy complimentary glasses of wine along with 5-minute massages from the employees of the onsite Aveda Spa.

Dining: Panzano, a restaurant with a separate lounge, features northern Italian cuisine and is open for breakfast, lunch and dinner daily.

Amenities: 24-hour room service, concierge, dual voice-modem lines and voice mail in each room, in-room fax/copier/printer, in-room massage (available for an extra charge), fitness center, gift shop, meeting facilities for 200 people.

Hotel Teatro. 1100 14th St. (at Arapahoe St.), Denver, CO 80202. ☎ **303/228-1100.** Fax 303/228-1101. www.hotelteatro.com. 116 units. A/C TV TEL. $195–$275 double; $325–$1,250 suites. AE, CB, DC, DISC, JCB, MC, V. Valet parking $18 a day.

Opening its doors in the spring of 2000, Hotel Teatro is Downtown Denver's newest upscale hotel. It's also the most dramatic, as the hotel's décor was inspired by the Denver Center for the Performing Arts (located right across the street), and features masks, photos, and wardrobe from past productions of its resident theatre company. The guest rooms cater to both business and leisure travelers and are exquisitely furnished with Indonesian marble, cherry-wood desks and fixtures, and fretta linens and towels. The nine-story building is a historic landmark, but the $18 million restoration brought with it perks more relevant to the 21st century, such as a combination fax/scanner/copier/printer and dedicated dataport in each room. Each room also features Aveda amenities, a hair dryer, and a shower massager.

Dining/Diversions: Restaurant Jou Jou offers casual American bistro fare for breakfast, lunch, and dinner in its dining room with 18-foot ceilings and European-style bar. Restaurant Kevin Taylor (eponymously named after one of Denver's best-known chefs, who runs both restaurants and the room service here) serves contemporary French cuisine for lunch and dinner. There is also a separate bar on the mezzanine level. All of the establishments are supplied by the hotel's 5,000-bottle wine cellar.

Amenities: Room service, concierge, valet laundry, and complimentary weekday newspaper. Two-line phones with caller identification, in-room fax/scanner/copier/printer, in-room data ports with high speed Internet access, in-room irons/boards, in-room coffeemakers. Fitness center, complimentary bathrobes. Meeting space for up to 88 people.

The Warwick. 1776 Grant St. (at E. 18th Ave.), Denver, CO 80203. ☎ **800/525-2888** or 303/861-2000. Fax 303/839-8504. www.warwickhotels.com/denver/. E-mail: res.denver@warwickhotels.com. 220 units, including 42 suites. A/C TV TEL. $169-$265 double; $179-$1200 suite. Weekend rates $99–$129 double. Children under 18 stay free in parents' room. AE, CB, DC, DISC, JCB, MC, V. Valet $23 per day, self-parking $18 per day, both underground.

One of six Warwicks in the United States (the others are in New York, Philadelphia, Washington, D.C., San Francisco, and Seattle), the exterior and rooms of this handsome midsize choice are reminiscent of hotels in Paris, where the corporate office is located. In contrast, the lobby is stylishly decorated to reflect the region, with contemporary Western furnishings and slate and redstone stonework. The hotel completed a major $20 million renovation in early summer 2000; everything in the hotel—from the plumbing to the bedding—was replaced.

Every room features a full private balcony with a great city view, and all are equipped with a fridge, wet bar, and dining table. Room furnishings include one king- or two queen-size beds, contemporary brass and mahogany furniture, floral prints on the walls, cable TV (with pay-per-view movies), and a phone with two incoming lines—one for a modem connection. There's also a phone in each bathroom. The standard rooms are very spacious, averaging 750 square feet, and the suites, which range from two-room parlor suites to grand luxury suites, are even more so.

Dining: The restaurant here serves contemporary American continental cuisine for breakfast and dinner daily, plus lunch weekdays. There is a seasonal garden terrace for outdoor dining. Lighter fare is offered in the lounge from 11am daily.

Amenities: 24-hour room service, concierge, valet laundry, courtesy town car service within the downtown area, and complimentary newspaper, in-room data ports and safes, fitness center, rooftop pool (open seasonally). Business center and meeting space for 300.

Westin Hotel at Tabor Center. 1672 Lawrence St., Denver, CO 80202. ☎ **800/ 228-3000** or 303/572-9100. Fax 303/572-7288. www.westin.com. E-mail: denve@westin.com. 420 units. A/C MINIBAR TV TEL. $250 double; $244–$1,200 suite; call for weekend rates and packages. Children under 18 stay free in parents' room. AE, CB, DC, DISC, MC, V. Parking $12–$26 per day.

The focal point of the two-square-block Tabor Center shopping and office complex, the 19-story Westin bridges the gap between the central business district and lower downtown, and is conveniently located near Coors Field. Its contemporary design incorporates architectural elements of nearby Victorian-era structures. The elegant second-floor lobby, reached by an elevator or long escalator, features three-dimensional murals and modern fountains. Personnel are very friendly and helpful.

The spacious guest rooms, three-quarters of which feature king-size beds, are beautifully appointed with modern European-style furnishings. Every room is equipped with a TV (with pay movie channels) and VCR, coffeemaker, stocked minibar, and hair dryer. The Executive Club on the hotel's top three floors provides upgraded features and amenities, including an in-room wet bar, continental breakfast, afternoon cocktails, and a resident concierge.

Dining: The award-winning Augusta still serves breakfast daily, but is reserved for private parties only for lunch and dinner. The Palm, located in the lower lobby, offers a variety of American fare and Italian specialties (see "Dining," below) for lunch and dinner.

Amenities: Room service; valet laundry; health club with indoor/outdoor swimming pool, hot tub, sauna, exercise and weight room, and racquetball courts; business center; refreshment center; meeting space for 400; beauty salon; and shopping arcade (open Monday through Saturday from 10am to 7pm, Sunday from noon to 5pm).

EXPENSIVE

Burnsley All Suite Hotel. 1000 Grant St. (at E. 10th Ave.), Denver, CO 80203. ☎ **800/ 231-3915** or 303/830-1000. Fax 303/830-7676. www.burnsley.com. 80 suites. A/C TV TEL. $109–$209 double. Rates include buffet breakfast. Weekend rates available. AE, CB, DC, MC, V. Free covered parking.

This small, elegant hotel offers suites with private balconies and separate living, bedroom, dining, and fully stocked kitchen areas. The units are handsomely furnished, with the recently renovated 64 upper-level suites featuring a rich hunter green color scheme, marble entrance floors, and antiques. Renovation of the remaining suites will be completed by the end of 2001.

The hotel restaurant serves breakfast, lunch, and dinner on weekdays, and breakfast and dinner on weekends. The menu features fresh salmon, tenderloin, Colorado game plate, and vegetarian dishes. Room service is available from 6:30am to 10:30pm. On the premises are a pool, self-service laundry, business center, and conference rooms; guests have privileges at a nearby health club. The hotel is conveniently situated near the Cherry Creek shopping areas and is only five blocks from downtown.

Embassy Suites. 1881 Curtis St., Denver, CO 80202. ☎ **800/733-3366** or 303/297-8888. Fax 303/298-1103. www.esdendt.com. 337 suites. TV TEL. $149–$179 double weekdays; $129–$159 double weekends; $239–$349 two-bedroom suite. Children (up to two) stay free in parents' room; extra adult $15. Rates include breakfast. AE, CB, DC, DISC, MC, V. Valet parking only, $17 weekdays, $14 weekends; 6 ft. 6 in. height limit.

Guests are welcomed in a large living room–style lobby with plush overstuffed chairs, numerous plants, and flags of the world. The spacious suites boast classic contemporary decor with mahogany wood furnishings and lovely views. The Foothills restaurant is a full-service establishment, serving Southwestern cuisine in three meals daily (dinner entrees range from $13 to $28). Breakfast is included in the room rate and is either full buffet or cooked to order, and evening cocktails are available. Extras include 8,000 square feet of meeting and banquet space, separate cocktail lounge, outdoor pool, exercise room, gift shop, and valet laundry. Modem hookups and Internet access (on TVs) are available. A connecting health club is available for a fee.

Holtze. 818 17th St., Denver, CO 80202. ☎ **800/422-2092** or 303/607-9000. Fax 303/607-0101. www.holtze.com. E-mail: stay@holtze.com. 244 units. A/C TV TEL. Mon–Thurs $139–$149 double, $169–$179 suite; Fri–Sun $109–$119 double, $119–$129 suite; monthly rates available. Rates include continental breakfast. AE, CB, DC, DISC, MC, V. Valet parking $18, self-parking $17; 6 ft. 10 in. height limit.

This upscale lodging aims to please the discerning business traveler, but it's a good choice for the sophisticated vacationer as well. The lobby has a cozy, almost library-like feel, with comfortable leather couches and wing chairs grouped around a marble fireplace. Included in the rates are an evening reception (Monday through Saturday) with cocktails and appetizers, and continental breakfast, which includes pancakes, waffles, cereals, and fresh fruit.

The rooms are decorated in contemporary European style; standard units have either two queen beds or one queen plus a couch or chair. All have coffeemakers and many have mini-refrigerators. The suites—one- or two-bedroom—boast full home-size kitchens, oversize tubs with showers, hair dryers, ironing boards and irons, and some have gas fireplaces. All phones have modem hookups and voice mail. Room service is available from noon until 10pm.

Oxford Hotel. 1600 17th St. (at Wazee St.), Denver, CO 80202. ☎ **800/228-5838** or 303/628-5400. Fax 303/628-5413. 80 units. A/C TV TEL. $135–$160 double; $180 suite. Children under 18 stay free in parents' room. AE, CB, DC, DISC, MC, V. Valet parking $14 per day.

Designed by the architect Frank Edbrooke, this is one of Denver's few hotels that has survived from the 19th century (another being the Brown Palace, described above). The facade is a simple red sandstone, but the interior boasts marble walls, stained-glass windows, frescoes, and silver chandeliers, all of which were restored between 1979 and 1983 using Edbrooke's original drawings. The hotel is listed on the National Register of Historic Places.

Antique pieces imported from England and France furnish 80 large rooms, which were created from the 200 original rooms during the restoration. No two units are alike, but all are equipped with stocked minibars, individual thermostats, hair dryers, dressing tables, and large closets. Although there is bedside lighting, the electrical outlets are limited. Local phone calls cost 75¢.

McCormick's Fish House & Bar (see "Dining," below) is open for lunch and dinner daily. The art-deco Cruise Room Bar, famous for Angus beef, is open daily from 4:30 to 10pm. The Corner Bar has enormous stained-glass panels on its back bar. Amenities include 24-hour room service, valet laundry, a fitness center, health spa, beauty salon, and meeting space for 150.

INEXPENSIVE

Denver International Youth Hostel. 630 E. 16th Ave. (at Washington St.), Denver, CO 80203. ☎ **303/832-9996.** Fax 303/861-1376. 160 dormitory beds. $9.75 per person per day plus a $10 key deposit. Discounts for members of American Association of International Hostels (☎ 602/774-6731) and for helping with chores at certain times; $1 off the first night for those carrying a current Frommer's guide to the area. Traveler's checks or cash only. (No credit cards.) Free parking.

This four-story brick building, in a generally quiet neighborhood four blocks east and one block north of the State Capitol, is perfect for those on a tight budget who don't mind sharing. In the hostel tradition, it provides friendly, relatively clean and safe accommodations in dormitory-style rooms, with shared bathrooms and limited amenities. The hostel also has a kitchen (free food is often available), television room, laundry, phone, game rooms, and library; transit schedules, maps, and other travel information are available. Separate dorm rooms house couples and families, and guests are given keys to the front door so they have access 24 hours a day. The office is open for check-in only from 8 to 10am and 5 to 10:30pm.

Hostel of the Rocky Mountains. 1530 Downing St., Denver, CO 80218. ☎ **800/909-4776, PIN 67** or 303/861-7777. E-mail: hostel_denver@sni.net. 78 beds. $14 per person. Rates include full breakfast. Free pickup and delivery at bus and train stations.

A member of Hostelling International, this centrally located hostel is in a bustling urban area just off of Colfax Avenue, within walking distance of more than 50 restaurants as well as all the major downtown attractions. As with most hostels, facilities here are shared, and have taken their fair share of use and abuse. They include a community room with TV, coin laundry, game room, a map room and snack and soda machines. Each dorm room has no more than four beds. The front door is always locked and someone is on the premises all night. The office is open from 8 to 10am and 5 to 10pm, but someone is always reachable by phone. Pay phones are located on the second and third floors.

BED-AND-BREAKFASTS

Those seeking an alternative to the standard or even luxurious hotel or motel might consider one of Denver's many bed-and-breakfast inns. Often located in historic 19th-century homes, bed-and-breakfasts offer a more personalized lodging experience than you could expect in all but the very best hotels because you rarely find more than 10 rooms in a B&B, and you are, quite literally, a guest in someone's home.

Capitol Hill Mansion Bed & Breakfast. 1207 Pennsylvania St., Denver, CO 80203. ☎ **303/839-5221** or 800/839-9329 outside the 303 and 720 area codes. Fax 303/839-8046. www.capitolhillmansion.com. E-mail: Info@capitolhillmansion.com. 8 units. A/C TEL TV. $95–$175 double; $145–$175 suite. Rates include full breakfast and afternoon refreshments. AE, CB, DC, DISC, MC, V.

Located on Denver's "Mansion Row" just southeast of downtown and the State Capitol, this turreted B&B exemplifies Richardsonian Romanesque design with its ruby sandstone exterior and curving front porch. The mansion (built in 1891) is listed on the National Register of Historic Places and still boasts the original woodwork and stained glass.

History aside, the inn is now outfitted for the 21st Century with refrigerators, color televisions, and split-line phones with data ports.

Each of the individually decorated rooms is named after a Western wildflower; some feature 2-person Jacuzzi tubs, fireplaces and private balconies. The elegant Elk Thistle Suite on the third floor features a panoramic view of the Rockies, a clawfoot tub, and a kitchen; the bedroom is subtly decorated in a Southwestern style. Honeymooners might enjoy the second floor Shooting Star Balcony Room, which has a separate whirlpool tub and brass and glass shower, and a private balcony with a city view. Smoking is not permitted inside the inn.

Castle Marne Bed & Breakfast. 1572 Race St., Denver, CO 80206. ☎ **800/92-MARNE** or 303/331-0621 for reservations. Fax 303/331-0623. www.castlemarne.com. 11 units. E-mail: Info@CastleMarne.com. A/C TEL. $95–$165 double; $200–$235 suite. Rates include full breakfast and afternoon tea. AE, CB, DC, DISC, MC, V. Ample street parking. Not suitable for children under 10.

A National Historic Landmark, Castle Marne is an impressive stone fortress designed and built in 1889 by the renowned architect William Lang for a contemporary silver baron. It was so named because a previous owner's son had fought in the Battle of the Marne during World War I.

The inn is furnished with antiques, fine reproductions, and family heirlooms. Two suites have whirlpool tubs for two, three rooms with private balconies are equipped with outdoor hot tubs for two, and 2000 saw the addition of a fourth suite with an outdoor hot tub for two. Three rooms have old-fashioned bathrooms with pedestal sinks and cast-iron clawfoot tubs. A gourmet breakfast is served in the original formal dining room (two seatings), and a proper afternoon tea is served daily in the parlor. The inn also provides a game room, small lending library, gift shop, and an office for business travelers' use. Smoking is not permitted.

Haus Berlin. 1651 Emerson St., Denver, CO 80218. ☎ **800/659-0253** or 303/837-9527. Fax 303/837-9527. www.hausberlinbandb.com. E-mail: haus.berlin@worldnet.att.net. 4 units (2 with shower only). A/C TV TEL. $100–$120 double; $140 suite. Rates include full breakfast. AE, CB, DC, DISC, MC, V. Free off-street parking. Not suitable for children.

A Victorian town house built in 1892, Haus Berlin is decorated with original art and collectibles gathered from around the world by owners Christiana and Dennis Brown. We particularly like the personal touches such as fresh flowers that give this property an elegant, romantic feel, and the fact that there are only four units provides an intimacy lacking in larger historic B&Bs. Rooms are furnished with queen- or king-size beds, fine linens, and down comforters. The suite, which encompasses the entire third floor, offers beautiful views of downtown Denver—it's ideal for honeymooners and others celebrating special occasions. Although located on a quiet tree-lined street of early-19th-century buildings, the Haus Berlin is just a 10-minute walk from the 16th Street Mall, State Capitol, several museums, and Denver's central business district. Smoking is not permitted and the only pet allowed is the resident cat.

✪ **Queen Anne Bed & Breakfast Inn.** 2147–51 Tremont Place, Denver, CO 80205. ☎ **800/432-4667** or 303/296-6666. Fax 303/296-2151. www.queenannebnb.com. E-mail: travel@queenannebnb.com. 14 units. A/C TEL. $75–$165 double; $155–$175 suite. Rates include hot breakfast and Colorado wine each evening. AE, DC, DISC, MC, V. Free off-street parking.

> ## ⓕ Family-Friendly Hotels
>
> **Loews Giorgio Hotel** (*see p. 55*)   Kids get a Teddy Bear when they arrive; there's also a special children's menu in the Tuscany Restaurant.
>
> **Quality Inn Denver South** (*see p. 48*)   This hotel has a great courtyard and provides free volleyball equipment.

A favorite of both business travelers and couples seeking a romantic getaway, the Queen Anne might be considered the perfect bed-and-breakfast in the perfect home. Actually, it consists of two Victorian homes: one built by the well-known architect Frank Edbrooke in 1879, and the other built in 1886. (Both houses are on the National Register of Historic Places.) Each room or suite is equipped with a phone and a writing desk. Innkeeper Tom King also provides piped-in chamber music, fresh flowers, and fax services. Each of the 10 double rooms in the 1879 Pierce–Tabor House is unique and decorated with period antiques. Three of the rooms boast original murals: All four walls of the Aspen Room are filled with aspen trees (what else?), giving the feeling that you are resting in an aspen grove; the third-floor Park Room overlooks a park and has a mural depicting the view that visitors would have seen in 1879; and the Tabor Room honors Augusta Pierce Tabor with a mural of an 1894 garden party she hosted at her mansion. Each of the four two-room suites in the adjacent 1886 Roberts house is dedicated to a famous artist (Norman Rockwell, Frederic Remington, John Audubon, and Alexander Calder). The suites have deep soaking tubs, and the Remington suite has its own hot tub. The Rooftop Room has a two-person jetted spa on its outdoor deck and the Fountain and Skyline Rooms each have a two-person jetted tub/shower in the bathroom.

Located in the Clements Historic District, the Queen Anne borders downtown Denver and is within easy walking distance of the State Capitol, 16th Street Mall, Convention Center, restaurants, theaters, and office buildings. Breakfast includes coffee, juice, fresh fruit, hot scones, granola, muffins, and a hot entree. Smoking is not permitted.

Victoria Oaks Inn. 1575 Race St., Denver, CO 80206. ☎ **800/662-6257** or 303/355-1818. Fax 303/331-1095. E-mail: vicoaksinn@aol.com. 9 units (7 with bathroom). A/C TEL. $60–$95 double. Rates include continental breakfast. AE, CB, DC, DISC, MC, V.

This circa-1896 Victorian home with handsome oak floors and leaded-glass windows is a favorite of European travelers, at least in part because it offers some of the lowest rates for a genuinely historic bed and breakfast in Denver. A bit more basic than some of the pricier B&Bs in the area, this is a good choice for those seeking a historic property but not wanting to pay for whirlpool tubs, gourmet food, and the other luxurious touches that seem to be finding their way into the region's bed and breakfast inns. The Victoria Oaks' first floor is built around a cozy shared TV room/parlor, which is eclectically decorated with stained glass lamps and an impressive array of antiques. Centrally located about 2 miles east of downtown (within easy walking distance to City Park), the inn provides a continental breakfast of fruit, Danish, muffins, cereals, coffee, tea, and juice. A veranda provides a pleasant sitting area, and guests have kitchen and laundry privileges.

OUTSIDE DOWNTOWN
VERY EXPENSIVE

Loews Giorgio Hotel. 4150 E. Mississippi Ave., Denver, CO 80246. ☎ **800/345-9172** or 303/782-9300. Fax 303/758-6542. www.loewshotels.com. 183 units. A/C TV TEL. $199–$229 double; $259–$1,000 suite; weekend rates from $89. Rates include continental breakfast. Children under 18 stay free in parents' room. AE, CB, DC, DISC, MC, V. Free valet and self-parking. Pets are accepted on 1 floor.

Located just east of Colorado Boulevard and south of Cherry Creek, the Loews Giorgio's exterior is black steel with a reflecting glass tower, but inside, it's bella Italia. Its columns are finished in imitation marble, and the Renaissance-style murals and paintings look 5 centuries old.

Throughout the hotel, much use has been made of floral patterns, Italian silk wall coverings, and marble-top furnishings. All of the spacious rooms have at least three phones, Spectravision movie channels, coffeemakers, and hair dryers. The west-facing rooms offer superb views of the Rocky Mountains.

Dining: The top-rated Tuscany Restaurant (see "Dining," below) serves three meals daily.

Amenities: 24-hour room service, concierge, dry cleaning, laundry service, newspapers in lobby, twice-daily maid service, baby-sitting, secretarial services, courtesy van. Game rooms, boutiques, a fitness center, jogging track, access to nearby health club, business center, and meeting facilities for 100. Each room on the two floors for business travelers is equipped with two phone lines (including modem hookups) and in-room fax, and there is complimentary newspaper delivery.

✪ **Renaissance Denver Hotel.** 3801 Quebec St., Denver, CO 80207. ☎ **800/HOTELS-1** or 303/399-7500. Fax 303/321-1966. www.renaissancehotels.com. 400 units. A/C MINIBAR TV TEL. $99–129 double; $195–$650 suite. AE, CB, DC, DISC, MC, V. Free self-parking; valet parking $5 per day.

The Renaissance is our pick for a comfortable but still somewhat elegant hotel, close to downtown, that offers all the amenities we might want. Particularly impressive is the architecture—a white double pyramid 12 stories high. The 10-story atrium lobby has tropical palms and fig trees growing beneath the central skylight, fountains, lots of marble and brass, and plants draping down from the balconies. Each spacious room— among the largest you'll find in Denver—is decorated in a contemporary style and contains an easy chair and ottoman, two phones, private balcony, coffeemaker, stocked minibar, and cable TV with Spectravision.

Dining: The restaurant is open daily from 6:30am to 10pm.

Amenities: Room service, concierge, dry cleaning and laundry service, self-serve laundry, newspaper delivery, express checkout, fax service. Indoor and outdoor pools, two whirlpools, steam room, exercise room, sundeck, gift shop, business center, and meeting facilities for 1,300. Nearby are four tennis courts and an 18-hole golf course.

MODERATE

Cameron Motel. 4500 E. Evans Ave. (I-25 exit 203), Denver, CO 80222. ☎ **303/ 757-2100.** Fax 303/757-0974. 35 units. A/C TV TEL. $52 double; $72 suite. AE, DISC, MC, V. Pets accepted with $5 fee each.

A small mom-and-pop motel located about 10 minutes from downtown, the Cameron provides a clean, quiet alternative to some of the more expensive chains. Built in the 1940s, the property has been completely renovated. The walls of the rooms are glazed brick; remote-control cable TVs offer 60 channels. Three rooms are equipped with kitchenettes. Fourteen rooms provide showers only, while 21 have tub/shower combinations. The owners live on-site and their pride of ownership shows.

CAMPING

Chatfield State Park. 11500 N. Roxborough Park Rd., Littleton, CO 80125. ☎ **303/ 791-7275** or 800/678-2267 for state park reservation service ($7 reservation fee). 193 sites. $10–$14, plus $4 day-use fee. MC, V only for advance reservations.

On the south side of Denver, 1 mile south of the intersection of Colo. 121 (Wadsworth) and Colo. 470, Chatfield offers a 1,550-acre reservoir with ample opportunities for boating, waterskiing, fishing, and swimming, plus 24 miles of trails for horseback riding, mountain biking, and hiking. Facilities include hot showers, picnic areas, a dump station, boat ramps and rentals, and electric hookups.

Delux R.V. Park. 5520 N. Federal Blvd., Denver, CO 80221. ☎ **303/433-0452.** 33 sites. $25 and up. AE, MC, V.

This campground, with shaded sites, hot showers, laundry, and full hookups, provides the best Denver location for travelers who take their homes with them. It's convenient to buses (no. 31 RTD), shopping, and recreational facilities. Open year-round, the campground is located five blocks north of I-70 exit 272, and two blocks south of I-76 exit 3, on the east side of Federal Boulevard.

Denver North Campground. 16700 N. Washington St., Broomfield, CO 80020. ☎ **800/ 851-6521** (reservations only) or 303/452-4120. www.campdenver.com. E-mail: campdenver@ aol.com. 150 sites. $19–$27. DISC, MC, V. Just off I-25 exit 229, 5 miles north of Denver.

Those seeking the amenities and easy accessibility of a commercial campground close to Denver will find newly renovated facilities at this well-laid-out campground, which offers sites in a variety of sizes. About half of the sites are pull through. Most sites have at least water and electric, and about half have full hookups. There's lots of grass and trees, and some tent sites are also available. All of the amenities—phone, showers, playground, pool, laundry, store, game room—are near the entrance. There are also two cabins ($35) and periodic entertainment such as cookouts and ice-cream socials.

4 Dining

Denver has been inundated with chain and franchise eateries, mostly family restaurants, where the food is reliably good, but seldom great. The restaurants we've listed here are mostly independent, unique to this area, and a cut above others in their price ranges. The price categories are defined as follows: **very expensive,** most dinner main courses are above $20; **expensive,** most dinner main courses are $15 to $20; **moderate,** dinner main courses run about $10 to $15; and **inexpensive,** dinner main courses are generally under $10.

DOWNTOWN
VERY EXPENSIVE

Broker Restaurant. 821 17th St. (near Champa St.). ☎ **303/292-5065.** Reservations recommended. Main courses $9–$16 lunch; $18–$35 dinner. AE, CB, DC, DISC, MC, V. Mon–Fri 11am–2:30pm; daily 5–11pm. STEAK/SEAFOOD.

The historic Denver National Bank building, with its circular 23-ton door still in place, is the site of the Broker. Patrons sit in cherry-wood booths once used by bank customers to inspect safe-deposit boxes, and historic photos of Denver line the walls. Famous for its generous portions, the Broker's house favorites include New York and porterhouse steaks, beef Wellington, prime rib, Rocky Mountain trout, rack of lamb, roast duck, Alaskan king-crab legs, and blackened catfish. Vegetarians can try the vegetarian pasta medley. The Broker's trademark is a complimentary large bowl of steamed gulf shrimp with a tasty and tangy sauce.

Two additional locations of Broker restaurants in Denver are: the **Airport Broker** (near DIA), 12100 E. 39th Ave., at Peoria just south of I-70 (☎ **303/371-6420**), and **DTC Broker,** 5111 DTC Parkway, east of I-25 in Greenwood Village(☎ **303/ 770-5111**). In Boulder, there's the **Broker Inn Restaurant**, 555 30th St., between the turnpike and Baseline Road (☎ **303/444-3330**).

Downtown Denver Dining

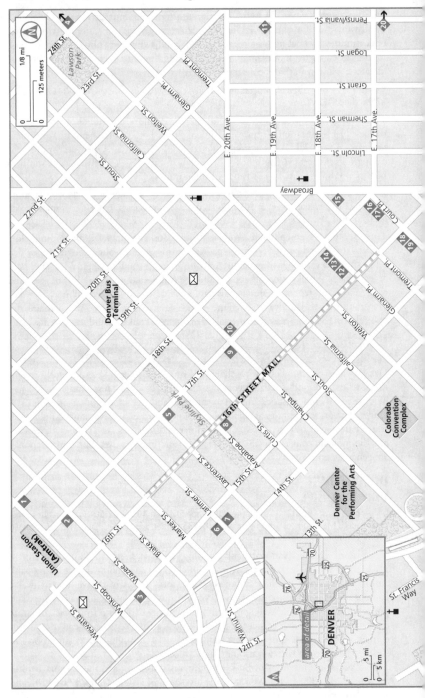

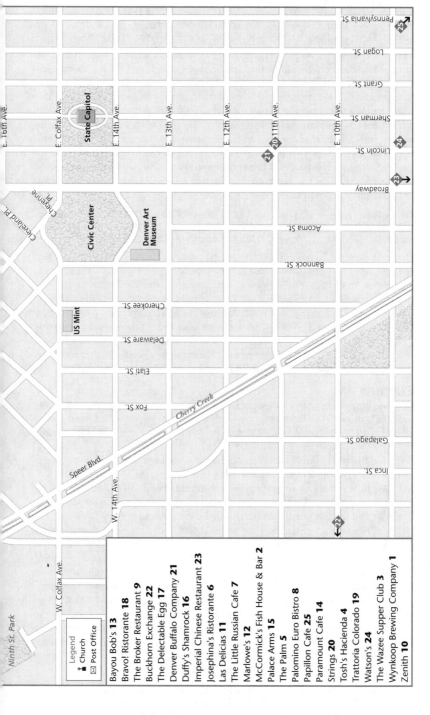

Legend
+ Church
☒ Post Office

Bayou Bob's **13**
Bravo! Ristorante **18**
The Broker Restaurant **9**
Buckhorn Exchange **22**
The Delectable Egg **17**
Denver Buffalo Company **21**
Duffy's Shamrock **16**
Imperial Chinese Restaurant **23**
Josephina's Ristorante **6**
Las Delicias **11**
The Little Russian Cafe **7**
Marlowe's **12**
McCormick's Fish House & Bar **2**
Palace Arms **15**
The Palm **5**
Palomino Euro Bistro **8**
Papillon Cafe **25**
Paramount Cafe **14**
Strings **20**
Tosh's Hacienda **4**
Trattoria Colorado **19**
Watson's **24**
The Wazee Supper Club **3**
Wynkoop Brewing Company **1**
Zenith **10**

59

Buckhorn Exchange. 1000 Osage St. (at W. 10th Ave.). ☎ **303/534-9505.** Reservations recommended. Main courses $6.75–$14 lunch, $18–$44 dinner. AE, CB, DC, DISC, MC, V. Mon–Fri 11am–2pm; Sun–Thurs 5:30–10:30pm, Fri–Sat 5:30–11pm. ROCKY MOUNTAIN.

Thanks to Denver's new light-rail system, this restaurant is just minutes from the 16th Street Mall, the Convention Center, and all downtown hotels. Still occupying the same premises since it was founded in 1893, the restaurant displays its Colorado Liquor License No. 1 over the 140-year-old hand-carved oak bar in the upstairs Victorian parlor and saloon. The dining room is definitively Western, packed with western art and an impressive taxidermy menagerie. Try the Buckhorn's Rocky Mountain oysters, fried alligator tail, or smoked buffalo sausage for starters, then choose from slow-roasted buffalo prime rib, lean and served medium rare, or elk or beef steaks for your main course. There are even large-portion steaks to serve two to five persons. And for those who just can't make up their minds, several combination plates are offered. For dessert, try the chocolate "moose."

Palace Arms. In the Brown Palace Hotel, 321 17th St. ☎ **303/297-3111.** Reservations recommended. Jacket and tie required at dinner. Main courses $10–$19 lunch, $27–$40 dinner. AE, CB, DC, DISC, MC, V. Mon–Fri 11:30am–2pm; daily 6–10pm. INTERNATIONAL.

Despite a dramatic Napoleonic decor—antiques dating from 1670 include a dispatch case and a pair of dueling pistols that may have belonged to Napoleon—the cuisine is a combination of traditional American, new American, classical French, and Southwestern. To begin, the lobster bisque is a special treat, or maybe you'd rather have the superb Caesar salad, prepared tableside for two. For an excellent main course, try the seasonally available cider-poached salmon with julienned vegetables and caviar potatoes, pan-seared venison with foie gras, or roast breast of guinea hen stuffed with wild rice and yams. There are a number of tasty "heart healthy" items on the menu, and the wine list has received *Wine Spectator's* award of excellence.

EXPENSIVE

✪ **Bravo! Ristorante.** Plaza Building of Adam's Mark Denver, 1550 Court Place. ☎ **303/626-2581,** or ext. 3164 from within the hotel. Reservations recommended. Main courses $4.50–$12.50 lunch, $12.50–$26 dinner. AE, CB, DC, DISC, MC, V. Mon–Fri 11:30am–2pm; Sun–Thurs 5:30–10:30pm, Fri–Sat 5:30–11pm. NORTHERN ITALIAN.

You'll feel like you're sitting on a piazza in Italy if you choose to dine here—the room is open and airy, with a high ceiling, windows overlooking the 16th Street Mall, potted trees, and quartet groupings of booths with etched-glass dividers. Glass chandeliers increase the sparkle, and the mood is enhanced by the music served with your meal: The wait staff are also fine singers of both Broadway tunes and opera.

The sauces here are lighter than you might expect, sometimes with unusual flavors enhancing the generous portions of al dente pasta. Also on the menu are several unique pizzas, such as prawn, shrimp, and prosciutto; and goat cheese, sun-dried tomatoes, and wild mushrooms. Several delightful pasta dishes are offered at both lunch and dinner. These include lasagna with fennel sausage, eggplant, and sweet peppers; fettuccine with diced tomatoes, roasted garlic, and red chiles; and shrimp, mussel, clams, and calamari tossed with angel hair. Other dinner selections include the specialty, filet Bravo! (tenderloin of beef with roasted cipollini onions, Gorgonzola cheese, balsamic-dressed arugula, and chianti), veal chop with wild mushroom sauce on soft polenta, rack of Colorado lamb in a mustard herb crust, char-grilled lemon basil tuna, and oak-roasted Atlantic salmon. Smoking is not permitted.

Denver Buffalo Company. 1109 Lincoln St. ☎ **303/832-0880.** Reservations recommended for dinner. Main courses $6–$12.50 lunch, $16–$38 dinner. AE, CB, DC, DISC, MC, V. Mon–Sat 11am–2:30pm; Mon–Thurs 5–9pm, Fri–Sat 5–10pm. AMERICAN.

You can't miss this busy restaurant, bar, deli, art gallery, and trading post—it's the one with the big bronze statue of a buffalo out front. The buffalo steaks, burgers, sausage, and even hot dogs come from the company's own Colorado ranch and are also available to take out or ship from the deli. For those not interested in buffalo, the restaurant also offers seafood, beef, poultry, and pasta dishes.

The bar is open all afternoon, serving a limited lunch menu, and there's live entertainment (country western, folk, or jazz) on Friday and Saturday nights.

Imperial Chinese Restaurant. 431 S. Broadway. ☎ **303/698-2800.** Reservations recommended. Individual dishes $8–$28. Complete multicourse dinners $15–$25. AE, CB, DC, MC, V. Mon–Thurs 11am–10pm, Fri 11am–10:30pm, Sat noon–10:30pm, Sun 4–10pm. CHINESE.

Considered by many local residents to be the best Chinese restaurant in Denver, the Imperial offers classic and innovative Szechuan, Hunan, Mandarin, and Cantonese dishes. A laughing Buddha greets diners at the entrance, while two rather large tropical fish tanks, an exquisite hand-carved panel, and Chinese ceramics provide the right atmosphere for a family-style Chinese meal. Specialties include Nanking pork loin, seafood bird's nest, and sesame chicken.

The Palm. In the Westin at Tabor Center, 1672 Lawrence St. ☎ **303/825-7256.** www.thepalm.com. Reservations recommended. Main courses $8.50–$17 lunch, $14–$30 dinner. AE, CB, DC, DISC, ER, JCB, MC, V. Mon–Fri 11am–11pm, Sat–Sun 5–11pm. ITALIAN/STEAK/SEAFOOD.

Pio Bozzi and John Ganzi opened the first Palm restaurant in New York City in 1926. It originally specialized in cuisine from their hometown of Parma, Italy, but whenever a customer requested steak, Ganzi ran to a nearby butcher shop, bought a steak, and cooked it to order! This eventually led to The Palm having its own meat wholesale company to ensure the quality of its steaks. Seafood was introduced to the menu by the current third-generation owners, who also expanded the business by opening a dozen more restaurants across the country. Most famous for its prime cuts of beef and huge lobsters, tradition holds firm at The Palm, with some of Ganzi's original Italian dishes still popular menu items. The dining room is decorated with fun on-the-wall drawings of celebrities; customers are seated at either booths or tables.

Palomino Euro Bistro. 1515 Arapahoe, on the 16th St. Mall. ☎ **303/534-7800.** Main courses $6–$14 lunch, $11–$28 dinner. AE, CB, DC, DISC, MC, V. Mon–Sat 11:15am–2:30pm; Sun–Thurs 5–10pm, Fri–Sat 5–11pm. Closed Thanksgiving and Dec 25. MEDITERRANEAN.

A lively, busy, and upbeat restaurant, with bright colors, rich wood, and hand-blown art-glass chandeliers, the Palomino also has a beautiful curving 48-foot bar of mahogany and marble. The menu changes monthly, with emphasis on wood-fired cooking. Specialties include spit-roasted garlic chicken; wood-oven–roasted prawns and fresh fish; and Roman-style pizza baked crisp in a 600° oven. Lunch also includes

ⓘ Family-Friendly Restaurants

Casa Bonita (*see p. 67*) If the kids' attention isn't on the tacos, they'll be enthralled by puppet shows, high divers, a fun house, and a video arcade.

White Fence Farm (*see p. 67*) Meals are served family style, with Mom or Dad doling out the vegetables, but the best part is outside with the live farm animals and playground.

sandwiches such as iron grill turkey with proscuitto, red onion, tomato, and provolone; grilled chicken club with bacon, lettuce, brie, and tomato on an onion kaiser roll; and daily fresh fish specials. Dinner entrees might include spit-roasted lamb shanks from the wood oven, applewood-grilled chicken, or Atlantic salmon. The Palomino also serves a large selection of beef, including prime rib and New York strip.

The Palomino offers a wide selection of draft beers and wines by the glass, plus their signature drinks: "Scratch Margarita," a succulent cocktail served up in a martini glass, and "Palomino Palini," a frozen blend of champagne, peach nectar, lemon, and cassis. And don't forget to save room for dessert: Try the rich chocolate tiramisù; wood-oven–roasted bread pudding with pears, golden raisins, and ice cream; or, for something lighter, the fruit sorbet.

Papillon Café. 250 Josephine St. (just north of the Cherry Creek Mall). ☎ **303/333-7166.** Reservations recommended. Main courses $10–$15 lunch, $14–$26 dinner. AE, MC, V. Mon–Fri 11am–3pm; Mon–Sat 5–10pm, Sun 5–9pm. MODERN FRENCH.

One of two restaurants in the city owned by noted Denver restaurateur Radek Cerny, this sleek, upscale eatery offers a creative twist on traditional pasta, poultry, seafood, and beef dishes. Lobster ravioli and foie gras are among the tempting appetizers on the menu, and the house specialties include charbroiled salmon with cannellini beans, Swiss chard and rosemary and tomato confit; Colorado trout with charbroiled veggies and garlic butter; and charbroiled pork with yellow curry. The lunch menu is packed with many similar offerings, as well as interesting salads, pastas, and sandwiches. The wine list is excellent. If you're on a budget, however, Cerny's other restaurant, Radex, 100 E. 9th Ave. (☎ **303/861-7999**), offers similar, albeit less expensive, dishes in a hip, bold space on Capitol Hill.

Strings. 1700 Humboldt St. (at E. 17th Ave.). ☎ **303/831-7310.** Reservations recommended. Main courses $9–$12 lunch, $15–$27 dinner. AE, CB, DC, DISC, MC, V. Mon–Thurs 11am–10pm, Fri–Sat 11am–11pm, Sun 5–10pm. CASUAL CONTEMPORARY.

Decorated in primary colors, Strings attracts a "with-it" crowd of 20- and 30-somethings, as well as visiting celebrities who continually contribute to a wall of autographed photos. Popular and usually crowded, the restaurant welcomes guests in T-shirts as well as tuxedos; it's especially busy during the before- and after-theater hours. The menu focuses on creative pasta dishes and fresh seafood, such as porcini-dusted Atlantic salmon. Another popular entree is pistachio-and-dijon-crusted lamb chops. Lunch specials change weekly to match the season and the mood of the chef. Strings has an outdoor patio for summer dining and five private rooms for parties of 16 to 65.

Zenith. 815 17th St. ☎ **303/293-2322.** Reservations recommended. Main courses $9–$12 lunch, $13–$24 dinner. AE, DC, MC, V. Mon–Fri 11am–10pm, Sat 5–10pm. CONTEMPORARY.

A favorite of Denver's movers and shakers, this new incarnation of Chef Kevin Taylor's Zenith is located in the former Guaranty National Bank building, a soaring space bedecked with columns and fine art. The relatively simple menu changes seasonally, with interesting variations on Mediterranean and southwestern standards. Recent dinner options included appetizers such as sashimi tuna and avocado terrine with ginger and sesame vinaigrette; and entrees ranging from peppered tenderloin with garlic mash to linguine with baby shrimp. There is also a good selection of soups, salads, and homemade desserts. The lunch menu features pasta, sandwiches, and light entrees.

MODERATE

Josephina's Ristorante. 1433 Larimer St. ☎ **303/623-0166.** Reservations recommended. Main courses $4–$18. AE, DC, DISC, MC, V. Mon–Fri 11am–2am, Sat–Sun noon–2am. ITALIAN.

A Larimer Square institution, Josephina's invokes nostalgia for decades past, with old advertising signs decorating the walls of the bar. House specialties include fettuccine Josephina's (with chicken, tomatoes, and wine sauce), eggplant parmigiana, and a specialty pizza, all prepared with northern Italian flair. There's also a good selection of seafood. Live rock or blues music is performed nightly from 9pm.

Little Russian Cafe. 1424H Larimer St. ☎ **303/595-8600.** $10–$16. AE, CB, DC, DISC, MC, V. Sun–Thurs 5:30–9pm; Fri–Sat 5–10pm. RUSSIAN.

This quiet, charming cafe combines old-world atmosphere with authentic Russian cuisine. Russian scenes grace the walls of the dimly lit dining room; there's also an outdoor patio. In the Russian tradition, you can, if you wish, begin your meal with a shot of ice-cold vodka and a bowl of borscht. Main dishes include beef Stroganoff, goulash, stuffed cabbage, lamb stew, and a variety of traditional Russian selections, many of them meatless.

There's a second **Little Russian Cafe** in Englewood, at 2500 E. Orchard Rd. (☎ **303/347-0300**).

Marlowe's. 501 16th St. (at Glenarm St.). ☎ **303/595-3700.** Reservations recommended. Main courses $7–$11 lunch, $9–$25 dinner. AE, DC, MC, V. Mon–Thurs 11am–midnight, Fri noon–1am, Sat 4–10pm. STEAK/SEAFOOD.

This popular eatery and saloon occupies a corner of the 1891 Kittredge Building (listed in the National Register of Historic Places), with an antique cherry-wood bar, granite pillars, and brass rails. It's a great spot for cocktails and appetizers, especially in warm weather, when tables are set up outside. House specialties include a Texas T-bone, filet mignon, chicken marsala, almond-crusted salmon, and live Maine lobster. The martinis are also held in high regard.

McCormick's Fish House & Bar. In the Oxford Hotel, 1659 Wazee St. ☎ **303/825-1107.** Reservations recommended. Lunch and light dishes $4–$12, dinner $9–$24. AE, CB, DC, DISC, MC, V. Mon–Fri 11am–2pm; Sun–Thurs 5–10pm, Fri–Sat 5–11pm; Sun brunch 10am–2pm. SEAFOOD.

Operating out of lower downtown's historic Oxford Hotel, McCormick's maintains a turn-of-the-century feel with stained-glass windows, oak booths, and a fine polished-wood bar. Come here for the best seafood in town—it's flown in daily, and might include Alaskan salmon and halibut, mussels from Florida, lobsters from Maine, Hawaiian mahimahi, red rockfish from Oregon, and trout from Idaho. The menu also offers pasta, chicken, and a full line of prime beef.

Tosh's Hacienda. 3090 Downing St. ☎ **303/295-1861.** Menu items $7–$14. AE, CB, DC, DISC, MC, V. Sun–Thurs 11am–9pm, Fri–Sat 11am–10pm. MEXICAN.

Open for more than half of a century in the Five Points neighborhood, Tosh's offers an easygoing atmosphere with tile and red brick decor. In a city brimming with Mexican restaurants, the food here stands out. The combination plates feature one or two main dishes with rice and beans, and are priced reasonably. You can't go wrong with the enchiladas, burritos, or rellenos, and the margaritas are both tart and strong.

There's a second **Tosh's Hacienda** in the Denver Tech Center, at 5071 S. Syracuse Pkwy. (☎ **303/770-8980**).

Trattoria Colorado. Plaza Building of Adam's Mark Denver, 1550 Court Place. ☎ **303/893-3333,** ext. 3172. Breakfast $4.50–$9, buffet (until 10am) $7 continental, $9 full; lunch $4–$10, buffet $9 (11am–2pm); dinner $7–$16. AE, CB, DC, DISC, MC, V. Daily 6am–10:30pm. ITALIAN/AMERICAN/REGIONAL.

Located just off the 16th Street Mall on the ground floor of the Adam's Mark Denver, the Trattoria offers cooked-to-order choices plus sumptuous buffets at almost every meal. Friday night is a grand seafood buffet, offering a variety of sushi, smoked trout, sturgeon, salmon, whitefish, and broiled lobster halves ($29 for adults, $12 for ages 6 to 11, free for age 5 and under). Saturday night, you can browse the international buffet, which generally has New England oysters, clams, and mussels; prime rib; Asian sushi and stir-fries; Italian-inspired pastas; Indian curries; French dishes such as veal ragout and pork loin with calvados sauce; Viennese pastries; and salads with flavors blended from around the world ($24 for adults, $12 for ages 6 to 11, free for age 5 and under). Both buffets are from 5 to 9:30pm. The "Sunday Brunch with Champagne" is open from 10:30am to 2:30pm ($22 for adults, $10 for ages 6 to 11, free for age 5 and under).

Breakfast includes cereals, simple to complex egg dishes, Danish pastries, croissants with a yummy selection of jams and marmalades, and griddle food—waffles, pancakes, and French toast. For lunch you might start with a soup, quesadilla, or seafood item such as smoked salmon or grilled mussels, or a caesar, California cobb, or niçoise tuna salad. Then choose a burger, chile-marinated chicken, or swordfish club sandwich.

Dinner brings choices such as Caribbean-style chicken breast; meat loaf made with pork, veal, and beef; grilled salmon in a lemon-herb crust; and slow-roasted prime rib. To round off your meal, try the wild-berry cheesecake or chocolate-raspberry truffle torte. Or add the salad and dessert bar option to your dinner entree for about $4, and try several delights!

Wynkoop Brewing Company. 1634 18th St. (at Wynkoop St.). ☎ **303/297-2700.** Reservations required for large parties. Menu items $5–$16. AE, CB, DC, DISC, MC, V. Mon–Sat 11am–2am, Sun 10am–midnight. REGIONAL AMERICAN/PUB.

When the Wynkoop opened its doors in 1988 as Denver's first new brewery in more than 50 years, it started a minirevolution: Since then, about 50 microbreweries have opened in Colorado. Wynkoop is located in a renovated warehouse across from Union Station and close to Coors Field. The menu offers pub fare, sandwiches, and soups and salads, plus dinners of steak, Denver cut elk medaillons, and honey-beer-mustard chicken breast. A hearty option is the "Field and Stream," a buffalo sirloin steak with a rainbow trout filet. See also "Denver After Dark," in chapter 5.

INEXPENSIVE

Bayou Bob's. 1635 Glenarm St. (in the Paramount Theatre Building). ☎ **303/573-6828.** Main courses $6–$9 lunch, $7–$12 dinner. AE, CB, DC, DISC, MC, V. Mon–Sat 11am–10pm, Sun 4–9:30pm. CAJUN.

Fishnets, street signs, and assorted Southern-tinged bric-a-brac cover the walls of Bayou Bob's, which serves Denverites reasonably priced Cajun food in its bar and dining room. Gumbo, red beans and rice, fresh crawfish etoufée, and jambalaya are all favorites, as are the huge Mardi Gras-style Hurricanes. The spicy fried alligator is a great starter, and the many combination plates are a good bet for almost any taste. Catfish, po'boys, and hamburgers are also available.

There's a second **Bayou Bob's** near the Denver Tech Center in Englewood, 9645 E. Arapahoe Rd. (☎ **303/740-7772**).

Delectable Egg. 1642 Market St. ☎ **303/572-8146.** Menu items $3.50–$6.25. AE, DC, DISC, MC, V. Mon–Fri 6:30am–2pm, Sat–Sun 7am–2pm. AMERICAN.

Every city should have a cafe like this: There are more than two dozen egg dishes, pancakes, waffles, and French toast. The lunch crowd can choose from a variety of salads and sandwiches as well. You can order eggs skillet-fried, baked in a frittata, scrambled into pita pockets, or smothered with chile or hollandaise. Accompany your meal with a coffee, latte, or espresso.

Another **Delectable Egg** can be found at 1625 Court Place (☎ 303/892-5720).

✪ **Duffy's Shamrock.** 1635 Court Place. ☎ **303/534-4935.** Breakfast $1.75–$4.50; lunch $4–$7; dinner $5–$12. AE, CB, DC, DISC, MC, V. Mon–Fri 7am–2am, Sat 8am–2am, Sun 11am–2am. AMERICAN.

This traditional Irish bar and restaurant with fast, cheerful service has been thriving since the late 1950s. Drink specialties include Irish coffees and imported Irish beers, but the food is mostly American. Daily specials may include prime rib, fried Louisiana prawns, broiled mahimahi, or grilled liver and onions. Sandwiches, on practically every kind of bread imaginable, include corned beef, Reuben, roast beef with gravy, and even a Dagwood.

Las Delicias. 439 E. 19th Ave. (at Pennsylvania St.). ☎ **303/839-5675.** Main courses $3–$10. AE, DISC, MC, V. Mon–Sat 8am–9pm, Sun 9am–9pm. MEXICAN.

Las Delicias, comprised of half a dozen red-brick-walled rooms, is known for its extensive menu of traditional Mexican dishes. Tamales, burritos, tacos, and fajitas are offered, along with generous portions of carne asada and carne de puerco adovado. Lots of fresh hot tortillas, chips, and salsa accompany each meal.

Other **Las Delicias** locations in Denver are at 7610 N. Conifer Rd. at Del Norte St., (☎ 303/430-0422), and 4301 E. Kentucky Ave. in Glendale (☎ 303/692-0912).

Paramount Cafe. 511 16th St. (at Glenarm St.). ☎ **303/893-2000.** Menu items $3–$9. AE, DC, DISC, MC, V. Mon–Sat 11am–1am, Sun 11am–midnight. AMERICAN.

Housed in the restored lobby of Denver's historic Paramount Theatre on the 16th Street Mall, this restaurant is popular, lively, and a bit noisy, with the jukebox playing both oldies and current pop music. The pool room contains five tables plus satellite trivia games, and the outdoor seating on the mall makes this a good choice for people watching. The menu features exotic subs, half-pound burgers, numerous sandwiches, large salads, and Tex-Mex fare. Leave room for the Kentucky bourbon pie.

Watson's. 900 Lincoln St. ☎ **303/837-1366.** Sandwiches (lunch and dinner) $5–$7. AE, DISC, MC, V. Mon–Thurs 8am–9pm, Fri 8am–10pm, Sat 10am–10pm. DELICATESSEN.

Established in 1951 as a soda fountain and pharmacy, Watson's evokes memories of that era. The walls are decorated with framed *Life* magazine covers and old-fashioned Coca-Cola advertising. While you can no longer get hand-dipped shakes and malts, Watson's still serves a great variety of hot and cold sandwiches, such as chicken caesar and ham and jarlsberg, and it's a great spot for a strong hit of nostalgia. In the store section you'll find about 200 microbrewed beers available for carry-out as well as a well-stocked wine gazebo, and you can choose from a wide selection of different postcards. The full-service pharmacy is still in business, and there's an in-store U.S. Post Office.

Wazee Supper Club. 1600 15th St. (at Wazee St.). ☎ **303/623-9518.** Menu items $3.50–$8 (large pizzas cost more). AE, MC, V. Mon–Sat 11am–2am. PIZZA/SANDWICHES.

A former plumbing-supply store in lower downtown, the Wazee is a Depression-era relic with a black-and-white tile floor and a bleached mahogany burl bar—a magnificent example of 1930s art deco. It's been popular for more than 20 years with artists, architects, theatergoers, entertainers, businesspeople, and others of good character. Pizza lovers throng the place (some believe the pizza here is the best in town, if not the world), but you'll also find an array of sandwiches from kielbasa to corned beef, plus buffalo burgers, and about a dozen draft beers will quench your thirst. Don't miss the dumbwaiter used to shuttle food and drinks to the mezzanine floor—it's a converted 1937 garage-door opener.

OUTSIDE DOWNTOWN
VERY EXPENSIVE

○ **Tuscany Restaurant.** In Loews Giorgio Hotel, 4150 E. Mississippi Ave. ☎ **303/ 782-9300.** Reservations recommended. Main courses $8–$17 lunch, $14–$32 dinner. AE, CB, DC, DISC, MC, V. Mon–Sat 6:30–10:30am and 11am–2pm, Sunday 7–10am and 11am–2pm (brunch); daily 6–10:30pm. ITALIAN.

Under the creative eye of Tim Fields (one of Colorado's top chefs, now the Loews Giorgio's food and beverage director), the Tuscany has become one of Denver's premier restaurants. Undergoing a $250,000 renovation in 2000, the elegant, contemporary and comfortable dining room reflects the hotel's Italian theme; it is decorated with a polished marble fireplace, fresh-cut flowers, and fine art. The food, which has tremendous visual and taste appeal, is Italian (or Italian style), and the service is excellent.

Breakfast includes a variety of egg dishes, pancakes, and waffles. On the lunch menu, you'll find innovative sandwiches like spicy chicken with grilled eggplant, entrees such as grilled salmon, and several pizzas. Dinner selections might include seafood linguine, garlic-crusted lamb chops with grilled zucchini, or skillet-roasted Sonoma County chicken breast with garlic potatoes and braised asparagus.

EXPENSIVE

○ **The Fort.** 19192 Colo. 8 (off W. Hampden Ave./U.S. 285), Morrison. ☎ **303/ 697-4771.** Reservations recommended. Main courses $18–$40. AE, CB, DC, DISC, MC, V. Mon– Fri 5–10pm, Sat 5:30–11pm, Sun 5–8pm. Call for special holiday hours. ROCKY MOUNTAIN.

There are several reasons to drive the 18 miles southwest from downtown Denver to visit The Fort. First is the atmosphere: The building was hand-built of adobe bricks in 1962 as a full-scale reproduction of Bent's Fort, Colorado's first fur-trading post. The interior is equally authentic, and the staff dress as 19th-century Cheyenne. A second reason is the owner Sam Arnold, a broadcast personality and master chef who has been known to open champagne bottles with a tomahawk. He's had the menu translated into French, German, Spanish, Japanese, and Russian.

The third (and best) reason to go is the food. The Fort built its reputation on high-quality, low-cholesterol buffalo, of which it claims to serve the largest variety and greatest quantity of any restaurant in the world. There's buffalo steak, buffalo tongue, broiled buffalo marrow bones, and even "buffalo eggs"—hard-boiled quail eggs wrapped in buffalo sausage. Other house specialties include Taos trout broiled with fresh mint and orange marmalade; "rattlesnake cakes," Texas diamondback meat prepared like a crab cake; and elk medallions with wild huckleberry sauce. Diehards can get beefsteak.

MODERATE

Bull & Bush Pub & Brewery. 4700 Cherry Creek Dr. S., Glendale. ☎ **303/759-0333.** Main courses $5–$15. AE, DC, MC, V. Mon–Fri 11am–closing, Sat–Sun 10am–closing. BREW PUB.

This re-creation of a famous London pub always has eight of its own award-winning brewed beers on tap. Sunday evenings bring traditional jazz by regional groups. The menu supports the brew-pub atmosphere with English fish-and-chips, "Brewmaster's Cowboy Steak" (a 16-ounce rib-eye), and a Henry VIII platter—a combination of St. Louis–style ribs, smoked chicken thigh, bacon-wrapped water chestnuts, smoked cheddar and gouda cheeses, and assorted fruit. Several burgers and other sandwiches are available, plus salads and Mexican dishes. Prime rib, top sirloin, or T-bone steaks appear as nightly specials. Saturday and Sunday, a brunch menu from 10am to 2:30pm features several egg plates, such as the popular Eggs Taos—eggs scrambled with avocados, scallions, and green chile, wrapped in a tortilla and smothered with green chile and melted cheddar. The Eggs Benedict is also touted as a house specialty. There are two Happy Hours most evenings. See also "Denver After Dark," in chapter 5.

Trail Dust Steak House. 7101 S. Clinton St., Tech Center, Englewood. ☎ **303/790-2420.** Reservations accepted for groups of 8 or more only. Main courses $5–$15 lunch, $8–$25 dinner. AE, DC, DISC, MC, V. Mon–Fri 11am–2pm; Mon–Thurs 5–10pm, Fri 5pm–11pm, Sat 4pm–11pm, Sun 11am–10pm. Exit I-25 south at Dry Creek Rd., drive 1 block east, and turn left onto Clinton St. STEAK.

Country-music lovers flock to the Trail Dust, which serves up live dance music along with mesquite-grilled steaks and ribs. Steaks range in size from 9 to 50 ounces and are accompanied by salad, beans, and bread. Chicken and fish are also available. The decor is made up of necktie tips and Western antiques interspersed with large photos of Hollywood western heroes. Destroyed by a kitchen fire in 1999, the Trail Dust was rebuilt on the same location and reopened in the summer of 2000.

There's a second **Trail Dust** at the north end of Denver, at 9101 Benton St., Westminster (☎ 303/427-1446), next to the Westminster Mall.

White Fence Farm. 6263 W. Jewell Ave., Lakewood. ☎ **303/935-5945.** Reservations accepted for parties of 15 or more. Meals $10–$18. DISC, MC, V. Tues–Sat 5–8:30pm, Sun noon–8pm. Closed January. AMERICAN.

Locals come here for the family-style fried-chicken dinners—a delicately fried half chicken per person plus heaping bowls of potatoes, corn fritters, homemade gravy, coleslaw, cottage cheese, pickled beets, and bean salad. Also available are T-bone steaks, deep-fried shrimp, broiled whitefish fillet, and liver and onions. For dessert, try the freshly baked pies. A children's menu is available, not to mention a children's playground, farm animals, carriage rides, and a country store, all in a beautiful country setting 20 minutes from downtown Denver.

INEXPENSIVE

Casa Bonita. In the JCRS Shopping Center, 6715 W. Colfax Ave., Lakewood. ☎ **303/232-5115.** Reservations not accepted. Lunch or dinner $6.50–$9. AE, CB, DC, DISC, MC, V. Daily 11am–9:30pm. MEXICAN/AMERICAN.

A west Denver landmark, Casa Bonita is more of a theme park than a restaurant. A pink Spanish cathedral-type bell tower greets visitors, who will discover nonstop action inside: divers plummeting into a pool beside a 30-foot waterfall, puppet shows, a video arcade, fun house, and strolling mariachi bands. Food is served cafeteria style, quite an undertaking for a restaurant that seats 1,100! There's standard Mexican fare—enchiladas, tacos, and fajitas—along with country-fried steak and fried chicken. Hot sopaipillas (deep-fried sweet dough), served with honey, are included with each meal.

Healthy Habits. 865 S. Colorado Blvd. ☎ **303/733-2105.** All you can eat $8. AE, DC, DISC, MC, V. Daily 11am–9pm. AMERICAN.

This award-winning cafeteria-style restaurant offers what may be Denver's best deal for salad and pasta. The 70-item salad bar displays everything you'd expect and more, including fresh fruit and a variety of pasta salads. A separate hot pasta bar offers a variety of pastas, fresh sauces, and pizza. The all-you-can-eat price includes fresh-baked desserts. Beverages, including beer and wine, are extra.

Additional Healthy Habits restaurants can be found at 7418 S. University Blvd., Littleton (☎ **303/740-7044**); 14195 W. Colfax Ave., Golden (☎ **303/277-9293**); and 4760 Baseline Rd., Boulder (☎ **303/494-9177**).

T-Wa Inn. 555 S. Federal Blvd. (3 blocks S of Alameda Ave.). ☎ **303/922-4584.** Lunch $5–$7; dinner $5.50–$13. AE, CB, DC, DISC, MC, V. Daily 11am–10pm. VIETNAMESE.

Denver's first Vietnamese restaurant still dishes up the authentic flavorful cuisine of Vietnam. The decor is simple but pleasant, with Viet folk songs providing atmospheric background. Try the egg rolls, with shrimp and crabmeat wrapped in rice paper; hearty meat-and-noodle soups; chicken salad; lemon beef and shrimp; or soft-shell crab. Several vegetarian dishes are also available, including the spicy Do Chay combination.

What to See & Do in Denver

An intriguing combination of modern American city and sprawling Old West town, Denver offers a wide variety of attractions, activities, and events. You'll discover art, history, sports, recreation, shopping, and, of course, dining, and it would be easy to spend a week in the city and never be bored. It's also a convenient base for easy day trips to Boulder, Colorado Springs, or up into the mountains.

Suggested Itineraries

If You Have 1 Day

Start at Larimer Square, Denver's birthplace, with a self-guided walking tour of the historic sites. Then stroll the 16th Street pedestrian mall and head toward the State Capitol, just across Broadway. En route, take a one-block detour for an early lunch or a cup of tea at the Brown Palace Hotel. After seeing the Capitol, explore other Civic Center sites, including the Denver Art Museum.

If You Have 2 Days

Spend your first day as suggested above. On Day 2, drive west. Venture into the old Rocky Mountain foothill mining towns of Idaho Springs and Georgetown. En route, visit the Red Rocks Amphitheatre near Morrison, where numerous hiking trails originate. On your return, tour the Coors Brewery or visit Buffalo Bill's Grave in Golden.

If You Have 3 Days

Spend your first 2 days as suggested above. On Day 3, explore more of Denver. The city has numerous historic homes, beautiful parks, attractive shopping centers, and several highly touted museums (for example, the Denver Museum of Nature and Science, the Museum of Western Art, the Botanic Gardens, and the Black American West Museum).

If You Have 4 Days or More

Spend Days 1 to 3 as suggested above. On Day 4, plan a daylong excursion to one of the nearby cities such as Colorado Springs (home of the Air Force Academy and the Pikes Peak Cog Railway) or Boulder.

For your fifth day, climb higher into the Rockies to resort communities such as Estes Park (gateway to Rocky Mountain National Park), or old mining towns like Idaho Springs.

1 The Top Attractions

✪ **Denver Art Museum.** 100 W. 14th Ave. (at Civic Center Park). ☎ **720/865-5000.** www.denverartmuseum.org. Admission $6 adults, $4 students and seniors, free for children under 6; free for everyone Sat. Tues–Sat 10am–5pm (until 9pm Wed), Sun noon–5pm. Bus: 7, 8, or 50.

Founded in 1893 and recently renovated, this seven-story museum is wrapped by a thin 28-sided wall faced with one million sparkling tiles designed by Gio Ponti of Italy and James Sudler Associates of Denver. The new main entrance on Acoma Plaza boasts a dramatic steel canopy and is more convenient to the parking lots at Acoma and 13th Avenue. The original Ponti entrance door on 14th Avenue is also accessible.

The museum's expanding collection of Western and regional works is housed on the seventh floor. Included are Frederic Remington's bronze The Cheyenne, Charles Russell's painting In the Enemy's Country, plus 19th-century photography, historical pieces, and works by Georgia O'Keeffe.

The American Indian collection consists of more than 17,000 pieces from 150 tribes of North America, spanning nearly 2,000 years. The collection is growing not only through the acquisition of historic pieces but also through the commissioning of works by contemporary artists. Other collections include architecture and design; graphics; and Asian, modern and contemporary, Pre-Colombian, and Spanish Colonial art.

The Bernadette Berger Discovery Libraries tantalize visitors with cozy reading nooks, display drawers of art objects and prints, and a costume closet where you can try on old-style clothing, hats, and wigs. Also scattered about are computer stations offering CD-ROM activities and access to the Denver Public Library's online catalogue.

Overview tours are available Tuesday through Sunday at 1:30pm, plus 11am on Saturday; an in-depth tour of a different area of the museum is offered each Wednesday and Friday at noon and 1pm; and a variety of child-oriented and family programs are scheduled regularly. The Museum Shop sells replicas of art treasures and books on art and Southwestern lore. A restaurant, Palettes, serves American meals, and a cafe offers lighter fare plus baked goods. Both are open from 11am to closing Monday through Saturday and noon to closing on Sunday.

✪ **Denver Museum of Nature and Science.** City Park, 2001 Colorado Blvd. ☎ **800/ 925-2250** outside Metro Denver, or 303/322-7009; 303/370-8257 for the hearing impaired. www.dmns.org. Admission to museum, $7 adults, $4.50 children 3–12 and seniors 60 and older; IMAX, $7 adults, $4.50 children and seniors; group rates available. Daily 9am–5pm. Closed Dec 25. Bus: 24, 32, or 40.

The fifth largest museum of its kind in the county, the Denver Museum of Nature and Science features 95 world-renowned dioramas, an extensive gems and minerals display, and several other award-winning exhibitions. The museum focuses on six sciences:

Impressions

. . . *Cash! Why they create it here.*
—Walt Whitman, on Denver in *Specimen Days* (1879)

Robbery at the Mint

A daring armed robbery took place at the Denver Mint in 1922, just 1 week before Christmas, and although police were certain they knew who the culprits were, no one ever served a day in jail for the crime. The most secure and theft-proof building in Denver, the Mint seemed an unlikely target for a robbery. In fact, the thieves did not rob the Mint itself—they simply waited for guards to carry the money out the front door.

A Federal Reserve Bank truck was parked outside the Mint on West Colfax Avenue at about 10:30am on December 18. It was being loaded with $200,000 worth of brand-new $5 bills, to be taken to a bank about 12 blocks away, when a black Buick touring car pulled up. Two men jumped out and began firing sawed-off shotguns, killing one guard and spraying the Mint and nearby buildings, while a third robber grabbed the bags of money. Guards inside the Mint quickly pulled their guns and returned fire, but within a minute and a half the robbers were gone—$200,000 richer.

Mint guards were certain they had hit one of the thieves, and 4 weeks later in a dusty Denver garage they found the Buick. Lying in the front seat was the frozen and bloody body of Nick Trainor, a convicted criminal who had recently been released on parole from the Nebraska State Penitentiary. Trainor had been shot several times.

Secret Service agents recovered $80,000 of the missing loot the following year in St. Paul, Minnesota, but no arrests were made, and little more was mentioned until 1934, when Denver police announced that they knew the identities of the other men involved. Still, no charges were filed. Two of the suspects were already serving life sentences for other crimes.

At the time, police said the robbery had been pulled off by a Midwest gang who had immediately fled to the Minneapolis–St. Paul area, where they gave the money to a prominent Minneapolis attorney, who also was never charged.

anthropology, health science, geology, paleontology, space science, and zoology.

The dioramas here depict Colorado wildlife, North American bears and sea life, Australian ecology and the habitats of Botswana, including a spectacular savanna diorama called "The Watering Hole."

The "Prehistoric Journey" traces the history of life on earth through 3.5 billion years. Dinosaur skeletons, fossils, interactive exhibits, and dioramas of ancient ecologies make this the museum's most popular attraction, especially enticing for children.

Another popular exhibit is the "Hall of Life," which focuses on the science of the human body—from fetal development and genetics to the senses and nutrition. Using a magnetic card, visitors gather information on themselves as they move through the interactive exhibits. When finished, they receive a printout about their own physical condition.

The "Egyptian Mummies" exhibition features two mummies displayed in open coffins, as well as a pair of mummified animals and other tomb goods. Beautifully illustrated panels reveal how and why the ancient Egyptians mummified and buried their dead.

The IMAX Theater (☎ 303/322-7009) presents science, nature, or technology-oriented films with sense-surround sound on a screen that measures 4½ by 6½ stories.

Downtown Denver Attractions

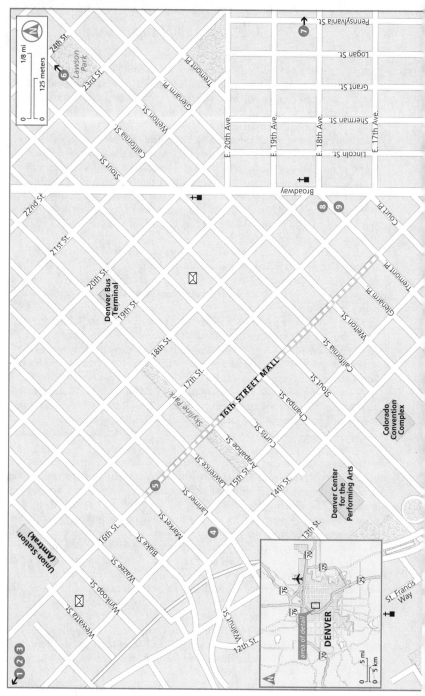

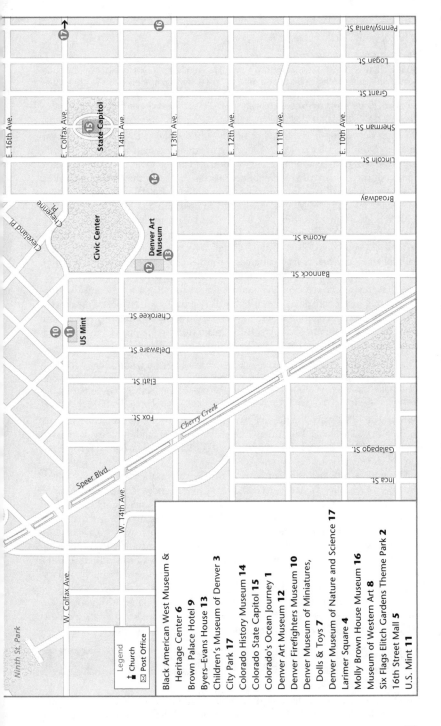

E. 16th Ave.
E. Colfax Ave.
E. 14th Ave.
E. 13th Ave.
E. 12th Ave.
E. 11th Ave.
E. 10th Ave.

Pennsylvania St.
Logan St.
Grant St.
Sherman St.
Lincoln St.
Broadway
Acoma St.
Bannock St.
Cherokee St.
Delaware St.
Elati St.
Fox St.
Galapago St.
Inca St.

State Capitol
Civic Center
Denver Art Museum
US Mint
Cheyenne Pl.
Cleveland Pl.
Speer Blvd.
Cherry Creek
W. 14th Ave.
W. Colfax Ave.
Ninth St. Park

⑰→
⑯
⑮
⑭
⑬
⑫
⑪
⑩

Legend
✚ Church
✉ Post Office

Black American West Museum &
    Heritage Center **6**
Brown Palace Hotel **9**
Byers–Evans House **13**
Children's Museum of Denver **3**
City Park **17**
Colorado History Museum **14**
Colorado State Capitol **15**
Colorado's Ocean Journey **1**
Denver Art Museum **12**
Denver Firefighters Museum **10**
Denver Museum of Miniatures,
    Dolls & Toys **7**
Denver Museum of Nature and Science **17**
Larimer Square **4**
Molly Brown House Museum **16**
Museum of Western Art **8**
Six Flags Elitch Gardens Theme Park **2**
16th Street Mall **5**
U.S. Mint **11**

The **Charles C. Gates Planetarium,** also onsite, has closed for major renovations and will reopen in 2002.

✪ **U.S. Mint.** 320 W. Colfax Ave. (between Cherokee and Delaware sts.). ☎ **303/ 405-4757** or 303/405-4761. www.usmint.gov. Free admission. Tickets available at the booth next to the visitor entrance on Cherokee St. Mon–Fri 8am–2pm; tours every 15–20 minutes depending on visitor volume. Tours run until 3pm during the winter. Reservations not accepted; June–Labor Day expect a 60 min. wait. Closed 2 weeks in summer for audit; call for exact date. Cultural Connection Trolley. Bus: 7.

Whether we worship it as our god or simply consider money to be a necessary commodity in our complex society, we all have to admit a certain fascination with the coins and bills that seem to make the world turn. There are four mints in the United States but the Denver Mint is one of only two (the other is the Philadelphia Mint) where we can actually see the process of turning lumps of metal into shiny coins.

Opened in 1863, the Mint originally melted gold dust and nuggets into bars. In 1904 the office moved to this site, and 2 years later began making gold and silver coins. Copper pennies were added a few years later. The last silver dollars (containing 90% silver) were coined in 1935. In 1970, all silver was eliminated from dollars and half dollars (today they're made of a copper-nickel alloy). The Denver Mint stamps about 10 billion coins a year, and each has a small D on it.

Although visitors today don't get quite as close as they might like (security, we suppose), a self-guided tour along the visitors' gallery provides a good look at the process, with video monitors offering a close-up view of the actual coin-minting process as it is taking place. A variety of displays help explain the minting process, and a shop at the end of the tour offers a variety of souvenirs.

✪ **Colorado State Capitol.** Broadway and E. Colfax Ave. ☎ **303/866-2604.** Free admission. 40- to 45-minute tours offered year-round (more frequently in summer), Memorial Day–Labor Day Mon–Fri 9am–3:40pm, Sat 9:30am–2:30pm; Labor Day–Memorial Day Mon–Fri 9:30am–2:30pm (the dome is locked at 3:30pm). Bus: 2, 7, 8, 12, or 15.

Built to last 1,000 years, the Capitol was constructed in 1886 of granite from a Colorado quarry. The dome, which rises 272 feet above the ground, was first sheathed in copper, but it was replaced with 200 ounces of gold after a public outcry: Copper was not a Colorado product.

Murals depicting the history of water in the state adorn the walls of the first-floor rotunda, which offers a splendid view upward to the underside of the dome. The rotunda resembles the layout of the national Capitol in Washington, D.C. South of the rotunda is the governor's office, paneled in walnut and lit by a massive chandelier.

On the first floor, the west lobby has a display case of dolls wearing ball gowns— miniature versions of those worn by various governors' wives. To the right of the main lobby is the governor's reception room. The second floor has main entrances to the House, Senate, and old Supreme Court chambers, and entrances to the public and visitor galleries for the House and Senate are on the third floor.

The Colorado Hall of Fame is located near the top of the dome, with stained-glass portraits of Colorado pioneers. On clear days, the views from the dome are spectacular. Capitol memorabilia is available for purchase at the tour guide desk.

2 More Attractions

HISTORIC BUILDINGS

There are 17 recognized historic districts in Denver, including Capitol Hill, the Clements District (around 21st Street and Tremont Street, just east of downtown), and 9th Street Park in Auraria (off 9th Street and West Colfax Avenue). **Historic Denver,** P.O. Box 480491, Denver, 80248-0491 (☎ **303/296-9887**), offers walking-tour maps of several of these areas. For additional information on some of Denver's historic areas, also see the "Neighborhoods in Brief" section in chapter 4.

Byers–Evans House. 1310 Bannock St. (in front of the Denver Art Museum). ☎ **303/620-4933.** Admission $3 adults, $2.50 seniors, $1.50 children 6–16, free for children under 6. Tues–Sun 11am–3pm. Closed state holidays. Bus: 8.

This elaborate Victorian home, built by the *Rocky Mountain News'* founding editor William Byers in 1883, has been restored to its 1912–24 period, when it was owned by William Gray Evans, son of Colorado's second territorial governor. Guided tours describe the architecture and explain the fascinating lives of these prominent Denver families. Admission to the Byers–Evans House includes the renovated service wing and carriage house, which now houses a living history exhibit. Here you will find changing displays and thousands of photos describing Denver's history, from the gold rush to World War II.

Larimer Square. 1400 block of Larimer St. ☎ **303/534-2367,** or 303/607-1276 for the events line. Bus: 2, 7, 12, 15, 16, 28, 31, 32, 38, or 44. The free Larimer Shuttle offers round-trip service to and from Coors Field and the Pepsi Center on game days

This is where Denver began. Larimer Street between 14th and 15th streets comprised the entire community of Denver City in 1858, with false-fronted stores, hotels, and saloons to serve gold-seekers and other pioneers. In the mid-1870s it was the main street of the city and the site of Denver's first post office, bank, theater, and streetcar line. By the 1930s, however, this part of Larimer Street had deteriorated so much that it had become a "skid row" of pawnshops, gin mills, and flophouses. Plans had been made to tear these structures down with a wrecking ball when the entire block was purchased by a group of investors in 1965.

The Larimer Square project became Denver's first major historic preservation effort. All 16 of the block's commercial buildings, constructed in the 1870s and 1880s, were

---

❷   **Did You Know?**

- Denver is exactly 1 mile high—the 15th step of the State Capitol Building is 5,280 feet above sea level.
- The first cheeseburger was grilled at Louis Ballast's Denver drive-in in 1944.
- Denver was named after Kansas Territorial Governor James Denver by boosters who hoped to gain political favors, but by the time they named the town, Denver had already resigned.
- The mountainous area of Colorado is six times the size of Switzerland.
- Golda Meir, former prime minister of Israel, attended North High School in Denver.
- The highest paved road in North America—to the top of 14,260-foot Mount Evans—is part of 20,000 acres of Denver's city parks.
- More Denverites have library cards than residents of any other city in the world, and the Tattered Cover Bookstore (see "Shopping," below) is the nation's largest independent bookstore with over 600,000 volumes.
- Douglas Fairbanks, famous movie star of the 1920s and 1930s, was expelled from Denver's East High School.

renovated, providing space for street-level retail shops, restaurants, and nightclubs, as well as upper-story offices. A series of inner courtyards and open spaces was created, and in 1973 it was added to the National Register of Historic Places.

Larimer Square hosts numerous special events. Free concerts take place on four Thursday evenings every summer; Oktoberfest (September and October) features beers from all around the globe, with an emphasis on Germany's finest; and December's Winterfest includes a huge tree-lighting, an outdoor ice-skating arena, and carolers.

✪ **Molly Brown House Museum.** 1340 Pennsylvania St. ☎ **303/832-4092.** www.mollybrown.org. Admission $6 adults, $4 seniors over 65, $2 children 6–12, free for children under 6. Tues–Sat 10am–4pm, Sun noon–4pm; June–Aug, also Mon 10am–4pm. Last tour of the day begins at 3:30pm. Closed major holidays. Cultural Connection Trolley. Bus: 2 on Logan St. to E. 13th, then 1 block east to Pennsylvania.

Built in 1889 of Colorado lava stone with sandstone trim, this was the residence of James and Margaret (Molly) Brown from 1894 to 1932. The "unsinkable" Molly Brown became a national heroine in 1912 when the Titanic sank. She took charge of a group of immigrant women in a lifeboat and later raised money for their benefit.

Restored to its 1910 appearance, the Molly Brown House has a large collection of turn-of-the-century furnishings and art objects, many of which belonged to the Brown family. A carriage house at the rear is also open to visitors.

MUSEUMS & GALLERIES

Black American West Museum & Heritage Center. 3091 California St. (at 31st St.) ☎ **303/292-2566.** Admission $4 adults, $3 seniors, $1 children 4–17, free for children 3 and under. May–Sept Daily 10am–5pm; Oct–Apr Wed–Fri 10am–2pm, Sat–Sun 10am–5pm. Light Rail stop no. 1.

Nearly one-third of the cowboys in the Old West were blacks, and this museum chronicles their little-known history, along with that of black doctors, teachers, miners, farmers, newspaper reporters, and state legislators. The 35,000-item collection is lodged in the Victorian home of Dr. Justina Ford, the first black woman licensed to practice medicine in Denver. Known locally as the "Lady Doctor," Ford delivered more than 7,000 babies, most of them at home since she was denied hospital privileges, and consistently served the disadvantaged and underprivileged of Denver.

Paul Stewart is a black man who loved to play cowboys and Indians as a boy, but his playmates always chose him to be an Indian because "There was no such thing as a black cowboy." He began researching the history of blacks in the West after meeting a black cowboy who had actually led cattle drives in the early part of the 20th century. Stewart explored almost every corner of the American West, gathering artifacts, memorabilia, photographs, oral histories—anything to document the existence of black cowboys—and his collection served as the nucleus for this museum when it opened in 1971.

Colorado History Museum. 1300 Broadway. ☎ **303/866-3682.** Admission $4.50 adults, $4 seniors and students, $2.50 children 6–16, free for children under 6. Mon–Sat 10am–4:30pm, Sun noon–4:30pm. Bus: 8.

The Colorado Historical Society's permanent exhibits include "The Colorado Chronicle," an 1800 to 1949 time line that uses biographical plaques and a remarkable collection of photographs, news clippings, and various paraphernalia to explain Colorado's past. Dozens of dioramas portray various episodes in state history, including an intricate re-creation of 19th-century Denver. There's also a life-size display of early transportation and industry.

Periodically changing exhibits fill two of the museum's three galleries. For 2001, exhibits on the lives of two Western luminaries—Buffalo Bill and Will Rogers—are scheduled; call for current information. The museum offers a series of lectures and statewide historical and archaeological tours. Its gift shop is also worth a visit.

Denver Firefighters Museum. 1326 Tremont Place. ☎ **303/892-1436.** Admission $3 adults, $2 children 12 and under. Mon–Sat 10am–2pm.

The history of the Denver Fire Department is preserved and displayed here in historic Fire Station No. 1. Built in 1909 for Engine Company No. 1, it was one of the largest firehouses in Denver, occupying 1,100 square feet on two floors. In its early years, it lodged men, fire engines, and horses. Motorized equipment replaced the horse-drawn engines by 1924, and in 1932 this firehouse was "modernized." Concrete replaced the wooden floor, the stables and hayloft were removed, and the plumbing was improved. Visitors today see firefighting equipment dating back to 1866, as well as historic photos and newspaper clippings.

Denver Museum of Miniatures, Dolls & Toys. 1880 Gaylord St. (just west of City Park). ☎ **303/322-1053.** Admission $4 adults, $3 seniors and children 2–16, free for children under 2. Tues–Sat 10am–4pm, Sun 1–4pm.

This early-20th-century property is home to an intriguing collection of antique and collectible dolls, from rag and wood to exquisite German bisque. Also on display are dollhouses, from a Santa Fe adobe with hand-carved furniture to a replica of a 16-room home in Newport, Rhode Island. The museum also displays wonderful old toys, from teddy bears to a full circus, complete with tent and animals. The gift shop is equally delightful.

✪ **Four Mile Historic Park.** 715 S. Forest St. ☎ **303/399-1859.** Admission $3.50 adults, $2 seniors and children 6–15, free for children under 6. Apr–Sept Wed–Fri noon–4pm, Sat–Sun 10am–4pm; Oct–Mar Sat–Sun noon–4pm. The park is 4 miles southeast of downtown Denver, at S. Forest St. and Exposition Ave.

The oldest log home (1859) still standing in Denver serves as the centerpiece for this 14-acre living-history facility. Everything is authentic for the period from 1859 to 1883, including the house (a former stagecoach stop), its furnishings, outbuildings, and farm equipment. There are draft horses and chickens in the barn and crops in the garden. Weekend visitors can enjoy stagecoach rides, weather permitting, and seasonal "Heritage Events" feature pioneer-era musicians and actors as well as many food and craft demonstrations. Call for dates and times of these upcoming special events.

Lakewood's Heritage Center at Belmar Park. 797 S. Wadsworth Blvd., Lakewood. ☎ **303/987-7850.** Admission $3 adults, $2 children 4–18, free for children 3 and under. Tues–Fri 10am–4pm, Sat–Sun noon–4pm. Bus: 76.

In Denver's early days, many of its wealthy residents maintained summer estates in the rural Lakewood area, and this historic village tells their story as well as that of others who lived and worked here. Your first stop should be the visitor center for an introduction to the museum; this is also where you can begin a personalized guided or self-guided tour. The village includes an 1870s farmhouse, a 1920s one-room school, and the Barn Gallery. There's an exhibit on "Lakewood People and Places," antique and vintage farm machinery, self-guided history walks through the surrounding 127-acre park, changing art exhibits, and a picnic area. An amphitheater and festival area opened for the 2000 season, hosting a summer concert series and a slate of seasonal fairs and celebrations, and a new visitors center was in the works at press time. The center presents year-round lecture-luncheon programs, plus children's programs on most summer Saturdays. There's also an excellent gift shop with unique handmade items.

Mizel Museum of Judaica. 560 S. Monaco Pkwy. ☎ **303/333-4156.** www.mizelmuseum. org. Free admission. Mon–Fri 10am–4pm, Sun noon–4pm. From downtown head east on Colfax Ave. for about 3½ miles, then south (right) on S. Monaco Pkwy. for about 2¼ miles to the museum; turn left onto Center Ave. and park in the east side lot.

The museum's permanent collection describes Jewish customs, ceremonies, and traditions in three groupings: *Torah, Hiddur Mitzvah,* and the Israel Arts and Crafts Movement. Part of this collection is on display at all times in the corridor cases. Changing exhibits discuss the history, culture, and art of Judaism around the world. Exhibitions in recent years include "Rage and Resolution," an exhibit marking and protesting violence against women; a display on modern Cuban Jewish art; and a remembrance of the horrors of the Holocaust including sculpture by Joe Nicrastri, paintings by Francia Tobacman offered as a *Kaddish* (memorial prayer) for the 6 million Jewish lives lost, and photographs by Judy Ellis Glickman that tell the story of Denmark's incredible feat in protecting 99% of its Jewish population.

Museum of Contemporary Art/Denver. 1275 19th St. at Sakura Square (19th and Larimer sts.) ☎ **303/298-7554.** www.mocadenver.com. Admission $3 adults, $2 seniors, free for children under 12. Tues–Sat 11am–5:30pm, Sun noon–5pm.

Rotating avant-garde exhibitions by numerous local and national artists are the main attraction at this downtown museum. Exhibitions from 1999 and 2000 included "Pleasure Seekers," works inspired by the personal pleasures of the artists, with no agenda except to offer a glimpse into what makes their creators smile; "We Are Named," a photo-based exploration of identity that questions Utopian visions; and "Western Vernacular," a survey of postmodern installation art in Colorado.

Wings Over the Rockies Air & Space Museum. 7711 E. Academy Pkwy., Hangar #1 in Lowry Air Force Base (gates at Sixth Ave. and Dayton St., Quebec St. and First Ave., and Alameda Ave. between Havana and Monaco sts.). ☎ **303/360-5360.** Admission $4 adults, $3 seniors, $2 children 6–17, free for children under 6. Group rates available. Mon–Sat 10am–5pm, Sun noon–5pm. Bus: 6.

More than 20 planes and spacecraft are housed in the cavernous Hangar No. 1, which became a museum when Lowry Air Force Base closed in 1995. On display are antique biplanes, a search-and-rescue helicopter, a massive B-1A bomber—one of only five ever built—and most of the F1 fighter series. You can also see a World War I uniform collection (as well as a special exhibit tracing the history of women's aviation uniforms), a Norden bomb sight, U3A Blue Canoe, and the Freedom space module, plus traveling exhibits and changing private collections. Once a month, the museum hosts "Open Cockpit Day," when children get to climb into the planes' cockpits. The store is filled with aviation- and space-oriented clothing, souvenirs, and toys for kids of all ages.

PARKS, GARDENS & ZOOS

✪ **Butterfly Pavilion & Insect Center.** 6252 W. 104th Ave., Westminster. ☎ **303/ 469-5441.** www.butterflies.org. Admission $6.95 adults, $4.95 seniors, $3.95 children 4–12, free for children under 4. Daily 9am–5pm. Take the Denver–Boulder Turnpike (U.S. 36) to West 104th Ave. and go east for about a block. The Pavilion is on your right.

A walk through the butterfly conservatory introduces the visitor to a world of grace and beauty. The constant mist creates a hazy habitat to support the lush green plants that are both food and home to the inhabitants. If you stand still for a few minutes, a resident butterfly might land on you, but don't try to pick them up—the oils on your hands contaminate their senses, interfering with their ability to find food. One display describes the differences among butterflies, moths, and skippers, and color charts are available to help with identification. (A butterfly guide is available for a nominal fee.)

In the insect room you'll discover that honeybees beat their wings some 200 times per second, and beetles comprise one-fifth of all living things on earth. Meet arthropods (the scientific name for insects) that are native to Colorado, and see exotic species from around the world. A fascinating "touch cart" allows you to get up close to a cockroach or tarantula—that is, if this is something you really want to do.

The walls of the entryway are lined with magnificent close-up photographs of insects by Fran Hall, many taken before macrolenses made such close-ups relatively easy. Hall started traveling and photographing in the mid-1930s, and many of the photos on display were taken with a special camera he designed with a toolmaker friend.

Also on the premises are a large gift shop and snack bar. Outside, a half-mile nature trail meanders among cactus and other desert-friendly plants.

City Park. E. 17th to E. 26th aves., between York St. and Colorado Blvd. Free admission to park, although the zoo, museum, golf course, and other sites charge independently. Daily 24 hours. Bus: 24 or 32.

Denver's largest urban park covers 314 acres (96 square blocks) on the east side of Uptown. Established in 1881, and with its Victorian touches still evident, it includes two lakes (with boat rentals), athletic fields, jogging and walking trails, playgrounds, tennis courts, picnic areas, and an 18-hole municipal golf course. In summer, band concerts are performed in the park, which is also the site of both the Denver Zoo and the Denver Museum of Nature and Science (including its IMAX Theater), discussed elsewhere in this chapter.

Colorado's Ocean Journey. 700 Water St, just east of I-25, exit 211. ☎ **303/561-4450.** www.oceanjourney.org. Admission $14.95 adults, $12.95 children 13–17 and seniors, $6.95 children 4–12, free for children under 4. Memorial Day–Labor Day Daily 9am–6pm; Labor Day–Memorial Day daily 10am–6pm. Closed Christmas.

A decade in the making, Denver's state-of-the-art aquarium—the largest between Chicago and Monterrey, California—opened in June 1999 and immediately emerged as one of the top regional attractions. Permanent exhibits include re-creations of two ecosystems that are on opposite sides of the planet: the Colorado River in North America and the Kampar River in Indonesia. Both exhibits have many separate tanks that showcase the wildlife in each river, from their mountainous origins to their oceanic destinations. The Colorado exhibit features the greenback cutthroat trout— the Colorado state fish—as well as river otters and innumerable other aquatic denizens. It culminates in a flash flood simulation and the 187,000-gallon Sea of Cortez display, populated with angelfish, moray eels, and rays. The Kampar River Display features endangered Sumatran tigers as well as the 320,000-gallon Depths of the Pacific exhibit, replete with a variety of sharks among its 3,000 fish. There is also a rotating exhibit space, which has featured traveling exhibits on sharks and sea otters, plus a restaurant, gift shop, and several hands-on displays aimed at children.

✪ **Denver Botanic Gardens.** 1005 York St. ☎ **303/331-4000** or 303/331-4010 (24-hour recording). www.botanicgardens.org. Admission May–Sept $5.50 adults, $3.50 seniors, $3 children 6–15; Oct–Apr $4.50 adults, $2.50 seniors, $2 children 6–15; free for children under 6. May–Sept. Sat–Tues 9am–8pm, Wed–Sat 9am–5pm; Oct.–Apr. Daily 9am–5pm. Closed Dec 25, Jan 1, and May 7. Cultural Connection Trolley. Bus: 2, 6, or 10.

Twenty-three acres of outstanding outdoor and indoor gardens display plants native to the desert, plains, mountain foothills, and alpine zones. There's also a traditional Japanese garden, herb garden, home-demonstration garden, water garden, "wingsong" garden to attract songbirds, and "Romantic Gardens" with a waterway, fragrance garden, and courtyard garden. New in 2000, the "Gardens of the World" contains collections of plants from Asia, Europe, Africa, Australia and the Tropics.

Even in the cold of winter, the dome-shaped, concrete-and-Plexiglas Tropical Botanica houses more than 1,000 species of tropical and subtropical plants. Huge, colorful orchids and bromeliads share space with a collection of plants used for food, fibers, dyes, building materials, and medicines. The Botanic Gardens also include a gift shop (open daily from 9:30am to 4:30pm), library, and auditorium. Special events are scheduled throughout the year; offerings range from garden concerts in summer to sunset strolls in mid-June to several holiday events.

✪ **Denver Mountain Parks.** Dept. of Parks and Recreation. ☎ **303/697-4545.** Free admission.

Formally established in August 1913, the city's Mountain Parks system immediately began acquiring land in the mountains near Denver to be set aside for recreational use. Today it includes more than 13,000 acres, with 31 developed mountain parks and 16 wilderness areas that are wonderful places for hiking, picnicking, bird-watching, golfing, or lazing in the grass and sun.

The first and largest, **Genesee Park,** is 20 miles west of Denver off I-70 exit 254; its 2,400 acres contain the Chief Hosa Lodge and Campground (the only overnight camping available in the system), picnic areas with fireplaces, a softball field, a scenic overlook, and an elk and buffalo enclosure.

Among the system's other parks is **Echo Lake,** located about 45 minutes from downtown Denver on Colo. 103. At 10,600 feet elevation on Mt. Evans, the park has good fishing, hiking, and picnicking, plus a restaurant and curio shop. Other parks include 1,000-acre **Daniels Park** (23 miles south of Denver via I-25 to Castle Pines Parkway, then west to the park), which offers picnic areas, a bison enclosure, and a scenic overlook; and **Dedisse Park** (2 miles west of Evergreen on Colo. 74), which provides picnic facilities, a golf course, restaurant and clubhouse, and opportunities for ice skating, fishing, and volleyball.

Denver Zoo. City Park, 23rd Ave. and Steele St. (main entrance is between Colorado Blvd. and York St.). ☎ **303/376-4800.** www.denverzoo.org. E-mail: zooinfo@denverzoo.org. Admission $6–$8 adults, $5–$6 seniors 62 and over, $3–$4 children 4–12 (accompanied by an adult), free for children under 4. Apr–Sept daily 9am–6pm; Oct–Mar daily 10am–5pm. Cultural Connection Trolley. Bus: 24 or 32.

More than 700 species of animals (more than 4,000 individuals) live in this very spacious zoological park. Feeding times are posted near the zoo entrance so you can time your visit to see the animals at their most active. Bear Mountain, when it was built in 1918, was the first animal exhibit in the United States to be constructed of simulated concrete rockwork. At the other end of the time line, Northern Shores (1987) allows underwater viewing of polar bears and sea lions, while Tropical Discovery (1994) re-creates an entire tropical ecosystem under glass, complete with crocodiles, piranhas, and king cobras, as well as the world's largest indoor habitat for the rare Komodo dragon. Exotic waterfowl inhabit several ponds, and 300 avians live in Bird World, which includes a hummingbird forest and a tropical aviary. The Primate Panorama is a 7-acre world-class primate exhibit with 29 species, ranging from a 6-ounce marmoset to a 581-pound gorilla.

The zoo is home to the nation's first natural gas–powered zoo train. The electric Safari Shuttle tours all zoo paths from spring through fall ($2.50 adult, $1.50 children). Another new attraction (in 2000) is an endangered species carousel, featuring wood-carved okapi, polar bears, Komodo dragons, and hippos.

Full meals are served at the Hungry Elephant, a zoo cafeteria with an outdoor eating area, and snack bars are scattered throughout the zoo. Many visitors bring picnic lunches to eat on the expansive lawns.

Rocky Mountain Arsenal National Wildlife Refuge. Quebec St. and 72nd Ave. ☎ **303/289-0232** (most activities require reservations). Free admission. Daylight hours. Bus: 48.

Once a site where the U.S. Army manufactured chemical weapons such as mustard gas and GB nerve agent, and later leased to a private enterprise to produce pesticides, the Rocky Mountain Arsenal has become an environmental success story. The 27-square-mile Superfund cleanup site, comprised of open grasslands and wetlands just west of Denver International Airport, is home to more than 330 species, including deer, coyotes, prairie dogs, and birds of prey. An estimated 100 bald eagles make this one of the country's largest eagle-roosting locales during the winter months.

The Rocky Mountain Arsenal Wildlife Society Bookstore is located at the visitor center. The U.S. Fish and Wildlife Service offers a drop-in visitor program on Saturdays as well as many other programs; for reservations, call ☎ **303/289-0232.** For a guided tour, it's best to call a week in advance. The U.S. Army (☎ **303/289-0467**) offers a program of environment cleanup information and tours.

3 Amusement Parks & Places Especially for Kids

Denver abounds in child-oriented activities, and the listings below will probably appeal to young travelers of any age. In addition, some sights listed in the previous sections may appeal to families as well. (Such as the Butterfly Pavilion and Insect Center; Colorado History Museum; Colorado's Ocean Journey; Denver Art Museum; Denver Museum of Miniatures, Dolls, and Toys; Denver Museum of Nature and Science; Denver Zoo; Four Mile Historic Park; and the U.S. Mint).

Adventure Golf. 9650 N. Sheridan Blvd. (at 96th Ave.). ☎ **303/650-7587.** Admission $5.95 adults, $5.45 seniors over 65, $4.75 children 4–12, free for children 3 and under. Easter–Halloween daily 10am–11pm, weather permitting. Hours may be shorter in spring and fall. Closed in winter. Bus: 51.

Each of the 54 holes at this miniature golf course has a theme to challenge you, such as a haunted house, pirate battle, fairy castle, fire-breathing dragon, and fiery volcano. Or perhaps you'd prefer to visit The Lost Continent, with "deadly" piranha pools and quicksand pits.

✪ **Children's Museum of Denver.** 2121 Children's Museum Dr. ☎ **303/433-7444.** www.cmdenver.org. Admission $5 ages 3–59, $3 seniors 60 and over, $2 children 1–2, free for children under 1 year. Memorial Day–Labor Day daily 10am–5pm plus Children's Museum Theatre, with evening performances every Sat and the first Fri of every month (call or see Website for times); Labor Day–Memorial Day Tues–Fri 9am–4pm, Sat–Sun 10am–5pm plus Mon school breaks and holidays. Take exit 211 (23rd Ave.) east off I-25; turn right on 7th St., and again on Children's Museum Dr.

Denver's best hands-on experience for children, this intriguing museum is both educational and just plain fun. Kids will enjoy the "Inventions" exhibit, which is comprised of an updated and expanded wood shop, where creative carpenters use wood and real tools and take home whatever they make; and an assembly line, where kids build a car and then test-drive it, fill the gas tank, check the air in the tires and water in the radiator, and even vacuum the interior. Another popular display helps children learn about biology and geology with help from characters such as Delores the Toothasaurus, who demonstrates the importance of dental hygiene by letting children floss and brush her teeth.

The Wild Oats Community Market is a grocery/deli/bakery where children learn to plan meals, create a shopping list, get a cart and choose items, and go through the checkout. (As items are "scanned" they go into a bin to be returned to the shelves.)

There's also a resource center that provides parenting information to adults; playscapes for 4- to 8-year-olds on the second floor; a mini-basketball court that teaches about good sportsmanship; an exhibit where participants play with letters and words on a large magnetic wall; and Arts á la Carte, where kids can sing, dance or put on a puppet show. The museum also has a cafe that serves sandwiches, snacks, and beverages. Special events such as story time and live theater take place periodically; call for schedules.

Fat City. 9670 W. Coal Mine Ave. (at Kipling St.), Littleton. ☎ **303/972-4344.** Admission varies by activity, $4–$6.50 (multiactivity tickets available). Sun–Thurs 9am–1am, Fri–Sat 9am–3am, call for activity availability. Bus: 67 or 76.

This 140,000 square foot indoor entertainment mall, completely renovated in 2000, bills itself as "bowling reinvented." Activities for adults as well as kids include 40 lanes of bowling, minigolf, Laser Tag, roller skating, 20 100-inch TVs, a large video arcade with virtual reality games and rides, billiards, a restaurant, and high-end martini bar.

Lakeside Amusement Park. I-70 exit 271 and Sheridan Blvd. ☎ **303/477-1621.** www.lakesideamusementpark.com. Gate admission $1.50. Ride coupons 25¢ (rides require 2 to 6 coupons each); unlimited rides $11.25 Mon–Fri, $14.75 Sat–Sun and holidays. May, Sat–Sun and holidays noon–11pm; June–Labor Day, Mon–Fri 6–11pm, Sat–Sun and holidays noon–11pm. Kiddie Playland, Mon–Fri 1–10pm, Sat–Sun and holidays noon–10pm. Closed Labor Day–Apr.

Among the largest amusement parks in the Rocky Mountains, Lakeside has about 40 rides, including a Cyclone roller coaster, a midway with carnival and arcade games, and a miniature train that circles the lake. There are also food stands and picnic facilities, plus a separate Kiddies Playland with 15 rides.

Six Flags Elitch Gardens Theme Park. Speer Blvd., at I-25 exit 212A. ☎ **303/595-4386.** www.sixflags.com/elitchgardens. Gate admission with unlimited rides $30 those taller than 4 feet; $17 seniors 55–69; $15 those 4 feet and under; free for children 3 and younger and seniors 70 and older. Memorial Day–Labor Day daily 10am–10pm. Call for off-season hours, Labor Day–Oct. 1.

A Denver tradition established in 1889, this amusement park moved to its present site just west of downtown in 1995. The 40-plus rides include Twister II, an unbelievable 10-story roller coaster with a 90-foot drop and dark tunnel; Mind Eraser, a suspension coaster that cruises at speeds in excess of 60 miles an hour; Island Kingdom, a waterslide park; the 220-foot, free-fall Tower of Doom; and a fully restored 1925 carousel with 67 hand-carved horses and chariots. Looney Tunes MovieTown is just for children under 54 inches tall, with rides sized to fit. There are also musical revues and other entertainment, games and arcades, food, shopping, and beautiful flower gardens.

Tiny Town. 6249 Turkey Creek Rd., Tiny Town, CO 80465. ☎ **303/697-6829.** www.designcircuit.com/eic/tiny.html. Admission $3 adults, $2 children 3–12, free for children under 3. Memorial Day–Labor Day daily 10am–5pm. Closed winter.

Originally built in 1920 at the site of a Denver-Leadville stagecoach stop, Tiny Town is exactly what its name implies—a one-sixth scale Western village. Nestled in a scenic mountain canyon about 20 miles southeast of Downtown Denver, Tiny Town is made up of 100 colorful buildings and a steam-powered locomotive kids can ride for an additional $1.

Water World. 88th Ave. and Pecos St., Federal Heights. ☎ **303/427-SURF.** www.hylandhills. org/waterworld.html. Admission $22.95 adults, $19.95 children 4–12, free for seniors and children under 4. Memorial Day–Labor Day daily 10am–6pm. Closed in winter. Take the Thornton exit (exit 219, 84th Ave.) off I-25 north.

This 64-acre complex, billed as America's largest family water park, has two ocean-like wave pools, river rapids for inner-tubing, twisting water slides, a small children's play area, plus other attractions—41 in all.

Walking Tour—Downtown Denver

Start: Denver Information Center, Civic Center Park.
Finish: State Capitol, Civic Center Park.
Time: 2 to 8 hours, depending on how much time you spend shopping, eating, and sightseeing.
Best Times: Any Tuesday through Friday in late spring.
Worst Times: Monday and holidays, when the museums are closed.

Start your tour of the downtown area at Civic Center Park, on West Colfax Avenue at 14th Street.

1. **Civic Center Park,** a two-square-block oasis, features a Greek amphitheater, fountains, statues, flower gardens, and 30 different species of trees, two of which (it is said) were originally planted by Abraham Lincoln at his Illinois home.

   Overlooking the park on its east side is the State Capitol. On its south side are the:

2. **Colorado History Museum,** a staircase-like building with exhibits that make the state's colorful history come to life; the Denver Public Library; and the:

3. **Denver Art Museum.** Designed by Gio Ponti of Milan, Italy, the art museum is a 28-sided, 10-story structure that resembles a medieval fortress with a skin of more than a million tiny glass tiles. Inside are 35,000 works of art, including a renowned American Indian collection.

   On the west side of Civic Center Park is the:

4. **City and County Building,** decorated in spectacular fashion with a rainbow of colored lights during the Christmas season.

   A block farther west is the:

5. **U.S. Mint.** Modeled in the Italian Renaissance style, the building resembles the Palazzo Riccardi in Florence. More than 60,000 cubic feet of granite and 1,000 tons of steel went into its construction in 1904.

   Cross over Colfax and go diagonally northwest up Court Place. Just two blocks ahead is the:

6. **Denver Pavilions,** the city's newest retail hotspot at the south end of the 16th Street Mall, featuring a Hard Rock Café, a 15-screen movie theatre, and a Barnes & Noble Superstore.

   Three blocks up the 16th Street Mall, head southwest two blocks on California St. past the Colorado Convention Center and turn right on 14th Street. Walk two blocks to the:

7. **Denver Center for the Performing Arts,** covering four square blocks between 14th Street and Cherry Creek, Champa Street and Arapahoe Street. The complex

is entered under a block-long, 80-foot–high glass archway. The center includes seven theaters, a symphony hall in the round, a voice research laboratory, and a smoking solar fountain. Free tours are offered.

Two more blocks up 14th past the arts center is:

8. **Larimer Square,** Denver's oldest commercial district. Restored turn-of-the-century Victorian buildings accommodate more than 30 shops and a dozen restaurants and clubs. Colorful awnings, hanging flower baskets, and quiet open courtyards accent the square, once home to such notables as Buffalo Bill Cody and Bat Masterson. Horse-drawn carriage rides originate here for trips up the 16th Street Mall or through lower downtown.

☕ **TAKE A BREAK**   Stop at Josephina's Ristorante (1433 Larimer St. between 14th and 15th streets) for some great specialty pizza. (See full review in chapter 4.)

A walkway at the east corner of Larimer and 15th leads through:

9. **Writer Square,** another shopping-and-dining complex with quaint gas lamps, brick walkways, and outdoor cafes.

At 16th Street, cross to the:

10. **Tabor Center,** a glass-enclosed shopping complex on three levels. In effect a two-block-long greenhouse (with the Westin Hotel rising from within), the Tabor Center was developed by the Rouse Company, the same firm that created Faneuil Hall in Boston, South Street Seaport in New York, and Harborplace in Baltimore.

To the east, the Tabor Center is anchored by the:

11. **D&F Tower,** a city landmark patterned after the campanile of St. Mark's Basilica in Venice, Italy, in 1910.

Here, begin a leisurely stroll down the:

12. **16th Street Mall,** with the State Capitol building to the southeast as your directional beacon. The $76-million pedestrian path is the finest people-watching spot in the city, where you'll see everyone from street entertainers to lunching office workers to travelers like yourself. Built of red and gray granite, it is lined with 200 red oak trees, a dozen fountains, and a lighting system straight out of Star Wars—not to mention the outdoor cafes, restored Victorian buildings, modern skyscrapers, and hundreds of shops—with an emphasis on sports—plus restaurants and department stores. Through it run sleek European-built shuttle buses, offering free transportation up and down the mall as often as every 90 seconds.

You'll walk seven blocks down 16th Street from the Tabor Center before reaching Tremont Place. Turn left, go one block farther, and across the street, on your right, you'll see the:

13. **Brown Palace Hotel.** One of the most beautiful grande dame hotels in the United States, it was built in 1892 and features a nine-story atrium lobby topped by a Tiffany stained-glass ceiling. Step into the lobby for a look, and if you're hungry...

☕ **TAKE A BREAK**   The Brown Palace Hotel serves lunch in several restaurants and also offers afternoon teas in its elegant lobby. Reservations are recommended for the English tea, which includes sandwiches and pastries from the Brown Palace bakery. (See full review in chapter 4.)

1 Civic Center Park
2 Colorado History Museum
3 Denver Art Museum
4 City and County Building
5 U.S. Mint
6 Denver Pavilions
7 Denver Center for
  the Performing Arts
8 Larimer Square
9 Writer Square
10 Tabor Center
11 D & F Tower
12 16th Street Mall
13 Brown Palace Hotel
14 State Capitol

Continue across Broadway on East 17th Avenue. Go two blocks to Sherman Street, turn right, and proceed two blocks south on Sherman to East Colfax Avenue.

You're back overlooking Civic Center Park, but this time you're at the:

14. State Capitol. If you stand on the 15th step on the west side of the building, you're exactly 5,280 feet (1 mile) above sea level. Architects modeled the Colorado capitol after the U.S. Capitol building in Washington, D.C., and used the world's entire known supply of rare rose onyx in its interior wainscoting. A winding 93-step staircase leads to an open-air viewing deck beneath the capitol dome; on a clear day, your view can extend from Pikes Peak near Colorado Springs to the Wyoming border.

4 Organized Tours

Visitors who want to be personally guided to the attractions of Denver and the surrounding areas by those in the know have a variety of choices. In addition to the following, see "Package Tours" under "Getting There," in chapter 2.

Half- and full-day bus tours of Denver and the nearby Rockies are offered by the ubiquitous **Gray Line,** P.O. Box 17646, Denver, CO 80217 (☎ **800/348-6877** for information only; **303/289-2841** for reservations and information). Fares for children 12 and under are half the adult prices listed below. Included in fares are entry fees but usually no food. Tours depart the Cherry Creek Shopping Center at 1st Ave. and Milwaukee St., as well as local hotels and hostels on a reservation basis.

A 4-hour tour (no. 27), leaving at 1:30pm, takes in Denver's mountain parks: Red Rocks Park, Bergen Park, and Buffalo Bill's grave atop Lookout Mountain. It costs $30 for adults. The Denver city tour (no. 28), which departs daily at 8:30am and takes about 3½ hours, gives you a taste of both old Denver—via Larimer Square and other historic buildings—and the modern-day city. It's $30 for adults, or you can combine this and the mountain parks tour for $55.

Highly recommended is the 10-hour Rocky Mountain National Park tour (no. 1), offered mid-May to mid-October, weather permitting, which takes visitors over the 12,183-foot summit of the park's Trail Ridge Road. Cost is $60 for adults; departure time is 8:30am. If you're not going to get to Colorado Springs on your own but would like to see Pikes Peak and the Air Force Academy, sign up for tour no. 31. This 10-hour tour departs at 8:30am daily and costs $70 for adults. From May to October, a 10-hour tour west to Georgetown is also offered for the same price.

Among other companies offering guided tours in and around Denver is **The Colorado Sightseer,** 6780 W. 84th Circle, Suite 60, Arvada, CO 80003 (☎ **303/423-8200,** www.coloradosightseer.com). The Historic Denver tour includes a visit to LoDo with some of the city's earliest buildings, the State Capitol, the Molly Brown House, and Four Mile Historic Park. It lasts about 4 hours and costs $35 for adults, $26 for children 5 to 12. A Rocky Mountain National Park tour, lasting about 9½ hours, costs $70 for adults and $55 for children 5 to 12, including a box lunch. The firm's 4½-hour Western Foothills Tour includes stops at Coors Brewery, the Buffalo Bill memorial, and scenic Red Rocks Park. Cost is $30 for adults and $22 for children 5 to 12.

SPECIALTY TOURS
FOUR-WHEEL-DRIVE TOURS

For those who want to get off the well-traveled path, a back-roads mountain tour is just the ticket. Several companies offer excursions in four-wheel-drive vehicles that depart from Denver and travel to remote areas with spectacular scenery; both half- and full-day trips are available. Many take visitors to ghost towns, old mining camps, historic wagon trails, and other historic sites. Nighttime star treks on mountaintops can also be arranged. One firm that offers these trips year-round is **Best Mountain Tours by the Mountain Men,** 3003 S. Macon Circle, Aurora, CO 80014 (☎ **303/750-5200** from 7am to 10pm). Destinations and daily availability vary. Typical rates are $40 per person for a 5-hour tour, $70 for an all-day tour. The Mountain Men also provide private group transportation to gambling casinos and ski resorts.

BICYCLING TOURS

A few companies operate bicycle tours out of the Denver area. **The World Outside** (☎ **800/488-8483** or 303/413-0938; www.theworldoutside.com) offers a 6-day, 5-night hut-to-hut tour that begins and ends in Vail (100 mi west of Denver). The huts, described by *Mountain Bike Magazine* as "luxurious backcountry accommodations," act as recreational headquarters for trip guests, who have plenty of fishing and sightseeing opportunities in between daily mountain biking treks.

The trips aren't cheap, running about $1,000 per rider, but this might be the best way for the biking enthusiast to enjoy the Rockies west of Denver. The trip is offered twice each summer, in June and August.

Another company that offers weeklong tours in the area is **Bicycle Tour of Colorado** (☎ **303/985-1180,** www.bicycletourcolo.com). For $360, a biker can join a tour involving in excess of 1,000 riders and 70 volunteers—including medical and bike-tech support as well as guiding services—on a 400-mile journey that hits six different cities each year, crossing the Continental Divide several times in the process. While accommodations can be prearranged at hotels, most riders elect to stay at facilities provided by the city: the local high school. Breakfast and lunch are provided, but you must find your own dinner in town.

Another good resource for bicyclists is the **Denver Bicycle Touring Club** (☎ **303/756-7240**), which organizes local rides and publishes a newsletter on the subject. See also "Bicycling," below.

5 Outdoor Activities

Denver's proximity to the Rocky Mountains makes it possible to spend a day skiing, snowmobiling, horseback riding, hiking, river running, sailing, fishing, hunting, mountain climbing, or rock-hounding and return to the city by nightfall. Within the city limits and nearby, visitors will find more than 200 miles of jogging and bicycle paths, over 100 free tennis courts, and several dozen public golf courses.

The city has an excellent system of **Mountain Parks** (☎ **303/697-4545**), covering some 13,488 acres, which are discussed earlier in this chapter in the "Parks, Gardens & Zoos" section.

Campsites are easily reached from Denver, as are suitable sites for hang gliding and hot-air ballooning. Sailing is popular within the city at Sloan's Lake and in Washington Park (both Denver City Parks), and the Platte River is clear for many miles of river running in rafts, kayaks, and canoes.

Detailed information can be obtained from the Denver Metro Convention and Visitors Bureau (see "Visitor Information," in chapter 4), and information on nearby outdoor activities is available from: **Colorado State Parks,** 1313 Sherman St., Suite 618, Denver, CO 80203 (☎ **303/866-3437;** www.coloradoparks.org); the **U.S. Forest Service,** Rocky Mountain Region, P.O. Box 25127, Lakewood, CO 80225 (☎ **303/275-5350;** www.fs.fed.us/r2); the **U.S. Bureau of Land Management,** 2850 Youngfield

St., Lakewood, CO 80215 (☎ **303/239-3600;** www.co.blm.gov); and the **National Park Service,** P.O. Box 25287, Denver, CO 80225 (☎ **303/969-2000;** www. nps.gov).

Visitors tempted by the Denver area's outdoor recreation opportunities but who neglected to bring the necessary equipment are in luck, with several rental sources available. **Sports Rent,** 8761 Wadsworth Blvd., Arvada, CO (☎ **303/467-0200;** fax 303/467-0359), has just about everything imaginable, including bikes, in-line skates, canoes, camping equipment, skis, snowboards, snowshoes, ski racks, and clothing. **Grand West Outfitters,** 801 Broadway, Denver, CO 80203 (☎ **303/825-0300**), rents camping gear and sells climbing gear, outdoor clothing, and other equipment. Grand West also has a rock-climbing wall in its store.

BALLOONING   You can't beat a hot-air balloon ride for viewing the magnificent Rocky Mountain scenery. **Life Cycle Balloon Adventures, Ltd.** (☎ **800/980-9272** or 303/216-1990, www.lifecycleballoons.com) offers sunrise champagne flights daily and has over 25 years of experience. **Colorado Balloon Rides** (☎ **800/873-8927**) generally schedules daily flights from all over Colorado's Front Range. **Looney Balloons** (☎ **303/979-9476**) offers daily 1-hour flights year-round.

BICYCLING   Denver is crisscrossed everywhere by paved bicycle paths, including a 12-mile scenic stretch along the bank of the South Platte River and along Cherry Creek beside Speer Boulevard. All told, the city has 85 miles of off-road trails for bikers and runners. Bike paths link the city's 205 parks, and many city streets are marked with bike lanes. In all, the city has more than 130 miles of designated bike paths and lanes. For more information, contact the Denver Convention and Visitors Bureau or **Bicycle Colorado** (☎ **719/530-0051;** www.bicyclecolo.org). Bike tours are available from several companies and clubs (see "Organized Tours," above).

BOATING   A quiet way to view some of downtown Denver is from a punt on scenic Cherry Creek. **Punt the Creek** (☎ **303/893-0750**) operates Tuesday through Sunday from 4 to 9pm, from June to August. Guides describe the history of the city while pointing out famous landmarks. Tickets are available at the kiosk at Creekfront Plaza, located at the intersection of Speer Boulevard and Larimer Street. It costs $12 for adults, $6 for children, and $11 for seniors for an hour-long trip. Half-hour trips are also available, for half the cost.

In 2000, commercial rafting companies began offering raft trips on the Platte River through Littleton and Englewood in Denver's south suburbs. **Flexible Flyers Rafting** (☎ **303/521-3567** or 970/247-4628) offers 2½ hour trips from early May to mid-June at 10:30am, 1:30pm and 4:30pm on Fridays through Sundays, as well as occasional weekday trips (call for availability). The cost is $40 adults, $20 children 12 and under.

Boaters enjoy the powerboat marinas at **Cherry Creek State Park,** 4201 S. Parker Rd., Aurora, CO 80014 (☎ **303/699-3860**), 11 miles from downtown off I-225; and **Chatfield State Park,** 11500 N. Roxborough Park Rd., Littleton, CO 80125 (☎ **303/791-7275**), 16 miles south of downtown Denver off Colo. 470. Jet skiing and sailboarding are also permitted at Cherry Creek and Chatfield State Parks. Sailboarding, canoeing, and other wakeless boating are popular at **Barr Lake State Park,** 13401 Picadilly Rd., Brighton, CO 80601 (☎ **303/659-6005**), 21 miles northeast of downtown via I-76.

For information on other boating opportunities, contact Colorado State Parks, the National Park Service, or the U.S. Forest Service (see above).

You Paid What?

47,000 hotels, 700 airlines, 50 rental car companies. And a few million ways to save money.

Travelocity.com

A Sabre Company

Go Virtually Anywhere.

AOL Keyword: Travel

Will you have enough stories to tell your grandchildren?

©2000 Yahoo! Inc.

Yahoo! Travel

BOWLING   One of Denver's biggest bowling centers is the 40-lane **Fat City,** 9670 W. Coal Mine Ave., Littleton (☎ **303/972-4344**), open Sundays through Thursdays 9am to 1am, Fridays and Saturdays 9am to 3am.

FISHING   A couple of good bets in the metropolitan area are Chatfield State Park, with trout, bass, and panfish, and Cherry Creek State Park, which boasts trout, walleye pike, bass, and crappie (see "Boating," above). In all, there are more than 7,100 miles of streams and in excess of 2,000 reservoirs and lakes in Colorado. For information, contact Colorado State Parks, the Colorado Division of Wildlife, or the U.S. Fish and Wildlife Service.

A number of sporting-goods stores can also provide more detailed information, including **The Flyfisher Ltd.,** 120 Madison St. (☎ **303/322-5014**). Their skilled and experienced staff can help with equipment choices and recommendations for where to go on any given day. Flyfisher also offers lessons, seminars, clinics, and guided wade and float trips.

GOLF   Throughout the Front Range, it's often said that you can play golf at least 320 days a year because the sun always seems to be shining, and even when it snows, what little snow that sticks melts quickly. With the resulting demand, there are more than 50 courses in the Denver area. These include seven municipal golf courses operated by the city, with nonresident greens fees up to $20 for 18 holes. City courses are: **City Park Golf Course,** East 25th Avenue and York Street (☎ **303/295-4420**); **Evergreen Golf Course,** 29614 Upper Bear Creek Rd., Evergreen (☎ **303/674-4128**); **Harvard Gulch Golf Course** (par 3), East Iliff Avenue and South Clarkson Street (☎ **303/698-4078**); **Kennedy Golf Course,** 10500 E. Hampden Ave. (☎ **303/751-0311**); **Overland Park Golf Course,** South Santa Fe Drive and West Jewell Avenue (☎ **303/698-4975**); **Wellshire Golf Course,** 3333 S. Colorado Blvd. (☎ **303/692-5636**); and **Willis Case Golf Course,** 4999 Vrain St. near West 50th Avenue (☎ **303/458-4877**). Wellshire is the best overall course, but we prefer Willis Case for its spectacular mountain views. Aside from same-day reservations, nonresident golfers must purchase a $10 card at any municipal course, then make reservations via an automated phone system (☎ 303/784-4000). The one exception to this policy is Evergreen Golf Course, where you can call the starter for reservations three days in advance. For information on any of them, you can also call the **Denver Department of Parks and Recreation** (☎ 303/964-2563).

For information on the state's major golf courses, contact the **Colorado Golf Resort Association,** 2110 S. Ash St., Denver, CO 80222 (☎ **303/680-9967;** www.cologolfresorts.com). Really serious golfers may want to subscribe to *The Colorado Golfer,* which carries information on courses throughout the state. An annual subscription (available at the number and address above) costs $6 and includes an excellent guide to the state's courses that is published each spring.

HIKING & BACKPACKING   The ✪ **Colorado Trail** is a hiking, horse, and mountain-biking route stretching 500 miles from Denver to Durango. The trail is also open to cross-country skiing, snowshoeing, and llama-pack hiking. Opened in 1988, the trail is still being fine-tuned. It took 15 years to establish using volunteer labor and crosses eight mountain ranges and five river systems, winding from rugged terrain to pristine meadows. For information, contact the Colorado Trail at 710 10th St., Room 210, Golden, CO 80401-1022(☎ **303/384-3729** ext. 113, fax 303/384-3743, www.coloradotrail.org). The **Colorado Trail Foundation,** (☎ **303/526-0809;** E-mail: ctf@ctf.coloradotrail.org) offers supported treks and accredited courses on the trail.

For hikes specific to the Denver area, contact the city **Department of Parks and Recreation** (☎ 303/964-2500) for information on Denver's park system. Or contact any of the following agencies: Colorado State Parks, Colorado Division of Wildlife, National Park Service, U.S. Bureau of Land Management, or U.S. Forest Service (see above). A good source for the many published area maps and hiking guides is **Mapsco Map and Travel Center,** 899 Broadway, Denver, CO 80203 (☎ **800/456-8703** or 303/623-4299), as are local sporting goods stores and bookstores (see "Shopping," below).

Mount Falcon Park offers excellent trails that are easy to moderate in difficulty, making this a good place for families with children. There are also picnic areas, shelters, and ruins of an old castlelike home. From Denver, go west on U.S. 285 and then south on Colo. 8; the park is open daily from dawn to dusk and admission is free. Mountain bikes and horseback riding are permitted, as are leashed dogs.

Other relatively easy trails near Denver can be found in **Roxborough State Park,** 10 miles south of Littleton—namely the 1-mile **Willow Trail** and the 2¼-mile ✪ **Fountain Valley Trail.** Three other trails at Roxborough are more strenuous, but worth the effort if you enjoy beautiful red rocks and the chance to see wildlife. To get to Roxborough Park, exit Colo. 470 south onto U.S. 85 and turn west onto Titan Road, then south again at Roxborough Park Road to the main entrance. Admission costs $4 per vehicle and the park is open daily from 8am to 8pm in summer, 8am to 6pm at other times. Dogs, bikes, and horseback riding are not permitted.

HORSEBACK RIDING   Equestrians can find a mount year-round at **Stockton's Plum Creek Stables,** 7479 W. Titan Rd., Littleton (☎ **303/791-1966**), near Chatfield State Park, 15 miles south of downtown. Stockton's offers hayrides and barbecue picnics, as well as lessons ($45 an hour). **Paint Horse Stables,** 4201 S. Parker Rd., Aurora (☎ **303/690-8235**), at Cherry Creek State Park, also rents horses, boards horses, and provides riding lessons, hayrides, and pony rides for kids.

RECREATION CENTERS   The **Denver Department of Parks and Recreation** (☎ **303/964-2500**) operates 29 recreation centers around the city, several of which have facilities oriented to seniors. Daily guest passes for all facilities, including swimming pools, cost $6 for adult nonresidents ($4 for Denver residents) and $2 for anyone 17 or younger. Facilities vary but may include basketball courts, indoor or outdoor pools, gyms, and weight rooms. A variety of fitness classes and other recreation programs is offered, including programs for those with special needs. Call ☎ 303/964-2496 for current program information.

Among the city's recreation centers are the following: **Berkeley Recreation Center,** 5031 W. 46th Ave. (☎ **303/458-4898**), which has both indoor and outdoor pools; **Martin Luther King Jr. Recreation Center,** 3880 Newport St. (☎ **303/331-4034**), which is the nearest full-service center to Denver International Airport and has an indoor pool, large gym, and racquetball court; **20th Street Recreation Center,** downtown at 1011 20th St., between Arapahoe and Curtis streets (☎ **303/295-4430**), with an indoor pool and weight room; and **Washington Park Recreation Center,** 701 S. Franklin St. (☎ **303/698-4962**), with an indoor pool, advanced weight room, large gym, and walking and jogging trails.

SKIING   Several ski resorts are close to Denver. These include **Eldora Mountain Resort,** 45 miles west via Boulder (☎ **888/235-3672** or 303/440-8700; fax 303/440-8797; www.eldora.com), which covers almost 500 acres and has 47 trails, with skiing rated 20% beginner, 50% intermediate, and 30% advanced. **Loveland Basin and Valley,** 56 miles west via I-70, exit 216 (☎ **800/736-3754** or 303/569-3203; fax 303/571-5580; www.skiloveland.com), covers 1,365 acres and has 70 trails, rated 17% beginner, 42% intermediate, and 41% advanced. ✪ **Winter Park Resort,** 73 miles west of Denver via I-70 and U.S. 40 (☎ **970/726-5514;** fax 970/726-1572;

www.winterparkresort.com), boasts 2,886 skiable acres with 121 trails, rated 9% beginner, 34% intermediate, 57% advanced. **Berthoud Pass Ski Area,** near Winter Park (☎ **800/SKI-BERTHOUD** or 970/569-0100), is billed as Colorado's first ski area. It recently reopened after being closed for 10 years, and redevelopment is underway. Call for current information.

Eldora and Winter Park offer Nordic as well as alpine terrain.

Full information on statewide skiing is available from **Colorado Ski Country USA,** 1560 Broadway, Suite 2000, Denver, CO 80202 (☎ **303/837-0793;** fax 303/837-1627; www.coloradoski.com), and the **Colorado Cross Country Ski Association,** which can be contacted via its Web site (www.colorado-xc.org).

Some useful Denver telephone numbers for skiers include: **ski-area information** ☎ 303/825-7669; **snow report** ☎ 303/573-7433; **weather report** ☎ 303/337-2500; **road conditions** ☎ 303/639-1111.

SWIMMING   The Denver Department of Parks and Recreation (☎ **303/964-2500**) operates 17 outdoor swimming pools (open daily June 15 to August 10) and 9 indoor pools (open Monday through Saturday year-round). See "Recreation Centers," above.

TENNIS   The Denver Department of Parks and Recreation (☎ **303/964-2500**) manages or owns close to 150 tennis courts, more than one-third of them lit for night play. In all, you'll find tennis courts at 26 city parks, with lighted courts at 11 parks. Among the most popular tennis courts are those located in City Park (York Street and East 17th Avenue), Berkeley Park (Tennyson Street and West 17th Avenue), Green Valley East Ranch Park (Jebel Street and East 45th Avenue), Washington Park (South Downing Street and East Louisiana Avenue), and Sloan's Lake Park (Sheridan Boulevard and West 17th Avenue). Most public courts are free, but some charge about $5 per hour. It's generally easier to find space at an outlying court than one in downtown Denver. For more information on tennis possibilities, contact the **Colorado Tennis Association,** 1191 S. Parker Rd., Suite 101, Denver, CO 80231 (☎ **303/695-4116**).

GREAT NEARBY STATE PARKS

Colorado has a number of excellent state parks offering a wide range of activities and scenery. Information on all the state's parks is available online at www.coloradoparks.org.

BARR LAKE STATE PARK   About 25 miles northeast of Denver via I-76 in Brighton, this wildlife sanctuary of 2,600 acres comprises a prairie reservoir and surrounding wetlands and uplands. Boats with motors exceeding 10 horsepower are not allowed, but you can sail, paddle, or row, as well as fish. A 9-mile hiking and biking trail circles the lake. A boardwalk from the nature center at the south parking lot leads to a good view of a heron rookery, and bird blinds along this trail allow wildlife observation and photography. Three picnic areas provide tables and grills; there's a commercial campground opposite the park on the west side. The entrance is at 13401 Picadilly Rd. Admission costs $4 per vehicle. Call ☎ **303/659-6005** for more information.

CASTLEWOOD CANYON STATE PARK   Steep canyons, a meandering stream, a waterfall, lush vegetation, and considerable wildlife distinguish this 1,000-acre park. You can see the remains of Castlewood Canyon Dam, which was built for irrigation in 1890; it collapsed in 1933, killing two people. The park, 30 miles south of Denver on Colo. 83, east of Castle Rock in Franktown, provides picnic facilities and hiking trails. The entrance is at 2989 S. State Highway 83; admission is $4 per vehicle. Call ☎ **303/688-5242** for more information.

CHATFIELD STATE PARK   Just 16 miles south of downtown Denver via U.S. 85 in Littleton, this park occupies 5,600 acres of prairie against a backdrop of the steeply rising Rocky Mountains. Chatfield Reservoir, with a 26-mile shoreline, invites swimming, boating, fishing, and other water sports. The area also has 18 miles of paved bicycle trails, plus hiking and horseback-riding paths. In winter, there's ice fishing and cross-country skiing.

An observation area on the south side of the park permits viewing of a 27-acre nature study grove. The park also has a hot-air balloon launch pad.

Facilities include 153 pull-through campsites, showers, laundry, and dump station. Admission is $4 per vehicle; the camping fee is $9 to $12 daily. The entrance is located one mile south of C-470 on Wadsworth Blvd. (☎ **303/791-7275**).

CHERRY CREEK STATE PARK   The 880-acre Cherry Creek Reservoir, created for flood control by the construction of a dam in 1950, is the central attraction of this popular park, which has become a mecca for 1.5 million visitors each year. Located at the southeast Denver city limits (off Parker Road and I-225) about 12 miles from downtown, the park comprises 5,000 acres: 3,900 of land, and 1,000 of water.

Water sports include swimming, waterskiing, boating, and fishing. There's a nature trail, dog-training area, model-airplane field with paved runways, jetski rental facility, rifle range, pistol range, and trap-shooting area. 10 miles of paved bicycle paths and 10 miles of bridle trails circle the reservoir (horse rentals are available). Rangers offer guided walks on a 1½-mile nature trail, as well as evening campfire programs in an amphitheater. Winter-sports enthusiasts enjoy skating, ice fishing, and ice boating.

Each of the park's 102 campsites has access to showers, laundry, and dump station. More than forty sites have electric hookups, but there are no water hookups. Also, many lakeshore day-use sites are supplied with picnic tables and grills.

Admission costs $5 per vehicle; the camping fee is $10 to $14 daily. Campgrounds are closed from November through March. The entrance is at 4201 S. Parker Rd. in Aurora. Call ☎ **303/690-3860** for general information or ☎ **800/678-2267** for camping reservations.

GOLDEN GATE STATE PARK   One hour west of Denver, this 14,000-acre park ranges in elevation from 7,400 to 10,400 feet and offers camping, picnicking, hiking, biking, fishing, hunting, and horseback-riding opportunities. A daily vehicle pass costs $4, and camping fees range from $10 to $14 in developed campgrounds, $6 for back-country camping. There are around 160 developed campsites, with a limited number of electrical hookups available. Coin-operated showers and laundry facilities are provided at Reverend's Ridge, the park's largest campground.

To get to Golden Gate, take Colo. 93 north from Golden 1 mile to Golden Gate Canyon Road. Then turn left and continue 15 miles to the park. For more information, call ☎ **303/582-3707.**

6 Spectator Sports

Tickets to many sporting events can be obtained from **The Ticketman,** 6800 N. Broadway, #103, Denver, CO 80221 (☎ **800/200-TIXS** or 303/430-1111), with delivery to your hotel available; or **Ticketmaster** (☎ **303/830-TIXS**), with several outlets in the Denver area.

AUTO RACING   Colorado National Speedway, at I-25 exit 232, 20 minutes north of Denver (☎ **303/665-4173**), has NASCAR Winston Racing, superstocks, and RMMRA Midgets on a three-eighth–mile asphalt oval track, weekends from April through September.

For drag racing, head to **Bandimere Speedway,** 3051 S. Rooney Rd., Morrison (☎ 303/697-6001, or 303/697-4870 for a 24-hour recording), with races scheduled from April through October. There are motorcycles, pickup trucks, street cars, and sports cars, plus car shows, swap meets, special events for high school students, and even a junior drag racing series for ages 8 to 17.

BASEBALL   The **Colorado Rockies,** which began life as a National League expansion team in 1993, still regularly sells out its home games. The team plays at Coors Field, in the historic lower downtown section of Denver. The 50,000-seat stadium, with its red brick exterior, was designed in the style of baseball stadiums of old. For information and tickets, call ROCKIES (☎ **800/388-7625** or 303/762-5437; www.coloradorockies.com).

BASKETBALL   The **Denver Nuggets** (☎ **303/405-1100** for ticket information) of the National Basketball Association play their home games at the state-of-the-art Pepsi Center (Speer Blvd. and Auraria Pkwy.), which opened in 1999. There are 41 home games a year between November and April, with playoffs continuing into June.

The **University of Denver** (☎ **303/871-2336** for ticket office) plays a competitive college basketball schedule from late November through March. Other university teams include women's gymnastics, men's hockey, and other sports.

FOOTBALL   The **Denver Broncos** (☎ **303/433-7466** for tickets) of the National Football League make their home at Mile High Stadium, part of a sports complex at exit 210B of I-25. After the Broncos' first-ever NFL Championship in 1998, Denver voters endorsed the construction of a new stadium. Ground broke in 1998 on the project, which is adjacent to Mile High and slated to be ready for the 2001 season. Home games are sold out months in advance, so call early. Your best bet may be to find someone hawking tickets outside the stadium entrance on game day.

You'll have better luck getting into a college game. The **University of Colorado Buffaloes** in Boulder play in the Big Eight Conference. For ticket information, call ☎ **303/492-8337.** Other top college football teams in the area can be found at Colorado State University in Fort Collins and at the Air Force Academy in Colorado Springs.

GREYHOUND RACING   **Wembley Park,** East 62nd Avenue and Colorado Boulevard, in Commerce City (☎ **303/288-1591**), has pari-mutuel dog races from June to February, with afternoon and evening events as well as simulcast horse racing year-round. Call for the current schedule.

HOCKEY   Denver's National Hockey League team, the **Colorado Avalanche** (☎ **303/893-6700** for ticket information), plays its home games at the luxurious and modern Pepsi Center (Speer Blvd. and Auraria Parkway), in a season that runs from October through April. Coloradans went wild in June 1996 when the Avalanche surprised everyone by winning the prestigious Stanley Cup, Colorado's first championship in any major-league sport. The team demolished the Florida Panthers to bring the Stanley Cup home to Denver, where they were met by a screaming throng of 450,000 fans and a ticker-tape parade.

HORSE RACING   **Arapahoe Park,** 26000 E. Quincy Ave., Aurora (☎ **303/690-2400**), offers pari-mutuel horse racing each summer with simulcast racing the rest of the year.

RODEO   The **National Western Stock Show and Rodeo** (☎ **303/297-1166**) is held the second and third weeks of January, with the rodeo at the Denver Coliseum and other activities at the National Western Complex and the Event Center. With more than $500,000 available in prize money, this is one of the world's richest rodeos.

SOCCER   The **Colorado Rapids** (☎ **800/844-7777** or 303/299-1599) brought soccer fame to Denver in 1997 with major-league soccer's Western Conference Championship. The team plays at Mile High Stadium from April to September, and will likely be tenants in the new Broncos' stadium for the 2002 season.

7 Shopping

If you're in Denver on foot, you'll find that most visitors do their shopping along the **16th Street Mall** (the mile-long pedestrian walkway between Market St. and Tremont Pl.), and adjacent areas, including **Larimer Square, The Shops at Tabor Center, Writer Square,** and the newest retail development downtown, **Denver Pavilions.**

For those who don't mind leaving the downtown area there are more options, primarily the huge **Cherry Creek Shopping Center**—a shopper's dream—located to the south of downtown. There are also numerous suburban shopping malls.

Business hours vary from store to store and from mall to mall. Generally, stores are open 6 days a week, with many open on Sunday, too; department stores usually stay open until 9pm at least one evening a week. Discount stores and supermarkets are often open later than other stores, and some supermarkets are open 24 hours a day.

SHOPPING A TO Z
ANTIQUES
Denver's main antiques area is **Antique Row,** along **South Broadway** between Mississippi and Iowa streets, with some 400 dealers selling all sorts of fine antiques, collectibles, and junk. It's great fun wandering through the gigantic rooms, where each dealer has his or her own little space. Just remember that prices are often negotiable; unless you're quite knowledgeable about antiques, it wouldn't hurt to do some comparison shopping before making a major purchase.

A major part of Antique Row is taken up by the **Antique Guild** (☎ **303/ 722-3365**), an antiques dealers' mall in the 1200 block of South Broadway; and the adjacent **Antique Market** (☎ **303/744-0281**). Together they have about 250 dealers selling every type of antique and collectible imaginable. There's also a historic soda fountain.

Serious antiques hunters will also want to explore the **Antique Mall of Lakewood,** 9635 W. Colfax Ave. (☎ **303/238-6940**), which has a 34,000-square-foot showroom where some 150 dealers display a wide variety of items from the 18th and 19th centuries, as well as more recent collectibles.

ART & FINE CRAFTS
The renaissance of Denver's Lower Downtown (LoDo) has resulted in the creation of the **Lower Downtown Arts District,** where you can explore more than two dozen galleries. The district runs from Larimer to Wynkoop streets between 14th and 20th streets. Art walks take place from 5 to 9pm on the first Friday of each month. Call ☎ **303/628-5424** for additional information.

Camera Obscura. 1309 Bannock St. ☎ **303/623-4059.** Closed Mon.

This highly respected photographic gallery exhibits vintage and contemporary photographs, including works by such renowned photographers as Henri Cartier-Bresson and Annie Liebowitz.

Core New Art Space. 2045 Larimer St. ☎ **303/297-8428.**

This lower downtown cooperative gallery features experimental art, including long themed engagements with works by many artists. One recent exhibit focused on art inspired by Elvis Presley.

Merrill Gallery of Fine Art, Ltd. 315 Detroit St. ☎ **303/333-1566.**

Established national and emerging regional artists are represented at this beautiful gallery in Cherry Creek North, which is known for its traditional and contemporary works of realism.

Mudhead Gallery. 321 17th St. ☎ **303/293-9977.**

This gallery, located in the Brown Palace Hotel, has contemporary and historic American Indian pottery, baskets, weavings, and jewelry, plus Western and Southwestern art. There's another location at the Hyatt Regency Hotel, 555 17th St. (☎ **303/293-0007**).

Native American Trading Company. 1301 Bannock St. ☎ **303/534-0771.**

Older weavings, pottery, baskets, jewelry, and other American Indian works from the Rocky Mountain region are sold at this fine gallery. Appropriately, it's across the street from the Denver Art Museum.

Pismo Contemporary Art Glass. 235 Fillmore St. ☎ **303/333-2879.**

Nationally renowned glass artists as well as emerging artists are represented in this gallery, located in Cherry Creek North.

Turner Art Gallery. 301 University Blvd. ☎ **303/355-1828.**

Colorado's oldest gallery specializes in traditional art forms, including oils and landscapes (many of Colorado scenes) by regional painters. Its collection also includes etchings and sculptures, as well as antique botanicals by European artists.

BOOKS

Barnes & Noble Booksellers. 500 16th St. (in the Denver Pavilions). ☎ **303/825-9166.**

Barnes & Noble has a large selection of all kinds of books and music, often at discounted prices. This two-story location opened in 1999 in an increasingly popular retail area on the south side of Downtown Denver. There's a particularly good travel section, where you'll find local and regional maps. The store also has, of course, a Starbucks Coffee attached.

Other Denver–area Barnes & Noble Booksellers are at 14015 E. Exposition Ave., Aurora (☎ **303/366-8928**); 8555 E. Arapahoe Rd., Englewood (☎ **303/796-8851**); 960 S. Colorado Blvd., Glendale (☎ **303/691-2998**); 8136 W. Bowles Ave., Littleton (☎ **303/948-9565**); County Line Rd. and Yosemite, Littleton (☎ **303/706-9660**); and 9370 N. Sheridan Blvd., Westminster (☎ **303/708-1735**).

Borders. 9515 E. County Line Rd. (at I-25 and E. County Line Rd., across from Park Meadows Shopping Center), Englewood. ☎ **303/708-1735.**

You'll find a large selection of books of all types plus recorded music at Borders. There's a well-stocked travel section, local and regional maps, and all the latest fiction and nonfiction. You can also stop at the in-store Cafe Espresso for a cup of coffee and a pastry.

Hue-Man Experience. 911 Park Ave. West (between Curtis and Champa sts.). ☎ **303/293-2665.**

This bookstore specializes in African and African American subjects, including children's books, fine art prints, and magazines.

Tattered Cover Book Store. 2955 E. First Ave. (opposite Cherry Creek Shopping Center). ☎ **800/833-9327** or 303/322-7727. www.tatteredcover.com.

This bookstore is so big, it supplies maps to help you find your way through its maze of shelves. Comfortable chairs are placed strategically throughout the building for those who want to check out the first chapter before buying or to rest up after a hike to the fourth floor. The store also provides a wide selection of newspapers and magazines, a bargain-book section, free gift wrapping, disabled access to all four floors via elevator, mail order, and out-of-print search services. In addition, there's a full-service coffee bar, an enclosed rooftop restaurant specializing in New American cuisine, and storytelling in the children's section every Tuesday at 11am and Saturday at 10:30am. Hours are Monday through Saturday from 9am to 11pm, Sunday from 10am to 6pm.

The **Tattered Cover** has a second location in Denver's LoDo at 16th and Wynkoop streets, on the 16th Street Mall (☎ **303/436-1070**).

FASHION

Eddie Bauer. 3000 E. Cherry Creek Ave. (in the Cherry Creek Mall). ☎ **303/377-2100.**

This is the place to come for good deals on the famous Eddie Bauer line of upscale outdoor clothing. This extra-large store features a wide variety of men's and women's fashions alongside outdoor-oriented gadgetry.

Lawrence Covell. 225 Steele St. (in Cherry Creek North). ☎ **303/320-1023.**

This renowned upscale shop, established in 1967 by Lawrence and Cathy Covell, offers the finest quality men's and women's fashions, including designer clothing by Ermenegildo Zegna, Vestimenta, Luciano Barbera, and Kiton.

Sheplers. 8500 E. Orchard Rd., Englewood. ☎ **303/773-3311.** www.sheplers.com. At I-25 exit 198.

Billing itself as the world's largest western clothing store, Sheplers sells boots, cowboy hats, western shirts, fancy skirts, belt buckles, scarves, jackets, plenty of jeans, and just about everything else western.

Another **Sheplers** is at 10300 Bannock St., Northglenn, at 104th Avenue (☎ **303/450-9999**).

Timbuktu Station. 1512 Larimer St. ☎ **303/820-3739.**

A good selection of upscale casual clothing and unique accessories is available here.

Woolrich Store. 6900 W. 117th Ave., Broomfield. ☎ **303/469-5257.**

This outlet store, located at the factory off U.S. 36 between Denver and Boulder, sells top-quality woolens and other outdoor clothing, plus accessories and wool blankets.

FOOD & DRINK

Safeway, King Soopers, and **Albertson's** are the main grocery store chains.

Alfalfa's. 201 University Blvd. ☎ **800/494-9453** or 303/320-9071. www.wildoats.com.

Already an institution in the Denver area, this huge natural-foods store—35,000 square feet in area—helps perpetuate Coloradans' healthy lifestyles. No food sold here contains artificial flavoring or preservatives, nor was any grown using pesticides, chemicals, or other additives. There's a juice and health-food bar as well. This Cherry Creek–area store opened in 1990; others are scattered throughout the metropolitan area.

Applejack Liquors. 3320 Youngfield St. (in the Applewood Shopping Center), Wheat Ridge (I-70 exit 264). ☎ **800/879-5225** or 303/233-3331.

This huge store, which covers some 40,000 square feet and claims to be Colorado's largest beer, wine, and liquor supermarket, offers some of the best prices in the area as well as delivery. The store has a wide choice of single malt scotches; an extensive wine section, which includes a number of Colorado wines; and a good selection of cigars. It's open Monday through Thursday until 10pm, and Friday and Saturday until 11pm.

Argonaut Wine & Liquor Supermarket. 700 E. Colfax Ave. (at Washington St.) ☎ 303/831-7788. www.spiritsusa.com.

You'll find an excellent selection of wines, as well as beer and liquor, at good prices at this large store, which is located just four blocks east of the State Capitol. It's open Monday through Thursday until 10pm and Friday and Saturday until 11:45pm.

Stephany's Chocolates. 6770 W. 52nd Ave., Arvada (north of I-70 via Wadsworth Blvd.) ☎ **800/888-1522** or 303/421-7229. www.stephanys-chocolates.com.

Denver's largest manufacturer and wholesaler of gourmet confections is best known for its Denver Mint and Colorado Almond Toffee. In business for more than 3 decades, it offers tours twice daily on weekdays, by advance reservation only. Retail outlets are located in malls throughout the city.

GIFTS & SOUVENIRS

Colorado History Museum Store. 1300 Broadway. ☎ **303/866-4993.**

This museum shop carries unique made-in-Colorado gifts and souvenirs, including American Indian jewelry and sand paintings, plus an excellent selection of books on Colorado.

Earth Works, Ltd. 1421-B Larimer Square. ☎ **303/825-3390.**

Here you'll find hand-crafted work by Colorado artisans, including pottery, jewelry, photos, candles, and prints. Of special note are the Colorado-made hot sauces and salsas and the aspen wood vases, also made in-state.

Made in Colorado. 4840 W. 29th Ave. (☎ **800/272-1046** or 303/480-9050. www.madeincolorado.com.

You can take home a piece of Colorado with a stop at this shop, which also has a mail-order department. The wide variety of gift and souvenir items ranges from Mesa Verde pottery and hand-blown glass to decorative oil candles, aspen wood vases, picture frames, and clocks, as well as art, jewelry, and foods of many descriptions, all made in Colorado.

JEWELRY

Atlantis Gems, Inc. 718 16th St. Mall. ☎ **800/659-6404** or 303/825-3366.

This store features unique custom jewelry plus a large selection of loose gemstones and exotic minerals. It also stocks fossils, estate jewelry, and vintage watches; a gemologist and watchmaker are on site.

Jeweler's Center at the University Building. 910 16th St. ☎ **303/534-6270.**

Here you'll find 12 floors of retail and wholesale outlets in what is billed as Denver's largest concentration of jewelers.

John Atencio. 1440 Larimer St. (on Larimer Square). ☎ **800/466-6944,** PIN 4277, or 303/534-4277.

A highly regarded Colorado artist, John Atencio has received several awards for his unique jewelry designs. Located on historic Larimer Square in downtown Denver, his store offers 14- and 18-karat gold jewelry accented with high-quality stones, plus special collections such as "Elements" which feature unusual combinations of gold, sterling silver, and stones.

MALLS & SHOPPING CENTERS

Cherry Creek Shopping Center. 3000 E. First Ave. (between University Blvd. and Steele St.). ☎ **800/424-6360** or 303/388-3900.

Saks Fifth Avenue, Neiman Marcus, Foley's, and Lord and Taylor anchor this deluxe million-square-foot mall, with more than 160 shops, restaurants, and services, including an eight-screen movie theater. Across the street is Cherry Creek North, an upscale neighborhood retail area. Open Monday through Friday from 10am to 9pm, Saturday from 10am to 7pm, and Sunday from 11am to 6pm.

Denver Pavilions. 500 16th St. (between Welton and Tremont sts.). ☎ **303/260-6001.**

Opened in 1998, the Pavilions are comprised of several massive retail structures on the southern end of the 16th Street Mall. A three-level complex jammed with entertainment and dining options, it features Denver's only Hard Rock and Wolfgang Puck Cafés, a movie-plex, and Nike Town, Virgin Records and Barnes & Noble megastores(see "Books," above). The store hours here are Monday to Thursday 10am to 9pm, Friday and Saturday 10am to 10pm, and Sunday 11am to 6pm; the restaurants and movie theatres are open later.

Larimer Square. 1400 block of Larimer St. ☎ **303/534-2367.**

This restored quarter of old Denver (see "More Attractions," earlier in this chapter) includes numerous art galleries, boutiques, restaurants, and nightclubs. Most shops are open Monday through Thursday from 10am to 8pm, Friday and Saturday from 10am to 9pm, and Sunday from noon to 5pm. Restaurant and nightclub hours vary, and hours are slightly shorter during the winter.

Mile High Flea Market. 7007 E. 88th Ave. (at I-76), Henderson. ☎ **303/289-4656.**

Just 10 minutes northeast of downtown Denver, this huge market attracts more than 1.5 million shoppers a year to its 80 paved acres. Besides close-outs, garage sales, and seasonal merchandise, it has more than a dozen places to eat and snack, plus family rides. It's open year-round on Wednesday, Saturday, and Sunday from 7am to 5pm. Admission is $2 Saturday and Sunday, $1 Wednesday, and free for children under 12.

Park Meadows Retail Resort. 8401 Park Meadows Center Dr., (just south of C-470 on Yosemite St.), Littleton. ☎ **303/792-2999** or 888/333-PARK. www.parkmeadows.com.

Located at the C-470/I-25 interchange south of Denver, this large specialty mall is at the heart of a burgeoning retail area. Very posh and upscale—the interior is reminiscent of a massive and luxurious lodge, with exposed timbers and stylish furnishings—Park Meadows features Nordstrom, Dillard's, Foley's, and 130 specialty shops and restaurants, as well as a large movie theatre and arcade. Stores are open Monday through Saturday, 10am to 9:30pm and Sunday 11am to 6pm.

The Prime Outlets at Castle Rock. I-25 exit 184, about 20 minutes south of Denver. ☎ **800/245-8351** or 303/688-4494. www.primeoutlets.com.

This outlet mall between Denver and Colorado Springs has well over 100 outlet stores, including Corning Revere, Levi's, Van Heusen, Calvin Klein, Eddie Bauer, Black & Decker, Sony, Bass, Nike, Big Dog, Guess?, Athlete's Foot, Farberware, the Gap, and Toy Liquidators, plus a food court. Although many prices are the same as you'd find during a sale at your local mall or discount store, there's a nice selection and a few real bargains—especially on end-of-season items, irregulars, and reconditioned Sony electronics and Black & Decker. Camp Coleman has practically every camping supply you can imagine, all manufactured by the reliable Coleman company. Wheelchair and stroller rentals are available, and there's an information booth in the food court with maps of the outlet center. Open Monday through Saturday from 10am to 9pm and Sunday from 11am to 6pm.

The Shops at Tabor Center. 16th Street Mall (at Lawrence St.). ☎ **303/572-6865.**

About 60 specialty shops, services, and eateries are in this two-block, glass-enclosed galleria. You'll find upscale clothing, toys, books, gifts and collectibles, as well as more than a dozen dining opportunities. Hours are Monday through Friday from 10am to 9pm, Saturday from 10am to 6pm, and Sunday from noon to 5pm.

Tivoli Student Union. 900 Auraria Pkwy. ☎ **303/556-6329** or 303/556-6330.

Transformed from a 19th-century brewery, this building has been home to Auraria's Student Union since 1994. It contains shops, cafes, restaurants, and movie theaters, plus a Ticketmaster outlet for both campus and city events and even ski-lift tickets. Shops are open Monday through Saturday from 10am to 9pm and Sunday from noon to 5pm.

Sporting Goods

Active travelers who want to pick up a few supplies will be pleased to discover that Denver has the world's largest sporting-goods store: **Gart Sports Castle,** on Broadway at 10th Avenue (☎ **303/861-1122;** www.gartsports.com). There are also a number of Gart outlets in the Denver area.

REI also has several stores in the metro area, including its flagship store just west of downtown, at 1416 Platte St.(☎ **303/756-3100;** www.rei.com). This gargantuan outdoor store features a climbing wall, an outdoor bike testing area, and a "cold room" to try out outerwear and sleeping bags. Those in need of a new bike may want to stop at **Bicycle Village,** 305 S. Kipling St. (☎ **303/988-3210;** www.bicyclevillage.com), which claims the distinction of being the largest Schwinn dealer west of the Mississippi River.

Sports fans looking for that Rockies cap or Broncos shirt will have no trouble finding exactly what they seek at the appropriately named **Sportsfan,** 1962 Blake St., across from Coors Field, (☎ **303/295-3460;** www.sportsteams.com). There are several other locations in the Denver area, and mail orders are accepted.

For information on where to rent sporting-goods equipment, see the "Outdoor Activities" section earlier in this chapter.

Toys & Hobbies

✪ **Caboose Hobbies.** 500 S. Broadway. ☎ **303/777-6766.**

Model-train buffs should plan to spend at least half a day here. Billed as the world's largest train store, there are electric trains, accessories, books, and so much train-related stuff that it's hard to know where to start. Knowledgeable employees will help you choose whatever you need, and they seem just as happy to talk about trains as to sell them. Naturally, there are model trains of every scale winding through the store, as well as test tracks so that you can check out a locomotive before purchasing it. There are also mugs, patches, and decals from just about every railroad line that ever existed in North America.

Wizard's Chest. 230 Fillmore St. ☎ **303/321-4304.**

This store's magical design—a castle with drawbridge and moat—and legendary wizard out front are worth the trip alone, but be sure to go inside. The Wizard's Chest, located in Cherry Creek North, is paradise for kids of all ages, specializing in games, toys, and puzzles. The costume department is fully stocked with costumes, wigs, masks, and professional makeup.

8 Denver After Dark

Denver's performing arts and nightlife scene, an important part of this increasingly sophisticated western city, is anchored by the four-square-block, $80-million **Denver Performing Arts Complex,** located downtown just a few blocks from major hotels. The complex houses nine theaters, a concert hall, and what may be the nation's first symphony hall in the round. It is home to the Colorado Symphony, Colorado Ballet, Opera Colorado, and the Denver Center for the Performing Arts (an umbrella organization for resident and touring theater companies).

In all, Denver has some 30 theaters, more than 100 cinemas, and dozens of concert halls, nightclubs, discos, and bars. Clubs offer country-and-western music, jazz, rock, and comedy acts.

Current entertainment listings are presented in special Friday morning sections of the two daily newspapers—the *Denver Post* and *Rocky Mountain News. Westword,* a weekly newspaper distributed free throughout the city every Wednesday, has perhaps the best listings of all since it focuses on the arts, entertainment, and local politics. *The Denver Post* provides information on movie show times and theaters; call ☎ **303/ 777-FILM** or check out www.777film.com.

You can get tickets for nearly all major entertainment and sporting events from **The Ticketman,** 6800 N. Broadway, #103, Denver, CO 80221 (☎ **303/430-1111**), with delivery to your hotel available. Also try **Ticketmaster** (☎ **303/830-TIXS**), which has several outlets in the Denver area.

THE CLUB & MUSIC SCENE
ROCK, JAZZ & BLUES

Bluebird Theater. 3317 E. Colfax Ave. (at Adams St.). ☎ **303/322-2308.**

This historic theater, built in 1913 to show silent movies, has been restored and now offers a diverse selection of jazz, rock, alternative, and other live music, as well as films.

El Chapultepec. 1962 Market St. ☎ **303/295-9126.**

Denver's oldest jazz club, the "Pec" offers live jazz nightly in a noisy, friendly atmosphere, where you'll often find standing room only.

Dead Beat Club. 4040 E. Evans Ave. ☎ **303/758-6853.**

Located southeast of downtown, this club features four different dance floors and seven bars scattered around a bizarre building—it's easy to get lost in this place. The main dance floor features alternative music, and the DJs also spin disco, Top 40, '80s and techno records. The offbeat décor and diverse crowd, in conjunction with the music, makes for near-sensory overload. There's also a patio to cool off on after dancing and several small lounges and atriums.

Fillmore Auditorium. 1510 Clarkson St. ☎ **303/860-7181.** www.thefillmore.com.

The 3,600-seat Fillmore is the former Mammoth Gardens, which was long considered to be one of Denver's worst music venues. The shift has been 180° since it was purchased and renovated by Bill Graham Presents–Chuck Morris Presents, the proprietors of the legendary Fillmore in San Francisco. Reopening in 1999, the venue is now one of Denver's best, loaded with bars and countless vintage rock photos. It attracts national rock acts such as Bob Dylan and Johnny Winter, as well as harder-edged bands.

Herman's Hideaway. 1578 S. Broadway (near Iowa Ave.). ☎ **303/777-5840.**

Considered one of the best spots in Denver to hear original rock music by bands on their way up, there's usually live music Wednesday through Saturday nights.

Mercury Cafe. 2199 California St. (at 22nd St.). ☎ **303/294-9281.** www.mercurycafe.com.

It's hard to classify the Mercury as specializing in any one genre of music, but there's always something exciting happening, even on poetry night. Offerings usually range from avant-garde jazz to classical violin and harp to big band to progressive rock.

Synergy. 3240 Larimer St. ☎ **303/296-9515.**

The high energy here will keep you dancing all night, and it may take several days before you can hear again after a night at Synergy. An after-hours club (it's open 'til 5am on Saturday and Sunday mornings, with a cover under $10), Synergy serves no alcohol, but offers juices and what it calls "smart drinks," blends designed to improve your alertness, memory, and mental capacity.

COUNTRY MUSIC

✪ **Grizzly Rose.** 5450 N. Valley Hwy. ☎ **303/295-1330.** www.grizzlyrose.com. At I-25 exit 215.

Known to locals as "the Griz" or "the Rose," its 5,000-square-foot dance floor beneath a 1-acre roof draws such national acts as George Thorogood, Garth Brooks, Willie Nelson, Don Williams, Leann Rimes, Tanya Tucker, and Johnny Paycheck. There's live music every night of the week; Sunday is family night. The cafe serves a full-service menu, and dance lessons are available.

Stampede Mesquite Grill & Dance Emporium. 2430 S. Havana St. (at Parker Rd.), Aurora. ☎ **303/337-6909.** www.stampedeclub.com.

There are free country-western dance lessons Wednesday through Saturday, a huge solid oak dance floor, pool tables, a restaurant, and seven bars at this nightclub, which is located off I-225 exit 4 (north on Parker Road about 2 miles to Havana Street). Local and national acts play the stage here Thursdays, Fridays, and Saturdays. Closed Mondays.

THE BAR SCENE

The first permanent structure built on the site of modern Denver was supposedly a saloon, and the city has been adding to that tradition ever since. Today, there are sports bars, dance bars, lots of brew pubs, outdoor cafe bars, English pubs, Old West saloons, city-overlook bars, art-deco bars, gay bars, and a few bars we don't want to discuss here.

Appropriately, the newest Denver "in" spot for barhopping is also the oldest part of the city—LoDo—which has been renovated and upgraded, and now attracts all the smart generation Xers and other young professionals. Its trendy nightspots are often noisy and crowded, but if you're looking for action, this is where it's at.

Glendale, an enclave completely surrounded by southeastern Denver where Colorado Boulevard crosses Cherry Creek, is another popular hangout for Denver's smart set. An unusual zoning situation has led to more than a dozen drinking establishments built into a small, concentrated area. In recent years, however, Glendale has become the Denver area's nexus for topless bars; the other bars have suffered.

Other "strips" can be found along North and South Broadway, and along East and West Colfax Avenue.

The following are among the popular bars and pubs, but there are plenty more, so be sure to check out the publications mentioned under "Denver after Dark," above.

Bull & Bush Pub & Brewery. 4700 Cherry Creek Dr. S., Glendale. ☎ **303/759-0333.**

This re-creation of a famous London pub always has eight of its own award-winning beers on tap—its ESB won the World Cup at the 1998 Great American Beer Festival—

Brewery Tours

Whether or not you drink beer, it can be fun to look behind the scenes and see how beer is made. Denver's first modern microbrewery—the **Wynkoop Brewing Co.,** 1634 18th St., at Wynkoop Street (☎ **303/297-2700**)—offers tours every Saturday between 1 and 5pm. Housed in the renovated 1898 J. S. Brown Mercantile Building across from Union Station, the Wynkoop is also a popular restaurant (see "Dining," in chapter 4). Ten beers are always on tap. If you can't decide which one to try, the "taster set" provides a nice sampling: six 4-ounce glasses of different brews. For nonbeer drinkers, the Wynkoop offers some of the best root beer in town. On the second floor is a top-notch pool hall with billiards, snooker, and darts.

Since it opened in November 1991, **Rock Bottom Brewery,** 1001 16th St. (☎ **303/534-7616**), has been one of the leading brew pubs in the area. Tours, which are given upon request, offer great views of the brewing process, plus a sampling of the product. The Rock Bottom also has eight billiard tables and a good brew-pub menu, starting at $7.50.

Another Denver brewery that lets you see the brewing process is **Breckenridge Brewery,** 471 Kalamath St. (☎ **303/623-BREW**), located a mile south of downtown. Brewery tours are given by appointment. In addition to its award-winning ales, you can get traditional pub fare. Breckenridge also has a downtown tasting room across from Coors Field, 2220 Blake St. (☎ **303/297-3644**).

Over in Cherry Creek, **Bull & Bush Pub & Brewery,** 4700 Cherry Creek Dr. S. (☎ **303/759-0333**), produces about eight hand-crafted ales and will give tours of its facilities upon request (see "Dining," in chapter 4). Northwest of Denver, in Arvada, the **Cheshire Cat,** 7803 Ralston Rd. (☎ 303/431-9000), an authentic English pub in a historic building (1891) also offers tours on request.

Those who are really serious about visiting Colorado's microbreweries should consider an organized tour with **"Actually Quite Nice Brew Tours"** (☎ **303/ 431-1440**). Traveling in a 23-passenger bus, participants sample the beers at Denver- and Boulder-area microbreweries on lunch and dinner tours, lasting 4 to 5 hours, or strike out on full-day excursions for breweries in Breckenridge and other mountain towns, or the Front Range cities of Colorado Springs and Fort Collins. Prices range from $50 to $75, and include beer samples, a sampling glass, and lunch or dinner. Custom tours are also available.

For a look at the other side of the coin, take a trip to nearby Golden for a look at **Coors,** the world's largest single-site brewery (see "A Side Trip to Colorado's Gold Circle Towns," below).

as well as Sunday evening traditional jazz by regional groups. A full brew-house menu is available.

Charlie Brown's Bar & Grill. 980 Grant St. (at 10th Ave.). ☎ **303/860-1655.**

Just south of downtown, Charlie Brown's is a popular piano bar, some version of which has been in existence since 1927. The atmosphere is casual, with Elvis decanters, a baby grand piano, and a large central bar that attracts a diverse array of Denverites. The pianist plays a wide range of tunes, from Henry Mancini to Billy Joel, and the bartenders are not stingy. The grill serves breakfast, lunch, and dinner, both inside and on a great patio. From June to September, Charlie Brown's hosts pig roasts on Friday evenings.

Churchill Bar. 321 17th St. (in the Brown Palace Hotel). ☎ **303/297-3111.**

You'll find an excellent selection of fine cigars, single malt Scotch, and after-dinner drinks at this refined cigar bar, which caters to older, well-to-do Establishment types.

Cruise Room Bar. In the Oxford Hotel, 1600 17th St. (at Wazee St.). ☎ **303/825-1107.**

Modeled after a 1930's era bar aboard the *Queen Mary*, the Cruise Room opened in 1934 on the day Prohibition ended. Recently restored to its art-deco best, it has a sophisticated atmosphere, a free jukebox, and one of the best martinis in town.

Falling Rock Tap House. 1919 Blake St. ☎ **303/293-8338.**

This LoDo pub has 69 beers on tap—one of the best selections in Denver. You'll also find darts and pool, cigars, happy hours, and occasional live music.

The Grand. 538 E. 17th Ave. ☎ **303/839-5390.**

This upscale gay bar just east of downtown features nightly piano music as background, but the proprietor's true aim was to create a "conversation bar." It's open seven nights a week and is especially popular on Friday nights. The garden patio here provides a great view of the Denver skyline.

Herb's Hideout. 2057 Larimer St. ☎ **303/299-9555.**

Herb's is a downtown bar with an atmosphere steeped in nostalgia. The checkerboard floors, dim lighting, lengthy bar, and intimate booths compliment the bar's specialties: martinis, cosmopolitans, and Manhattans, served with the icy remainder in a shaker. During the week, Herb's is a local hangout with an emphasis on the pool table; weekends bring lively crowds out for the live jazz and blues for (usually a $3 cover). Closed Sunday and Monday.

SandLot Brewery. 2145 Blake St. ☎ **303/298-1587.**

Located at Coors Field, home of the Colorado Rockies, this is believed to be America's first microbrewery located in a ballpark. Owned by the Coors Brewery in nearby Golden, you might get a sample of new products being tested by Coors. There's a restaurant nearby. Unless you're attending a ball game, stay away on game days—you can't get in without tickets.

Sing Sing. 1735 19th St. ☎ **303/291-0880.**

Noisy college students dominate the scene at this LoDo hot spot, located beneath the Denver ChopHouse Restaurant. You'll often find low-priced beer specials, which encourage the partying college types to sing along (loudly and badly) with the dueling pianos. A fun place, but hang on tight. Closed Sunday and Monday.

Wynkoop Brewing Company. 1634 18th St. (at Wynkoop St.). ☎ **303/297-2700.**

Denver's first modern brew pub, many real beer fans say this is still the city's best. Among its most interesting offerings are its India pale ale and Scotch ale, but you can't go wrong here. An added attraction is a large pool hall.

THE PERFORMING ARTS
CLASSICAL MUSIC & OPERA

Colorado Symphony Orchestra. 821 17th St., #700. ☎ **303/98-MUSIC.**

This international-caliber orchestra performs more than 100 classical, pops, and family concerts each year at various locations throughout the metropolitan area.

Opera Colorado. 695 S. Colorado Blvd., #20. ☎ **303/893-4100** or 303/778-1500. www.operacolorado.org.

Each season three operas (12 performances each) are staged with English supertitles at the Denver Performing Arts Complex. Internationally renowned singers and local favorites sing the lead roles. The typical schedule is three evening performances and one matinee each week from February through May.

THEATER & COMEDY

Avenue Theater. 2119 E. 17th Ave. ☎ **303/321-5925.**

Original and off-Broadway plays are presented in an intimate 99-seat theater.

Chicken Lips Comedy Theater. Performances at Jackson's, 20th and Blake sts. ☎ **303/ 534-4440.** www.chickenlips.com.

At 7pm on Saturdays, this improv group performs a 1½ hour comedy show at Jackson's, a spacious sports bar across the street from Coors Field.

Comedy Works, Inc. 1226 15th St. ☎ **303/595-3637.** www.comedyworks.com.

Considered one of the region's top comedy clubs, this is your best bet for seeing America's hot comics at work.

Denver Center for the Performing Arts. 14th and Curtis sts. ☎ **800/641-1222** or 303/893-4100, or 303/893-DCPA for recorded information. www.denvercenter.org.

An umbrella organization for resident and touring theater, youth outreach, and conservatory training, the DCPA includes the **Denver Center Theatre Company,** the largest professional resident theater company in the Rockies. With 40 artists on its payroll, the troupe performs about a dozen plays in repertory from October through June, including classical and contemporary dramas, musicals, and premieres of new plays.

El Centro Su Teatro. 4725 High St. ☎ **303/296-0219.** www.suteatro.org.

A Hispanic theater and cultural center, El Centro presents bilingual productions on a regular basis.

Germinal Stage Denver. 44th and Alcott sts. ☎ **303/455-7108.** www2.privatei.com/ ~gsden.

In this 100-seat theater, plays by modern playwrights such as Brecht, Albee, and Pinter are presented.

Hunger Artists Ensemble Theatre. ☎ **303/893-5438.**

This award-winning theater group presents contemporary works at various locations throughout the city.

DANCE

Cleo Parker Robinson Dance. 119 Park Ave. W. ☎ **303/295-1759.** www.cleoparkerdance.org.

A highly acclaimed multicultural modern-dance ensemble and school, the Cleo Parker Robinson group performs a varied selection of programs each year, both on tour around the world and at several Denver locations.

Colorado Ballet. 1278 Lincoln St. ☎ **303/837-8888.** www.coloradoballet.org.

The state's premier professional resident ballet company performs in the Auditorium Theatre and Temple Hoyne Buell Theatre at the Denver Performing Arts Complex.

The company presents four productions during its fall-through-spring season—a balance of classical and contemporary works that always includes *The Nutcracker* at Christmastime.

MAJOR CONCERT HALLS & ALL-PURPOSE AUDITORIUMS

Arvada Center for the Arts & Humanities. 6901 Wadsworth Blvd., Arvada (2½ miles north of I-70). ☎ **303/431-3939.** Fax 303/431-3083. www.arvadacenter.org.

This multidisciplinary arts center is in use almost every day of the year for performances by internationally known artists and its own theater companies; its historical museum and art gallery exhibitions; and hands-on education programs for all ages. In addition, the children's theater program performs in front of an annual audience of 60,000. A fully handicapped-accessible playground has recently been added and features a 343-foot sea creature by the name of Squiggles. The 1998–99 theater season included *Wait Until Dark, Sweet Charity,* and *Joseph and the Amazing Technicolor Dreamcoat.* Visiting musicians included the Iguanas, Asleep at the Wheel, and Rita Coolidge. The indoor theater seats 500 and the outdoor amphitheater seats 1,200.

Denver Performing Arts Complex. 14th and Curtis sts. ☎ **800/641-1222** or 303/893-4100, or 303/893-DCPA for recorded information. www. denvercenter.org.

Covering four square blocks in downtown Denver from Speer Boulevard to 14th Street and Champa to Arapahoe streets, the Center for the Performing Arts (called the "PLEX" by locals) is impressive even to those not attending a performance. Its numerous theaters seat from 157 to 2,800, and there's also a restaurant and shopping promenade.

Fiddler's Green Amphitheatre. 6350 Greenwood Plaza Blvd., Englewood. ☎ **303/220-7000.**

Alfresco summer concerts here feature national and international stars in rock, jazz, classical, and country music. The amphitheater has 7,500 reserved seats and room for plenty more on its spacious lawn. Located in the southwestern section of the metropolitan area, just west of I-25 between Arapahoe and Orchard roads, it's open from May through September.

Paramount Theatre. 1631 Glenarm Place. ☎ **303/825-4904** or 303/892-7016 for recorded information.

A performing arts center since 1929, this restored 2,000-seat downtown theater is a wonderful place to enjoy jazz, pop, and folk performances, as well as comedy and films. Recent entertainers have included Tom Waits and Emmylou Harris.

Red Rocks Amphitheatre. I-70 exit 259 S., 16351 County Rd. 93, Morrison. ☎ **303/295-4444.**

Denver's favorite venue for top-name outdoor summer concerts is set in the foothills of the Rocky Mountains, 15 miles southwest of the city. The 9,000-seat amphitheater is flanked by 400-foot-high red sandstone rocks, and at night, with the lights of Denver spread across the horizon, the atmosphere is magical.

The Beatles performed here, as have U2, Paul Simon, Sting, Bonnie Raitt, Lyle Lovett, Merle Haggard, and top symphony orchestras from around the world. Visit the **Red Rocks Trading Post/Visitor Center** (☎ **303/697-8935**) to learn about the varied performances that have taken place here since it opened in 1941. The trading post also has a good selection of American Indian jewelry and pottery, plus a variety of other curios and souvenirs.

9 A Side Trip to Colorado's Gold Circle Towns

Golden, Georgetown, and **Idaho Springs** comprise most of the fabled Gold Circle—
those towns that boomed with the first strikes of the gold rush in 1859. The circle
would be complete with the inclusion of Central City, once the richest of the four
towns, but now the least attractive for today's visitor. Central City is trying to relive
its glory days with a return to gambling, largely supported by locals from Denver, and
although the exteriors of its historic buildings remain appealing, the rows of electronic
slot machines and other gambling devices inside are a turn-off. Visitors to the area
might like to make a brief stop, and then move on to Idaho Springs, where they can
actively experience the area's past by panning for gold, riding a replica of a turn-of-the-
century locomotive (the *Argo Express*), or donning a hard hat and following a working miner through the narrow tunnels of the **Phoenix Gold Mine** (see "What to See
& Do," in "Idaho Springs" below).

GOLDEN

Golden, 15 miles west of downtown Denver via U.S. 6 or Colo. 58 off I-70, is better
known for the Coors Brewery (founded in 1873) and the Colorado School of Mines
(established in 1874) than for its years as territorial capital.

For tourist information, contact the **Greater Golden Area Chamber of Commerce,** 1010 Washington Ave., Golden, CO 80401 (☎ **800/590-3113** or 303/
279-3113; www.goldencochamber.org).

WHAT TO SEE & DO

Historic downtown Golden centers on the **Territorial Capitol** in the **Loveland
Building** at 12th Street and Washington Avenue. Built in 1861, it housed the first
state legislature from 1862 to 1867, when the capital was moved to Denver. Today it
houses offices and a restaurant. The **Armory,** 13th and Arapahoe streets, is probably
the largest cobblestone structure in the United States; 3,300 wagon loads of stone and
quartz were used in its construction. **The Rock Flour Mill Warehouse,** Eighth and
Cheyenne streets, dates from 1863; it was built with red granite from nearby Golden
Gate Canyon and still has its original cedar beams and wooden floors.

In addition to the attractions listed below, see the section on Golden Gate State
Park in the Denver "Outdoor Activities" section above.

Astor House Museum. 822 12th St. ☎ **303/278-3557.** www.astorhousemuseum.org.
Admission $3 adults, $1 children 12 and under. Tues–Sat 10am–4:30pm

This handsome native stone structure, believed to be the first stone hotel built west of
the Mississippi River, was constructed in 1867 to house legislators when Golden was
the Territorial capital. Scheduled for demolition to make space for a parking lot, the
Astor House was instead restored in the 1970s and is now listed on the National Register of Historic Places. Today this western-style Victorian hotel offers glimpses into
life in Golden during the town's heyday in the late 19th century.

While there, you can obtain a walking-tour guide for the 12th Street Historic District or visit the Victorian Gift Shop, whose proceeds benefit the museum.

Boettcher Mansion. 900 Colorow Rd. (on Lookout Mountain). ☎ **303/526-0855.**
http://mansion.co.jefferson.co.us. Free admission, donations accepted. Mon–Sat 8am–5pm,
or by appointment.

This historic Jefferson County estate was built by Charles Boettcher in 1917 as a summer home and hunting lodge and contains displays of furnishings and other items

from the American Arts and Crafts period of the late 1800s and early 1900s. Other exhibits explore the history of Golden and the Boettcher family.

Buffalo Bill Museum & Grave. 987½ Lookout Mountain Rd. ☎ **303/526-0747.** Admission $3 adults, $2 seniors, $1 children 6–15, free for children under 6. May–Oct daily 9am–5pm; Nov–Apr Tues–Sun 9am–4pm. Closed Dec 25. I-70 exit 256.

William Frederick Cody, the famous western scout, is buried atop Lookout Mountain, south of Golden. The adjacent museum contains memorabilia from the life and legend of Buffalo Bill, who rode for the Pony Express, organized buffalo hunts for foreign royalty, and toured the world with his Wild West Show. There are also displays of American Indian artifacts, guns, and western art; and an observation deck provides a great view of Denver. The museum is in 66-acre **Lookout Mountain Park,** a Denver municipal park popular for picnicking.

Clear Creek History Park. 11th and Arapahoe sts. in Downtown Golden. ☎ **303/278-3557.** www.clearcreekhistorypark.org. Admission $3 adults, $2 children 12 and under. May–Oct. Wed–Sun 11am–4pm; by appointment rest of year.

Opened in 1999, this 3-acre creekside park illustrates the history of the area's ranching, with two log cabins, several animal barns, a blacksmith's shop, and a one-room schoolhouse from the 1870s. The buildings were moved to this site to save them from development in nearby Golden Gate Canyon, their original location.

Colorado Railroad Museum. 17155 W. 44th Ave. ☎ **800/365-6263** or 303/279-4591. www.cmm.org. Admission $4 adults, $3.50 seniors over 60, $2 children under 16, $9.50 families. June–Aug daily 9am–6pm; Sept–May daily 9am–5pm. Closed New Year's morning, Thanksgiving, and Dec 25. The museum is located 2 miles east of Golden. Follow the signs from I-70 exit 265 westbound, exit 266 eastbound.

Housed in a replica of an 1880 railroad depot, this museum is a must-see for railroad buffs. On display are more than four dozen narrow- and standard-gauge locomotives and cars, plus other historic equipment, artifacts, photos, documents, and model trains. The exhibits cover 12 acres, including the two-story depot. You can climb into many of the old locomotives and wander through the parlor cars. The excellent gift and souvenir shop sells hundreds of railroad-related items, from coffee mugs to posters to T-shirts.

✪ **Colorado School of Mines Geology Museum.** 16th and Maple sts. ☎ **303/273-3815.** Free admission. School year, Mon–Sat 9am–4pm, Sun 1–4pm; summer, Mon–Sat 9am–4pm. Closed for Colorado School of Mines holidays.

Exhibits here help explain the history of mining in Colorado with a replica of a gold mine and other displays. There are some 50,000 minerals, gems, fossils, and artifacts from around the world exhibited, plus displays of geology, earth history, and paleontology. There's also a kids' corner. The Colorado School of Mines, founded in 1874, has an enrollment of about 3,000.

Coors Brewing Company. 13th and Ford sts. ☎ **303/277-2337.** Free admission. Tours, Mon–Sat 10am–4pm; shop, Mon–Sat 10am–5pm. Closed holidays. Visitors under 18 must be accompanied by an adult.

This is the world's largest single-site brewery, producing 1½ million gallons of beer each day. Coors conducts free public tours of its brewery, followed by free samples of the various beers produced by Coors. The entire presentation lasts about 1½ hours. Tours leave a central parking lot at 13th and Ford streets, where visitors board a bus for a short drive through historic Golden before arriving at the brewery. There, a 30-minute walking tour covers the history of the Coors family and company, the barley malting process, the 13,640-gallon gleaming copper kettles, and the entire production process all the way to packaging. Children are welcome, and arrangements can be made for disabled or non-English-speaking visitors. There's also a gift shop and an interactive time line in the reception area.

Foothills Art Center. 809 15th St. ☎ **303/279-3922.** Free admission. Mon–Sat 10am–5pm, Sun 1–5pm.

Housed in an 1872 Gothic-style Presbyterian church (which is on the National Historic Register), this exhibition center evolved from the annual Golden Sidewalk Art Show and features changing national and regional exhibits. A gift shop next door—Foothills Two—sells crafts by local artisans.

Golden Pioneer Museum. 923 10th St. ☎ **303/278-7151.** www.henge.com/~goldenpm. Free admission. Mon–Sat 10am–4:30pm. Closed major holidays.

This museum exhibits an impressive collection of furniture, household articles, photographs, and other items, including a re-created 19th-century parlor and boudoir. Especially impressive is its collection of 200 American Indian dolls, representing 42 different groups from all around North America. There is also a genealogical and historic research library and a small gift shop.

Heritage Square. 18301 Colfax Ave. (U.S. 40) ☎ **303/279-2789.** Free admission, but individual activities impose their own charges. Memorial Day–Labor Day daily 10am–9pm; Labor Day–Memorial Day daily 10am–6pm. I-70, exit 259.

A shopping, dining, and entertainment village with a Wild West theme, Heritage Square features 30 Victorian specialty shops, a Ferris wheel, a stocked fishing pond, several fine restaurants, and a dinner theater. Warm-weather activities include go-carts, bumper boats, a water slide, a bungee tower, mountain-bike rentals, white-water rafting, and a 2,350-foot alpine slide with bobsled-style carts. Heritage Square Music Hall offers shows for both adults and children, plus there's an ice-cream parlor and a grill with an outdoor stage that features live music on summer weekends.

Lookout Mountain Nature Center. 910 Colorow Rd. (on Lookout Mountain). ☎ **303/526-0594.** Free admission. Trail, daily 8am–dusk; Nature Center, Tues–Sun 10am–4pm.

A 1¼-mile self-guided nature trail winds through this 110-acre preserve among ponderosa pines and pretty mountain meadows. A free trail guide is available at the Nature Center (when it's open), and a map is on display at a kiosk for those walking the trail at other times. The nonprofit Nature Center has displays on the pine beetle, pollenation, and Colorado wildlife, plus an interactive exhibit on the ponderosa pine forest. Children will also enjoy the "Treasure Hunt," an engaging look at the food chain. The building, which opened in 1997, is also worth a look—it's constructed of used and recycled materials such as ground-up plastic soda containers and the pulp of aspen trees. A variety of free naturalist-guided environmental education activities is offered year-round, mostly on weekends. Topics vary, but could include the flowers, butterflies, or wildlife of the area, or a look at the night sky. Advance registration is required, and some age restrictions may apply for certain programs. Call for details.

Mother Cabrini Shrine. 20189 Cabrini Blvd. (I-70 exit 259), Lookout Mountain. ☎ **303/526-0758.** www.den-cabrini-shrine.org. Free admission, donations welcome. Summer daily 7am–7pm; winter daily 7am–5pm; masses Mon–Sat 7:30am, Sun 7:30am and 11am.

A 22-foot statue of Christ stands at the top of a 373-step stairway adorned by carvings representing the stations of the cross and mysteries of the rosary. Terra-cotta benches provide rest stops along the way. The shrine is dedicated to the country's first citizen saint, St. Frances Xavier Cabrini, who founded the Order of the Missionary Sisters of the Sacred Heart. The order has a convent here with a gift shop, open 9am to 5pm daily.

National Earthquake Information Center. 1711 Illinois St. ☎ **303/273-8500.** neic.usgs.gov. Free admission. Tues–Thurs, by appointment only.

The U.S. Geological Survey operates this facility to collect rapid earthquake information, transmit warnings via the Earthquake Early Alerting Service, and publish and disseminate earthquake data. Tours of 30 to 45 minutes can be scheduled by appointment when a guide is available. They include information about the NEIC, the Earthquake Early Alerting Service, and earthquakes in general.

Rocky Mountain Quilt Museum. 1111 Washington Ave. ☎ **303/277-0377.** Admission $3; free for children under 6. Mon–Sat 10am–4pm.

This museum presents changing exhibits, including works from its permanent collection of more than 200 quilts. Consigned works can be purchased in the gift shop.

WHERE TO STAY & DINE

La Quinta Inn–Golden, just off I-70 exit 264, at 3301 Youngfield Service Rd. (☎ **800/531-5900** or 303/279-5565), is a dependable choice for the night, with 129 units and rates of $69 to $79 single or double. **Table Mountain Inn,** 1310 Washington Ave. (☎ **800/762-9898** or 303/277-9898), is a slightly more expensive, if smaller, alternative, with 65 rooms and 9 suites, and rates of $99 to $109 single or double; $138 to $168 suite. Open since 1992, it features Southwest charm, beautiful views of the surrounding mesas, and a restaurant serving three meals daily.

For a good meal in a historic setting, try the **Old Capitol Grill** in downtown Golden, 1122 Washington Ave. at 12th Street (☎ **303/279-6390**), offering steak and burgers plus a good selection of sandwiches. Located in the Territorial Capitol Building constructed in 1862, the restaurant is open daily for lunch and dinner, with dinner prices in the $8 to $18 range.

IDAHO SPRINGS

For visitor information, contact the **Idaho Springs Chamber of Commerce,** P.O. Box 97, Idaho Springs, CO 80452 (☎ **800/685-7785** or 303/567-4382; www.idahospringschamber.com). Information on Idaho Springs and the nearby towns of Empire, Georgetown, and Silver Plume can be obtained from the **Clear Creek County Tourism Board,** Box 100, Idaho Springs, CO 80452 (☎ **800/88-BLAST** or 303/567-4660).

WHAT TO SEE & DO

The scenic "Oh My God" dirt road winds from Central City through Virginia Canyon to Idaho Springs, although most visitors prefer to take I-70 directly to this community, located 35 miles west of Denver. Site of a major gold strike in 1859, today Idaho Springs beckons visitors to try their luck at panning for any gold that may still remain.

The **Argo Gold Mine, Mill, and Museum,** 2350 Riverside Dr. (☎ **303/567-2421;** www.historicargotours.com), is listed on the National Register of Historic Places, and offers tours daily in the summer from 9am to 6pm. Visitors can see the Double Eagle Gold Mine, relatively unchanged since the early miners first worked it more than 100 years ago, and the mill, where ore was processed into gold. Everyone is welcome to take part in gold and gemstone panning. Allow at least 45 minutes. It costs $9 for adults, $5 for children 7 to 12, and free for kids 6 and under.

Still being worked—albeit barely—is ✪ **Phoenix Gold Mine** on Trail Creek Road (☎ **303/567-0422**), where you can don a hard hat and follow a working miner through narrow tunnels to see what mining 100 years ago was really all about. You can also pan for gold on the property and relax in the picnic area. Open daily from 10am to 6pm in the summer (it closes at 5pm in the winter), the tours are informal and entertaining. Cost is $9 for adults, $8 for seniors, $5 for children 5 to 11, and free for children 4 and younger.

The Colorado School of Mines in Golden uses the **Edgar Experimental Mine,** less than a mile north of Idaho Springs on 8th Avenue (☎ **303/567-2911**), as a research area and teaching facility for high-tech mining practices. Underground walking tours of 1 to 1½ hours are offered from mid-June to mid-August, by appointment only; tour hours were not set at press time, so call ahead for current information. Group tours are available year-round by appointment, subject to guide availability. Tours are $8 for adults, $5 for children 6 to 16 and seniors, and free for kids under 6.

Just outside of Idaho Springs is **Indian Springs Resort,** 302 Soda Creek Rd. (☎ **303/567-2191;** www.indianspringsresort.com), a fine spot for a relaxing soak in the hot springs after a long day of skiing or hiking. The resort has a covered swimming pool, indoor and outdoor private baths, and a vapor cave with soaking pools. Rates are $14 per person per hour for the private baths, $14 for all-day use of the vapor cave, and $10 for all-day use of the pool. Lodging ($55 to $95 for two), meals, and weekend entertainment are also offered. The resort is open daily from 7am to 10:30pm year-round.

Idaho Springs is the starting point for a 28-mile drive to the summit of 14,260-foot **Mount Evans.** From I-70 exit 240, follow Colo. 103—also called Mt. Evans Highway—as it winds along Chicago Creek through Arapahoe National Forest to **Echo Lake Park,** another Denver mountain park with fireplaces, hiking trails, and fishing. From here, Colo. 5—the highest paved auto road in North America—climbs to the Mount Evans summit. It is generally open from Memorial Day to Labor Day.

Another way to see this area's great scenery is by horseback. **A&A Historical Trails Stables,** 5 miles up Virginia Canyon from Idaho Springs at 2380 Riverside Dr. (☎ **303/567-4808**), offers a variety of trail rides, including breakfast and moonlight rides. Rides are usually offered from May through November, weather permitting. A 1-hour ride costs $20 per person, and a 2-hour ride costs $35.

WHERE TO STAY & DINE

H&H Motor Lodge, 2445 Colorado Blvd. (P.O. Box 1359), Idaho Springs, CO 80452 (☎ **800/445-2893** or 303/567-2838), is a mom-and-pop motel on the east side of town. It offers bright and cheery rooms, TVs with HBO, a hot tub, and a sauna. The 34 rooms and suites here include several larger family units. Rates are $44 to $54 double for a standard room, kitchenettes $10 extra; two-bedroom suites start at $69. Pets are welcome for a $5 fee.

Beau Jo's Colorado Style Pizza, 1517 Miner St. (☎ **303/567-4376**), offers a wide variety of so-called mountain pizzas, including standard pepperoni; "Skier Mike's," with Canadian bacon, green peppers, and chicken breast; and a roasted garlic and veggie combo. Sandwiches are also available, plus a soup and salad bar set up in a pair of old clawfoot bathtubs. The bill usually comes out to $6 to $12 per person. Smoking is not permitted.

GEORGETOWN

A pretty village of Victorian-era houses and stores, Georgetown, 45 miles west of Denver on I-70 at an elevation of 8,500 feet, is named for an 1860 gold camp. Among the best preserved of the foothill mining towns, Georgetown is one of the few that didn't suffer a major fire during its formative years. Perhaps to acknowledge their blessings, townspeople built eye-catching steeples on top of their firehouses, not their churches.

For information on attractions and travel services, drop by or contact the **Georgetown Chamber of Commerce,** P.O. Box 444, Georgetown, CO 80444 (☎ **800/ 472-8230** or 303/569-2888), which runs a visitor information center at 6th and Argentine streets across from the Georgetown post office; or **Historic Georgetown, Inc.,** at 15th and Argentine streets, P.O. Box 667, Georgetown, CO 80444-0667 (☎ **303/569-2405;** www.historicgeorgetown.org).

WHAT TO SEE & DO

The Georgetown–Silver Plume Mining Area was declared a National Historic Landmark District in 1966, and more than 200 of its buildings have been restored.

A convenient place to begin a **walking tour** is the Old County Courthouse at Sixth and Argentine streets. Now the Community Center and tourist information office, it was built in 1867. Across Argentine Street is the Old Stone Jail (1868); three blocks south, at Third and Argentine, is the Hamill House (see below).

Sixth Street is Georgetown's main commercial strip. Walk east from the Old Courthouse to, on your left, the Masonic Hall (1891), the Fish Block (1886), the Monti and Guanella Building (1868), and the Cushman Block (1874); and on your right, the Hamill Block (1881) and the Kneisel & Anderson Building (1893). The Hotel de Paris (see below) is at the corner of Sixth and Taos. Nearly opposite, at Sixth and Griffith, is the Star Hook and Ladder Building (1886), along with the town hall and marshal's office.

If you turn south on Taos Street, you'll find Grace Episcopal Church (1869) at Fifth Street, and the Maxwell House (1890) a couple of steps east on Fourth. Glance west on Fifth to see Alpine Hose Company No. 2 (1874) and the Courier Building (1875). North on Taos Street from the Hotel de Paris are the Old Georgetown School (1874) at Eighth Street, First Presbyterian Church (1874) at Ninth, Our Lady of Lourdes Catholic Church (1918) at Ninth, and the Old Missouri Firehouse (1870) at 10th and Taos.

If you turn west on Ninth at the Catholic church, you'll find two more historic structures: the Bowman–White House (1892) at Rose and Ninth, and the Tucker–Rutherford House (ca. 1860), a miner's log cabin with four small rooms and a trapper's cabin in back, located on Ninth Street at Clear Creek.

Georgetown Energy Museum. 600 Griffith St. in downtown Georgetown. ☎ **303/ 569-3557.** E-mail: gtnem@juno.com. Free admission, donations accepted. June–Sept. Mon–Sat 10am–4pm, Sun noon–4pm; Oct.–May Mon–Fri 10am–noon and 1–4pm.

This small museum is dedicated to educating people about the history of hydro-power in Georgetown and Colorado. Located at Georgetown's still-operating power plant—built in 1900—the museum allows visitors to get an up-close look at a pair of hydroelectric generating units in action. The museum also features photographic and text displays detailing the history of similar plants in the region, as well as a collection of relevant antiques: washing machines, stoves, and generator meters.

Georgetown Loop Railroad. 1106 Rose St., Georgetown. I-70, exit 228. ☎ **800/ 691-4FUN** outside the 303 and 720 area codes, 303/569-2403, or 303/670-1686 in Denver. Fax 303/569-2894. www.georgetownloop.com. Admission for train ride, $12.95 adults, $8.50 children 3–15, free for children under 3 not occupying a seat; mine tour (only accessible by train), $5 adults, $3 children 3–15. There's no mine tour on the final run. Memorial Day–Labor Day daily 9:20am–4pm; Labor Day–early Oct, full schedule on weekends, limited during the week. Departures from Georgetown and from Silver Plume.

An 1884 railroad bridge serves this restored narrow-gauge line, which runs daily trips in summer between Georgetown and Silver Plume. The steel bridge, 300 feet long and 95 feet high, was considered an engineering miracle a century ago. Although the direct distance between the terminals is 2.1 miles, the track covers 3.5 miles, climbing 638 feet in 14 sharp curves and switchbacks, crossing Clear Creek four times, and culminating with a 360° spiraling knot. Passengers may make a round-trip from either end: The whole trip takes about 2½ hours, including an optional walking tour of the Lebanon Mine and Mill, which can be reached only by train.

There is a restaurant in the Georgetown depot that serves standard American fare ($3.50 to $7.00 for a main course at lunch). A model re-creation of the Georgetown Loop circles above the diners here.

Hamill House. Third and Argentine sts. ☎ **303/569-2840,** or 303/569-2111 in Denver. www.historicgeorgetown.org/houses/hamill.htm. Admission $5 adults, $4 seniors 60 and older, $4 students of all ages, free for children under 6. Memorial Day–Sept 30, daily 10am–4pm; Oct–Dec Sat–Sun noon–4pm; closed Jan–Memorial Day except for prearranged tours.

Built in Country Gothic Revival style, this house dates from 1867, when it was owned by silver speculator William Hamill. When acquired by Historic Georgetown, Inc. (in 1971), the house had its original woodwork, fireplaces, and wallpaper. A delicately carved outhouse had two sections: one with walnut seats for the family; the other with pine seats for servants.

Hotel de Paris. 409 6th St. (at Taos St.). ☎ **303/569-2311.** Admission $4 adults, $3 seniors 60 and older, $2 children 6–16, free for children under 6. Memorial Day–Labor Day, daily 11am–4:30pm; rest of year, Sat–Sun noon–4pm, weather permitting. Closed major holidays.

The builder of the hotel, Louis Dupuy, once explained his desire to build a French inn so far away from his homeland: "I love these mountains and I love America, but you will pardon me if I bring into this community a remembrance of my youth and my country." The hotel opened in 1875 and soon became famous for its French provincial luxury.

Today it's a historic museum run by the National Society of Colonial Dames of America, embellished with many of its original furnishings, including Haviland china, a big pendulum clock, paintings and etchings of the past century, photographs by William Henry Jackson, and carved walnut furniture. The kitchen contains an antique stove and other cooking equipment, and the wine cellar houses early wine barrels, with their labels still in place.

WHERE TO STAY & DINE

Colorado's oldest continuously operating hotel, about 5 minutes from Georgetown, is the **Peck House Hotel and Restaurant,** on U.S. 40 off I-70 exit 232, at 83 Sunny Ave., P.O. Box 428, Empire, CO 80438 (☎ **303/569-9870;** fax 303/569-2743; www.thepeckhouse.com). Established in 1862 as a stagecoach stop for travelers and immigrants from the East Coast, the hotel has an antique-filled parlor lined with photos of the Peck family and their late-19th- and early–20th-century guests. The rooms are comfortable and quaint (clawfoot tubs grace many bathrooms), and one of the best parts of a stay here is the fine panoramic view of the Empire Valley afforded by the wide veranda. There are 11 rooms (9 with private bathroom), and rates for two are in the $70 to $100 range. The hotel's excellent **restaurant** serves fish and steak entrees and seriously delicious hot-fudge cake and raspberries Romanoff. The restaurant serves dinner and Sunday brunch (during the summer) only; prices for dinner entrees are $16 to $28, and the brunch costs $15.

Back in Georgetown, **The Happy Cooker,** 412 6th St. (☎ **303/569-3166**), serves unusual soups, sandwiches on homemade breads, crepes, quiches, and more substantial fare such as fritattas and eggs Benedict in a converted home in Georgetown's historic business district. It's open Monday through Friday from 7am to 4pm, Saturday and Sunday from 7am to 5pm. Prices are in the $4 to $8 range and breakfast is served all day long.

6 Boulder

Although Boulder is known primarily as a college town (the University of Colorado is here), it would be inaccurate to describe the town as just that. Sophisticated and artsy, Boulder is home to numerous high-tech companies and research concerns; it has also attracted countless outdoor sports enthusiasts, who have been drawn by Boulder's delightful climate, vast open spaces, and close proximity to Rocky Mountain National Park.

Set at the foot of the Flatirons of the Rocky Mountains, just 30 miles northwest of downtown Denver and only 74 feet higher than the "Mile High City," Boulder was settled by hopeful miners in 1858 and named for the large rocks in the area. Welcomed by Chief Niwot and the resident southern Arapaho, the miners struck gold in the nearby hills the following year. By the 1870s, Boulder had become a regional rail and trade center for mining and farming. The university, founded in 1877, became the economic mainstay of the community after mining collapsed around the beginning of the 20th century.

Since the 1950s, Boulder has grown as a center for scientific and environmental research. The National Center for Atmospheric Research and the National Institute of Standards and Technology are located here, as are IBM, Storage Tek, and Ball Aerospace, among other companies.

Today's residents are a mix of students attending the University of Colorado (called C.U. by locals); employees of the many computer, biotech, and research firms in the area; and others who were attracted by the casual, environmentally aware, and hip lifestyle that prevails here. Whatever differences exist among the residents, they are united by a common love of the outdoors. Boulder has 30,000 acres of open space within its city limits, 56 parks, and 200 miles of trails. On any given day, seemingly three-quarters of the population is outside making great use of this land, generally from the vantage point of a bicycle seat, the preferred mode of transport—there are nearly 100,000 bicycles in Boulder, which is more than one per resident.

1 Orientation

ARRIVING
BY PLANE

Boulder doesn't have its own commercial airport. Air travelers must fly into Denver International Airport, then make ground connections to Boulder, a trip of about an hour.

GETTING TO & FROM THE AIRPORT   The **SuperShuttle Boulder** (☎ 303/444-0808 or 303/227-0000) leaves Denver hourly from 7:10am to 11:10pm, and Boulder hourly between 4am and 9pm, with fewer departures on holidays. Scheduled pickups in Boulder are made from the University of Colorado campus and area hotels; pickups from other locations are made on call. The one-way fare from a scheduled pickup point to the airport is $18 per person, or $22 for residential pickup service from other points; children ride for free. Super Shuttle Boulder also provides statewide charter services.

Boulder Yellow Cab (☎ 303/777-7777) charges $60 one-way to the airport for up to five passengers.

Buses operated by the **Regional Transportation District,** known locally as **RTD** (☎ 800/366-7433 or 303/299-6000, TDD 303/299-6089; www.rtd-denver.com), charge $8 for a one-way trip to the airport (exact change required). Buses leave from, and return to, the main terminal at 14th and Walnut streets daily every hour from 6am to 11pm.

Boulder Limousine Service (☎ 800/910-7433 or 303/449-5466; www.whitedovelimo.com) charges $97 to take up to three people from Boulder to Denver Airport in a sedan limousine, $127 for a six-passenger stretch limo, $163 for an eight-passenger stretch limo, $187 for a 10-passenger stretch limo, and $247 for a 12-passenger stretch limo. Charter services are also available.

BY CAR

The Boulder Turnpike (U.S. 36) branches off I-25 north of Denver and passes through the suburbs of Westminster, Broomfield, and Louisville before reaching Boulder some 25 minutes later.

If you're arriving from the north, take the Longmont exit from I-25 and follow Colo. 119 all the way. Longmont is 7 miles due west of the freeway; Boulder is another 15 miles southwest via the Longmont Diagonal Highway.

VISITOR INFORMATION

The **Boulder Convention and Visitors Bureau,** 2440 Pearl St. (at Folsom Street), Boulder, CO 80302 (☎ 800/444-0447 or 303/442-2911; www.bouldercoloradousa.com), is open Monday through Thursday from 8:30am to 5pm, Friday 8:30am to 4pm, and can provide excellent maps, brochures, and general information on the city.

There are also visitor information kiosks on **Pearl Street Mall** and at the **Davidson Mesa overlook,** several miles southeast of Boulder on U.S. 36. Brochures are available at those sites year-round.

CITY LAYOUT

The north–south streets increase in number going from west to east, beginning with Third Street. (The eastern city limit is at 61st Street, although the numbers continue to the Boulder County line at 124th Street in Broomfield.) Where U.S. 36 enters Boulder (and does a 45-degree turn to the north), it becomes 28th Street, a major commercial artery. The Longmont Diagonal Highway (Colo. 119) enters Boulder from the northeast and intersects 28th Street at the north end of the city.

To reach downtown Boulder from U.S. 36, turn west on Canyon Boulevard (Colo. 119 west) and north on Broadway, which would be 12th Street if it had a number. It's two blocks to the Pearl Street Mall, a four-block pedestrians-only strip from 11th to 15th streets that constitutes the historic downtown district. Boulder's few one-way streets circle the mall: 13th and 15th streets are one-way north, 11th and 14th one-way south, Walnut Street (a block south of the Mall) one-way east, and Spruce Street (a block north) one-way west.

Broadway continues across the Mall, eventually joining U.S. 36 north of the city. South of Arapahoe Avenue, Broadway turns to the southeast, skirting the University of Colorado campus and becoming Colo. 93 (the Foothills Highway to Golden) after crossing Baseline Road. Baseline follows a straight line from east Boulder, across U.S. 36 and Broadway, past Chautauqua Park and up the mountain slopes. To the south, Table Mesa Drive takes a similar course.

The Foothills Parkway (not to be confused with the Foothills Highway) is the principal north–south route on the east side of Boulder, extending from U.S. 36 at Table Mesa Drive to the Longmont Diagonal; Arapahoe Avenue, a block south of Canyon Boulevard, continues east across 28th Street as Arapahoe Road.

2 Getting Around

BY PUBLIC TRANSPORTATION

The **Regional Transportation District,** better known locally as the **RTD** (☎ **800/ 366-7433** or 303/299-6000; www.rtd-denver.com), provides bus service throughout Boulder as well as the Denver greater metropolitan area. The Boulder Transit Center, 14th and Walnut streets, is open Monday through Friday from 5am to midnight and Saturday and Sunday from 6am to midnight. Fares within the city are 75¢ for adults and children (25¢ for seniors and disabled persons during off-peak hours); schedules are available at the Transit Center, the Chamber of Commerce, and other locations. Buses are wheelchair accessible.

The City of Boulder runs two shuttle bus services, called **HOP** and **SKIP** (☎ **303/ 447-8282**), connecting downtown, University Hill, the University of Colorado, and Crossroads Mall. HOP operates Monday through Wednesday from 7am to 7pm, Thursday and Friday from 7am to 10pm, and Saturday from 9am to 10pm. While the University of Colorado is in session, the night HOP runs Thursday through Saturday from 10pm to 3am, to every destination except Crossroads Mall. Buses run about every 10 minutes during the day, every 15 to 20 minutes at night; fares are 75¢ (25¢ for seniors).

SKIP operates Monday through Friday from 5:30am to midnight, Saturday 7:30am to midnight, and Sunday 7:30am to 10:30pm. Buses run north and south along Broadway, with a loop through the west Table Mesa neighborhood, every 6 to 10 minutes during peak weekday times and less frequently in the evenings and on weekends. Fares are also 75¢ (25¢ for seniors).

BY CAR

The **American Automobile Association (AAA)** has an office at 1933 28th St. #200 (☎ **303/753-8800,** ext. 8600). It's open Monday through Friday from 8:30am to 5:30pm, Saturday from 9am to 1pm.

CAR RENTALS   Although most people who fly to Colorado will land at Denver International Airport and rent a car there before proceeding to Boulder, those who find themselves in need of a car in Boulder can contact **Avis** (☎ 800/331-1212), **Budget** (☎ 800/527-0700), **Dollar** (☎ 800/800-4000), **Enterprise** (☎ 800/ 736-8222), **Hertz** (☎ 800/654-3131), or **National** (☎ 888/227-7368).

PARKING   Most downtown streets have parking meters, with rates of about 25¢ per half hour. Downtown parking lots cost about $1 to $3 for 3 hours before 5pm. Parking is generally hard to find around the Pearl Street Mall. Outside downtown, free parking is generally available on side streets.

BY BICYCLE

Boulder is a wonderful place for bicycling; there are bike paths throughout the city and an extensive trail system leading for miles beyond Boulder's borders (see "Bicycling" under "Outdoor Activities," below).

Among shops where you can rent and repair mountain bikes and buy copies of the handy *Boulder Bicycling Map* ($10) are **Doc's Ski and Sports,** 627 S. Broadway (☎ **303/499-0963**), and **Full Cycle,** 1211 13th St., near the campus (☎ **303/440-7771**). Bike rentals cost $16 to $30 daily. Maps and other information are also available at the **Boulder Chamber of Commerce,** 2440 Pearl St. (☎ 303/442-1044).

BY TAXI

You can get 24-hour taxi service from **Boulder Yellow Cab** (☎ **303/442-2277**), but you'll need to call for service since there are no taxi stands and taxis won't stop for you on the street. Another company that serves Boulder is **Metro Taxi** (☎ **303/666-6666**).

ON FOOT

Most of what's worth seeing in downtown Boulder can be reached by simple foot power, especially around the Pearl Street Mall and University of Colorado campus.

Fast Facts: Boulder

Area Code   Area codes are **303** and **720,** and local calls require 10-digit dialing. See the "Telephone/Fax" section under "Fast Facts," in chapter 2.

Baby-sitters   The front desk at a major hotel often can make arrangements on your behalf. Boulder's **Child Care Referral Service** (☎ **303/441-3180**), open Monday through Friday from 8am to 5pm, can also help.

Business Hours   Most banks are open Monday through Friday from 9am to 5pm, and some have Saturday hours, too. Major stores are open Monday through Saturday from 9 or 10am until 5 or 6pm, and often Sunday from noon until 5pm. Department and discount stores often have later closing times.

Car Rentals   See "Getting Around," above.

Drugstores   Reliable prescription services are available at the Medical Center Pharmacy in the **Boulder Medical Center,** 2750 N. Broadway (☎ **303/440-3111**), and **Jones Drug and Camera Center,** 1370 College Ave. (☎ **303/443-4420**). The pharmacy at **King Soopers Supermarket,** 1650 30th St. (in Sunrise Plaza), is open from 8am to 10pm (☎ **303/444-0164**).

Emergencies   For police, fire, or medical emergencies, call ☎ **911.** For the **Poison Control Center,** call ☎ **800/332-3073** or 303/739-1123. For the **Rape Crisis Hotline,** call ☎ **303/443-7300.**

Eyeglasses   You can get fast repair or replacement of your glasses at **Boulder Optical,** 1928 14th St. (☎ **303/442-4521**), just off the Pearl Street Mall.

Hospitals   Full medical services, including 24-hour emergency treatment, are available at **Boulder Community Hospital,** 1100 Balsam Ave., at North Broadway (☎ **303/440-2273**).

Newspapers/Magazines   Boulder's *Daily Camera* is an award-winning daily newspaper, and the new *Boulder Weekly* is a weekly local paper. Many townspeople also read the campus paper, the *Colorado Daily,* available all over town.

Both Denver dailies—the *Denver Post* and *Rocky Mountain News*—are available at newsstands throughout the city. You can also find the *New York Times, Wall Street Journal,* and *Christian Science Monitor* at many newsstands. The free *Boulder* magazine, published three times a year, lists seasonal events and other information on restaurants and the arts.

Photographic Needs   For standard processing requirements (including 2-hour slide processing) as well as custom lab work, contact **Photo Craft,** 3550 Arapahoe Ave. (☎ **303/442-6410**). For equipment, supplies, and repairs, visit **Mike's Camera,** 2500 Pearl St. (☎ **303/443-1715**).

Post Office   The main downtown post office is at 15th and Walnut streets; call the U.S. Postal Service (☎ **800/275-8777**) for hours and other locations.

Radio/TV   Boulder radio stations include KBCO (97.3 FM) for alternative rock; KBVI (1490 AM) for local news, sports, and contemporary rock; and KGNU (88.5 FM) for Boulder and national public radio. Boulder is also within reception range of most Denver stations.

The following Denver television stations can be received in Boulder: Channels 2 (KWGN/WB), 4 (KCNC/CBS), 6 (KRMA/PBS), 7 (KMGH/ABC), 9 (KUSA/NBC), and 31 (KDVR/FOX). Boulder has two independent stations: Channel 20 (KTVD) and 59 (KUBD/PAX). Cable or satellite service is available at most motels.

Safety   Although Boulder is generally a safe city—safer than Denver, for instance—it is not crime-free. Many locals say they avoid walking alone late at night along the Boulder Creek Path because of the transients who tend to hang out there.

Taxes   State and city sales tax total almost 7%.

Useful Telephone Numbers   Call ☎ **303/639-1111** for **road conditions;** ☎ **303/825-7669** for **ski reports;** and ☎ **303/494-4221** for **weather reports.**

3 Accommodations

You'll find a good selection of comfortable lodgings in Boulder, with a wide range of rates to suit almost every budget. Be aware, though, that the town literally fills up during the popular summer season, making advance reservations essential. It's also almost impossible to find a place to sleep during any major event at the University of Colorado, particularly graduation. Those who do find themselves in Boulder without lodging can check with the Boulder Convention and Visitors Bureau (see "Visitor Information," under "Orientation," above), which keeps track of availability. Of course, you can usually find a room in Denver, a half hour or so away.

Major chains and franchises that provide reasonably priced lodging in Boulder include **Ramada Inn Boulder,** 800 28th St., Boulder, CO 80303 (☎ **800/542-0304** or 303/443-3322), with 165 units and rates of $82 to $99 double; **Best Western Golden Buff Lodge,** 1725 28th St., Boulder, CO 80301 (☎ **800/528-1234** or 303/442-7450), with 112 units, charging $66 to $101 double; **Best Western Boulder Inn,** 770 28th St., Boulder, CO 80303 (☎ **800/233-8469** or 303/449-3800), with 98 units and rates for two of $66 to $103; **Quality Inn and Suites—Boulder Creek,** 2020 Arapahoe Ave., Boulder, CO 80302 (☎ **888/449-7550** or 303/449-7550), with 46 units and rates for two of $89 to $150; and **Super 8,** 970 28th St., Boulder, CO 80303 (☎ **303/443-7800** or 800/525-2149), with 71 units and rates of $70 to $90 double. A locally-owned, low-end option is the **University**

Inn, 1632 Broadway (near Arapahoe Ave.), Boulder, CO 80302. (☎ **800/258-7917** or 303/442-3830), with 39 units and a double rate of $70 to $110.

For the accommodations listed below, the price categories have been defined as follows: **expensive,** more than $100 per night for two persons; **moderate,** $70 to $100; **inexpensive,** less than $70. These rates do not include the 9.5% sales tax that is added to all accommodations bills. Parking is free at all the hotels listed below unless otherwise specified.

EXPENSIVE

✪ The Alps. 38619 Boulder Canyon Dr., Boulder, CO 80302. ☎ **800/414-2577** or 303/ 444-5445. Fax 303/444-5522. www.bedandbreakfastinns.org/alps. E-mail: alpsinn@aol.com. 12 units. TEL. $133–$216 double. Rates include full breakfast. AE, CB, DC, DISC, MC, V.

A stage stop in the late 1800s, this historic log lodge sits on a mountainside about 7 minutes west of downtown Boulder. It has been turned into a beautiful bed-and-breakfast decorated with British antiques by its owners, Jeannine and John Vanderhart. Each room is different, although all have functional fireplaces with Victorian mantels, queen beds with down comforters, individual thermostats, and hair dryers. Most are spacious, with either a clawfoot or double whirlpool tub plus a double shower. Many rooms have private porches. Shared spaces include a beautiful lounge with a huge rock fireplace and VCR, plus delightful gardens and patio areas. The entryway to The Alps is the original log cabin built in the 1870s. Smoking is not permitted.

Boulder Marriott. 2660 Canyon Blvd., Boulder, CO 80303 (1 block west of Canyon and 28th St.). ☎ **303/440-8877.** Fax 303/440-3377. www.marriott.com/DENBO. 155 units. A/C TV TEL. $109–$199 double; $139–$209 suite. AE, CB, DC, DISC, MC, V. Free valet and self-parking.

The newest full-service hotel in the city (it opened in May 1997), this property's customer service was ranked in the top 1% by Marriott. It is conveniently located a block off 28th St. (U.S. 36), providing great access to everything in town. Subtly furnished with Southwestern touches, the rooms are geared at the business traveler, with multi-line phones, large work desks, and ergonomic chairs.

Half the rooms are on two concierge levels, with a private lounge that offers a complimentary continental breakfast, happy hour, and hors d'oeuvres. Three-quarters of the rooms feature mountain views.

Dining: JW's Steakhouse, specializing in steaks, seafood, and regional specialties for dinner, serves three meals a day and has a lounge and extensive wine list.

Amenities: Room service, valet laundry and dry cleaning, on-call masseur, health spa, gift shop, shopping arcade, pool and hot tub, fitness center, 24-hour business center, meeting space for 120.

Boulder Victoria. 1305 Pine St., Boulder, CO 80302. ☎ **303/938-1300.** Fax 303/ 938-1435. www.bouldervictoria.com. 7 rooms, including 1 suite (all with showers only). A/C TV TEL. $119–$169 double, $159–$189 suite. Rates include continental breakfast, afternoon tea, and evening port. AE, MC, V. Not suitable for children under 12.

This B&B, located two blocks north of downtown and the Pearl Street Mall, began as a simple dwelling (built in 1876) that was expanded by a local banker 20 years later, then became apartments in the 1920s. After a meticulous renovation it was reborn in 1990 as the Victoria. The rooms feature rich wallpapering, queen-sized brass beds with down comforters and pillows, and period antiques. Some rooms have fireplaces; one has a private balcony. The grounds are lovely, with bountiful flowerbeds and outdoor seating on a canopied patio. There is also a shared second-floor balcony guests can use for relaxing.

Boulder Accommodations & Dining

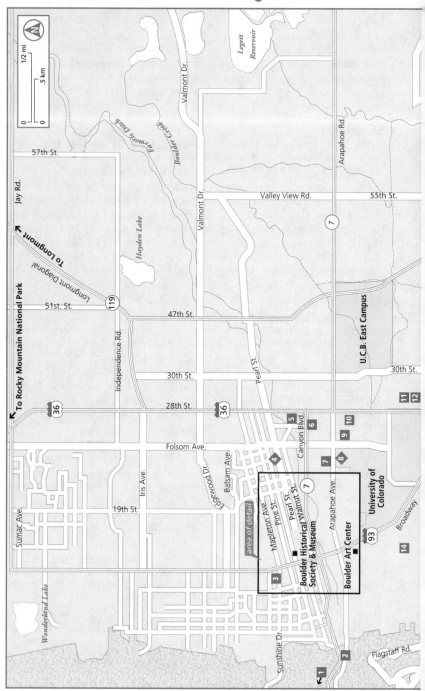

ACCOMMODATIONS

The Alps **1**
Best Western Boulder Inn **13**
Best Western Golden Buff Lodge **5**
Boulder International Hostel **14**
Boulder Marriott **6**
Boulder Victoria **23**
Briar Rose **7**
Colorado Chautauqua Association **16**
Days Inn Boulder **18**
Earl House **3**
Foot of the Mountain Motel **2**
Hotel Boulderado **24**
Quality Inn and Suites — Boulder Creek **9**
Ramada Inn Boulder **12**
Regal Harvest House **10**
Super 8 **11**
University Inn **32**

DINING

Antica Roma **27**
Boulder Dushanbe Teahouse **31**
Corner Bar **24**
Flagstaff House Restaurant **15**
14th Street Bar & Grill **28**
Healthy Habits **17**
Illegal Pete's **29**
Jax Fish House **20**
John's Restaurant **4**
La Estrellita **26**
Nick-N-Willy's **19**
Q's Restaurant **24**
Sunflower **30**
Sushi Zanmai **25**
Tom's Tavern **21**
Turley's **8**
Walnut Brewery **22**

Baseline Reservoir

Cherryvale Rd.

Boulder
Denver
COLORADO
Colorado Springs

Baseline Rd.

Foothills Pkwy.

S. Boulder Rd.

To Denver →

157

18

17

36

Moorehead Ave.

Martin Park

Bear Canyon Creek

Univ. of Colorado
Williams Village

13

93

S. Broadway

Baseline Rd.

16

15

Harlow C.
Platts Park

BOULDER MOUNTAIN
PARK

Table Mesa Dr.

DOWNTOWN BOULDER

18th St.
17th St.
16th St.
15th St.
14th St.
13th St.
11th St.
10th St.
9th St.
8th St.

Pine St.
Spruce St.
Pearl St.
Walnut St.
Marine St.

N. Broadway
Canyon Blvd.
Arapahoe Ave.

Breakfast is served either outside or in a dining room with large bay windows, and the afternoon tea is served with scones, lemon curd, shortbread, and cakes. Business services such as faxing and copying are also available, as is a small meeting space. There is also a 24-hour messaging service. Smoking is not permitted.

Briar Rose. 2151 Arapahoe Ave., Boulder, CO 80302. ☎ **303/442-3007.** Fax 303/786-8440. www.globalmall.com/brose. E-mail: brbbx@aol.com. 10 units, including 1 suite (6 with shower only). A/C TEL. May–Dec $114–$164 double, $189 suite; Dec–Apr $99–$149 double, $159 suite. Rates include continental breakfast. AE, DC, MC, V.

A country-style brick home built in the 1890s, this midcity bed-and-breakfast might remind you of Grandma's. Every room is furnished with antiques, from the bedrooms to the parlor to the back sunporch, and the lovely gardens offer a quiet escape. Amenities to accommodate the business traveler, such as modem hookups, large work table, and super lighting, have been added to several rooms. A fax/copy machine is also available.

Six rooms are in the main house, four in a separate cottage. Two in the main house have fireplaces, all are furnished with feather comforters, and the cottage rooms come with either a patio or a balcony. The newly renovated suite is designed for extended executive stays, but it is also popular with families. It can sleep four, and features a full kitchen and dining room. Weekly and monthly rates are available.

The continental breakfast is gourmet quality: croissants, granola, fresh nut breads, yogurt with fruit, and much more. Refreshments are available in the lobby from 8am to 10pm. Smoking is permitted only in the outside garden areas.

Earl House. 2429 Broadway, Boulder, CO 80304. ☎ **303/938-1400.** Fax 303/938-9710. www.earlhouse.com. 6 rooms (including 1 suite; 3 rooms with showers only) and 2 carriage houses. A/C TV TEL. $129–$169 double, $159–$189 suite, $199–$299 carriage house. Rates include full breakfast, afternoon tea, and evening port. AE, MC, V. Not suitable for children under 12.

The sister property of the Boulder Victoria (see above), the main house of this inn inhabits a historic 1880s Gothic Revival mansion, awash in sunny public rooms and period antiques. The inn takes its name from a wealthy English cattleman who bought the property in 1916, but the original owners are the ones that made the inn what it is today by adding such touches as hiring an East Coast artist to carve the cherry, mahogany, and oak woodwork. The original fireplaces are also intact and quite impressive.

The rooms here—five queens and one double—feature antique furnishings, leaded glass windows, Gothic arches, and inlaid floors; most have Jacuzzi tubs (or steam showers), fireplaces and private balconies. There are two separate three-story carriage houses out back available for nightly, weekly, and monthly rentals. These are of modern construction in an English Victorian style, what we might call casual elegance. They are decorated in a more contemporary and rustic style than the main house, with sleigh beds and oak desks and tables. Each has three bedrooms—two with queen-size beds and one with two twins—plus two bathrooms and full kitchen, as well as the modern conveniences of a television, VCR, answering machine, stereo, washer, and dryer.

Breakfast includes such delicacies as homemade baked goods, granola and smoked ham. (The complimentary breakfast is not available with the carriage house rentals.) Copying and faxing services are available, and smoking is not permitted.

✪ **Hotel Boulderado.** 2115 13th St. (at Spruce St.), Boulder, CO 80302. ☎ **800/433-4344** or 303/442-4344. Fax 303/442-4378. www.boulderado.com. E-mail: info@boulderado. com. 160 units. A/C TV TEL. $166–$211 double; $229–$265 suite. Extra person $12. AE, CB, DC, DISC, MC, V.

Opened on January 1, 1909, this elegant and historic hotel still has the same Otis elevator that wowed visiting dignitaries on opening day. The colorful leaded-glass ceiling and cantilevered cherry-wood staircase are other reminders of days past, along with the rich woodwork of the balusters around the mezzanine and the handsome armchairs and settees in the main-floor lobby. The hotel's Christmas tree, a 35-footer with 1,000 white lights, is a Boulder tradition.

The five-story hotel, just a block off the Pearl Street Mall, has 42 bright and cozy guest rooms, every one a little bit different. Although all rooms have recently been renovated down to the wiring and plumbing, they retain a Victorian flavor. The construction of a spacious North Wing a few years ago almost quadrupled the number of rooms, while continuing the early twentieth century feel in the wallpaper and reproduction antiques. All units have electronic locks, hair dryers, and two-line phones with data ports and voice mail; some rooms have refrigerators and coffeemakers.

The hotel offers a full range of amenities, including a business center, laundry service, access to a nearby health club, and bike rentals in summer. Facilities include restaurants (see "Dining," below), bars (see "Boulder After Dark," below), shops, and more.

Regal Harvest House. 1345 28th St., Boulder, CO 80302. ☎ **800/545-6285** or 303/443-3850. Fax 303/443-1480. 269 units. A/C TV TEL. $129–$145 double; $175–$395 suite. AE, CB, DC, DISC, MC, V.

Harvest House is exceptional in that it's a downtown hotel and yet has spacious and lovely grounds. Located on the west side of U.S. 36, the Harvest House looks like almost any other four-story hotel from the front—but its backyard melts into a park that surrounds the east end of the 10-mile Boulder Creek Path (see "Attractions," below).

All rooms are furnished with one king-size or two double beds, a lounge chair and ottoman, remote-control cable TV, and direct-dial phone (local calls cost 50¢). Spacious VIP Tower accommodations provide upgraded amenities such as hair dryers and bathrobes, daily newspapers, and an extra phone jack for a modem; they also include a continental breakfast and cocktail hour in the Regal Club Room. Our favorite rooms here are the two dozen that look out on the Boulder Creek Path.

Dining/Diversions: The hotel's restaurant, the Fancy Moose, has the look and feel of a mountain lodge, with large windows looking out on a waterfall along Boulder Creek Path. The cuisine is what the chef calls "Rocky Mountain Continental," with an emphasis on Colorado fish and game, and dinner selections such as baked Colorado trout, buffalo rib-eye steak, and elk sausage. Lunch brings variations on the

---

ⓗ   Family-Friendly Hotels

Regal Harvest House (*see p. 123*)   A good place to stay with the kids, especially in the summer. The Harvest House has a nice swimming pool and lots of nearby green space; it's also next to the Boulder Creek Path and within walking distance of the Crossroads Mall.

Foot of the Mountain Motel (*see p. 124*)   There's lots of space here where the kids can expend their energy. Across the street is a lovely park with a playground, as well as the Boulder Creek Path.

Ramada Inn Boulder (*see p. 118*)   At this former "Holidome," kids can use the pool and play inside even when the weather is bad.

dinner menu along with sandwiches and lighter items, and breakfasts feature standard American fare. The hotel also has a seasonal outdoor dining patio overlooking a waterfall.

Amenities: Room service, valet and self-service laundry, on-call masseur, airport shuttle, 15 tennis courts (five indoors), indoor lap pool and hot tub, outdoor swimming pool and hot tub, baby pool, fitness center, bicycle rentals at Boulder Creek Path, business center, and meeting space for 200.

MODERATE

✪ **Days Inn Boulder.** 5397 S. Boulder Rd., Boulder, CO 80303. ☎ **800/329-7466** or 303/499-4422. Fax 303/494-0269. www.daysinn.com. 74 units. A/C TV TEL. $69–$109 double. Rates include continental breakfast. AE, CB, DC, DISC, MC, V. Small pets accepted.

One of the best values around, this four-story hotel offers great views of the mountains. Perhaps the reason it looks and feels as though it should cost a lot more is because unlike in many franchise hotels, the owner is also the manager. The rooms are large, with night tables on each side of the beds. All units have irons and boards, blow dryers, cable TV, desks, and phones with modem hookups; many rooms also have microwaves and refrigerators; and fax and photocopy services are available at the 24-hour front desk. The continental breakfast is excellent, and there's a seasonal outdoor heated pool.

Foot of the Mountain Motel. 200 Arapahoe Ave., Boulder, CO 80302. ☎ **303/442-5688.** 18 units (2 with shower only). TV TEL. $75 double. AE, DISC, MC, V. Pets accepted ($5 nightly).

This motel, a series of log cabins with bright red trim near the east gate of Boulder Canyon, dates from 1930 but has been fully modernized. Across the street is Eben Fine Park, at the top end of the Boulder Creek Path. The motel serves free coffee in the lobby and offers bicycle rentals to guests. The pleasant pine-walled cabins are furnished with queen or double beds, cable TV, refrigerators, and individual water heaters.

INEXPENSIVE

Boulder International Hostel. 1107 12th St., Boulder, CO 80302-7029. ☎ **888/442-0522** or 303/442-0522. Fax 303/442-0523. E-mail: boulder.hostel@mail.com. 50 units. $15 dorm bed; $32–$40 private room. AE, DISC, MC, V.

As at most hostels, guests come here expecting to share—and they do. The toilets, showers, kitchen, laundry, and TV room are communal. Individual phones can be arranged for private rooms (with a deposit), but others share a phone. Just two blocks from the University of Colorado campus, the hostel is open for registration daily from 7am to midnight. (To stay here, you must present identification proving you are not a resident of Colorado.)

Colorado Chautauqua Association. 900 Baseline Rd. (at 9th St.), Boulder, CO 80302. ☎ **303/442-3282,** ext. 11 for lodging, 303/440-3776 for restaurant, 303/545-6924 for general information. Fax 303/449-0790. www.chautauqua.com. E-mail: chau@usa.net. 87 units. June–Aug. $57–$73 room, $63–$73 apartment, $68–$120 cottage (minimum 4-night stay); from Sept.–May, many of the accommodations are rented for the entire season, but some cottages are available, $95–$145. MC. V. Bus: 203. Pets accepted in cottages for $100 fee; pets not permitted in lodges.

During the late 19th and early 20th centuries, more than 400 Chautauquas—adult education and cultural entertainment centers—sprang up around the United States. This 26-acre park, on a hillside southwest of downtown, is one of the few remaining

Chautauqua parks in the country. In summer, it hosts a wide-ranging program of music, dance, theater, and film, including the Colorado Music Festival (see "Boulder After Dark," below).

Lodging is available in attractive but basic cottages and in rooms and apartments in two historic lodges owned by the Chautauqua Association. All units are completely furnished and come with linens, towels, coffeemakers, balconies or porches, and either private or shared kitchens. Cottages range from efficiencies to three-bedroom, two-bathroom units.

Guests have access to a self-service laundry as well as the park's playgrounds, picnic grounds, tennis courts, and hiking trailheads. The historic Chautauqua Dining Hall, which first opened on July 4, 1898, serves three meals daily at moderate prices from Memorial Day to Labor Day.

4 Dining

Partly because Boulder is a young, hip community, it has attracted a variety of small, with-it restaurants—chef-owned and -operated—where innovative and often-changing cuisine is the rule. You'll find a lot of California influences here, but also a number of top-notch chefs doing their own thing.

In the following listings, the price categories are defined as follows: **very expensive,** most dinner main courses are above $25; **expensive,** most dinner main courses are $17 to $25; **moderate,** dinner main courses run about $10 to $17; and **inexpensive,** dinner main courses are generally under $10.

A Boulder city ordinance prohibits smoking inside restaurants.

VERY EXPENSIVE

✪ **Flagstaff House Restaurant.** 1138 Flagstaff Rd. (west up Baseline Rd.). ☎ **303/442-4640.** www.flagstaffhouse.com. E-mail: flagstaffrestaurant@earthlink.net. Reservations recommended. Main courses $25–$45. AE, DC, MC, V. Sun–Fri 6–10pm, Sat 5–10pm. NEW AMERICAN/REGIONAL.

People come to the Flagstaff House from across the state and nation to partake of its excellent cuisine and service, and enjoy its spectacular nighttime view of the lights of Boulder spread out 1,000 feet below. A local institution since 1951, this family-owned and -operated restaurant has an elegant, candlelit dining room with glass walls that maximize the view.

The menu, which changes daily, offers an excellent selection of seafood and Rocky Mountain game, all prepared with a creative flair. Typical appetizers include smoked rabbit or duck, oysters, wild mushrooms, and cheeses. Entrees, many of which are seasonal, might include Colorado buffalo, ahi tuna, Canadian halibut, and soft-shell crabs. The restaurant also boasts dessert soufflés, a genuinely world-renowned wine cellar (undoubtedly the best in Colorado), and an impressive selection of after-dinner drinks.

EXPENSIVE

John's Restaurant. 2328 Pearl St. ☎ **303/444-5232.** www.johnsrestaurantboulder.com. Reservations recommended. Main courses $15–$28. AE, DISC, MC, V. Tues–Sat from 5:30pm. CONTINENTAL/AMERICAN.

This small, charming restaurant has been winning awards and raves since it opened in 1974. Chef-owned, the restaurant serves the classic dishes of France, Italy, and Spain, along with contemporary American cuisine. House specialties include filet mignon with Stilton ale sauce, which is topped with grilled Bermuda onions; Texas tournedos with succulent cactus leaves; and large shrimp pan-grilled with artichoke hearts and fried Sicilian olives. The menu also includes vegetarian items, such as porcini-like mushrooms with a nutty brown butter sauce. Homemade desserts include a caramel cheesecake that people rave over. There's a well-chosen wine list, microbrewery and other beers, and cocktails.

Q's Restaurant. In the Hotel Boulderado, 2115 13th St. (at Spruce St.). ☎ **303/442-4880.** Reservations recommended. Breakfast $7–$10, lunch $8–$13, dinner $12–$22. AE, DC, DISC, MC, V. Mon–Fri 6:30am–2pm and 5–10pm, Sat–Sun 7am–2pm and 5–10pm. CONTEMPO-RARY AMERICAN.

The historic ambience that makes the Hotel Boulderado such a delightful place to stay also makes its way into Q's, the hotel's main restaurant. The dining room combines both the old—rich polished wood and stained glass—with the comfortable, casually elegant feel of today. Of course, the important thing is the food, and chef/owner John Platt does an excellent job, using locally grown organic vegetables whenever possible.

Platt, who claims seafood as his specialty after years at Cape Cod, always includes several fresh fish selections on the menu, such as roasted Atlantic cod served with parsnip puree, sweet corn broth, and a warm salad of French beans, wild mushrooms, apple bacon, and winter greens. Rotisseried meats are also offered, such as the cumin-roasted pork loin served with a sweet-potato tamale, sautéed squashes, and red chile jus. You'll also likely find several pasta dishes, roasted chicken and quail, venison, and beef.

Sushi Zanmai. 1221 Spruce St. (at Broadway). ☎ **303/440-0733.** Reservations requested for groups of four or more. Lunch $7–$11, dinner $12–$20. AE, DC, MC, V. Mon–Fri 11:30am–2pm; Sun–Fri 5–10pm, Sat 5pm–midnight. JAPANESE.

For years local newspaper readers have rated Sushi Zanmai as Boulder's best Japanese restaurant. All of the food is traditionally prepared while you watch—at the sushi bar or tableside. There are lunch specials as well as sushi happy-hour specials during lunch and dinner. Karaoke sing-along takes place every Saturday from 10pm to midnight.

MODERATE

Antica Roma. 1308 Pearl St. (on the Mall). ☎ **303/442-0378.** Reservations accepted. Main courses $8–$20, pizza $8–$10. AE, DISC, MC, V. Daily 11:30am–3pm; 5–10pm. ROMAN ITALIAN.

Walking into Antica Roma is like entering a piazza in Rome: There's a lovely fountain in the main dining room, and the brick walls are finished like the outside of Roman homes—there's even laundry hanging on the balcony. The food is equally authentic, with all the pasta made on the premises and hand-thrown pizza baked in the wood-burning oven. Particularly popular are the seafood dishes, such as salmon Mediter-ranean (a fresh salmon fillet marinated in white wine and fresh herbs, then broiled with tomatoes, fresh mint, and thyme), plus the pasta al pesto (homemade pasta tossed in a puree of fresh basil, pine nuts, garlic, Parmesan, and olive oil), and the award-winning lasagna. There's a full bar and more than 250 Italian wines.

Boulder Dushanbe Teahouse. 1770 13th St. ☎ **303/442-4993.** Lunch $6–$13, dinner $8–$18. AE, DISC, MC, V. Mon–Fri 11am–3pm, 5–10pm; Sat–Sun 8am–3pm, 5pm–10pm. Tea and coffee bar open from 8am–10pm daily. ETHNIC WORLD CUISINE.

In 1990, 200 crates were shipped to Colorado as a gift from Dushanbe, Tajikistan, Boulder's sister city. Containing ornately hand-carved and painted pieces of a Persian teahouse, the building was assembled at its present site—with help from four on-site

ⓘ   Family-Friendly Restaurants

Sushi Zanmai (*see p. 126*)   Flashing knives and tableside cooking keep kids fully entertained.

Turley's (*see p. 129*)   Breakfast is served all day long here, plus there are fresh-squeezed juices, soups, salads, interesting entrees, burgers, and sandwiches. There's a great kid's menu and a sunny, social atmosphere.

Tajik artisans—making it the only teahouse of its kind in the Western Hemisphere. Lavishly and authentically decorated with 14 pillars carved from Siberian cedar and a grand central fountain, the teahouse serves lunch and dinner during the week and brunch and dinner on weekends. The cuisine includes Persian, Indonesian, Greek, Indian, and Thai dishes; Persian chickpea fritters, moo shu vegetables, and Thai curry noodles are among the most popular dishes. Pastries, coffees, and more than 50 teas are also available, as are wine and beer.

14th Street Bar & Grill. 1400 Pearl St. ☎ **303/444-5854.** Main courses $7–$21. AE, CB, DC, DISC, MC, V. Mon–Sat 11:30am–10pm. AMERICAN.

An open restaurant with big windows facing the corner of 14th and Pearl streets, this is a great spot for people watching as well as dining. The open wood grill and pizza oven, the long and crowded bar, and a changing display of abstract art let you know that this is a fun place. The constantly evolving menu centers around what chef/owner Kathy Andrade calls "American grill" cuisine, which includes grilled sandwiches, Southwestern chicken salads, and unusual homemade pizzas, such as a pie topped with chorizo sausage, garlic, and roasted green chiles. A variety of pasta dishes are also offered, plus changing dinner specials such as beef tenderloin stuffed with cheese and cilantro.

Jax Fish House. 928 Pearl St. (1 block west of the Mall). ☎ **303/444-1811.** Main courses $10–$24. MC, V. Mon–Thurs 4–10pm, Fri–Sat 4–11pm, Sun 4–9pm. SEAFOOD.

Fresh seafood is flown in daily from the East and West Coasts to supply this restaurant, a lively space with colored chalk graffiti and oceanic art on its brick walls, social patrons, and a booming stereo system. At patio, bar and table seating, you can order one of the house specialties—the Mississippi catfish platter is a good bet—or simply slurp down raw oysters and martinis to your heart's content. Entrees usually include shrimp, Alaskan halibut, Rocky Mountain trout, South American sea bass, and Hawaiian tuna, along with lobster and soft-shell crab when available. Clam, rock shrimp, catfish and calamari po'boys are also served, with slaw and your choice of potatoes or red beans and rice. Those who prefer beef can choose from New York strip steak and hamburgers.

Sunflower. 1701 Pearl St. (2 blocks east of the mall). ☎ **303/440-0220.** Lunch $7–$9, dinner $12–$21. AE, MC, V. Daily 5–10pm; Mon–Sat 11am–2:30pm, Sun brunch 10am–2:30pm. CONTEMPORARY/ORGANIC.

This pleasant and contemporary eatery, eclectically decorated with murals, Asian art, and a flagstone floor, touts itself as "Boulder's most unique restaurant," based on its dedication to organic produce and free-range chicken. (The menu is without red meat or refined sugars.) Owner-chef John Pell takes a multicultural approach, as Sunflower features a diverse selection of dinner entrees, including grilled ahi tuna served with seared pineapple salsa, corn and sage stuffed chicken breast, enchiladas with spiced organic black beans and chipotle pepper sauce, and Szechuan vegetable stir fry. Lunch includes fresh variations on sandwiches—such as a blackened salmon burger—as well as ethnic specialties like pad Thai and penne pomodoro.

Walnut Brewery. 1123 Walnut St. (near Broadway). ☎ **303/447-1345.** Lunch $4.50– $9.25, dinner $6.50–$17.50. AE, DC, DISC, MC, V. Food service available Sun–Thurs 11am– 10:30pm, Fri–Sat 11am–1am. Bar open until 1am Sun–Wed, until 2am Thurs–Sat. AMERICAN.

Walnut Brewery looks as a brewery should: brick walls, prominent brew tanks, warehouse-like decor, and big beer-label signs. Order an appetizing taster of the brewery's eight hand-crafted beers (including root beer), but don't ignore the food. Lunches feature a Caesar salad (available plain or with chicken or salmon), the brew burger, and the brewer's club, as well as excellent beer-batter fish and chips made with cold-smoked salmon. The dinner menu includes the same brewery favorites, plus pasta and such entrees as brown ale chicken, tenderloin with roasted garlic, and St. Louis–style ribs.

INEXPENSIVE

In addition to the choices below, see chapter 4 for a complete review of **Healthy Habits,** 4760 Baseline Rd. (☎ **303/494-9177**), a cafeteria-style restaurant that offers all-you-can-eat salad, pasta, and more.

Corner Bar. In the Hotel Boulderado, 2115 13th St. (at Spruce St.). ☎ **303/442-4566.** Entrees $6–$12. AE, DC, DISC, MC, V. Daily 11am–midnight. CONTEMPORARY AMERICAN.

With the same chef as the highly rated Q's Restaurant (see above), the Hotel Boulderado's Corner Bar is far above your average sandwich shop, although sandwiches and burgers are on the menu, too. Here you can savor a peppered salmon-fillet sandwich, served with red-onion marmalade, spinach, and mustard-dressed gold potato salad. Or you might try spaghettini with Prince Edward Island mussels, garlic, capers, parsley, lemon, and tomato; or mango barbecued shrimp salad with cucumber, Napa slaw, lo mein noodles, and miso vinaigrette. Those not in search of a full meal can opt for just an appetizer, such as Chesapeake Bay oysters baked with spinach, or Boulderado nachos.

Illegal Pete's. 1447 Pearl St. ☎ **303/440-3955.** AE, DISC, MC, V. Menu items $4–$5. Daily 11am–10pm. Take-out and delivery available. MEXICAN.

Located at the far east end of the of the Pearl Street Mall, Illegal Pete's is renowned locally for its selection of creative and healthy burritos, packed with chicken, steak, veggies, or fish. The menu also includes a similar range of tacos, as well as salads, quesadillas, and chile. Margaritas and domestic and Mexican beers are available.

La Estrellita. 1718 Broadway (at Arapahoe Ave.). ☎ **303/939-8822.** Meals $4–$14. AE, DISC, MC, V. Sun–Thurs 11am–10pm, Fri–Sat 11am–11pm. MEXICAN.

John Montoya established this restaurant in 1986 using recipes developed by his parents at the original La Estrellita in Fort Lupton in the 1950s and 1960s. You'll find all the standards, such as tacos, tostadas, enchiladas, tamales, and chile rellenos, in generous portions, as well as a few surprises: costillas adobadas (Mexican-style ribs), Indian tacos, and stuffed sopaipillas. Fajitas are also a big seller. In recent years Hispanic Magazine chose La Estrellita as one of the 50 Best Mexican Restaurants in the United States. The restaurant has a delightful outdoor patio.

Nick-N-Willy's. 801 Pearl St. (2 blocks west of the Mall). ☎ **303/444-9898.** Slices $1.25–$3.95, medium (12-inch) pizza (uncooked, to take out) $6.50–$15. MC V. Sun–Thurs 11:30am–9pm, Fri–Sat 11:30am–9:30pm. PIZZA.

This tiny spot is a favorite of pizza-loving locals. The dough and sauces are homemade, and the cheese is grated fresh daily. You can get slices to eat at the restaurant, or whole, uncooked pies to bake at home (or anywhere else with an oven). Sandwiches and salads are also served.

There's a second Nick-N-Willy's in south Boulder at 4800 Baseline Rd. (☎ 303/499-9898).

✪ **Tom's Tavern.** 1047 Pearl St. ☎ **303/443-3893.** Menu items $5–$10. AE, CB, DC, DISC, MC, V. Mon–Thur 11am–10pm, Fri–Sat 11am–11pm, Sun noon–8:30pm. AMERICAN.

Boulder's most popular place for a good hamburger, Tom's has been a neighborhood institution for almost 40 years. Located in a turn-of-the-century building that once housed an undertaker, the tavern has vinyl-upholstered booths and patio seating outdoors. Besides the one-third–pound burgers and other sandwiches, you can get a 10-ounce steak, fried chicken, or a veggie burger. Tom's serves dinner anytime.

Turley's. 2350 Arapahoe Ave. ☎ **303/442-2800.** Menu items $4–$10. AE, DC, DISC, MC, V. Mon–Sat 6:30am–9pm, Sun 7am–9pm. AMERICAN

A feel-good family diner with a healthier menu than the norm, Turley's is a Boulder landmark. Its sunny atmosphere and friendly staff provide a pleasant, homey backdrop for any meal, and breakfast is served all day. There are full espresso and juice bars serving everything from café latte to fresh-squeezed celery juice to fruit smoothies. A menu featuring omelets, burgers, sandwiches, wraps, and dinner entrees ranging from buffalo meatloaf to tofu scramble ensures that everyone's tastes will be satisfied.

ESPRESSO BARS, COFFEE HOUSES, AND RELATED ESTABLISHMENTS

Espresso fans will have no problem finding a decent espresso, cappuccino, or latte, since there are five **Starbucks** establishments**,** as well as many more interesting independent coffeehouses, throughout Boulder. Many of the independents, located in the vicinity of the Pearl Street Mall, provide outdoor seating in nice weather. **Bookend Cafe,** 1115 Pearl Street Mall (☎ 303/440-6699), offers a variety of coffee drinks; a delightful array of baked goods and egg dishes for breakfast; and soups, salads, and sandwiches (such as the Mediterranean grilled panini) for lunch and supper. At the east end of the mall (at 18th Street) is the somewhat bohemian **Penny Lane** (☎ 303/443-9516), a gathering place for talking, playing chess, or reading while you sip regular coffee, espresso, cappuccino, or latte, and munch on a bagel or muffin. There's a wide variety of newspapers and nightly live entertainment including poetry, an open stage, and a diverse range of music by local and regional performers. See also "Boulder After Dark," below. Also, the **Boulder Dushanbe Teahouse,** 1770 13th St., (☎ 303/442-4993) offers an authentic Persian setting for quaffing 50 varieties of tea and a good selection of coffees from 8am to 10pm daily. Homemade baked goods are also available.

5 Attractions

THE TOP ATTRACTIONS

✪ **Boulder Creek Path.** 55th St. and Pearl Pkwy. to the mouth of Boulder Canyon. ☎ **303/413-7200.** Free admission. Daily 24 hours. Bus: HOP.

Following Boulder Creek, this nature corridor provides about a 16-mile-long oasis and recreation area through the city and west into the mountains. With no street crossings (there are bridges and underpasses instead), the path is popular with Boulder residents, especially on weekends, when you'll see numerous walkers, runners, bicyclists, and in-line skaters. (Walkers should stay to the right since the left lane is for faster traffic.) The C.U. campus and several city parks are linked by the path, as are local office

Boulder Attractions

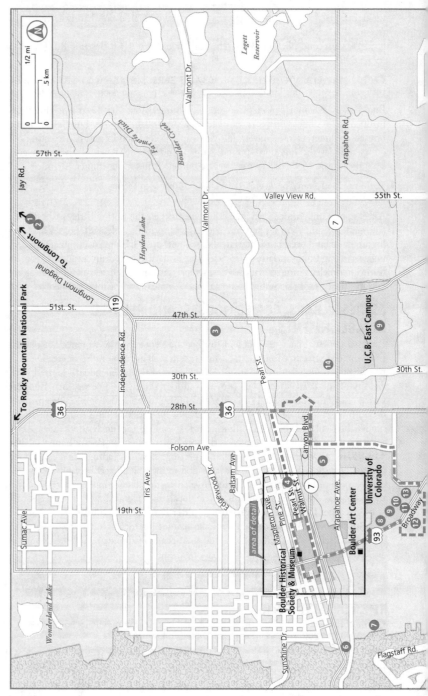

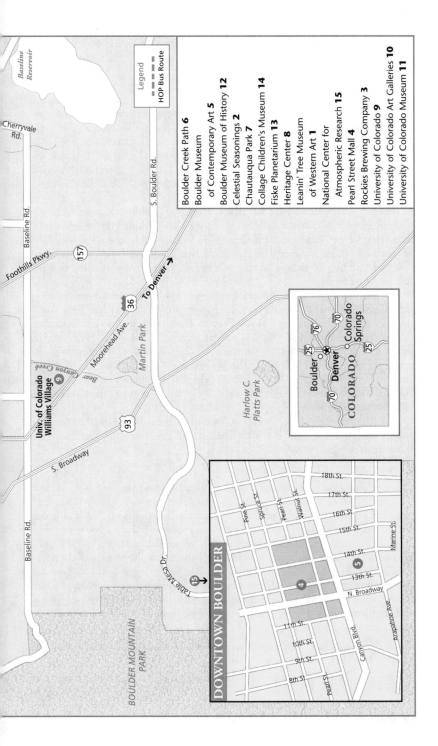

Legend

- - - HOP Bus Route

Boulder Creek Path **6**
Boulder Museum
  of Contemporary Art **5**
Boulder Museum of History **12**
Celestial Seasonings **2**
Chautauqua Park **7**
Collage Children's Museum **14**
Fiske Planetarium **13**
Heritage Center **8**
Leanin' Tree Museum
  of Western Art **1**
National Center for
  Atmospheric Research **15**
Pearl Street Mall **4**
Rockies Brewing Company **3**
University of Colorado **9**
University of Colorado Art Galleries **10**
University of Colorado Museum **11**

Baseline Reservoir

Cherryvale Rd.

Foothills Pkwy.

To Denver →

Moorehead Ave.

Martin Park

Bear Canyon Creek

Univ. of Colorado
Williams Village **9**

S. Broadway

Baseline Rd.

Table Mesa Dr.

15 →

BOULDER MOUNTAIN PARK

Harlow C. Platts Park

COLORADO

Boulder

Denver

Colorado Springs

DOWNTOWN BOULDER

18th St.
17th St.
16th St.
15th St.
14th St.
13th St.

Pine St.
Spruce St.
Pearl St.
Walnut St.

Marine St.

N. Broadway

Canyon Blvd.

Arapahoe Ave.

11th St.
10th St.
9th St.
8th St.

Pearl St.

4

5

buildings. Near the east end, watch for deer, prairie dog colonies, and wetlands, where some 150 species of birds have been spotted. You may see Canada geese, mallard ducks, spotted sandpipers, owls, and woodpeckers.

At 30th Street, south of Arapahoe Road, the path cuts through **Scott Carpenter Park** (named for Colorado's native-son astronaut), where you can swim in summer and sled in winter. Just west of Scott Carpenter Park you'll find **Boulder Creek Stream Observatory,** which is adjacent to and maintained by the Regal Harvest House (see "Accommodations," above). In addition to observing trout and other aquatic wildlife, you're invited to feed the fish with trout food purchased from a vending machine (25¢). **Central Park,** at Broadway and Canyon Boulevard, preserves some of Boulder's history with a restored steam locomotive. The **Boulder Public Library** is also in this area.

Traveling west, watch for the **Charles A. Heartling Sculpture Garden** (with the stone image of local Indian Chief Niwot) and the **Kids' Fishing Ponds;** these ponds are stocked by the Boulder Fish and Game Club and open only to children under 12, who can fish for free and keep what they catch. Near Third Street and Canyon Boulevard you'll find the **Xeriscape Garden,** where drought-tolerant plants are tested for reduced water intake.

The **Eben G. Fine Park** is named for the Boulder pharmacist who discovered Arapaho Glacier on nearby Arapaho Peak. To the west, **Red Rocks Settlers' Park** marks the beginning of the **Boulder Canyon Pioneer Trail,** which leads to a continuation of Boulder Creek Path. The park is named for Missouri gold-seekers who camped at this spot in 1858 and later found gold about 12 miles farther west. Watch for explanatory signs along the 1.2-mile path. The **Whitewater Kayak Course** has 20 slalom gates for kayakers and canoeists to use free; to the west, **Elephant Buttresses** is one of Boulder's more popular rock-climbing areas. The path ends at **Four Mile Canyon,** the old town site of Orodell.

Note: Although the path is generally well populated and quite safe, Boulderites warn against using it late at night if you are alone; one of the problems is the number of transients who take refuge there.

✪ **Pearl Street Mall.** Pearl St. from 11th to 15th sts. Bus: HOP.

This four-block-long tree-lined pedestrian mall marks Boulder's downtown core and its center for dining, shopping, strolling, and people watching. Musicians, mimes, jugglers, and other street entertainers hold court on the landscaped mall day and night, year-round. Buy your lunch from one of the many vendors and sprawl on the grass in front of the courthouse to relax and eat. Locally owned businesses and galleries share the mall with trendy boutiques, sidewalk cafes, and major chains including Peppercorn, Banana Republic, and Abercrombie & Fitch. There's a wonderful play area for youngsters, with climbable boulders set in gravel. Don't miss the bronze bust of Chief Niwot (of the southern Arapaho) in front of the Boulder County Courthouse between 13th and 14th streets. Niwot, who welcomed the first Boulder settlers, was killed in southeastern Colorado during the Sand Creek Massacre of 1864.

University of Colorado. East side of Broadway, between Arapahoe Ave. and Baseline Rd. ☎ **303/492-1411.** www.colorado.edu. Bus: HOP, SKIP.

The largest university in the state with 25,000 students (including 4,600 graduate students), the University of Colorado dominates the city. Its student population, cultural and sports events, and intellectual atmosphere have helped to shape Boulder into the city it is today. The school boasts 15 alumni astronauts who have flown in space, plus one in training.

If heaven has a college town, it's probably as beautiful as Boulder.

—Sunset Magazine

Old Main, on the Norlin Quadrangle, was the first building erected after the university was established in 1876; at that time, it housed the entire school. Later, pink-sandstone Italian Renaissance–style buildings came to dominate the campus. Visitors may want to take in the university's **Heritage Center,** on the third floor of Old Main; the **University of Colorado Museum** (see "More Attractions," below), a natural history museum in the Henderson Building on Broadway; the **Mary Rippon Outdoor Theatre,** behind the Henderson Building, site of the annual Colorado Shakespeare Festival; **Fiske Planetarium and Science Center,** between Kittredge Loop Drive and Regent Drive on the south side of campus; and the **Norlin Library,** on the Norlin Quadrangle, the largest research library in the state, with extensive holdings of American and English literature. Other attractions include the Fine Arts Galleries, University Memorial (the student center), and the new Integrated Teaching and Learning Laboratory in the College of Engineering. Prospective students and their parents can arrange campus tours by contacting the admissions office (☎ 303/492-6301).

Tours are available weekdays at the **Laboratory for Atmospheric and Space Physics** (☎ 303/492-6412), on the east campus, with at least 1 week's advance notice. The **Sommers–Bausch Observatory** (☎ 303/492-6372 during the day, 303/492-2020 at night) offers tours and Friday evening open houses. Among the telescopes there are 16-, 18-, and 24-inch Cassegrain reflectors and a 10-inch aperture heliostat.

National Center for Atmospheric Research. 1850 Table Mesa Dr. ☎ **303/497-1174.** www.ncar.ucar.edu. Free admission. Self-guided tours, Mon–Fri 8am–5pm, Sat–Sun and holidays 9am–4pm. One hour guided tours, June–Sept Mon–Sat at noon; rest of year, Mon and Wed at noon. Take Broadway heading southwest out of town to Table Mesa Dr., and follow it west to the center.

I. M. Pei designed this striking pink-sandstone building, which overlooks Boulder from high atop Table Mesa in the southwestern foothills. (You might recognize the center from Woody Allen's *Sleeper,* scenes from which were shot on location here.) Scientists study such phenomena as the greenhouse effect, wind shear, and ozone depletion to gain a better understanding of the earth's atmosphere. Among the technological tools on display are satellites, weather balloons, interactive computer monitors, robots, and supercomputers that can simulate the world's climate. There are also hands-on, weather-oriented exhibits from the San Francisco Exploratorium Museum, now on permanent display. The **Weather Trail** outside the building's west doors takes visitors on a 0.4-mile loop along a path with interpretive signs describing various aspects of weather and climate plus the plants and animals of the area. The center also hosts a changing art exhibit.

MORE ATTRACTIONS
INDUSTRIAL TOURS

✪ **Celestial Seasonings.** 4600 Sleepytime Dr. (off Spine Rd. at Colo. 119, Longmont Diagonal). ☎ **303/581-1202.** Free admission. Mon–Sat 10am–3pm, Sun 11am–3pm; tours on the hour. Reservations required for groups of 8 or more. Bus: J.

The nation's leading producer of herbal teas, housed in a modern new building in northeastern Boulder, offers tours that are an experience for the senses. The company, which began in a Boulder garage in the 1970s, now produces more than 50 varieties of tea from more than 100 different herbs and spices imported from 35 foreign countries. You'll understand why they invite you to "see, taste, and smell the world of Celestial Seasonings" as you move from a consumer taste test in the lobby, to marketing displays, and finally into the production plant where milling, packaging, and shipping can be seen. The overpowering "Mint Room" is a highlight. The tour lasts about an hour.

Rockies Brewing Company. 2880 Wilderness Place. ☎ **303/444-8448.** Free admission. Tours, Mon–Sat at 2pm; pub, Mon–Sat 11am–10pm. Take U.S. 36 north to Valmont Rd. and then head east to Wilderness Place.

From the grinding of the grain to the bottling of the beer, the 25-minute tour of this attractive "designer" microbrewery ends as all brewery tours should: in the pub. Tours pass by glistening copper vats that turn out 300 to 400 kegs of Boulder Beer a day. The pub is actually a restaurant that overlooks the bottling area, so even if you visit without taking a tour, you still get a good view of the brewing process. The menu includes munchies, soup, fresh salads, and sandwiches; lunches run $5 to $8.

MUSEUMS & GALLERIES

There are three art galleries on the University of Colorado campus, all with free admission. The **C.U. Art Gallery,** in the Sibell Wolle Fine Arts Building (☎ **303/ 492-8300**), is home to the Colorado Collection of about 5,000 works by international artists including Warhol, Durer, Rembrandt, Tiepolo, Hogarth, Hiroshige, Matisse, and Picasso. There are also rotating exhibits. The gallery is open Monday to Friday from 10am to 5pm and Saturday from noon to 4pm. Tuesday the gallery is open until 7:30pm. Bus: HOP, SKIP.

At the University Memorial Center, **UMC Art Gallery** (☎ 303/492-7465) organizes and hosts a variety of exhibitions featuring regional and national artists. In the music-listening rooms, visitors can peruse current periodicals while listening to modern and classical music. The gallery is on the second floor of the center, just left of the information desk; it's open Monday to Thursday from 9am to 9pm and Friday from 9am to 5pm. Bus: HOP, SKIP.

The **Andrew J. Macky Gallery** (☎ 303/492-8423), at the main entrance of Macky Auditorium, shows touring exhibits and works by local artists. It's open Wednesday from 9am to 4pm. Bus: HOP, SKIP.

Boulder Museum of Contemporary Art. 1750 13th St. ☎ **303/443-2122.** www. bmoca.org. Admission $2 adults, $1.50 students and seniors. Tues–Fri 11am–5pm, Sat 9am–5pm, Sun noon–5pm. Hours fluctuate seasonally; call ahead for current information. Closed major holidays. Bus: HOP, SKIP.

This multidisciplinary art center, originally created to exhibit the work of local artists, has gradually evolved to become an exciting venue where one can expect to see almost anything art related, from the lighthearted to the elegant, by local, regional, and international contemporary artists. There are special programs for young children and a variety of other arts events throughout the year. Performing arts—from poetry and dance to music and drama—are presented in the museum's award-winning performance venue, featuring local, national, and international performers. In addition, on Saturday evenings in summer, classic movies such as *Citizen Kane* and cult classics are shown outside ($5 per person). Take a lawn chair or blanket.

Boulder Museum of History. 1206 Euclid Ave. ☎ **303/449-3464.** bcn.boulder.co.us/ arts/bmh. Admission $2 adults; $1 children, students, and seniors. Guided and self-guided Tues–Fri 10am–4pm, Sat–Sun noon–4pm. Closed major holidays. Bus: HOP, SKIP.

Ensconced on University Hill in the 1899–1900 Harbeck-Bergheim House, a French château-style sandstone mansion with a Dutch-style front door and Italian tile fireplaces, this museum has an impressive collection of more than 20,000 artifacts, plus hundreds of thousands of photographs and historical documents from Colorado's early days up to the present. Built by a New York financier, it features a Tiffany window on the stairway landing, a built-in buffet with leaded-glass doors, and hand-carved mantels. Mannequins are used to depict cooking in the authentic old-fashioned kitchen. The wardrobes in the upstairs bedrooms contain an extensive collection of Victorian and Edwardian clothing, and there is also a unique collection of antique farm equipment.

Operated by the Boulder Historical Society, the museum presents lecture programs, classes on subjects such as quilting and historic photo preservation, and events such as a Victorian Fair with barbershop quartets, carriage rides, quilting, and an old-time women's baseball game complete with long skirts.

Collage Children's Museum. 2065 30th St. ☎ **303/440-9894.** Admission $3.50 adults and children, $1.75 seniors, free for children under 2, $12 maximum per family. Mon and Wed–Sat 10am–5pm, Sun 1–5pm. Across from Crossroads Mall on the north side.

With 4,700 square feet of custom-designed interactive exhibits created to stimulate the imagination, children from preschool through elementary grades are encouraged to touch, dress up, and get involved here. There's a 20-foot fire engine for climbing on and learning about firefighting, plenty of art supplies, and changing hands-on exhibits dealing with science, technology, cultural diversity, and other subjects. Call for times of the museum's numerous planned activities. Children under 12 must be accompanied by an adult, but adults can play, too.

Heritage Center. Third floor of Old Main, University of Colorado. ☎ **303/492-6329.** Free admission. Tues–Fri 10am–4pm; Sat 10am–2pm. Bus: HOP.

Located in the oldest building on campus, this museum reflects the history of the university. Within seven galleries are exhibits on early student life (together with a complete set of yearbooks), C.U.'s contributions to space exploration, campus architecture, distinguished C.U. alumni, and an overview of the university's history.

Leanin' Tree Museum of Western Art. 6055 Longbow Dr. (off Spine Rd. and Longmont Diagonal). ☎ **800/777-8716 ext. 299** or 303/530-1442 ext. 299. www.leanintree.com. Free admission. Mon–Fri 8am–4:30pm, Sat–Sun 10am–4pm. Bus: 205.

You may know Leanin' Tree as the world's largest publisher of western art greeting cards. What's not so well known is that here in the company's headquarters is an outstanding collection of original paintings and bronze sculptures by contemporary artists—all depicting scenes from the Old or New West, including a collection of humorous cowboy art. Some of the works have been reproduced on the company's greeting cards that are offered for sale in the gift shop. Free guided tours are available.

University of Colorado Museum. University of Colorado, Henderson Bldg., Broadway at 15th St. ☎ **303/492-6892.** Free admission, but donations accepted. Mon–Fri 9am–5pm, Sat 9am–4pm, Sun 10am–4pm. Bus: HOP.

The natural history and anthropology of the Rocky Mountains and Southwest are the focus of this campus museum, founded in 1902. Featured exhibits include ancestral Puebloan pottery and collections pertaining to dinosaurs, geology, paleontology, botany, entomology, and zoology. A children's area has interactive exhibits, and one gallery is devoted to special displays that change throughout the year.

ESPECIALLY FOR KIDS

City parks (see "Outdoor Activities," below), and **Collage Children's Museum** (see above) offer the best diversions for children.

On the **Boulder Creek Path** (see "The Top Attractions," above), youngsters are fascinated by the underwater fish observatory behind the Regal Harvest House. They can feed the huge trout swimming behind a glass barrier on the creek (machines cough up handfuls of fish food for 25¢). Farther up the path, on the south bank around 6th Street, Kids' Fishing Ponds, stocked by the Boulder Fish and Game Club, are open to children under 12. There's no charge for either activity.

The **Fiske Planetarium** (☎ 303/492-5001) offers visitors a walk through the Solar System. Dedicated to the memory of C.U. alumnus Ellison Onizuka and the six other astronauts who died in the space shuttle Challenger explosion, the outdoor scale model of the system begins at the entrance to the planetarium with the sun and inner planets, and continues across Regent Drive to the outer planets, located along the walkway to the Engineering Center. Admission is free; allow at least a half hour. The planetarium also offers after-school and summer discovery programs for kids, as well as star shows and other programs where you get a chance to look at the sky through the planetarium's telescopes. Admission charge for these events is usually $2 to $4 per person; call for the latest schedule. Bus: HOP.

6 Outdoor Activities

Boulder is clearly one of the leading spots for outdoor sports in North America. The city manages over 38,000 acres of parklands, including more than 200 miles of hiking trails and bicycle paths. Several canyons lead down from the Rockies directly into Boulder, attracting mountaineers and rock climbers. Families enjoy picnicking and camping in the beautiful surroundings. It seems that everywhere you look, people of all ages are running, walking, biking, skiing, or engaged in other active sports.

The **Boulder Parks and Recreation Department** (☎ 303/413-7200) schedules many year-round activities for children as well as adults. Seasonal booklets on activities and city parks are available free from the Chamber of Commerce office. Although many of the programs last for several weeks or months, some are half- or full-day activities that visiting children can join, although usually at a slightly higher price than charged for city residents. The department sponsors hikes, fitness programs, ski trips, water sports, special holiday events, and performances in local parks. (TV trivia buffs, take note: Mork of *Mork and Mindy* first touched down on Planet Earth in Chautauqua Park, on the city's south side).

One destination where you can enjoy several kinds of outdoor activities is **Eldorado Canyon State Park.** This mountain park, just 8 miles southwest of Boulder in Eldorado Springs, is a favorite of technical rock climbers, but the 850-foot-high canyon's beauty makes it just as popular with hikers, picnickers, and others who want to get away from it all. The 1,165-acre park includes 12 miles of hiking and horseback-riding trails, plus 9 miles of trails suitable for mountain bikes; fishing is permitted, but not camping. Exhibits at the visitor center describe the canyon's geologic formations, bats, and the history of the park. There's also a climbing wall. Admission is $4 per vehicle; the park is open daily from dawn to dusk. For further information, contact Eldorado Canyon State Park, Box B, Eldorado Springs, CO 80025 (☎ **303/494-3943;** www.coloradoparks.org).

BALLOONING Float above the majestic Rocky Mountains in a hot-air balloon, watching as the early morning light gradually brightens to full day. Flights often include complimentary champagne and an elaborate continental breakfast. **Fair Winds Hot Air Balloon Flights** (☎ 303/939-9323; www.fairwindsinc.com) flies 7 days a week year-round, weather permitting. Prices are about $150 per person.

BICYCLING   On some days, you can see more bikes than cars in Boulder. Paths run along many of the city's major arteries, and local racing and touring events are scheduled year-round. Bicyclists riding at night are required to have lights; perhaps because of the large number of bicyclists in Boulder, the local police actively enforce traffic regulations that apply to them. Generally, bicyclists must obey the same laws that apply to operators of motor vehicles.

For current information on biking events, tips on the best places to ride, and equipment sales and repairs, check with **University Bicycles,** 839 Pearl St., about two blocks west of the Pearl Street Mall (☎ 303/444-4196; www.ubikes.com). The shop also provides bike rentals for about $20 per day, and has maps of the city's 90 miles of bike lanes, paths, and routes. See also "By Bicycle" under "Getting Around," above.

CLIMBING   If you would like to tackle the nearby mountains and cliffs with ropes and pitons, contact **Mountain Sports,** 2835 Pearl St. (☎ 303/442-8355), which sells clothing and technical equipment, and can also provide maps and advice on climbing and trail running. There's a second location at 1821 Pearl St. (☎ 303/443-6700). Another good information source is **Colorado Athletic Training School,** 2800 30th St. (☎ 303/939-9699).

The Flatiron Range (easily visible from downtown Boulder) and nearby Eldorado Canyon are two favorite destinations among expert rock scalers. The so-called "amphitheatre" in the Flatirons is among the most revered of the nearby climbing areas. For bouldering, Carter Lake (30 miles north on U.S. 36) and Boulder Canyon (west of the city on Canyon Boulevard) are two of the top spots.

FISHING   Favored fishing areas near Boulder include **Boulder Reservoir,** managed by the Boulder Parks and Recreation Department (☎ 303/441-3461), North 51st Street, northeast of the city off the Longmont Diagonal, where you can try your luck for walleye, catfish, largemouth bass, bluegill, crappie, and carp. Other favorite fishing holes include **Lagerman Reservoir,** west of North 73rd Street off Pike Road, about 15 miles northeast of the city, where only nonmotorized boats can be used; **Barker Reservoir,** just east of Nederland on the Boulder Canyon Drive (Colo. 119), for bank fishing; and **Walden Ponds Wildlife Habitat,** about 6 miles east of downtown on North 75th Street.

GLIDER FLYING & SOARING   The atmospheric conditions generated by the peaks of the Front Range are ideal for year-round soaring and gliding. **Mile High Gliding,** 5534 Independence Rd. (☎ 303/527-1122), offers rides and lessons on the north side of Boulder Municipal Airport, 2 miles northeast of downtown. Rides for one person range from $60 to $160 and last from 15 minutes to an hour or more; a half-hour ride for two costs $160.

GOLF   Local courses include **Flatirons Golf Course** (run by Boulder Parks and Recreation Dept.), 5706 E. Arapahoe Ave. (☎ 303/442-7851), and **Lake Valley Golf Course,** 4400 Lake Valley Dr., three miles north of Boulder off Neva Road (☎ 303/444-2114). Nonresident greens fees for 18 holes range from $26.50 to $50.

HIKING & BACKPACKING   There are plenty of opportunities for hiking and backpacking in the Boulder area—the Boulder Mountain Parks system includes 4,625 acres bordering the Boulder city limits, including the Flatirons and Flagstaff Mountain. You can obtain a map with descriptions of more than 60 trails from the **Boulder Convention and Visitors Bureau,** 2440 Pearl St. (☎ 303/442-2911).

Numerous Roosevelt National Forest trailheads leave the Peak to Peak Scenic Byway (Colo. 72) west of Boulder. Check with the **U.S. Forest Service,** Boulder Ranger District, 2140 Yarmouth Ave. (☎ **303/444-6600**), for hiking and backpacking information, and during dry weather check on possible fire and smoking restrictions before heading into the forest. The trailheads leading to Long, Mitchell, and Brainard lakes are among the most popular, as is the 2-mile hike to Isabel Glacier.

About 70 miles west of Boulder, on the Continental Divide, is the **Indian Peaks Wilderness Area** (☎ **303/541-2519** for recorded information). More than half of the area is fragile alpine tundra; permits are required for camping from June 1 to September 15. North of Boulder, via Estes Park, is **Rocky Mountain National Park** (☎ **970/586-1206**), one of the state's prime destinations for hikers and those seeking beautiful mountain scenery. The **Mills Lake Trail,** one of our favorites, is located here; see "A Side Trip to Estes Park & Rocky Mountain National Park," later in this chapter. Another good hike is the Mesa Trail, which departs from the National Center for Atmospheric Research (see "The Top Attractions," above).

RUNNING The Boulder Creek Path (see "The Top Attractions," above) is one of the most popular routes for runners in Boulder. A local group that is a good resource for the traveling runner is **Boulder Road Runners** (☎ **303/499-2061;** www.boulderroadrunners.org). They organize group runs in the area and also are a good resource for information. The **Bolder Boulder** (☎ **303/444-RACE**), held every Memorial Day, attracts 40,000 runners who circle its 10-kilometer (6.2-mile) course.

SKIING Friendly **Eldora Mountain Resort,** P.O. Box 1697, Nederland, CO 80466 (☎ **888/235-3672** or 303/440-8700; fax 303/440/8797; www.eldora.com), is just 21 miles (about a 40-minute drive) west of downtown Boulder via Colo. 119 through Nederland. RTD buses leave Boulder for Eldora four times daily during ski season. For downhill skiers and snowboarders, Eldora has 47 trails, rated 20% novice, 50% intermediate, and 30% expert terrain among its 495 acres. It has snowmaking on 320 acres. The area has two quad lifts, one triple and four double chairlifts, three surface lifts, and a vertical rise of 1,400 feet. Lift tickets (1999–2000 rates) are $38 for adults, $17 for children 6 to 12 and seniors 65 to 69, and free for those under 6 and over 69. There are also discount packages that include lessons and rental equipment for both skiers and snowboarders. Snowshoeing is also gaining popularity in the area. The season runs from mid-November to mid-April, snow permitting.

For cross-country skiers, Eldora has 45 kilometers of groomed and backcountry trails, and an overnight hut available by reservation. Snowmaking equipment serves two 5-kilometer loops. About 15% of the trails are rated easy, 50% intermediate, and 35% difficult. The trail fee is $10, or $7 for seniors 65 to 69.

You can rent all your ski, snowboard, and snowshoeing equipment at the ski-rental center, and Nordic equipment at the Eldora Nordic Center. A free base-area shuttle runs throughout the day from the Lodge to the Little Hawk area and the Nordic Center.

In Boulder, you can rent or buy telemark and alpine touring equipment from **Mountain Sports,** 2835 Pearl St. (☎ **303/442-8355**) or 821 Pearl St. (☎ **303/443-6770**).

SWIMMING Five public pools are located within the city. Indoor pools, all open daily year-round, are at the **North Boulder Recreation Center,** 3170 N. Broadway (☎ 303/441-3444), the **East Boulder Community Center,** 5660 Sioux Dr. (☎ 303/441-4400), and the **South Boulder Recreation Center,** 1360 Gillaspie Dr. (☎ 303/441-3448). The two outdoor pools (both open daily from Memorial Day to Labor

Day) are **Scott Carpenter Pool,** 30th Street and Arapahoe Avenue (☎ 303/ 441-3427), and **Spruce Pool,** 2102 Spruce St. (☎ 303/441-3426). Swimming fees for all municipal pools are $4.75 for adults, $2 for children, and $2.75 for seniors.

TENNIS   There are more than 30 public courts in the city. The North and South Boulder Recreation Centers (see "Swimming," above) each have four lighted courts and accept reservations ($8 an hour). The North Boulder Recreation Center also has two platform tennis courts. Play is free if you arrive and there's no one using the courts or with a reservation. For locations of other public tennis courts, contact the Boulder Parks and Recreation Department (☎ **303/413-7200**).

WATER SPORTS   For both powerboating and non-powerboating, sailboard instruction, or swimming at a sandy beach, head for the 1,400-acre **Boulder Reservoir** (☎ **303/441-3461**), on North 51st Street off the Longmont Diagonal northeast of the city. Nonpowered boats and canoes (sorry—no personal watercraft) can be rented starting at $5 an hour, with sailboards at $10 an hour. There's also a boat ramp and other facilities.

7 Spectator Sports

The major attractions are **University of Colorado football, women's volleyball,** and **men's and women's basketball.** For tickets, contact the Ticket Office, Campus Box 372, Boulder, CO 80309 (☎ **303/49-BUFFS**; www.cu-sports.com). Football tickets sell out early, particularly for homecoming and games with Nebraska, Texas A&M, and Oklahoma, so it would be wise to make reservations far in advance—perhaps even months ahead.

8 Shopping

For the best shopping in Boulder, head to the **Pearl Street Mall** (see "The Top Attractions," above), where you'll find not only shops and galleries galore but also street entertainers.

The indoor/outdoor, 1.5-million square foot **FlatIrons Crossing** (☎ 720/ 887-9900; www.flatironcrossing.com), a thoroughly modern, upscale mall featuring Nordstrom, Dillard's, and Lord & Taylor, is a more comprehensive option for the devout shopper. It opened in August 2000, 9 miles southeast of Boulder off U.S. 36 in Broomfield.

SHOPPING A TO Z
ARTS & CRAFTS
Art Source International. 1237 Pearl St. ☎ **303/444-4080.**

Natural history prints, maps, and other items relevant to western Americana, mainly from the 18th and 19th centuries, are the specialty here, along with a collection of hundred-year-old Colorado photographs. The store also features a great selection of globes, as well as reproductions.

Boulder Arts & Crafts Cooperative. 1421 Pearl St. ☎ **303/443-3683.**

This shop, owned and operated by its artist members since 1971, features a wide variety of original hand-crafted works, ranging from watercolors, serigraphs, and other fine art, to top-quality crafts including blown glass, stained glass, handmade jewelry, and functional pottery. Many of the items are made in Colorado or the Rocky Mountain region, and this is a good place to find a unique gift or souvenir.

Handmade in Colorado. 1426 Pearl St. ☎ **303/938-8394.**

This cooperative gallery offers pottery, glass, wood, quilts, photographs, jewelry, dried-flower arrangements, and other unique items made by more than 20 artists, all living in Colorado.

Maclaren Markowitz Gallery. 1011 Pearl St. ☎ **303/449-6807.**

Works by local and national artists in a variety of media and styles are presented here, including fine paintings, sculpture, ceramics, and wearable art jewelry.

BOOKS

Being a college town, Boulder is one of the best cities in the world for a browsing bookworm. It is said that Boulder has more used bookstores per capita than any other U.S. city.

Barnes & Noble Booksellers. 2915 Pearl St. ☎ **303/442-1665.**

You'll find all the usual best-sellers and other titles at this large bookstore, which also stocks a good selection of local and regional titles. If you want to find out about Colorado and Boulder history, area hiking trails, and the like, this is the place to come. It's also a good source for maps—from downtown Boulder to world atlases—and the music section stocks Colorado artists as well as all the usual big names. There's a cafe with fresh-baked pastries and a variety of coffees, and the store sponsors special readings and kids' events.

Boulder Book Store. 1107 Pearl St. ☎ **303/447-2074.** www.boulderbookstore.com.

This meandering, four-story, 20,000 square foot bookstore has been locally owned and operated for more than 25 years. It attracts students, bohemians, and businessmen alike with its homey vibe, and features great selections of Buddhism tomes and travel guides. It is attached to a coffeehouse with patio seating on the Pearl Street Mall, The Bookend Café (see "Espresso Bars, Coffee Shops, and Related Establishments," above.)

FASHION

Alpaca Connection. 1326 Pearl St. ☎ **303/447-2047.**

Natural fiber clothing from around the world, including alpaca-and-wool sweaters from South America, are featured at this shop.

Fresh Produce Sportswear. 1136 Pearl St. ☎ **303/442-7507.**

Colorful clothing for both kids and adults is available at this outlet store for the Boulder-based brand. The style is casual resort-ware, and there are seasonal selections and sales year-round.

FOOD & DRINK

Alfalfa's. 1651 Broadway. ☎ **303/442-0909.**

The original Alfalfa's, a natural-foods supermarket, sells excellent produce (much of it certified organic) and chemical-free groceries; there's also a deli, a soup-and-salad bar, a juice-and-espresso bar, and a hot-food case.

Boulder Wine Merchant. 2690 Broadway. ☎ **303/443-6761.** www.boulderwine.com.

This store has a solid wine selection with more than 2,000 varieties from around the world, plus knowledgeable salespeople who can help you make the right choice.

Liquor Mart. 1750 15th St. (at Canyon Blvd.). ☎ **800/597-4440** or 303/449-3374. www.
liquormart.com.

Here you'll find a huge choice of discounted wine and liquor, with more than 5,000
wines and 900 beers, including a wide selection of imported and microbrewed beers.

GIFTS & SOUVENIRS
Nature's Own Imagination. 1133 Pearl St. Mall. ☎ **303/443-4430.**

This shop has a unique collection of candles, aromatherapy oils, and wind chimes,
plus birdhouses, jewelry, picture frames, T-shirts, fossils, minerals, and geodes.

HARDWARE
✪ **McGuckin Hardware.** 2525 Arapahoe Ave. ☎ **303/443-1822.**

McGuckin's claims to have the world's largest hardware selection, with more than
200,000 items in stock. In addition to the nuts, bolts, brackets, paints, tools, and
assorted whatchamacallits that most hardware stores carry, here you'll also find sporting goods, kitchen gizmos, automotive supplies, stationery, some clothing, electronics,
outdoor furniture, fresh flowers, and a whole lot of other stuff.

JEWELRY
Antiquariat. 2014 Broadway. ☎ **303/443-6311.**

This shop focuses on American Indian jewelry, including many hard-to-find pieces.
You'll also find estate and fine jewelry, sterling silver, figurines, and other collectibles.

KITCHENWARE
Peppercorn. 1235 Pearl St. ☎ **800/447-6905** or 303/449-5847.

From cookbooks to pasta makers, you can find virtually everything for the kitchen
here, along with china, glassware, flatware, and table linens. This vast store has hundreds of kitchen gadgets and appliances—everything you might need to prepare, serve,
and consume the simplest or most exotic meal.

MUSIC
✪ **Boulder Early Music Shop.** 3200 Valmont Rd. #7. ☎ **800/499-1301** or 303/
449-9231. www.bems.com.

Musicians and music lovers from across North America rely on this shop for sheet music,
recordings, books, musical gifts, and instruments (including recorders, flutes, harpsi-
chords, dulcimers, and viols). Browsing is loads of fun, and the musician-shopkeepers
are friendly, highly knowledgeable folks who obviously love their work.

Motherland Music. 2028 14th St. (immediately adjacent to the Boulder Theater). ☎ **303/
440-4661.** www.motherlandmusic.com.

This shop specializes in imported handcrafted African musical instruments and art,
with a focus on drums and other high-quality items from Ghana, Nigeria, and Mali.
It often hosts drumming classes in the evening.

SPORTING GOODS
There are a number of well-established sporting-goods stores in the city. **Mountain
Sports,** 821 Pearl St. (☎ **800/558-6770** or 303/443-6770), which boasts of being
Boulder's oldest mountaineering shop (it opened in 1958), specializes in equipment,
clothing, and accessories for backpacking, camping, rock and ice climbing, moun-
taineering, backcountry and telemark skiing, skate skiing, and snowshoeing. Equipment

rentals include sleeping bags, tents, backpacks, and snowshoes; backcountry and tele-mark ski packages are available. Mountain Sports also sells maps and guidebooks, and the knowledgeable staff—which includes several trained guides—can help you plan your trip. There's a second location at 2835 Pearl St. (☎ **303/442-8355**).

A staff of outdoor enthusiasts can also help you at **Doc's Ski and Sport,** 627 S. Broadway (☎ **303/499-0963**), which sells, rents, and repairs skis, snowboards, snow-shoes, mountain bikes, and in-line skates. **Boulder Army Store,** 1545 Pearl St. (☎ **303/442-7616**), has the best stock of camping gear in the city, along with a lim-ited amount of fishing equipment, plus a good supply of outdoor clothing and mili-tary surplus items such as fatigues, helmets, and that disarmed hand grenade you've always wanted. **Gart Sports,** 3320 N. 28th St.(☎ **303/449-9021**), is a good all-purpose sporting-goods source.

9 Boulder After Dark

As a cultured and well-educated community (59% of Boulder's adult residents have at least one college degree), Boulder is especially noted for its summer music, dance, and Shakespeare festivals. Of course, major entertainment events take place here year-round, both downtown and on the University of Colorado campus. There's also a wide choice of nightclubs and bars, but it hasn't always been so: Boulder was dry for 60 years, from 1907 (13 years before national Prohibition) to 1967. The first new bar in the city opened in 1969, in the Hotel Boulderado. The notoriously healthy city banned smok-ing in 1995; only a few establishments allow patrons to ignore the policy.

Entertainment schedules can be found in the *Daily Camera's* weekly *Friday Maga-zine;* in either of the Denver dailies, the *Denver Post* or the *Rocky Mountain News;* in *Westword,* the Denver weekly; or in the free *Boulder Weekly.*

THE CLUB & MUSIC SCENE

Boulder Theater. 14th and Pearl sts. ☎ **303/786-7030.** www.bouldertheater.com.

Country, rock, jazz, and who knows what else is performed here by musicians such as Michael Martin Murphey, Ravi Shankar, and Arturo Sandoval.

The Catacombs. In the basement of the Hotel Boulderado, 13th and Spruce sts. ☎ **303/443-0486.**

This popular bar attracts a crowd to listen to live blues and jazz by local and regional performers. The loud, somewhat raucous atmosphere makes this a favorite of C.U. students.

Fox Theatre and Cafe. 1135 13th St. ☎ **303/443-3399** or 303/447-0095. www.foxtheatre.com.

A variety of live music (including, but not limited to, bluegrass, funk, blues, and alter-native) is presented here seven nights a week, featuring a mix of local, regional, and national talent. You'll find three bars at this converted movie theater, which is revered for its great acoustics.

Penny Lane Coffee House. Pearl and 18th sts. ☎ **303/443-9516.**

By day a somewhat bohemian gathering place for talking, playing chess, or reading while sipping espresso, this Greenwich Village–style coffeehouse comes alive at night. There's usually a poetry reading on Monday, one night of live jazz each week, several open-stage evenings, and a diverse mixture of live music by local and regional artists on Friday and Saturday. See also "Espresso Bars," in section 4 above.

Soma. 1915 Broadway. ☎ **303/938-8600.**

Voted the "best place to dance" in town by both the *Boulder Weekly* and *Daily Camera*, Soma attracts the rave set, featuring techno and electronic DJs playing cutting-edge dance music 7 days a week. There are great beer specials here every night and free sushi happy hours on Fridays 5 to 8pm.

Tulagi. 1129 13th St. ☎ **303/938-9090** or 303/443-3399. www.tulagis.com.

An informal college bar on the Hill off campus, Tulagi features live rock music most nights, has frequent beer and drink specials, and offers open-mike nights and workshops for singers and songwriters.

West End Tavern. 926 Pearl St. (between 9th and 10th sts.). ☎ **303/444-3535.**

The West End seems to have a lock on the annual "best neighborhood bar" balloting conducted by the *Daily Camera*. Sunny afternoons find dozens of Boulderites on the tavern's roof garden, and evenings see them tuned into a wide-ranging selection of jazz, blues, or other live music in the trendy bar. Fare includes hot chili, pizza, and charbroiled sandwiches.

THE BAR SCENE

Barrel House. 2860 Arapahoe Rd. ☎ **303/444-9464.**

Consistently voted the number-one sports bar in Boulder by local newspaper readers, the Barrel House offers a choice of 25 beers on tap, most of which are Colorado microbrews. There are close to three dozen TVs, including four big-screen sets, and a huge menu. The bar is a traditional pre-game meeting place for University of Colorado football fans.

✪ Conor O'Neill's. 1922 13th St. ☎ **303/449-1922.**

Everything in this pub—from the bar to the art to the timber floors—was designed and built in Ireland. The atmosphere is rich, with a "shop pub" up front and two back rooms centered around a pair of fireplaces that were constructed by visiting Irish stonemasons. There are over a dozen beers on tap, primarily from Ireland (where else?), and the pub menu features fish and chips, burgers, and a mean shepherd's pie. There are live Irish music sessions on Tuesday through Wednesday and Sunday evenings.

✪ Corner Bar. In the Hotel Boulderado, 13th and Spruce sts. ☎ **303/442-4344.**

Probably the best Boulder bar for people watching, the Corner Bar serves sandwiches, soups, and other items from the Boulderado's main restaurant, Q's, and features occasional live music. Also see "Dining," above.

Mountain Sun Pub & Brewery. 1535 Pearl St. (east of the Mall). ☎ **303/546-0886.**

An English-style neighborhood pub and microbrewery, Mountain Sun produces 35 barrels of beer each week and provides tours on request. The menu features soups, salads, burgers, sandwiches, and a few Mexican dishes, and there's live folk, acoustic, and bluegrass music on Sunday night (no cover).

Oasis II Brewery. 1061 Canyon Blvd. ☎ **303/449-0363.**

Probably the only brew pub with an Egyptian motif, Oasis II brews good beer. Try the award-winning Tut Brown Ale. The happy hour (4 to 6pm daily) features great food and drink specials.

Rio Grande. 1101 Walnut St. ☎ **303/444-3690.**

This popular neighborhood bar, just south of the Pearl Street Mall, is best known for its huge, award-winning margaritas. Frequented by college students and Boulder's under-30 crowd, the Rio is bustling for reasons beyond its alcoholic concoctions—namely the loud and social atmosphere, and the food, a good variety of oversized Mexican entrees and combos.

'Round Midnight. 1005 Pearl St. (1 block west of the Pearl St. Mall). **303/442-2176.**

A basement bar with two areas—a barroom and a stage room—'Round Midnight features two pool tables and an eclectic mix of live music and DJs several nights a week. With a classy vibe, the emphasis here is on cocktails and single-malt scotches. There's also a smoking room here.

The Sink. 1165 13th St. ☎ **303/444-SINK.**

This off-campus establishment has been open since 1949, but updated with new spacey wall murals that help make this one of Boulder's funniest—as well as most fun—nightspots. There's a full bar with more than a dozen regional microbrews, live music, and fare such as Sinkburgers and "ugly crust" pizza.

Sundown Saloon. 1136 Pearl St. **303/449-4987.**

This raucous dive is a C.U. institution. Situated in a spacious basement on the west end of the Pearl Street Mall, pool is the pastime of choice and the drinks are reasonably priced. The Sundown Saloon is one of the few establishments that averts its eyes from guests violating Boulder's smoking ban, resulting in one of the smokiest bars known to man.

Walnut Brewery. 1123 Walnut St. (near Broadway). ☎ **303/447-1345.**

This large microbrewery—popular with the after-work crowd, both young and old—has its restaurant/bar/brewery in a historic brick warehouse a block from the Pearl Street Mall. At least six beers, from a pale ale to a stout, and including two cask-conditioned ales, are always available. Several seasonal specials are also brewed here, and the brewery produces its own root beer. See also "Dining," above.

The Yard. 2690 28th St., Unit C. ☎ **303/443-1987.**

A gay bar that attracts a diverse crowd, The Yard features dancing (no cover) on Friday and Saturday, as well as pool and a daily happy hour.

THE PERFORMING ARTS

Music, dance, and theater are important aspects of life for Boulder residents, and visitors are welcome to take full advantage of the numerous events scheduled. Many of these activities take place at **Macky Auditorium** at the University of Colorado (☎ **303/492-8008;** www.colorado.edu/music), and other campus venues, as well as the **Chautauqua Auditorium,** 900 Baseline Rd. (☎ **303/442-3282**), and the Dairy Center for the Arts, 2590 Walnut St. (☎ **303/440-7826;** www.thedairy.org).

CLASSICAL MUSIC & OPERA

✪ **Boulder Bach Festival.** P.O. Box 1896, Boulder, CO 80306. ☎ **303/494-3159.** www.boulderbachfest.org.

First presented in 1981, this celebration of the music of Johann Sebastian Bach includes not only a late January festival but also concerts and other events year-round. Individual adult tickets cost $25, students pay $10, and series tickets are also available.

Boulder Philharmonic Orchestra. Dairy Center for the Arts, 2590 Walnut St. ☎ **303/ 449-1343.**

This acclaimed community orchestra performs an annual fall-to-spring season, with world-class artists that have included singer Marilyn Horne, guitarist Carlos Montoya, cellist Mstislav Rostropovich, and violinist Itzhak Perlman. Tickets are $10 to $40.

Colorado MahlerFest. P.O. Box 1314, Boulder, CO 80306. ☎ **303/447-0513** for information, 303/449-1343 for box office. www.mahlerfest.org.

Begun in 1988, this international festival is the only one of its kind in the world. For a week each January it celebrates the work of Gustav Mahler with a performance of one of his symphonies as well as films, discussions, seminars, and other musical programs. Some events are free; admission to orchestra concerts ranges from $8 to $30.

Colorado Music Festival. 1525 Spruce St., Suite 101, Boulder, CO 80302. ☎ **303/ 449-1397** for general information, or 303/449-2413 for tickets; tickets also available online. www.coloradomusicfest.com.

Begun in 1976, this series is the single biggest annual arts event in Boulder, with visiting musicians from around the world performing in the acoustically revered Chautauqua Auditorium. The festival presents works by classical through modern composers, such as Bach, Beethoven, Mozart, Dvorak, and Gershwin, plus living composers. It usually runs from mid-June to mid-August, with symphony orchestra performances Thursday and Friday at 8pm, chamber orchestra concerts Sunday at 7pm, and a chamber music series Tuesday at 8pm. There's also a children's concert in late June and a free Independence Day concert. Adult ticket prices range from $12 to $35.

C.U. Concerts. University of Colorado. ☎ **303/492-8008.** www.colorado.edu/music.

The university's College of Music presents the Artist Series, Lyric Theatre, University of Colorado Summer Opera, Takács String Quartet Series, and Holiday Festival at Macky Auditorium and Grusin Music Hall. General admission tickets usually range from $10 to $32. The Artist Series features an outstanding lineup of classical soloists, jazz artists, dance companies, and multidisciplinary events. These include several concerts by the renowned Takács String Quartet (call early for tickets) and the annual Holiday Festival, including the University Symphony Orchestra, University choirs, several smaller ensembles, and soloists from the College of Music's student body and faculty.

THEATER & DANCE

Boulder Ballet Ensemble. Dairy Center for the Arts, 2590 Walnut St. ☎ **303/442-6944.**

This community group, established in 1984, presents classical ballet with professional as well as semiprofessional and amateur dancers. It is best known for its production of The Nutcracker with the Boulder Philharmonic each Thanksgiving weekend.

Colorado Dance Festival. P.O. Box 356, Boulder, CO 80306. ☎ **303/442-7666.** E-mail: colodancefest@earthlink.net.

Dancers from around the world flock to Boulder for this 4-week event each July. Varied performances (tickets range from $15 to $20) are interspersed with classes, workshops, lectures, film and video screenings, and panel discussions.

✪ **Colorado Shakespeare Festival.** Campus Box 277, University of Colorado, Boulder, CO 80309. ☎ **303/492-0554** for information and the box office. www.coloradoshakes.org.

Considered one of the top three Shakespearean festivals in the United States, this 2-month annual event attracts more than 40,000 theatergoers between late June and late August. Held since 1958 in the University of Colorado's Mary Rippon Outdoor Theatre, and indoors at University Theatre Main Stage, it offers more than a dozen performances of each of four Shakespearean plays. Actors, directors, designers, and everyone associated with the productions are fully schooled Shakespearean professionals. Tickets run from $14 to $40 for single performances, with series packages also available. During the festival, company members conduct one-hour backstage tours before each show; and there are also special events including staged readings of new plays.

Guild Theatre. Dairy Center for the Arts, 2590 Walnut St. ☎ **303/442-1415.**

The Guild Theatre is actually the umbrella for four resident theater companies—the Upstart Crow, Actors Ensemble, Boulder Conservatory Theater, and Mystyk Hande—which perform on two stages: a 100-seat theater (where no seat is more than three rows from the stage) and an 80-seat proscenium theater.

10 A Side Trip to Estes Park & Rocky Mountain National Park

34 miles NW of Boulder, 71 miles NW of Denver

The northern half of the Colorado Rockies is truly the country's ultimate mountain wilderness, the crown on the head of the great range that dominates the American West. This is rugged beauty at its best, extending on either side of the meandering Continental Divide down sawtooth ridgelines, through precipitous river canyons, and across broad alpine plains. Here, snowfall is measured in feet, not inches, and when spring's sun finally melts away the frost, amazing arrays of alpine wildflowers herald the new beginning. Although this can be a fairly easy day trip from Boulder or Denver, we heartily recommend spending at least 2 or 3 days here, perhaps staying in Estes Park while exploring the trails and spectacular views of the national park.

ESTES PARK

Unlike other Colorado mountain towns, most of which began as mining communities, Estes Park (elevation 7,522 feet) has always been a resort town. Long known by the Utes and Arapahos, this area was explored in 1859 by rancher Joel Estes. Soon thereafter, he sold his homestead to Griff Evans, who built it into a dude ranch. One of Evans' guests, the Earl of Dunraven (a Welshman), was so enchanted with the region that he purchased most of the valley and operated it as his private game reserve until thwarted by such settlers as W. E. James, who built Elkhorn Lodge as a "fish ranch" to supply Denver restaurants.

But the growth of Estes Park is inextricably linked with two individuals: Freelan Stanley and Enos Mills. Stanley, a Bostonian who, together with his brother Francis, invented the kerosene-powered Stanley Steamer automobile in 1899, settled in Estes Park in 1907, launched a Stanley Steamer shuttle service from Denver, and in 1909 built the landmark Stanley Hotel. Mills, an innkeeper-turned-conservationist, was one of the prime advocates for the establishment of Rocky Mountain National Park. President Woodrow Wilson signed the bill creating the 400-square-mile park in 1915; today it attracts some 3 million visitors annually.

ESSENTIALS

GETTING THERE By Car The most direct route is U.S. 36 from Denver and Boulder. At Estes Park, U.S. 36 joins U.S. 34, which runs up the Big Thompson

Canyon from I-25 and Loveland, and continues through Rocky Mountain National Park to Granby. An alternative scenic route to Estes Park is Colo. 7, the "Peak-to-Peak Scenic Byway" that goes, under different designations, through Central City (Colo. 119), Nederland (Colo. 72), and Allenspark (Colo. 7).

By Plane   Visitors can fly into Denver International Airport, then rent a car or contact Charles Tour and Travel Services (see below) to continue to Boulder and Estes Park.

By Bus   Estes Park Shuttle (☎ **800/586-5009** or 970/586-5151; www. estesparkco.com) connects the town with Boulder and Denver.

VISITOR INFORMATION   The **Estes Park Chamber Resort Association,** 500 Big Thompson Ave., Estes Park, CO 80517 (☎ **800/44-ESTES** or 970/586-4431; fax 970/586-6336; www.estesparkresort.com), has a visitor center on U.S. 34, just east of its junction with U.S. 36, with access from both highways.

CITY LAYOUT   U.S. 34 and U.S. 36 enter Estes Park from the east, on either side of Lake Estes. The highways proceed together through downtown Estes Park as Elkhorn Avenue; U.S. 34 Bypass branches to the north and west as Wonderview Avenue, rejoining Elkhorn on the west side of town as Fall River Road and paralleling Fall River as it climbs into Rocky Mountain National Park. U.S. 36, also known as Moraine Avenue, turns south and west off Elkhorn at a town-center intersection; it follows Glacier Creek to the junction of Bear Creek Road, then ascends to the national park entrance.

GETTING AROUND   In summer, a free national park **shuttle bus** runs from Moraine Park Campground, Moraine Park Museum, and the Glacier Basin parking area to Bear Lake, with departures every 15 to 30 minutes.

There's year-round taxi service with **Estes Park Shuttle** (see "Getting There," above), which also provides tours into Rocky Mountain National Park during the summer. Similar services are offered by **Emerald Taxi, Shuttle, Tour, and Travel Service** (☎ **970/586-1992** for taxi service, 970/586-1991 for tour information).

SPECIAL EVENTS   Area events include the Stanley Steamer Tour in May; the Art-Walk and Jazz Festival in mid-May; the Wool Market in mid-June; the Scandinavian Mid-Summer Festival on the weekend closest to the summer solstice; the Rooftop Rodeo during the third week of July; the Scottish–Irish Highland Festival on the weekend after Labor Day; the Chamber Music Festival on the third weekend in September; the Autumn Gold Brats and Bands in late September; and the Elk Festival in October.

FAST FACTS   In an **emergency,** dial ☎ **911.** In the national park, call ☎ **970/586-1399** for emergencies. The hospital, **Estes Park Medical Center,** which has a 24-hour emergency room, is at 555 Prospect Ave. (☎ **970/586-2317**). The **post office** is at 215 W. Riverside Dr. (☎ **800/275-8777**). For statewide **road conditions,** call ☎ **303/639-1111.** For **local weather and road conditions,** call ☎ **970/586-5555.**

On the radio, tune in to 1610AM for local wildlife-watching suggestions and other park information; on TV, cable channel 8 also presents a calendar of events. State and local taxes will add about 8% to hotel bills.

WHAT TO SEE & DO

Enos Mills Homestead Cabin. 6760 Colo. 7 (opposite Longs Peak Inn). ☎ **970/586-4706.** home.earthlink.net/~enosmillscbn. E-mail: enosmillscbn@earthlink.net. Free admission (but donations welcome). Memorial Day–Labor Day, usually Tues–Sun 11am–4pm, but call to confirm. By appointment in other seasons.

This 1885 cabin and homestead belonged to the late-19th- and early-20th-century conservationist Enos Mills, an enthusiastic advocate for the outdoors in general and the Rocky Mountains in particular, and a major force behind the establishment of Rocky Mountain National Park. A short walk down a nature trail brings you to the cabin, where members of the Mills family discuss his life and work. Memorabilia in the cabin include copies of the 15 books written by Mills and the cameras he used to take thousands of photos of the mountains he loved. Summer nature walks (call for current schedule and rates) are available by appointment, and evening talks are scheduled during the winter. Also on the premises are a book shop, photo gallery, and nature center.

Estes Park Aerial Tramway. 420 E. Riverside Dr. ☎ **970/586-3675.** Admission $8 adults, $4 children 6–11, free for children 5 and under. Summer daily 9am–6:30pm.

This lift provides panoramic views of Longs Peak and the Continental Divide, plus Estes Park village itself. The lower terminal is one block south of the post office. Its upper terminal has a gift shop, snack bar, and observation deck with binoculars (25¢). Numerous trails converge atop the mountain.

Estes Park Area Historical Museum. 200 Fourth St. at U.S. 36. ☎ **970/586-6256** or 970/586-6029. www.estesnet.com/Museum. E-mail: epmuseum@juno.com. Admission $2.50 adults, $2 seniors 60 and older, $1 children 12 and under, $10 maximum for families. May–Oct Mon–Sat 10am–5pm, Sun 1–5pm; Nov–Apr Fri–Sat 10am–5pm, Sun 1–5pm; extended Dec holiday hours.

The lives of early homesteaders in Estes Park are depicted in this excellent small museum, which includes a completely furnished turn-of-the-century log cabin, an original Stanley Steamer Car, and a changing exhibit gallery. The museum also features a permanent "Tracks in Time" exhibit that helps visitors see the impact that ordinary peoples, from the region's American Indians and women pioneers to today's area residents and travelers, have had on Estes Park. You can also see the Rocky Mountain National Park's original headquarters building, which has been moved here. In addition, the museum sponsors a variety of programs and distributes a historical walking-tour brochure on downtown Estes Park.

Michael Ricker Pewter Casting Studio & Museum. 2050 Big Thompson Ave. ☎ **800/ 373-9837** or 970/586-2030. www.ricker.com. Free admission. Summer Mon–Thurs 9am–9pm, Fri–Sat 9am–8pm, Sun 10am–6pm; winter Mon–Sat 9am–5pm, Sun 11am–5pm.

Ricker is an internationally recognized artist and sculptor whose works have been displayed in the Great Hall of Commerce in Washington, D.C. and at both Disneyland and Disney World. This museum and gallery has more than 1,000 pewter sculptures, including Ricker's masterpiece, Park City, claimed to be the world's largest miniature pewter sculpture. Free guided tours are available daily.

Stanley Museum of Colorado. Downstairs lobby of the Stanley Hotel, 333 Wonderview Ave. ☎ **970/577-1903.** Free admission. Daily 10am–4pm.

At this branch of the Stanley Museum of Kingfield, Maine, you can see exhibits on the life and work of F. O. Stanley and his family. Stanley, with his brother Francis, invented the Stanley Steam Car (more popularly known as the Stanley Steamer) in 1899, and in 1907 brought a fleet of his cars to Estes Park, built the Stanley Hotel, and began a shuttle service from Denver to bring tourists to the area.

SHOPPING

The **Art Center of Estes Park** in the Stanley Village Shopping Center, 517 Big Thompson Ave. (☎ 970/586-5882), is a community visual arts center—the only nonprofit art gallery in town—that features changing exhibits of a wide variety of local and regional art, including paintings, sculpture, photography, textiles, glass work, and wood carvings. Works are for sale, and the center also presents workshops and classes, lasting from several hours to a full day, on subjects such as oil painting, sketching, stained glass, and jewelry making. Cost is usually in the $40 to $75 range, including materials. The Art Center is a bit hard to find; once you get to the shopping center, go up the stairs behind the fountain. It's open daily from 10am to 5pm from May through September; and 10am to 4pm Friday through Monday the rest of the year.

Among the notable galleries and gift shops are those in the **Old Church Shops,** 157 W. Elkhorn Ave. Also worth looking for are **The Glassworks,** 323 W. Elkhorn Ave. (☎ **800/490-6695** or 970/586-8619; www.garthsglassworks.com), a gallery and studio with hand-glass-blowing demonstrations, and **Serendipity Trading Company,** 117 E. Elkhorn Ave. (☎ **800/832-8980** or 970/586-8410; www.serendipitytrading.com), traders in American Indian arts and crafts.

Ten miles south of Estes Park is **Eagle Plume's** store and museum, 9853 Colo. 7, Allenspark (☎ **303/747-2861;** www.eagleplume.com). A University of Colorado graduate (now deceased), Charles Eagle Plume was one-quarter Blackfeet (a Montana tribe, not the better-known Blackfoots of Canada) and an entertainer and entrepreneur. His fascinating collection of museum-quality artifacts is not for sale, but here in the museum (where admission is free) you'll get to see antique Indian beadwork and quill work, historic and prehistoric pottery, Navajo and Pueblo textiles dating from the 1870s, plus old pawn jewelry. In the trading post, you can purchase contemporary works by American and Canadian Indians, including crafts, pottery, jewelry, baskets, beadwork, and rugs. Eagle Plume's is open April through December, daily from 9am to 5pm; Saturday and Sunday 9am to 5pm, and by appointment from January through March.

WHERE TO STAY

For help in finding accommodations, call the **Estes Park Chamber Resort Association Lodging Referral Service** (☎ **800/44-ESTES** or 970/586-4431; www.estesparkresort.com). National chains represented here include **Best Western Lake Estes Resort,** 1650 Big Thompson Hwy. (U.S. 34), Estes Park, CO 80517 (☎ **800/292-8439** or 970/586-3386), with rates of $120 to $130 double from mid-June to mid-September, and $50 to $85 single or double the rest of the year; and **Holiday Inn,** U.S. 36 and Colo. 7 (P.O. Box 1468), Estes Park, CO 80517 (☎ **800/803-7837** or 970/586-2332), charging $129 to $139 double in summer, and $75 to $119 double the rest of the year. See also the National Park Resort, Cabins, and Campground in the "Camping" section, below.

Although many lodging facilities in the Estes Park area do not have air conditioning, it is seldom needed at this elevation. Unless otherwise noted, pets are not permitted in the following properties.

Expensive

✪ **Aspen Lodge at Estes Park.** 6120 Colo. 7, Longs Peak Route, Estes Park, CO 80517. ☎ **800/332-6867** (reservations only) from outside Colorado, or 970/586-8133. Direct from Denver ☎ 303/440-3371. Fax 970/586-8133. www.aspenlodge.net. E-mail aspen@aspenlodge. net. 59 units. June– Aug: 2-day minimum, packages include 3 meals, children's program, entertainment, and recreation (horseback riding extra). 2 days shared rm $300 each adult, $180 each child 3–12 years, children under 3 free; single adult $380. 3 days shared rm $450 each adult, $270 each child 3–12 years, children under 3 free; single adult $580. 7 days shared rm $930 each adult, $610 each child 3–12 years, children under 3 free; single adult $1345. Sept–May $79–$129 double per night for lodge rooms or one-room cabins, including full breakfast. Holiday rates higher. Call for 2- and 3-room cabin rates. AE, DISC, DC, MC, V.

Among Colorado's top dude ranches, Aspen Lodge is a full-service western-style resort, offering horseback riding, tennis, hiking, mountain biking, fishing, cross-country skiing, ice skating, snowshoeing, and a myriad of other activities. Guests stay in the handsome log lodge, which has a commanding stone fireplace in the lobby, or in cozy one-, two-, or three-room cabins nestled among the aspens. All lodge rooms have balconies, and most rooms and cabins have splendid views of Longs Peak, the tallest mountain in Rocky Mountain National Park. Trails on the lodge's 82 acres of grounds lead directly into the national park. Guests can also enjoy an outdoor heated swimming pool and hot tub, as well as the sports center, which has racquetball, a weight room, and a sauna. Meals are varied and delicious. The lodge also schedules numerous activities to entertain both children and teens.

✪ **Boulder Brook.** 1900 Fall River Rd., Estes Park, CO 80517. ☎ **800/238-0910** or 970/586-0910. Fax 970/586-8067. www.estes-park.com/boulderbrook. 16 suites. TV TEL. 89–$199 double; $129–$229 spa suites. AE, DISC, MC, V.

It would be hard to find a more beautiful setting for lodging than this. Surrounded by tall pines, all suites face the Fall River, and all feature private riverfront decks and either full or partial kitchens. The spa suites are equipped with two-person spas, fireplaces, sitting rooms with cathedral ceilings, and king-size beds. One-bedroom suites offer king-size beds, window seats, two TVs, and bathrooms with whirlpool tub and shower combinations. There's also a year-round outdoor hot tub. VCRs, in-room movies, and fax service are available, and special-occasion packages can be arranged year-round.

Romantic RiverSong Inn. P.O. Box 1910, Estes Park, CO 80517. ☎ **970/586-4666.** Fax 970/577-0699. www.romanticriversong.com. E-mail: riversng@frii.com. 9 units. $150–$275 double. Rates include full breakfast. MC, V. Not suitable for small children.

A 1920 Craftsman mansion on the Big Thompson River, this elegant bed-and-breakfast has 27 forested acres with hiking trails and a trout pond, as well as prolific wildlife and beautiful wildflowers. Very quiet, the inn is at the end of a country lane, the first right off Mary's Lake Road after it branches off U.S. 36 south. The cozy bedrooms are decorated with a blend of antique and modern country furniture. Some feature ornate brass beds and clawfoot tubs; all have large tubs and separate showers; and several units offer jetted tubs for two. All come with fireplaces. Smoking is not permitted. Gourmet candlelight dinners are available by advance arrangement ($69 per couple), but you must supply your own alcoholic beverages.

Stanley Hotel. 333 Wonderview Ave. (P.O. Box 1767), Estes Park, CO 80517. ☎ **800/976-1377** or 970/586-3371. Fax 970/586-3673. 135 units. TV TEL. Late May to mid-Oct $159–$209 double, $269–$299 suite; mid-Oct to late May $129–$179 double, $219–$249 suite. AE, DISC, MC, V.

F. O. Stanley, inventor of the Stanley Steam Car (the Stanley Steamer), built this elegant, white-pillared hotel in 1909. The equal of European resorts of the time, it was constructed into solid rock at a height of 7,800 feet on the eastern slope of the Colorado Rockies. Today the hotel and its grounds are listed on the National Register of Historic Places, designated the Stanley Historic District. The entire building, including guest rooms and public spaces, was remodeled in 1997. As is often the case in historic hotels, each room differs in size and shape, offering a variety of views of Longs Peak, Lake Estes, and surrounding hillsides. Amenities include a heated outdoor pool, tennis and volleyball courts, sundeck, access to a nearby health club, two restaurants, shops, and a business center. Rooms come with hair dryers.

Streamside Cabins. 1260 Fall River Rd., Moraine Rte. (P.O. Box 2930), Estes Park, CO 80517. ☎ **800/321-3303** or 970/586-6464. Fax 970/586-6272. www.streamsidecabins. com. E-mail: resv@streamsidecabins.com. 19 units. TV. Late Oct–early May $75–$145 double; early May–late Oct $95–$225 double; extra person $15. AE, DISC, MC, V.

These cabin suites, on 17 acres along the Fall River, about a mile west of Estes Park on U.S. 34, are surrounded by woods and meadows of wildflowers. Deer, elk, and occasional bighorn sheep are such regular visitors that many have been given names.

Everything is top drawer inside these cabins. All have king- or queen-size beds, fireplaces, cable TV, VCRs, and decks or patios with gas grills. Most also have full kitchens, and many have beamed cathedral ceilings, skylights, and whirlpool tubs or steam showers.

Guests also have use of an indoor hot tub/swim spa and can wander the nature trails on the property. A variety of special-occasion packages are offered.

Moderate

All Budget Inn. 945 Moraine Ave., Estes Park, CO 80517. ☎ **800/628-3438** or 970/586-3485. www.allbudgetinn.com. 15 units. TV TEL. Summer $69–$99; rest of year $49–$69. MC, V. Pets accepted.

This pleasant motel offers simple rooms with homey touches such as fresh flowers, and nature prints adorning the white walls. Units have firm queen beds, a coffee pot and coffee, small refrigerator, and shower-tub combos; some units have kitchenettes and private balconies.

Allenspark Lodge Bed & Breakfast. 184 Main St., Colo. 7 Business Loop (P.O. Box 247), Allenspark, CO 80510. ☎ **303/747-2552.** 14 units (7 with bathroom). $65–$135 double. Rates include breakfast. AE, DISC, MC, V. Children 14 and older welcome.

There's a historic ambience to this three-story lodge, which was built in 1933 of hand-hewn ponderosa pine logs and includes a large native stone fireplace. Located 16 miles south of Estes Park, in a tiny village at the southeast corner of the national park, all lodge rooms offer mountain views and original handmade 1930s pine furniture. At the top end is the Hideaway Room, with a queen-size brass bed, bear-claw-footed tub, fine linens, and a gas-log stove. Guests share the large sunroom, the stone fireplace in the Great Room, Ping-Pong and videos in the recreation room, and books in the library. A hot family-style breakfast, afternoon and evening coffee, tea, and cookies are complimentary. There's also a hot tub, self-service laundry, conference rooms, espresso coffee shop, and wine and beer bar.

Baldpate Inn. 4900 S. Colo. 7 (P.O. Box 4445), Estes Park, CO 80517. ☎ **970/586-6151.** www.baldpateinn.com. E-mail: baldpatein@aol.com. 13 units (4 with bathroom), 3 cabins. $85 double with shared bathroom, $100 double with private bathroom; $140 cabin. Rates include full breakfast. DISC, MC, V. Closed Nov–Apr.

Built in 1917, the Baldpate was named for the novel Seven Keys to Baldpate, a murder mystery in which seven visitors believe each possesses the only key to the hotel. In 1996, the Baldpate was added to the National Register of Historic Places. Guests today can watch several movie versions of the story, read the book, and add their keys to the hotel's collection of more than 20,000 keys.

Baldpate is located 7 miles south of Estes Park, adjacent to Rocky Mountain National Park at an elevation of 9,000 feet. Guests can enjoy complimentary refreshments by the handsome stone fireplace in the lobby, relax on the large sundeck, or view free videos on the library VCR. But it might be difficult to stay inside once you experience the spectacular views from the inn's spacious porch and see the nature trails beckoning. Each of the early-20th-century–style rooms is unique, with handmade quilts on the beds. In summer, an excellent soup-and-salad buffet is served for lunch and dinner daily (see "Where to Dine," below). Smoking is not permitted.

✪ **Estes Park Center/YMCA of the Rockies.** 2515 Tunnel Rd., Estes Park, CO 80511-2550. ☎ **970/586-3341,** or 303/448-1616 direct from Denver. www.ymcarockies. org. E-mail: info@ymcarockies.org. 510 lodge rms (450 with bathroom), 205 cabins. Lodge rooms, summer $52–$120, winter $41–$92; cabins, year-round $60–$239. YMCA membership required (available at a nominal charge). No credit cards. Pets are permitted in the cabins, but not the lodge rooms.

This extremely popular family resort is an ideal place to get away from it all, and serves as a great home base while exploring the Estes Park area. Lodge units are basic but perfectly adequate, and many were completely renovated in 1998. The spacious mountain cabins are equipped with two to four bedrooms (accommodating up to 10), complete kitchens, and phones; some have fireplaces. The center, which occupies 860 wooded acres, offers hiking, horseback riding, miniature golf, an indoor heated swimming pool and children's pool, fishing, bicycling (rentals available), three tennis courts, and cross-country skiing. Other facilities include conference rooms and a self-service laundry.

Glacier Lodge. Colo. 66 (P.O. Box 2656), Estes Park, CO 80517. ☎ **800/523-3920** or 970/586-4401; www.glacierlodge.com. 28 units. TV. Early June–late Aug $95–$160; late May–early June and late Aug–late Sept $85–$130. Early May–late May and late Sept–Oct $80–$98. Closed Nov–Apr. MC, V.

Deer and elk frequently visit these lovely cottages, which are spread across 15 acres of woodland along the Big Thompson River. Poolside chalets sleep up to six; cozy, homey river duplexes with outside decks overlook the stream; and river triplexes range from earthy to country quaint in decor. All have a porch or patio, and almost all feature kitchens and fireplaces, with a bundle of wood delivered daily. Facilities include a swimming pool, sport court, playground, fishing, gift shop, ice cream shop, lending library, and stables. Breakfast cookouts, barbecues, and special kids' activities are held in summer, at an extra charge.

Camping
In addition to the following commercial campgrounds in the Estes Park area, see "Camping," in "Rocky Mountain National Park," later in this section.

Estes Park KOA. 2051 Big Thompson Ave., Estes Park, CO 80517. ☎ **800/562-1887** for reservations, or 970/586-2888. www.estes-park.com/koa. E-mail: koa@estes-park.com. 62 sites. $22–$30 per campsite for two people. Extra person $3. Rates include cable TV hookups. Open mid-Apr through late Oct.

This member of the reliable national KOA campground chain is located across the street from Lake Estes and within walking distance of the Big Thompson River, about 1 mile east of Estes Park on U.S. 34. Although it lacks a swimming pool, it does offer a scenic location, cable TV hookups, a basketball court, and a game room. It also sells LP gas. In addition to the campsites, there are 16 cabins ($44–$52 double) and five teepees ($32 double). There are fire pits in the tent and cabin areas, but not at RV sites.

Mary's Lake Campground. 2120 Mary's Lake Rd. (P.O. Box 2514), Estes Park, CO 80517. ☎ **800/445-6279** or 970/586-4411. Fax 970/586-4493. www.gocampingamerica.com/maryslake. E-mail: maryslake@gocampingamerica.com. 150 sites. $21–$27 per campsite for two people. Extra person (over age 5) $2. Rates include cable TV hookups; $2 extra for A/C or electric heater use. Open May–Sept. AE, DISC, MC, V.

Campsites are available here for everything from tents to 40-foot RVs, with full hookups available. Facilities include bathhouses, laundry, dump station, playground, basketball court, small store, heated swimming pool, and game room. Fishing licenses as well as bait and tackle can be obtained for shore fishing at the lake as well as stream fishing in the national park.

National Park Resort, Cabins, and Campground. 3501 Fall River Rd., Estes Park, CO 80517. ☎ **970/586-4563.** www.estes-park.com/nationalparkresort. 100 sites; 9 cabins. $25–$27 per campsite for two people; extra person $2. Cabins $90–$150; extra person $10. DISC, MC, V. Campground open May–Sept; cabins open year-round.

This wooded campground can accommodate both tents and RVs. Full hookups include electric, water, sewer, and cable TV. Facilities include bathhouses, laundry, grocery store, and a livery stable. There are also some pleasant cabins with TVs.

Spruce Lake R.V. Park. U.S. 36 and Mary's Lake Rd. (P.O. Box 2497), Estes Park, CO 80517. ☎ **970/586-2889.** www.estes-park.com/sprucelake. E-mail: sprucelake@estes-park.com. 110 sites. $19–$32. Extra fees for cable TV and A/C or electric heater use. MC, V. Open Apr–Oct 15.

The meticulously well-maintained Spruce Lake offers a heated pool, free miniature golf, large playground, stocked private fishing lake, large sites, and spotless rest room/shower facilities. There are Sunday pancake breakfasts and weekly ice cream socials. Ground tents are not permitted. Reservations are strongly recommended, especially in summer.

WHERE TO DINE

In addition to the restaurants described here, see the discussion on the Lazy B Ranch under "Arts & Entertainment," below.

✪ **Baldpate Inn.** 4900 S. Colo. 7. ☎ **970/586-6151.** www.baldpateinn.com. Reservations recommended. Buffet $10.75 adults, $8.25 children under 10. DISC, MC, V. Memorial Day–Sept daily 11:30am–8pm. SOUP/SALAD.

Don't be misled by the simple cuisine—the buffet is deliciously filling and plentiful. Everything is freshly prepared on the premises, with the cooks barely staying one muffin ahead of the guests. Soups—a choice of two is offered each day—include hearty stews, chili, a marvelous chicken rice, garden vegetable, and classic French onion. The salad bar provides fresh greens and an array of toppings, chunks of cheese, and fruit and vegetable salads. Honey-wheat bread is a staple, plus wonderful rolls, muffins, and cornbread. Topping off the meal are fresh homemade pies and cappuccino. Smoking is not permitted. See also the listing for the Baldpate Inn under "Where to Stay," above.

Dunraven Inn. 2470 Colo. 66. ☎ **970/586-6409.** Reservations highly recommended. Main courses $7–$32. AE, DISC, MC, V. Sun–Thurs 5–10pm, Fri–Sat 5–11pm; closes slightly earlier in winter. ITALIAN.

The decor here is eclectic, to say the least: Images of the Mona Lisa are scattered about, ranging from a mustachioed lady to opera posters, and autographed dollar bills are posted in the lounge area. House specialties include shrimp scampi, linguine with white clam sauce, and Dunraven Italiano (an 11-ounce charbroiled sirloin steak in a sauce of peppers, onions, and tomatoes). There's a wide choice of pastas, seafood, vegetarian plates, and desserts, plus a children's menu.

Estes Park Brewery. 470 Prospect Village Dr. ☎ **970/586-5421.** Sandwiches and salads $4.95–$6.95; dinners $9.95–$15.95. AE, CB, DC, DISC, MC, V. Summer daily 11am–midnight; closes earlier in winter. AMERICAN.

Pizzas, burgers, sandwiches—including meatball and grilled turkey—and bratwurst made with the brewery's own beer are the fare here. Vegetarians can order a veggie burger and a variety of salads; kids can choose from a children's menu. In addition, a number of full dinners are also offered, ranging from barbecued chicken to Rocky Mountain rainbow trout to steak. The brewery specializes in Belgian-style ales, such as Longs Peak Raspberry Wheat, and also produces an excellent India pale ale.

Grumpy Gringo. 1560 Big Thompson Ave. (U.S. 34). ☎ **970/586-7705.** www.grumpygringo. com. E-mail: eat@grumpygringo.com. $4.95–$14.95. AE, DISC, MC, V. Daily 11am–10pm summer, 11am–8pm the rest of the year. Closed last week of Jan and first week of Feb. On U.S. 34, 1 mile east of the junction of U.S. highways 34 and 36. MEXICAN.

This classy restaurant has private booths, white-washed plaster walls, green plants and bright poppies for a splash of color, and a few choice sculptures that give the feeling of high-cost dining. And although the food is excellent and portions are large, the prices are surprisingly low. The most popular item is the burrito—and there are several varieties; the enchilada olé is huge and is actually three enchiladas: one each of cheese, beef, and chicken; and the fajitas—either chicken or beef—are delicious. There are six sauces to choose from, each homemade, and rated mild, semi-hot, or hot. Burgers and sandwiches are also offered. The house specialty drink is the Gringo Margarita—made with Jose Cuervo gold tequila from an original (and secret) recipe.

Molly B. 200 Moraine Ave. ☎ **970/586-2766.** Reservations recommended for dinner. Breakfast $3–$7, lunch $5–$8, dinner $8–$17. AE, MC, V. Year-round Thurs–Tues 6:30am–3pm; May–Oct 4–9pm. AMERICAN.

The friendly staff makes you feel right at home in this casual, popular restaurant. Menu choices include vegetarian entrees, fresh seafood, pasta, prime rib, and steak. Desserts are homemade, and a children's menu is available. In good weather, you can sit on the patio.

Arts & Entertainment

There is no lack of entertainment in Estes Park, especially in summer. Choices range from chamber music concerts to Broadway musicals to knee-slapping western music. For details on what's going on when you plan to be in town, contact the **Cultural Arts Council of Estes Park,** P.O. Box 4135, Estes Park, CO 80517 (☎ **970/586-9203,** an umbrella organization for about 30 area arts groups.

Among individual organizations presenting live productions is the **Fine Arts Guild of the Rockies,** which sponsors a musical and two plays each year; in the past these have included *South Pacific, Crimes of the Heart, Mame,* and *Harvey.* The Guild also produces arts-and-crafts shows and festivals. **Estes Park Music Festival** presents a series of classical music concerts each summer, and the **Chamber Music Society of Estes Park** offers several concerts in September.

The historic **Stanley Hotel,** 333 Wonderview Ave. (☎ **800/ROCKIES** or 970/586-3371), offers free concerts Sunday afternoon from September through April, plus a variety of other live performances. See "Where to Stay," above.

The **Lazy B Ranch,** 1915 Dry Gulch Rd. (☎ **800/228-2116** or 970/586-5371), serves a chuck-wagon supper with a show of live western music and comedy. There's also a program on the history of western music. Cost is $15 for everyone 13 and older, $12 for those 10 to 12 years old, and $8 for children 3 to 9. To reach Lazy B, take U.S. 34 east from Estes Park about 1½ miles, turn left at Sombrero Stables, and follow the signs. The ranch is open from late May through September, but the schedule varies so call for specific times and days.

For live rock music and dancing, check out **Lonigan's Saloon,** 110 W. Elkhorn Ave. (☎ **970/586-4346**).

✪ ROCKY MOUNTAIN NATIONAL PARK

Snow-covered peaks—17 mountains above 13,000 feet—stand over lush valleys and shimmering alpine lakes in the 415 square miles (265,727 acres) that comprise Rocky Mountain National Park. The highest, at 14,255 feet, is Longs Peak.

But what really sets the park apart (after all, this sort of eye-popping beauty is not unusual in the Rockies) is its variety of distinct ecological zones. As you rise and descend in altitude, the landscape of the park changes dramatically. In relatively low areas, from about 7,500 to 9,000 feet, a lush forest of ponderosa pine and juniper cloaks the sunny southern slopes, with Douglas fir on the cooler northern slopes. Thirstier blue spruce and lodgepole pine cling to streamsides, with occasional groves of aspen. Elk and mule deer thrive. On higher slopes, a subalpine ecosystem exists, dominated by forests of Engelmann spruce and subalpine fir, but interspersed with wide meadows alive with wildflowers during spring and summer. This is also home to bighorn sheep, which have become unofficial mascots of the park. Above 11,500 feet, the trees become increasingly gnarled and stunted, until they disappear altogether and alpine tundra predominates. Fully one-third of the park is at this altitude, and in this bleak, rocky world, many of the plants are identical to those found in the Arctic.

Trail Ridge Road, which cuts west through the middle of the park from Estes Park, then south down its western boundary to Grand Lake, is one of America's great alpine highways. Climbing to 12,183 feet near Fall River Pass, it's the highest continuous paved highway in the United States. The road is usually open from Memorial Day into October, depending on the snowfall. The 48-mile scenic drive from Estes Park to Grand Lake takes about 3 hours, allowing for stops at numerous scenic outlooks. Exhibits at the **Alpine Visitor Center** (open in summer daily from 9am to 5pm) at Fall River Pass, 11,796 feet above sea level, explain life on the alpine tundra.

Fall River Road, the original park road, leads to Fall River Pass from Estes Park via Horseshoe Park Junction. West of the Endovalley picnic area, the road is one-way uphill, and closed to trailers and motor homes. As you negotiate its gravelly switchbacks, you get a clear idea of what early auto travel was like in the West. This road, too, is closed in winter.

One of the few paved roads in the Rockies that leads into a high mountain basin is **Bear Lake Road;** it is kept open year-round, with occasional half-day closings to clear snow. Numerous trails converge at Bear Lake, southwest of the Park Headquarters/Visitor Center, via Moraine Park.

JUST THE FACTS

ENTRY POINTS   Entry into the park is from either the east (through Estes Park) or the west (through Grand Lake). The two sides are connected by the **Trail Ridge Road.** Most visitors enter the park from the Estes Park side. The **Beaver Meadows entrance,** west of Estes Park via U.S. 36, is the national park's main entrance. U.S. 34 west from Estes Park takes you to the **Fall River entrance** (north of the Beaver Meadows entrance). Those entering the park from the west side should take U.S. 40 to Granby and then follow U.S. 34 north to the **Grand Lake entrance.**

VISITOR CENTERS & INFORMATION   Entering the park from Estes Park, the **Beaver Meadows Visitor Center,** U.S. 36, west of Colo. 66 (☎ **970/586-1206**), has knowledgeable people to answer questions and give advice, a wide choice of books and maps for sale, and interpretive exhibits, including a relief model of the park and an audiovisual program. In summer, this center is open daily from 8am to 9pm; in winter, daily from 8am to 5pm.

Just outside the park, just east of the Fall River entrance, is the new **Fall River Visitor Center,** which was completed in the summer of 2000. Located in a beautiful mountain lodge-style building, it was built with private funds but is staffed by park rangers and volunteers from the Rocky Mountain Nature Association. It contains exhibits on park wildlife, including some spectacular full-size bronzes of elk and other animals, plus information and a bookstore. Next door is a large (but somewhat pricey) souvenir and clothing shop plus a cafeteria-style restaurant with snacks and sandwiches. Summer hours are 8am to 8pm daily, with shorter hours at other times.

Near the park's west side entrance is the **Kawuneeche Visitor Center** (☎ 970/627-3471), open in summer daily from 8am to 6pm, in winter daily from 8am to 4:30pm. Located high in the mountains (11,796 feet above sea level) is the **Alpine Visitor Center,** at Fall River Pass, open in summer only, daily from 9am to 5pm; exhibits here explain life on the alpine tundra. Visitor facilities are also available at the **Moraine Park Museum** on Bear Lake Road, open mid-April to mid-October, daily from 9am to 5pm.

For more specifics on planning a trip, contact Superintendent, Rocky Mountain National Park, Estes Park, CO 80517 (☎ **970/586-1206;** www.nps.gov/romo). You can also get detailed information from the **Rocky Mountain Nature Association,** P.O. Box 3100, Estes Park, CO 80517 (☎ **800/816-7662** or 970/586-0108; www.rmna.org/bookstore), which sells a variety of maps, guides, books, and videos (including some in PAL format). Those who would like to help this nonprofit association and receive a 15% discount on purchases at this and most other national parks and monuments can join. Memberships cost $25 for individuals and $35 for families.

FEES & REGULATIONS   Park admission is $10 per week per vehicle, $5 for bicyclists and pedestrians. An annual park pass costs $25.

As is true for most of the national parks, wilderness permits are required for all overnight backpacking trips, and camping is allowed only in specified campsites. Pets must be leashed at all times and are not permitted on trails or in the backcountry. Both motor vehicles and bicycles must remain on the roads or in parking areas. Do not feed or touch any park animals, and do not pick any wildflowers.

SEASONS   Even though the park is technically open daily year-round, Trail Ridge Road, the main east–west thoroughfare through the park, is almost always closed in winter. The road is usually open by late May (after the snow has been cleared) and closes again between mid- and late October. However, it is not uncommon for snowstorms to close the road for several hours or even a full day at any time, especially in early June and October. The high country is open during the summer and as snow conditions permit in winter.

AVOIDING THE CROWDS   Because large portions of the park are closed half the year, practically everyone visits during the other half of the year—spring and summer. The busiest period, though, is from mid-June to mid-August—essentially during school vacations. In order to avoid the largest crowds, try to visit just before or just after that period. For those who don't mind chilly evenings, late September and early October are less crowded and can be beautiful, although there's always the chance of an early winter storm. Regardless of when you visit, the absolute best way to avoid crowds is by putting on a backpack or climbing onto a horse. Rocky Mountain has almost 350 miles of trails leading into all corners of the park (see "Sports & Outdoor Activities In & Around the Park," below).

RANGER PROGRAMS   Campfire talks and other programs are offered at each visitor center between June and September. Consult the park's free High Country

Rocky Mountain National Park

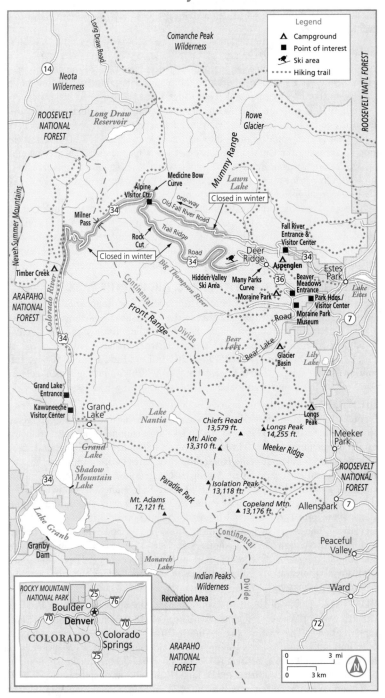

Legend
- △ Campground
- ■ Point of interest
- 🎿 Ski area
- ·········· Hiking trail

Comanche Peak Wilderness

Long Draw Road

14 Neota Wilderness

ROOSEVELT NATIONAL FOREST

Long Draw Reservoir

Rowe Glacier

Mummy Range

Lawn Lake

Closed in winter

Medicine Bow Curve

Alpine Visitor Ctr.

one-way

Old Fall River Road

34

Milner Pass

Trail Ridge

Rock Cut

Road

34

Closed in winter

Big Thompson River

Continental

Front Range

Divide

Neversummer Mountains

Timber Creek △

Colorado River

ARAPAHO NATIONAL FOREST

34

Fall River Entrance & Visitor Center

Deer Ridge

■ Aspenglen

Beaver Meadows Entrance

34

Many Parks Curve

Hidden Valley Ski Area

36

Moraine Park ■

Park Hdqs./ Visitor Center

Moraine Park Museum

Estes Park

Lake Estes

7

Bear Lake

Road

Bear Lake

△ Glacier Basin

Lily Lake

Grand Lake Entrance ■

Kawuneeche Visitor Center

Grand Lake

Lake Nantia

Chiefs Head 13,579 ft.
△

Mt. Alice 13,310 ft. △

Longs Peak 14,255 ft. △

Longs Peak ○

Meeker Park ○

Grand Lake

Shadow Mountain Lake

34

Meeker Ridge

ROOSEVELT NATIONAL FOREST

Paradise Park

Isolation Peak 13,118 ft. △

Allenspark ○

7

Mt. Adams 12,121 ft. △

Copeland Mtn. 13,176 ft. △

Lake Granby

Granby Dam

Monarch Lake

Continental

Divide

Indian Peaks Wilderness Recreation Area

ARAPAHO NATIONAL FOREST

Peaceful Valley ○

Ward ○

72

ROCKY MOUNTAIN NATIONAL PARK

25

76

Boulder

70 ★ Denver 70

COLORADO

Colorado Springs

25

0   3 mi
0   3 km

ROOSEVELT NAT'L FOREST

Headlines newspaper for scheduled activities, which vary from photo walks to fly-fishing and orienteering.

SEEING THE HIGHLIGHTS

Although Rocky Mountain National Park is generally considered the domain of hikers and climbers, it's surprisingly easy to thoroughly enjoy this park without working up a sweat. For that we can thank **Trail Ridge Road.**

Built in 1932 and undoubtedly one of America's most scenic highways, it provides expansive and sometimes dizzying views in all directions. The drive from Estes Park to Grand Lake covers some 48 miles through the park, rising above 12,000 feet in elevation and crossing the Continental Divide. It offers spectacular vistas of snowcapped peaks, deep forests, and meadows of wildflowers, where bighorn sheep, elk, and deer browse. Allow at least 3 hours for the drive, and possibly more if you'd like to take a short hike from one of the many vista points.

To get a close look at the tundra, pull off Trail Ridge Road into the **Rock Cut** parking area (elevation 12,110 feet), about halfway along the scenic drive. The views of glacially carved peaks along the Continental Divide are spectacular, and signs on the half-mile Tundra Nature Trail identify the hardy plants and animals that inhabit the region and explain how they have adapted to the harsh environment.

SPORTS & OUTDOOR ACTIVITIES IN & AROUND THE PARK

Estes Park is a major center for outdoor recreation. In addition to Rocky Mountain National Park, many activities take place in the 1,240-square-mile Roosevelt National Forest. Obtain information on hiking, horseback riding, fishing, and other activities in advance from the **Canyon Lakes Ranger District Office,** 1311 S. College Ave., Fort Collins, CO 80524 (☎ **970/498-2770**). In Estes Park, a **Forest Service Information Center** is located at 161 Second St. (☎ **970/586-3440**); it's open daily from 9am to 5pm in summer, and is also open occasionally in winter.

BICYCLING   Bicyclists must pay a $5 weekly fee to enter Rocky Mountain National Park, and in most cases will have to share the roadways with motor vehicles along narrow roads with 5% to 7% grades. Like most national parks, bikes are not permitted off established roads. However, bicyclists still enjoy the challenge and scenery. One popular 16-mile ride is the **Horseshoe Park/Estes Park Loop,** which goes from Estes Park west on U.S. 34 past Aspenglen Campground and the park's Fall River entrance, and then heads east again at the Deer Ridge Junction, following U.S. 36 through the Beaver Meadows park entrance. There are plenty of beautiful mountain views; allow from 1 to 3 hours. A free park brochure provides information on safety, regulations, and other suggested routes. Tours, rentals, and repairs are available at **Colorado Bicycling,** 184 E. Elkhorn Ave., Estes Park (☎ **970/586-4241;** www.coloradobicycling.com). Bike rentals start at about $5 per hour ($21 per day), and the company also offers guided downhill trips in the park ranging in price from about $50 to $70 per person.

BOATING   The small Lake Estes, with a marina a half-mile east of Estes Park along U.S. 34, covers 185 acres. It's popular with boaters and fishermen, although a bit cool for swimming. The marina (☎ **970/586-2011;** www.estesvalleyrecreation.com), open during the summer, sells fishing licenses and supplies (plus a few groceries) and rents boats and bikes. Canoes rent for $10 an hour, paddleboats for $15 an hour, fishing boats with a small outboard motor for $17 an hour, small sport boats for $19 an hour, and seven-person pontoon boats for $31 an hour. Rental mountain bikes cost $5 per hour, tandem bikes cost $6 an hour, and surrey bikes cost $12 per hour.

CLIMBING & MOUNTAINEERING **Colorado Mountain School,** P.O. Box 1846, Estes Park, CO 80517 (☎ **888/CMS-7783** or 970/586-5758; www. www.2. gorp.com/cms; E-mail cmschool@cmschool.com), is an AMGA accredited year-round guide service, and the sole concessionaire for technical climbing and instruction in Rocky Mountain National Park. The school has programs for all ages. The most popular climb is Longs Peak (the highest mountain in the park). It can be ascended by those without experience via the "Keyhole," but its north and east faces are for experts only. Rates vary, and the larger the group the less per person, but the base rates for one person for half- and full-day excursions ranges from $75 to $300. The school also offers lodging in a hostel-type setting, at about $20 per night per person. (See also "Hiking & Backpacking," below.) Be sure to stop at the ranger station at the Longs Peak trailhead for current trail and weather information before attempting to ascend Longs Peak.

EDUCATIONAL PROGRAMS The **Rocky Mountain Nature Association** (see contact information under "Visitor Centers & Information," above), offers a wide variety of seminars and workshops, ranging from one full day to several days. Subjects vary, but might include songbirds, flower identification, edible and medicinal herbs, painting, wildlife photography, tracking park animals, and edible mushrooms. Rates are about $55 to $65 for full-day programs, and $85 to $195 for multiday programs. There is also a series of special kids' programs at a cost of $15. Nature Association members receive 10% discounts.

FISHING Four species of trout are fished in national park and national forest streams and lakes: brown, rainbow, brook, and cutthroat. A state fishing license is required, and only artificial lures or flies are permitted in the park. A number of lakes and streams in the national park are closed to fishing, including Bear Lake; you'll find a list of open and closed bodies of water plus regulations and other information in a free park brochure that's available at visitor centers. Trout fishermen also head to Lake Estes (see "Boating," above).

GOLF There are two nearby courses: **Estes Park Golf Course** (18 holes), 1080 S. St. Vrain St. (☎ **970/586-8146**), just off Colo. 7, charges a nonresident fee of $33 for 18 holes; and **Lake Estes 9 Hole Golf Course,** 690 Big Thompson Hwy. (☎ **970/586-8176**), along U.S. 34 east of downtown Estes Park, charges nonresidents $11 for 9 holes. Information on both courses is available online at www. estesvalleyrecreation.com

HIKING & BACKPACKING Park visitor centers offer U.S. Geological Survey topographic maps and guidebooks for sale, and rangers can direct you to lesser-used trails. Keep in mind that all trails here start at over—sometimes well over—7,000 feet elevation, and even the easiest and flattest walks will likely be tiring for those accustomed to lower elevations.

One particularly enjoyable (and easy) hike is the **Alberta Falls Trail** from the Glacier Gorge Parking Area (0.6 miles one-way), which rises in elevation only 160 feet as it follows Glacier Creek to pretty Alberta Falls.

A slightly more difficult option is the **Bierstadt Lake Trail,** accessible from the north side of Bear Lake Road about 6.4 miles from Beaver Meadows. This 1.4-mile (one-way) trail climbs 566 feet through an aspen forest to Bierstadt Lake, where you'll find excellent views of Longs Peak.

Starting at Bear Lake, the trail up to **Emerald Lake** offers spectacular scenery en route, past Nymph and Dream lakes. The half-mile hike to Nymph Lake is easy, climbing 225 feet; from there the trail is rated moderate to Dream Lake (another

0.6 miles) and then on to Emerald Lake (another 0.7 miles), which is 605 feet higher than the starting point at Bear Lake. Another moderate hike is the relatively uncrowded **Ouzel Falls Trail,** which leaves from Wild Basin Ranger Station and climbs about 950 feet to a picture-perfect waterfall. The distance one-way is 2.7 miles.

Among our favorite moderate hikes here is the **Mills Lake Trail,** a 2½-mile (one-way) hike, with a rise in elevation of about 700 feet. Starting from Glacier Gorge Junction, the trail goes up to a picturesque mountain lake, nestled in a valley among towering mountain peaks. This lake is an excellent spot for photographing dramatic Longs Peak, especially in late afternoon or early evening, and it's the perfect place for a picnic.

If you prefer a more strenuous adventure, you'll work hard but be amply rewarded with views of timberline lakes and alpine tundra on the **Timber Lake Trail,** in the western part of the park. It's 4.8 miles one-way, with an elevation gain of 2,060 feet. Another strenuous trail, only for experienced mountain hikers and climbers in top physical condition, is the 8-mile (one-way) **East Longs Peak Trail,** which climbs some 4,855 feet along steep ledges and through narrows to the top of Longs Peak.

Backcountry permits (required for all overnight hikes) can be obtained at Park Headquarters and ranger stations (in summer) for $15 from May through October, and free from November through April; for information call ☎ **970/586-1242.** There is a 7-night backcountry camping limit from June to September, with no more than 3 nights at any one spot. Tents are not permitted in the backcountry in summer.

HORSEBACK RIDING   Many of the national park's trails are open to horseback riders, and a number of outfitters provide guided rides both within and outside the park ranging from 1 hour (about $20) to all day (about $80), plus breakfast and dinner rides and multiday pack trips. Recommended companies include **Sombrero Ranch Riding Stables,** opposite the Lake Estes dam at 1895 Big Thompson Hwy. (U.S. 34) (☎ **970/586-4577;** www.sombrero.com); the **National Park Village Stables** at the Fall River entrance of the national park on U.S. 34 (☎ **970/586-5269**); and the **Cowpoke Corner Corral,** at Glacier Lodge 3 miles west of town, 2166 Colo. 66 (☎ **970/586-5890**). **Hi Country Stables** operates two stables inside the park: **Glacier Creek Stables** (☎ **970/586-3244**) and **Moraine Park Stables** (☎ **970/ 586-2327**).

RIVER RAFTING   For trips down the Colorado or Poudre rivers, contact **Rapid Transit Rafting,** P.O. Box 4095, Estes Park, CO 80517 (☎ **800/367-8523** or 970/586-8852); they provide half-day and full-day river trips with transportation from Estes Park, starting at about $45 per person.

SKIING & SNOWSHOEING   Much of the park is closed to vehicular travel during the winter, when deep snow covers roads and trails. Snow is usually best from January through March. A popular spot for cross-country skiing and snowshoeing in the park is Bear Lake, south of the Beaver Meadows entrance. A lesser-known area of the park is Wild Basin, south of the park's east entrances off Colo. 7, about a mile north of the community of Allenspark. A 2-mile road, closed to motor vehicles for the last mile in winter, winds through a subalpine forest to the Wild Basin Trailhead, which follows a creek to a waterfall, a rustic bridge, and eventually to another waterfall. Total distance to the second falls is 2.7 miles. Along the trail, your chances are good for spotting birds such as Clark's nutcrackers, Steller's jays, and the American dipper. On winter weekends, the Colorado Mountain Club often opens a warming hut at the Wild Basin Ranger Station.

Before you set forth, stop by Park Headquarters for maps, information on where the snow is best, and a permit if you plan to stay out overnight. Ski rentals, instruction, and guide service are available from **Colorado Mountain School** (see contact information under "Climbing & Mountaineering," above). Rangers often lead guided snowshoe walks on winter weekends.

SWIMMING   The **Estes Park Aquatic Center,** 660 Community Dr. (☎ 970/586-2340), is open for public and lap swims, lessons, and water aerobics. Call for current schedules and fees.

WILDLIFE VIEWING & BIRD WATCHING   Rocky Mountain National Park is a premier wildlife viewing area; fall, winter, and spring are the best times, although we saw plenty of elk and squirrels, plus a few deer, a marmot, and a coyote during a recent mid-July visit. Large herds of elk and bighorn sheep can often be seen in the meadows and on mountainsides. In addition, you may spot mule deer, beavers, coyotes, and river otters. Watch for moose among the willows on the west side of the park. In the forests are lots of songbirds and small mammals; particularly plentiful are gray and Steller's jays, Clark's nutcrackers, chipmunks, and golden-mantled ground squirrels. There's a good chance of seeing bighorn sheep, marmots, pikas, and ptarmigan along Trail Ridge Road. For detailed and current wildlife viewing information, stop by one of the park's visitor centers, and check on the many interpretive programs, including bird walks. Rangers stress that it is both illegal and foolish to feed any wildlife.

CAMPING

The park has five campgrounds with a total of almost 600 sites. Nearly half (247 sites) are at **Moraine Park;** another 150 are at **Glacier Basin.** Moraine Park, **Timber Creek** (100 sites), and **Longs Peak** (26 tent sites) are open year-round; Glacier Basin and **Aspenglen** (54 sites) are seasonal. Camping in summer is limited to 3 days at Longs Peak and 7 days at other campgrounds; and 14 days at all the park's campgrounds in winter. Arrive early in summer if you hope to snare one of these first-come, first-served campsites. Reservations for Moraine Park and Glacier Basin are accepted from Memorial Day through early September and are usually completely booked well in advance. However, any sites not reserved are available on a first-come first-served basis. Contact the **National Park Reservation Service** (☎ 800/365-2267), or make reservations through the park's website (www.nps.gov/romo). Campsites cost $16 per night during the summer, $10 in the off-season when water is turned off. No showers or RV hookups are available.

7

Colorado Springs

Magnificent scenic beauty, a favorable climate, and dreams of gold have lured visitors to Colorado Springs and neighboring Pikes Peak Country for well over 100 years.

Nearly two centuries ago, in 1806, army lieutenant Zebulon Pike led a company of soldiers on a trek around the base of an enormous mountain. He called it "Grand Peak," declared it unconquerable, and moved on. Today, the 14,110-foot mountain we now know as Pikes Peak has been conquered so often that an auto highway and a cog railway have been built to take visitors to the top.

Unlike many Colorado towns, neither mineral wealth nor ranching was the cornerstone of Colorado Springs' economy during the 19th century—tourism was. In fact, when founded in 1871, Colorado Springs was the first genuine resort community west of Chicago. General William J. Palmer, builder of the Denver & Rio Grande Railroad, established the resort on his rail line, at an elevation of 6,035 feet. The state's growing reputation as a health center, with its high mountains and mineral springs, convinced him to build at the foot of Pikes Peak. In an attempt to lure affluent easterners, he named the resort Colorado Springs, because most fashionable eastern resorts were called "springs." The mineral waters at Manitou Springs were only 5 miles away, and soon Palmer exploited them by installing a resident physician, Dr. Samuel Solly, who exuberantly trumpeted the benefits of Manitou's springs both in print and in person.

The 1890s gold strikes at Cripple Creek, on the southwestern slope of Pikes Peak, added a new dimension to life in Colorado Springs. Among those who cashed in on the boom was Spencer Penrose, a middle-aged Philadelphian and Harvard graduate who arrived in the Springs in 1892, made some astute investments, and became quite rich. Penrose, who believed that the automobile would revolutionize life in the United States, promoted the creation of new highways. To show the effectiveness of motor cars in the mountains, he built (from 1913 to 1915) the Pikes Peak highway, using more than $250,000 of his own money. Then, during World War I, at a cost of more than $2 million, he built the luxurious Broadmoor hotel at the foot of Cheyenne Mountain. World War II brought the military and defense industry to this area, and in 1958 the $200-million U.S. Air Force Academy opened.

Modern Colorado Springs is a growing city of 357,000, with over half a million people in the metropolitan area. The majority of its residents are conservative (one-third of its residents are active or retired military personnel), and in recent years it has developed a reputation for right-wing political activism. The city is also home to some of the country's largest nondenominational churches and conservative groups, such as Focus on the Family.

To many visitors, the city retains the feel and mood of a small western town. Most tourists come to see the Air Force Academy, marvel at the scenery at Garden of the Gods and Pikes Peak, and explore the history of America's West.

1 Orientation

ARRIVING
BY PLANE
Major airlines offer some 100 flights a day to **Colorado Springs Airport,** located north of Drennan Road and east of Powers Boulevard in the southeastern part of the city (☎ **719/550-1900**).

Airlines serving Colorado Springs include **American** (☎ 800/433-7300), **America West** (☎ 800/235-9292), **Continental** (☎ 800/525-0280; www.flycontinental. com), **Delta** (☎ 800/221-1212; www.delta.com), **Mesa** (☎ 800/637-2247), **Northwest** (☎ 800/225-2525), **TWA** (☎ 800/221-2000), and **United** (☎ 800/241-6522).

GETTING TO & FROM THE AIRPORT   The **Colorado Springs Airport Shuttle** (☎ **719/578-5232**) operates direct ground service from Colorado Springs Airport to local hotels and the Denver airport.

BY BUS
Greyhound, Trailways, and **TNM&O Coaches,** 120 S. Weber St. (☎ **719/635-1505**), provide regular service to communities throughout the state.

BY CAR
The principal artery to and from the north (Denver: 70 miles) and south (Pueblo: 42 miles), I-25 bisects Colorado Springs. U.S. 24 is the principal east–west route through the city.

Visitors arriving via I-70 from the east can take exit 359 at Limon and follow U.S. 24 into the Springs. Arriving on I-70 from the west, the most direct route is exit 201 at Frisco, then Colo. 9 through Breckenridge 53 miles to U.S. 24 (at Hartsel), and then east 66 miles to the Springs. This route is mountainous, so check road conditions before setting out in winter.

VISITOR INFORMATION
The **Colorado Springs Convention and Visitors Bureau** is located at 104 S. Cascade Ave., Colorado Springs, CO 80903 (☎ **800/DO-VISIT** or 719/635-7506; fax 719/635-4968; www.coloradosprings-travel.com). Ask for the free *Official Visitor Guide to Colorado Springs and the Pikes Peak Region,* a colorful booklet with a comprehensive listing of accommodations, restaurants, and other visitor services in the area, as well as a basic but efficient map. Inquire at the Visitor Information Center or local bookstores for more detailed maps (an excellent one is the Pierson Graphics Corporation's *Colorado Springs and Monument Valley Street Map*).

The **Visitor Information Center,** located in the Sun Plaza Building at the corner of Cascade and Colorado avenues, is open in summer, daily from 8:30am to 5pm; in winter, Monday through Friday from 8:30am to 5pm. From I-25, take the Bijou Street exit, head east, and turn right at the second stoplight onto Cascade. Just past

the Antlers Adam's Mark Hotel, turn right onto Colorado Avenue, and almost immediately left into the parking lot for the Visitor Information Center. The center also
operates a weekly events line with a 24-hour recording (☎ **719/635-1723**).

Additional information on regional attractions plus accommodations, restaurants,
and special events in the Manitou Springs area can be obtained from the **Manitou
Springs Chamber of Commerce,** 354 Manitou Ave., Manitou Springs, CO 80829
(☎ **800/642-2567** or 719/685-5089; fax 719/685-0355; www.manitousprings.org;
E-mail: manitou@pikespeak.com). You can also contact the **Pikes Peak Country
Attractions Association** at the same address (☎ **800/ 525-2250** or 719/685-5894;
fax 719/685-5873; www.pikes-peak.com; e-mail: ppcaa@pikes-peak.com).

CITY LAYOUT

It's easy to get around central Colorado Springs, since it is laid out on a classic grid
pattern.

If you focus on the intersection of I-25 and U.S. 24, downtown Colorado Springs
lies in the northeast quadrant—bounded on the west by I-25 and on the south by U.S. 24
(Cimarron Street). Boulder Street to the north and Wahsatch Avenue to the east complete the downtown frame. Nevada Avenue (U.S. 85) parallels the freeway for 15 miles
through the city, intersecting it twice; Tejon Street and Cascade Avenue also run
north–south through downtown between Nevada Avenue and the freeway. **Colorado
Avenue** and **Platte Avenue** are the busiest east–west downtown cross streets.

West of downtown, Colorado Avenue extends through the historic Old Colorado
City district and the quaint foothill community of **Manitou Springs,** rejoining
U.S. 24—itself a busy but less interesting artery—as it enters Pike National Forest.

South of downtown, **Nevada Avenue** intersects **Lake Avenue,** the principal boulevard into the Broadmoor, and proceeds south as Colo. 115 past Fort Carson.

North and east of downtown, **Academy Boulevard** (Colo. 83) is the street name to
remember. From the south gate of the Air Force Academy north of the Springs, it
winds through residential hills, crosses Austin Bluff Parkway, then runs without a
curve 8 miles due south, finally bending west to intersect I-25 and Colo. 115 at Fort
Carson. U.S. 24, which exits downtown east as Platte Avenue, and Fountain Boulevard, which leads to the airport, are among its cross streets. Austin Bluffs Parkway
extends west of I-25 as **Garden of the Gods Road,** leading to that natural wonder.

City street addresses are divided by Pikes Peak Avenue into "north" and "south"; by
Nevada Avenue into "east" and "west."

2 Getting Around

Although Colorado Springs has public transportation, most visitors prefer to drive.
Parking and roads are good, and some of the best attractions, such as the Garden of
the Gods, are accessible only by car (or foot or bike for the truly ambitious).

BY CAR

For regulations and advice on driving in Colorado, see "Getting Around," in chap-
ter 2. The **American Automobile Association (AAA)** maintains an office in Colorado
Springs at 3525 N. Carefree Circle (☎ **800/283-5222** or 719/591-2222), open
Monday through Friday from 8:30am to 5:30pm and Saturday from 9am to 1pm.

CAR RENTALS   Car-rental agencies in Colorado Springs, some of which have
offices in or near downtown as well as at the airport, include **Avis** (☎ 800/831-2847
or 719/596-2751), **Budget** (☎ 800/527-0700 or 719/574-7400), **Dollar** (☎ 800/
800-4000 or 719/637-2620), **Enterprise** (☎ 800/736-8222 or 719/636-3900),

Hertz (☎ 800/654-3131 or 719/596-1863), **National** (☎ 800/ 227-7368 or 719/ 596-1519), and **Thrifty** (☎ 800/367-2277 or 719/390-9800).

PARKING   Most downtown streets have parking meters; the rate is 25¢ for a half hour. Look for city-run parking lots, which charge 25¢ per half hour and also offer day rates. Outside of downtown, free parking is generally available on side streets.

BY BUS

City bus service is provided by **Colorado Springs Transit** (☎ **719/385-7433**). Buses operate Monday through Friday from 6am to 10pm, and Saturday from 7am to 2pm, except holidays. Fares on in-city routes are $1.25 for adults; 95¢ students; 60¢ for children 6 to 11, seniors, and the disabled; and free for children under 6. Fares for routes outside the city limits are 35¢ higher. Bus schedules can be obtained at terminals, city libraries, and the Colorado Springs Convention and Visitors Bureau.

In Manitou Springs, the **Town Trolley** (☎ **719/685-1573**) operates daily from early June to Labor Day from 10am to 8pm, and on weekends during September and October, weather permitting. The open-sided trolleys provide 1-hour guided tours through Manitou Springs and the perimeter of Garden of the Gods. A 1-day pass ($2 for adults, $1 for children) allows riders to stop to see the sights and then resume the tour later. The trolleys (named Morris and Charlie) depart from Seven Minute Springs Park every 30 minutes.

BY TAXI

Call **Yellow Cab** (☎ **719/634-5000**) or **American Cab** (☎ **719/637-1111**) for taxi service and tours.

ON FOOT

Each of the main sections of town can easily be explored without a vehicle. It's fun, for instance, to wander the winding streets of Manitou Springs or explore the Old Colorado City "strip." Between neighborhoods, however, distances are considerable. Unless you're particularly fit, it's wise to drive or take a bus or taxi.

Fast Facts: Colorado Springs

American Express   To report a lost card, call ☎ **800/528-4800;** to report lost traveler's checks, call ☎ **800/221-7282.**

Area Code   The telephone area code is **719.**

Baby-sitters   Front desks at major hotels often can make arrangements on your behalf.

Business Hours   Most banks are open Monday through Friday from 9am to 5pm, and some have Saturday hours as well. Major stores are open Monday through Saturday from 9 or 10am until 5 or 6pm, and often Sunday from noon until 5pm. Stores that cater to tourists are usually open longer in the summer with shorter hours in winter. Some may close completely between October and April.

Car Rentals   See "Getting Around," above.

Dentists   For 24-hour referrals, contact Colorado Springs Dental Society Emergency and Referral Service (☎ **719/598-5161**).

Doctors   For referrals, call Healthlink Physician Referral (☎ **719/444-2273**).

Drugstores   Walgreens Drug Stores has a 24-hour prescription service at 920 N. Circle Dr. (☎ **719/473-9090**).

Emergencies   For police, fire, or medical emergencies, call ☎ **911.** To reach **Poison Control,** dial ☎ **800/332-3073.**

Eyeglasses   You can get 1-hour replacement of lost or broken glasses at **Pearle Vision Express** in Citadel Mall (☎ **719/550-0300**). Another good choice is **LensCrafters,** in Erindale Centre on N. Academy Blvd. (☎ **719/548-8650**).

Hospitals   Full medical services, including 24-hour emergency treatment, are offered by **Memorial Hospital,** 1400 E. Boulder St. (☎ **719/365-5000**). The **Penrose–St. Francis Health System** (☎ **719/776-5000**) operates health-care facilities throughout the city.

Newspapers/Magazines   The *Gazette Telegraph,* published daily in Colorado Springs, is the city's most widely read newspaper. Both Denver dailies—the *Denver Post* and *Rocky Mountain News*—are available at newsstands throughout the city. *Springs* magazine and the *Independent* are free arts-and-entertainment tabloids. *USA Today* and the *Wall Street Journal* can be purchased on the streets and at major hotels.

Photographic Needs   There are dozens of photo finishing outlets throughout the city, including **Walgreens Drug Stores** and **Shewmaker's Camera Shop,** in the Woodmen Valley Shopping Center at 6902 N. Academy Blvd. (☎ **719/598-6412**). For camera and video supplies and repairs, as well as photo finishing, go to **Wolf Camera,** 1850 N. Academy Blvd. (☎ **719/597-1575**), or the central location of **Shewmaker's Camera Shop,** downtown at 30 N. Tejon St. (☎ **719/636-1696**).

Post Office   The main post office is downtown at 201 E. Pikes Peak Ave. Call the U.S. Postal Service (☎ **800/275-8777**) for hours and locations of other post offices.

Radio/TV   More than a dozen AM and FM radio stations in the Colorado Springs area cater to all tastes in music, news, sports, and entertainment, including KCME (88.7 FM) for classical and jazz, KSPZ (92.9 FM) for oldies, KILO (94.3 FM) for album-oriented hard rock, KKFM (98.1 FM) for classic rock, KGFT (100.7 FM) and KCBR (1040 AM) for contemporary Christian, KCMN (1530 AM) for big band and hit parade, KKCS (101.9 FM) for country, KRDO (1240 AM) for sports talk, KKLI (106.3 FM) for adult contemporary, and KVOR (1300 AM) for all news.

Major television stations include Channels 5 (NBC), 8 (PBS), 11 (CBS), 13 (ABC), and 21 (FOX). Cable or satellite service is available at most hotels.

Safety   Although Colorado Springs is generally a safe city, it is not crime-free. Try to be aware of your surroundings at all times, and ask at your hotel or the visitor center about the safety of neighborhoods you plan to explore, especially after dark.

Taxes   The Colorado state sales tax is 3%. In Colorado Springs the sales tax is about 7% and the lodging tax is about 9%. Rates in Manitou Springs are about 7.5% for general sales tax and almost 10% for lodging.

Useful Telephone Numbers   For **road conditions** and time, call ☎ **719/630-1111.** For **ski conditions** statewide, call ☎ **303/825-7669.** For **weather** information, phone ☎ **719/475-7599.**

3 Accommodations

You'll find a wide range of lodging possibilities here, from Colorado's fanciest resort—The Broadmoor—to clean, basic budget motels. There are also several particularly nice bed-and-breakfasts. The rates listed here are the officially quoted prices ("rack rates") and don't take into account any individual or group discounts. Generally, rates are highest from Memorial Day to Labor Day, and lowest in the spring. During graduation and other special events at the Air Force Academy, rates will be at their absolute highest, and you may have trouble finding a room at any price.

In addition to the accommodations described below, a number of chain and franchise motels in Colorado Springs offer reliable, moderately priced lodging. These include the **Best Western Palmer House,** 3010 N. Chestnut St., Colorado Springs, CO 80907 (☎ **800/223-9127** or 719/636-5201), which charges $49 to $99 double; **Econo Lodge Downtown,** 714 N. Nevada Ave., Colorado Springs, CO 80903 (☎ **800/553-2666** or 719/636-3385), with rates for two ranging from $35 to $75; and **Super 8,** 4604 Rusina Rd., Colorado Springs, CO 80907 (☎ **800/800-8000** or 719/594-0964), which charges $47 to $80 double.

In these listings, the price ranges, based on the summer rate for a double room, have been defined as follows: **very expensive,** more than $200 per night; **expensive,** $120 to $200; **moderate,** $65 to $120; and **inexpensive,** less than $65. A lodging tax (about 9% in Colorado Springs, almost 10% in Manitou Springs) will be added to all bills.

VERY EXPENSIVE

✪ The Broadmoor. Lake Circle, at Lake Ave. (P.O. Box 1439), Colorado Springs, CO 80901. ☎ **800/634-7711** or 719/634-7711. Fax 719/577-5779. www.broadmoor.com. E-mail: info@broadmoor.com. 700 units. A/C TV TEL. Summer $295–$450 double; $450–$2,000 suite. Winter $195–$325 double; $350–$1,575 suite. Winter packages may cost as little as $99 per person per night. AE, CB, DC, DISC, MC, V. Free parking.

A Colorado Springs institution and a tourist attraction in its own right, The Broadmoor is a sprawling resort complex of historic pink Mediterranean-style buildings with modern additions, set at the foot of Cheyenne Mountain about 3.5 miles southwest of downtown Colorado Springs. Built in the Italian Renaissance style, The Broadmoor opened in 1918. Its marble staircase, chandeliers, della Robbia tile, hand-painted beams and ceilings, and carved-marble fountain remain spectacles today, along with a priceless art collection featuring original work by Toulouse-Lautrec and Ming dynasty ceramicists. The first names entered on the guest register were those of John D. Rockefeller Jr. and his party.

The guest rooms are located in four separate buildings on the 3,000-acre grounds—our favorite, Broadmoor Main, which contains the luxurious lobby, plus adjacent Broadmoor South, Broadmoor West across Cheyenne Lake, and Broadmoor West Tower. The spacious and luxurious rooms are decorated with early–20th-century antiques and original works of art. Most units are furnished with two double beds or one king-size bed, desks and tables, plush seating, secluded luggage areas, and excellent lighting. The service is impeccable: The hotel staffs two employees for every guest.

Dining/Diversions: The elegant Penrose Room, in Broadmoor South, is the hotel's finest restaurant, serving breakfast and dinner daily. Charles Court (see "Dining," below), in Broadmoor West, serves breakfast, high tea, and American continental cuisine for dinner. The Tavern (see "Dining," below), in Broadmoor Main, serves steak and seafood in an informal setting. Offering breakfast daily, the Lake Terrace Dining Room also serves the hotel's award-winning Sunday brunch. More casual are the

Colorado Springs Accommodations & Dining

ACCOMMODATIONS ■

The Antlers Adam's Mark
  Hotel **3**
Best Western Palmer House **25**
The Broadmoor **36**
Cliff House Inn **16**
DoubleTree Hotel World
  Arena **35**
Eastholme in the Rockies **19**
Econo Lodge Downtown **10**
El Colorado Lodge **14**
Hearthstone Inn **2**
Holden House 1902
  Bed & Breakfast Inn **28**
Old Town GuestHouse **29**
Radisson Inn North **3**
Sheraton Colorado
  Springs Hotel **34**
Super 8 **23**
Travel Inn **31**
Two Sisters Inn **11**

DINING ◆

Adams Mountain Cafe **12**
Anthony's **27**
The Blue Star **33**
Briarhurst Manor **13**
Charles Court **37**
Cliff House Inn Dining Room **17**
Craftwood Inn **15**
Dutch Kitchen **18**
Edelweiss Restaurant **32**
Giuseppe's Old Depot
  Restaurant **1**
The Hungry Farmer **24**
Judge Baldwin's Brewing
  Company **4**
La Petite Maison **30**
MacKenzie's Chop House **6**
The Margarita at PineCreek **21**
Marigold's Café & Bakery **22**
Michelle's **9**
Phantom Canyon Brewing
  Co. **5**
Primitivo Wine Bar **7**
The Ritz Grill **8**
Steaksmith **26**
The Tavern **38**

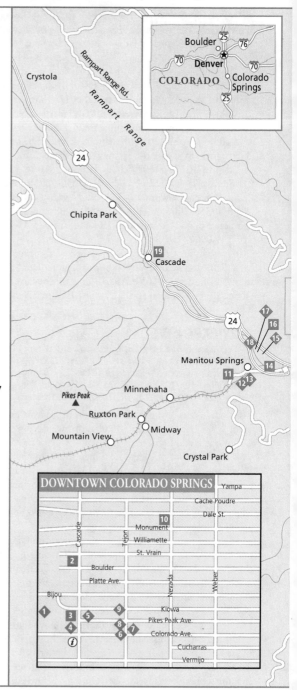

Crystola

Rampart Range Rd.

Rampart Range

24

Chipita Park

Cascade **19**

24

17
16
18
15
Manitou Springs
14
11
12 13

Pikes Peak ▲

Minnehaha

Ruxton Park

Mountain View

Midway

Crystal Park

Boulder 25 76
70 Denver 70
COLORADO Colorado Springs
25

DOWNTOWN COLORADO SPRINGS

Yampa
Cache Poudre
Dale St.
Monument **10**
Williamette
St. Vrain
Cascade
Tejon
Boulder **2**
Platte Ave.
Bijou
Nevada
Weber
Kiowa **9**
Pikes Peak Ave. **3** **5** **8** **7**
Colorado Ave. **4** **6**
ⓘ
Cucharras
Vermijo
1

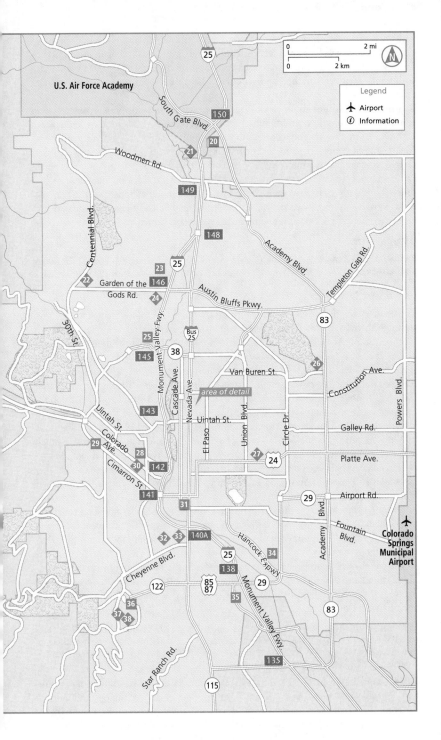

U.S. Air Force Academy

South Gate Blvd.

25

150

20

21

Woodmen Rd.

149

148

Academy Blvd.

Templeton Gap Rd.

25

23

146

22

Garden of the
Gods Rd.

24

Austin Bluffs Pkwy.

83

Monument Valley Fwy.

Bus
25

25

26

145

38

Van Buren St.

Constitution Ave.

30th St.

143

Cascade Ave.

Nevada Ave.

area of detail

Powers Blvd.

Uintah St.

Uintah St.

Union Blvd.

Circle Dr.

Galley Rd.

Colorado
Ave.

El Paso

29

28

30

142

27

24

Platte Ave.

Cimarron St.

141

29

Airport Rd.

31

29

Academy Blvd.

Fountain
Blvd.

✈ Colorado
Springs
Municipal
Airport

32

33

140A

Hancock Expwy.

34

Cheyenne Blvd.

25

138

122

85
87

29

35

83

36

37

38

Monument Valley Fwy.

Star Ranch Rd.

135

115

Golden Bee (see "Colorado Springs After Dark," below), an authentic English pub; Café Julie, a sidewalk eatery serving continental breakfast and light lunches; the Espresso cafe, with gourmet coffee, pastries, and sandwiches; and The Broadmoor Golf Club (members and hotel guests only). There are also six lounges, each to fit a different mood.

Amenities: 24-hour room service, full concierge service, in-room massage, valet laundry, shuttle bus between buildings. Sports and recreational facilities include three 18-hole championship golf courses, three swimming pools, 12 all-weather tennis courts, bicycle rentals, a state-of-the-art fitness center and full-service spa, aerobics classes, saunas, and whirlpool tub. Horseback riding, paddleboating on Cheyenne Lake, and hot-air ballooning are also available. Other facilities include close to 30 shops (boutiques, galleries, jeweler, florist, hair salon, and gift shops), a theater, a car-rental agency, and a service station. Up to 1,600 people can be accommodated for meetings; there are 46 meeting rooms and a conference center.

EXPENSIVE

Antlers Adam's Mark Hotel. 4 S. Cascade Ave., Colorado Springs, CO 80903. ☎ **800/ 444-ADAM** or 719/473-5600. Fax 719/444-0417. www.adamsmark.com. 292 units. A/C TV TEL. $99–$205 double; $250–$700 suite. AE, CB, DC, DISC, ER, JCB, MC, V. Self-parking $6 per day, valet $10.

The Antlers has been a Colorado Springs landmark for more than a century—although there have been three different Antlers on the same site. The first, a turreted Victorian showcase built in 1883, was named for General William Palmer's collection of deer and elk trophies. After it was destroyed by fire in 1898, Palmer built an extravagant Italian Renaissance–style building that survived until 1964, when it was leveled to make room for the more contemporary Antlers Plaza, set off from the street and featuring a modern, 13-story hotel with a rich marble- and woodwork-laden lobby, and spectacular mountain views. That in turn was closed for more than a year after it was purchased by Doubletree Hotels; it reopened in October 1990 after a dramatic face-lift that included the construction of a covered arcade that connects the hotel with a pair of adjacent office buildings In 1998, the property was sold to Adam's Mark. Despite all the changes in ownership and architecture, the Antlers remains one of the top hotels in Colorado Springs, a most impressive facility that is a cut above other high-end chain properties.

Antique black-walnut nightstands from the preceding Antlers provide a touch of historic continuity in guest rooms, which also have two telephones, coffeemakers, and ample closet space. The corner rooms are larger, and the west-side rooms provide great views of the mountains.

The hotel offers a full range of services, including a beauty salon, fitness center, indoor pool, and whirlpool. It has two restaurants, including Colorado Springs' first microbrewery: Judge Baldwin's Brewing Company (see "Dining," and "Colorado Springs After Dark," below).

Cliff House Inn. 306 Cañon Ave., Manitou Springs, CO 80829. ☎ **888/212-7000** or 719/ 685-3000. Fax 719/685-3913. www.thecliffhouse.com. E-mail: information@thecliffhouse. com. 57 units. A/C TV TEL. $129–$189 double, $169–$400 suite. Rates include continental breakfast. AE, CB, DC, DISC, MC, V.

Before reopening in July 1999, the Cliff House underwent a $10-million restoration and renovation to marry its Victorian charm to modern-day technology and amenities. Built in 1873, the Cliff House was designated a National Historic Landmark in 1980, and has hosted such eminent guests as Theodore Roosevelt, Clark Gable, and Thomas Edison. (A fire forced The Cliff House to close in 1982.)

The reconstruction—which began in 1997—incorporated several pieces of the hotel's original decor, including ornate woodwork and a tile fireplace. What the fire destroyed at the hotel was replicated with an emphasis on attention to detail. The net result is a hotel grand both in its public areas and guest rooms.

Today, the lovely, uniquely decorated accommodations vary in size and personality, offering a wide variety of choices from studio to celebrity suites. Some units have gas fireplaces, two-person spas, steam showers, and terrific views of the mountains. All have robes, heated toilet seats, Internet access and modem ports, coffeemakers, hair dryers, and irons and ironing boards. The "Celebrity Suites" are named after famed guests from the hotel's 19th-century heyday, including P.T. Barnum and Katharine Lee Bates, the writer of "America the Beautiful." (It is said that Bates penned a portion of the poem on the hotel's veranda.)

Services include airport pickup, valet parking, valet laundry service, and room service between 7am and 11pm. The Cliff House Inn Dining Room (see "Dining," below) serves breakfast and dinner daily, plus Sunday brunch.

Doubletree Hotel World Arena. 1775 E. Cheyenne Mountain Blvd. (I-25 exit 138), Colorado Springs, CO 80906. ☎ **800/222-TREE** or 719/576-8900. Fax 716/576-4450. www. doubletreehotels.com. 299 units. A/C TV TEL. $69–$149 double; $299–$450 suite. AE, CB, DC, DISC, MC, V. Pets accepted with deposit and by prior arrangement.

This attractive five-story hotel is conveniently located south of downtown Colorado Springs, with easy access to all the sights, particularly the World Arena and Cheyenne Mountain Zoo. Of course, guests receive the Doubletree welcome: freshly baked chocolate-chip cookies.

The oversized rooms are comfortably furnished in contemporary style, with two phones (one with data port), coffeemaker, and iron and ironing board, as well as a hairdryer in the bathroom. Some units have sliding-glass doors leading onto private balconies. West-facing rooms have magnificent views of the mountains, particularly Pikes Peak.

The large indoor pool and whirlpool are very inviting, and adjacent are a delightful patio and fountain, which draw guests outdoors on sunny days—a frequent occurrence in the Springs. Nearby are a spa, dry sauna, and exercise room. Handicap-accessible rooms are available—two have roll-in showers. Other amenities include laundry facilities, a gift shop, business services, valet and room service. The Atrium Cafe serves three meals daily in a pleasant, casual atmosphere, and guests can relax in their Quiet Bar or inhabit a more upbeat scene at Maxi's Lounge, which offers dancing and disc jockeys Thursday through Sunday for the livelier crowd.

✪ Old Town GuestHouse. 115 S. 26th St., Colorado Springs, CO 80904. ☎ **888/ 375-4210** or 719/632-9194. Fax 719/632-9026. www.bbonline.com/co/oldtown. E-mail: oldtown@rmi.net. 8 units. A/C TEL TV. $95–$175 double. AE, DISC, MC, V. Off-road parking. Not recommended for children under 12.

Just a half-block south of the main street of Colorado Springs' historic Old Colorado City stands this three-story red-brick inn. It may appear to be from the 19th century, but innkeepers Kaye and David Caster designed and built it in 1997 to provide all the modern amenities in a warm and inviting atmosphere. To the right of the entryway is an attractive library with fireplace, music, and overstuffed chairs that entice you to relax and stay awhile.

All eight of the guest rooms are individually decorated and named for flowers: for example, Colorado Columbine with an attractive red, white, and blue quilt on the king bed, Moroccan Jasmine with a Sahara Desert theme, Oriental Poppy decorated in collectibles from the Orient, and Victorian Rose with a romantic ambience. Each room has individual climate control, VCR, CD player, coffeemaker with your choice of coffee, refrigerator, robes, ironing board and iron, and a queen or king bed. Several have gas-log fireplaces, seven have either a private porch or balcony, and some have either steam showers for two or private outdoor hot tubs. There's an elevator, and one room is ADA approved.

Across from the library is the dining room, with a patio out front for pleasant alfresco dining in warm weather. Wine and hors d'oeuvres are offered in the afternoon. Full homemade breakfasts are served, with lighter fare available, and special dietary needs can be accommodated with advance notice. Downstairs is a game room with pool table and exercise equipment, plus a 50-person private conference room for small business and social activities. On many weekends, Dave parks his 1936 Cadillac in front to add a festively historic touch.

Sheraton Colorado Springs Hotel. 2886 S. Circle Dr. (I-25 exit 138), Colorado Springs, CO 80906. ☎ **800/981-4012** or 719/576-5900, 800/325-3535 worldwide. www.asgusa. com/scsh. Fax 719/576-7695. 500 units. A/C TV TEL. $99–$169 double; $250–$660 suite. AE, DC, DISC, JCB, MC, V. Free outdoor parking.

Eleven acres of landscaped grounds and a beautiful sky-lit indoor garden set this Sheraton apart from others. The estatelike grounds feature trees, waterfalls, and three plaza-style courtyards. The indoor garden has a pool and whirlpool tub, while the outdoor garden features a second pool, sunbathing area, and children's play area. All guest rooms are equipped with coffeemakers, full-size mirrors, and vanities, with refrigerators available on request. Some have balconies and stocked minibars, and many offer views of the indoor or outdoor pool. A half-dozen bilevel suites are furnished with a king-size bed in a loft and a sleeper sofa downstairs.

Amenities include a concierge, 24-hour room service, newspaper delivery, dry cleaning, secretarial services, and express checkout. Also on the premises are a restaurant and lounge, business center, car-rental desk, conference rooms, game rooms, health club, and two tennis courts. The Executive Club Level rooms include in-room fax, large work desk with an ergonomic chair, complimentary continental breakfast, and evening hors d'oeuvres.

MODERATE

Eastholme in the Rockies. 4445 Haggerman Ave. (P.O. Box 98), Cascade, CO 80809. ☎ **800/672-9901** or 719/684-9901. www.eastholme.com. E-mail: eastholme@rmi.net. 8 units (2 with shared bath), including 2 cottages. $75–$99 double; $140–$150 cottage; $109 suite. Rates include full breakfast. AE, DISC, MC, V. Free parking. 10 mi west of I-25 on U.S. 24 in Cascade.

Nestled in the quaint Pikes Peak mountain village of Cascade a mere 10 miles west of Downtown Colorado Springs, this Victorian B&B gives guests an opportunity to see the city and get away from it all in the same day. Originally built in 1885 as a resort hotel, this property has a storied history that includes a stint as a boarding house before becoming a guest inn in 1988.

The parlor is decorated with antiques, including historic photos of the property's second owner and an ornately carved fireplace. All of the inn's rooms feature ten-foot ceilings, plush quilts, and remarkable views. The Marriott and Eisenhower suites feature original furnishings and a plethora of interesting antiques, and the cottages offer cable television, VCRs, and spacious bathrooms. Guest amenities include a shared kitchen, library, and hot tub.

Located a mere mile from the turnoff off the Pikes Peak Highway off U.S. 24, Eastholme is surrounded by the mountainous pine scenery of the Pike National Forest.

Stargazers love the night views from the second floor balcony, free from the light pollution of the city. Aside from the innkeeper's Akita, Mojo, and miniature horse, Ringo, pets are not accepted. Smoking is not permitted.

⭐ **Hearthstone Inn.** 506 N. Cascade Ave., Colorado Springs, CO 80903. ☎ **800/521-1885** or 719/473-4413. Fax 719/473-1322. www.hearthstoneinn.com. E-mail: hearthstone@worldnet.att.net. 25 units (2 with shared bathroom). A/C. $99–$159 double with private bathroom, $69 double with shared bathroom; $199 suite. Rates include full breakfast. AE, DISC, MC, V. Free off-street lighted parking.

This comfortably elegant small downtown inn is actually two historic homes, built in 1885 and 1900, connected by a carriage house. Listed on the National Register of Historic Places and the winner of numerous preservation awards, the inn is decorated with old photographs, many antiques, and reproductions. Some of the comfortably furnished rooms can accommodate three or four people, and each unit has its own distinct personality. The Study, for instance, is a parlor-style room with built-in bookcases and a fireplace. The Solarium features an open-air latticed porch, and the third-floor Loft has three dormer windows, a queen-size brass bed, and a tiny child's bed with a child-size rocking chair. Breakfasts are wonderful: imaginative variations on the standard egg entrees, plus home-baked breads, fruit, and hot and cold cereals. The restaurant, which is open to the public, also serves lunch and dinner. A common parlor has games, a piano, and fresh coffee. There weren't any televisions in the 1890s, and there still aren't any here. Smoking is not permitted inside the inn, but there is an outside porch designated for smokers.

⭐ **Holden House 1902 Bed & Breakfast Inn.** 1102 W. Pikes Peak Ave., Colorado Springs, CO 80904. ☎ **888/565-3980** or 719/471-3980. www.holdenhouse.com. E-mail: mail@holdenhouse.com. 5 suites. A/C TEL. $125–$140 double. Rates include full breakfast. AE, CB, DC, DISC, MC, V. Not suitable for children.

Innkeepers Sallie and Welling Clark restored this storybook Colonial Revival–style Victorian house and its adjacent 1906 carriage house, and filled the rooms with antiques and family heirlooms. Located near Old Colorado City, the inn has a living room with a tile fireplace, a front parlor with a TV, and verandas. Guests enjoy a 24-hour coffee/tea service with a bottomless cookie jar, plus a gourmet breakfast in the formal dining room. Smoking is not allowed and pets are not permitted—the two resident cats, Mingtoy and Muffin, claim prior tenancy.

Each guest room, which is named after a Colorado mining area, contains memorabilia of that district. All have private sitting areas, queen-size beds, fireplaces, and tubs for two. The Cripple Creek suite features Victorian fretwork in the sitting area, a mahogany fireplace, and a magnificent Roman marble tub for two. Ask about their 2-night "breakfast in bed" Romance Package. The Independence Suite, in the adjacent building, is accessible to the disabled and is cat-free for those with allergies. There's also a gazebo out back set in a lovely garden.

🏨 Family-Friendly Hotels

Radisson Inn North (*see p. 174*)   Kids love the 24-hour pool; for teens who want to hang out, Chapel Hills Mall is right across the street.

Sheraton Colorado Springs Hotel (*see p. 172*)   Two swimming pools, a separate children's pool, shuffleboard, and a putting green should keep most kids occupied.

Radisson Inn North. 8110 N. Academy Blvd. (I-25 exit 150), Colorado Springs, CO 80920. ☎ **800/333-3333** or 719/598-5770. Fax 719/598-3434. 200 units. A/C TV TEL. $80–$120 double; $149–$249 suite. AE, CB, DC, DISC, MC, V. Free parking.

As the nearest full-service hotel to the Air Force Academy, this Radisson Inn's location makes it an attractive option. It has a large and beautiful atrium, with fountains beneath a skylight. Guest rooms are outfitted with king or double beds, light-wood furnishings, dressing tables, and TVs with in-house movies. Facilities include a restaurant and lounge, indoor pool, fitness center, whirlpool, sauna, and guest laundry; a complimentary airport shuttle is available. Chapel Hills Mall is within easy walking distance.

✪ Two Sisters Inn. 10 Otoe Place, Manitou Springs, CO 80829. ☎ **800/2SISINN** or 719/685-9684. www.twosisinn.com. 5 units (3 with private bathroom). $69 room with shared bathroom, $95 room with private bathroom; $115 cottage. Rates include full breakfast. DISC, MC, V. Suitable for well-supervised children over 10. Located 1 block north of the town clock on Manitou Ave.

Built by two sisters in 1919 as a boarding house, this award-winning bed-and-breakfast is still owned and operated by two women—sisters in spirit if not actually in blood. Wendy Goldstein and Sharon Smith have furnished the four bedrooms and separate honeymoon cottage with family heirlooms and photographs, in a style best described as "informal elegance." The rooms in the main house feature Victorian frills and furnishings, such as quilts and clawfoot bathtubs. Located across a splendid garden area, the cottage, with a separate bedroom and living room, has a feather bed, gas-log fireplace, refrigerator, and shower with skylight. Fresh flowers adorn each room, and homemade chocolates and baked goods are served upon arrival. The proprietors describe their breakfasts as "healthy decadence." They often cook with herbs and vegetables from their garden, and never serve the same thing twice. In the summer, Wendy and Sharon's lemonade, made fresh with the naturally-sparkling Manitou Springs water, is the perfect refreshment. Smoking is not permitted.

INEXPENSIVE

El Colorado Lodge. 23 Manitou Ave., Manitou Springs, CO 80829. ☎ **800/782-2246** or 719/685-5485. 26 cabins (8 with kitchen, 11 with shower only). A/C TV TEL. Summer $54– $125 cabin. Winter rates are lower; call for details. AE, CB, DC, DISC, MC, V. Free parking by cabins.

Most of the cabins in this Southwestern-style lodge have fireplaces and beamed ceilings. Each has from one to three clean, well-appointed rooms and can accommodate from two to six people. The lodge boasts the largest outdoor swimming pool in Manitou Springs and an outdoor pavilion for groups. Complimentary coffee is served during the summer.

Travel Inn. 512 S. Nevada Ave., Colorado Springs, CO 80903. ☎ **719/636-3986.** Fax 719/636-3980. 34 units. A/C TV TEL. Summer $45–$52 double; winter $32–$37 double. Rates include continental breakfast. AE, DC, DISC, MC, V. Free parking.

This two-story motel with bright turquoise trim is conveniently located near downtown Colorado Springs, with easy access to all the area attractions via I-25 and U.S. 24. The recently remodeled rooms are simple, clean, and comfortable, with white stucco walls and dark-wood furnishings. About a third of the units have tub/shower combinations, others have showers only. A self-serve laundry is available.

CAMPING

Garden of the Gods Campground. 3704 W. Colorado Ave., Colorado Springs, CO 80904. ☎ **800/248-9451** or 719/475-9450. www.coloradovacation.com/camp/gogc. $25–$35 for

2 people. Extra person $2. DISC, MC, V. Closed mid-Oct to mid-Apr. Take I-25 exit 141, head west on U.S. 24, then north (right) on 31st St., then left on Colorado Ave. for 6 blocks (keep right), and turn right to gate.

Located near Garden of the Gods (see "Attractions," below), this large tree-shaded campground offers 250 full RV hookups (30- and 50-amp service), an adults-only section, and additional tent sites. Facilities include tables, a barbecue pit, bathhouses, a grocery store, laundry, heated swimming pool, whirlpool tub, playground, and clubhouse with pool tables and game room.

Mueller State Park. P.O. Box 49, Divide, CO 80814. ☎ **800/678-2267** for reservations, or 719/687-2366. 132 sites. $4 per vehicle park entrance fee, plus camping fee of $10 for walk-in sites, $14 for drive-in sites with electricity. DISC, MC, V for reservations, cash or check only at the park. To reach the park entrance, take U.S. 24 west from Colorado Springs to Divide (25 miles), then go 3½ miles south on Colo. 67.

Located on the west slope of Pikes Peak, this park is ideal for campers who want to get away from it all but still enjoy a hot shower and modern rest room at the end of the day (the bathhouse is open from late May to mid-October only). Hikers, equestrians, and mountain bikers share 75 miles of trails in this 12,000-acre park, and the scenery and wildlife-viewing opportunities rival those at Rocky Mountain National Park. Trails north of the campground are closed for elk calving from June 1 to June 20.

4 Dining

Colorado Springs has an excellent variety of above-average restaurants, and surprisingly, almost all of them put a lot of effort into creating exciting desserts. The restaurant price categories used below are defined as follows: **very expensive,** most dinner main courses are over $22; **expensive,** dinner main courses range from $15 to $22; **moderate,** dinner main courses are $10 to $15; and **inexpensive,** dinner main courses are generally under $10. See also the section on dinner theaters in "Colorado Springs After Dark," later in this chapter.

VERY EXPENSIVE

Charles Court. Broadmoor West, in The Broadmoor, Lake Circle. ☎ **719/634-7711.** Reservations recommended. Breakfast $7.75–$15.50; dinner main courses $18–$36. AE, CB, DC, DISC, MC, V. Daily 7–11am and 6–9:30pm. PROGRESSIVE AMERICAN.

The English country-manor atmosphere of this outstanding restaurant, with picture windows looking across Cheyenne Lake to the renowned Broadmoor hotel, lends itself to a fine dining experience complete with attentive service. The creative menu changes seasonally, but you'll usually find such delicacies as Colorado lamb chops, beef tenderloin, salmon fillet, and a wild-game selection such as Colorado elk. The wine list includes more than 600 selections, and the desserts are extraordinary. In 2000, the restaurant was renovated to feature a seasonal outdoor patio.

Cliff House Inn Dining Room. Cliff House Inn, 306 Cañon Ave., Manitou Springs. ☎ **719/785-2415.** Reservations recommended. Breakfast $7–$15; lunch $7–$19, fixed-price lunch $18; dinner main courses $18–$32, fixed-price dinner $45. AE, CB, DC, DISC, MC, V. Daily 7–10am, lunch 11:30am–2:30pm, dinner 5:30–9:30pm; Sun brunch 11am–2pm. NEW AMERICAN/UNIVERSAL CUISINE.

Reopening with the historic hotel in 1999, the Cliff House Dining Room is decorated in western Victorian style, in keeping with its location in the newly restored historic Cliff House Inn. The Villeroy and Boch china, damask linen, crystal glassware, and 19th-century tiled fireplace evoke the charm of the Victorian era.

Chef Craig Hartman defines the cuisine as "universal" because it doesn't limit itself to regional or ethnic categories—instead, it combines flavors to create new taste sensations. For dinner, house specialties include grill-roasted loins of lamb topped with a leek-tomato compote and fresh cheese pesto; chateaubriand with black truffle butter and a Cabernet glaze; and crab cakes served with tomatoes, arugula, fresh horseradish, and balsamic vinegar. The lunch menu features an array of light entrees and salads; one highlight is the Caesar salad with pan-fried rainbow trout. The prix fixe lunch and dinner menus change daily and the wine list features 310 varieties, uncorked by a pair of sommeliers.

EXPENSIVE

The Blue Star. 1645 S. Tejon St. ☎ **719/632-1086.** Reservations recommended. Main courses $15–$24. AE, MC, V. Sun–Thurs 5:30–9pm, Fri–Sat 5:30–10pm. MEDITERRANEAN.

Relocating from Old Colorado City to a building in a quiet area just south of downtown in 1998, Blue Star is revered for its food. The menu changes weekly, but it always includes filet mignon, fresh fish (flown in three times a week from Boston), pasta, pork, and chicken. The culinary inspiration for the dishes comes from both Mediterranean and Pacific Rim cultures; the restaurant might serve Thai beef tips one week and beef bourguinonne the next. The dining room here is open for dinner nightly, and the adjacent bar serves lunch, dinner, tapas, and drinks from 11:30 am to midnight during the week. The dining room features sleek wood-and-metal decor and well-lighted artwork on the walls, while the bar atmosphere is louder and more casual.

Briarhurst Manor. 404 Manitou Ave., Manitou Springs. ☎ **719/685-1864** or 877/ 6851448. www.briarhurst.com. E-mail: info@briarhurst.com. Reservations suggested. Main courses $10.50–$30. Lower prices for seniors' and children's portions. AE, CB, DC, MC, V. Mon–Sat from 5:30pm; plus May–Labor Day Sun 5–7pm. CONTINENTAL/AMERICAN.

The original 1876 stone home of Manitou Springs founder Dr. William Bell, this incredible Tudor mansion sits elegantly on the main street of town. Scheduled for demolition in 1975, this landmark building was purchased by Chef Sigi Krauss, an East German who came to Colorado Springs after 10 years in Vail. Krauss restored its rich wood interior, including a Gothic oak staircase, and turned it into a world-renowned restaurant. Diners are welcome to tour the manor.

The Briarhurst features selections ranging from Rocky Mountain rainbow trout to Colorado lamb chops to a vegetarian platter. The menu also offers homemade pastas, chicken, seafood, and a variety of beef dishes. A special treat is the Wednesday night all-you-can-eat candlelight buffet ($18), with a marvelous array of delicacies from around the world, from appetizers to dessert. Also available are several fixed-price meals, which include everything from appetizer to dessert.

✪ **Craftwood Inn.** 404 El Paso Blvd., Manitou Springs. ☎ **719/685-9000.** www. craftwood.com. Reservations recommended. Main courses $12–$32. AE, DC, DISC, MC, V. Daily 5–10pm. Turn north off Manitou Ave. onto Mayfair Ave., go uphill 1 block, and turn left onto El Paso Blvd.; the Craftwood is on your right. COLORADO CUISINE.

Ensconced in an English Tudor building with beamed ceilings, stained-glass windows, and a copper-hooded fireplace, the casually elegant Craftwood Inn, built in 1912, was originally a coppersmith's shop. Today this excellent restaurant specializes in regional game, plus offerings of steak, seafood, chicken, and vegetarian dishes. Their extensive selection of game attracts the most acclaim: the restaurant serves elk, venison, pheasant, quail, caribou, antelope, wild boar, ostrich, and buffalo. Be sure to save room for one of the superb—and somewhat unusual—desserts, such as jalapeño white-chocolate mousse with raspberry sauce, or prickly pear sorbet.

❂ **La Petite Maison.** 1015 W. Colorado Ave. ☎ **719/632-4887.** Reservations recommended. Main courses $17–$26. AE. CB, DC, DISC, MC, V. Tues–Sat 5–10pm. FRENCH/ CONTEMPORARY.

This delightful 1894 Victorian cottage houses a gem of a restaurant, providing a blend of classic French and eclectic modern cuisine, served in a friendly, intimate setting to the strains of chamber music. The food is top rate and the service impeccable; this is where locals go to celebrate special occasions. Our recommendations include herb crab cakes with fresh greens and an orange and raspberry sauce; sake-cured yellowfin tuna salad; and pork tournedos wrapped in Applewood bacon with a peppercorn marsala sauce. Other choices include the evening's pasta selection and fresh fish; in addition, several lighter dishes are offered between 5 and 6:30pm. Desserts, all made in-house, might include white-chocolate mousse with fresh berries, a fresh fruit tart with almond paste, or crème brûlée.

❂ **MacKenzie's Chop House.** 128 S. Tejon St. ☎ **719/635-3536.** Reservations highly recommended. Main courses $5–$15 lunch, $16–$35 dinner. AE, MC, V. Mon–Fri 11am–3pm; Sun–Thurs 5–10pm, Fri–Sat 5–11pm. STEAK HOUSE.

Located downstairs in a handsome brick building in downtown Colorado Springs, MacKenzie's draws diners into its large dining room, which is divided into numerous intimate sections. Dark woods such as mahogany and antique-like upholstery on the booths add to the ambience; the library section even has a fireplace and, of course, books lining the walls. The open-air patio may be below ground level, but it gives one the feeling of dining in a grotto, with flowering plants, trees, and a lovely waterfall cascading over rocks, plus old streetlamps casting a gentle glow at night. MacKenzie's makes a great stop before or after a night at the theater.

The food lives up to its surroundings—both tasty and casually elegant. The crusty breads are made by a local bakery, fresh seafood is flown in daily, and the chops are special-ordered and cooked to perfection. You might start with the shrimp cocktail of jumbo prawns, served in a chilled martini glass, and then move on to a fresh Atlantic salmon, oven roasted on a cedar plank and coined with a garlic-herb butter sauce. Or select the fresh ahi tuna or one of the signature charbroiled chops such as the 24-ounce porterhouse. The most popular item at MacKenzie's is the surf and turf—filet mignon alongside a 9-ounce Brazilian lobster tail. The lunch menu features sandwiches and burgers, pasta, pizza, plus a few steak, fish, and chicken offerings.

MacKenzie's Martini Menu lists some three dozen martinis—shaken, not stirred— from the traditional to the exotic, and even so-called dessert martinis. The bar lounge offers a full menu and seating at high tables. The cigar lounge is furnished with over-stuffed chairs and sofas arranged in intimate groupings, and has a fragrant walk-in humidor. The large selection of cigars range in price from $7 to $30. See also "Colorado Springs After Dark," below.

The Margarita at PineCreek. 7350 Pine Creek Rd. ☎ **719/598-8667.** Reservations recommended. Fixed-price lunch $7.75; fixed-price dinner $23–$27. AE, DISC, MC, V. Tues–Fri 11:30am–2pm; Tues–Sat 6–9pm, Sun 5–8pm. ECLECTIC FINE DINING.

A delightful spot to sit and watch the sun setting over Pikes Peak, the Margarita is tucked away above two creeks on the north side of the city. Decor is attractively simple, with tile floors and stucco walls; a tree-shaded outdoor patio is open in summer. Saturday evenings bring live harpsichord music in the dining room, and Friday nights often feature live acoustic music—bluegrass to Celtic.

The emphasis here is on fresh ingredients and everything prepared "from scratch," including fish, vegetables, herbs, and homemade breads and stocks. Lunches feature a choice of soup (usually a beef barley and a seafood or mushroom bisque), salad, and freshly baked bread; there's also a Southwestern special. Six-course dinners offer three entree choices, usually fresh fish, veal, steak, pasta, lamb, or duckling, and a Mexican dish on weeknights.

Marigold's Café and Bakery. 4605 Centennial Blvd. (at Garden of the Gods Rd.). ☎ **719/ 599-4776.** Breakfast $4–$6.75, lunch $5.50–$9.50, dinner $9.25–$22.50. AE, DC, DISC, MC, V. Daily 7–10:30am; 11am–2:30pm; 5–9pm. Coffee bar and bakery open from 6am–9pm daily. Box lunches available. CONTINENTAL.

A relatively new restaurant—it opened in this burgeoning area northwest of down-town in November 1998—Marigold's is a simple, contemporary eatery that offers something for everyone. Breakfast and lunch are casual, featuring traditional menus infused with gourmet-savvy items such as breakfast casseroles and white pizzas. The bakery counter bustles through the early afternoon: coffee, bread, pastries, sandwiches, and box lunches are available. The generous dinners include fresh ingredients and are inspired by a wide range of international influences. Favorites include veal scaloppini marsala and "Papillotte Salmon" baked with sun-dried tomato pesto, fresh lemon, dill, and leeks.

Primitivo Wine Bar. 28 S. Tejon St. ☎ **719/473-4900.** Reservations recommended. Main courses $6–$14 lunch, $14–$26 dinner. Fixed price dinner $45–$52 without wine, $68–$78 with wine. AE, DISC, MC, V. Tues–Fri 11am–2pm; mid-May to early Sept Mon, Wed, Thurs 5–11pm, Tues, Fri, Sat 5pm–midnight; early Sept to mid-May Mon, Wed, Thurs 5–10pm, Tues, Fri, Sat 5–11pm. MEDITERRANEAN.

"Celebrating the marriage of food and wine" is Primitivo's slogan. It's not just mar-keting, either, as *Wine Spectator* has awarded the establishment their "Best of ..." award for several years running. Elegant yet subtle in atmosphere with red velvet curtains at the entryway, the restaurant prides itself on its food: French, Spanish, and Italian cui-sine prepared with fresh American ingredients. The menu changes monthly; recent dinner entrees included roasted duck with lentil ragout, sweet potato puree, greens and apricot curry sauce; house-made cappellini pasta with shrimp, capers, garlic, roasted tomato, and basil; and a grilled organic pork chop with snap peas, roasted apples, and a whole grain mustard sauce. Lunch offerings range from gourmet sand-wiches to entrée salads, with a good selection of appetizers. The restaurant also hosts monthly wine tasting events.

Steaksmith. 3802 Maizeland Rd. (at Academy Blvd.). ☎ **719/596-9300** or 800/201-2736. www.steaksmith.com. E-mail: steak@frii.com. Reservations recommended. Main courses $13.50–$35. AE, DISC, MC, V. Daily 5–10pm. Open for cocktails from 4:30pm daily. STEAK/ SEAFOOD.

Reputed to serve some of the best steaks and seafood in Colorado Springs, the Steak-smith works hard to maintain that reputation. In addition to a wide choice of top-quality choice-aged and house-cut beef, the restaurant offers excellent fresh fish and seafood, often including North Atlantic king salmon, East Coast oysters, and stuffed trout. Be warned that the prime rib and other specials often sell out early in the evening—a sure sign of success. The menu, which changes seasonally, also features Colorado lamb chops, vegetarian entrees, homemade soups, and delicious homemade desserts. For Valentine's Day, for example, the dessert might be "Kissing Swans for Two"—two puff pastries, one filled with chocolate mousse and the other with white-chocolate mousse, garnished with crème anglaise and strawberries. There's a full-service bar and an extensive wine list. Smoking is allowed only in the fireside cocktail lounge.

---

① Family-Friendly Restaurants

Edelweiss Restaurant (*see p. 179*)   Kids will enjoy the strolling musicians who play German folk music on weekends, and they'll love the apple and cherry strudels.

Giuseppe's Old Depot Restaurant (*see p. 179*)   An original locomotive stands outside this old Denver & Rio Grande Railroad station. Most kids will adore the spaghetti and pizza.

✪ **The Tavern.** Broadmoor Main, at The Broadmoor, Lake Circle. ☎ **719/634-7711.** Reservations recommended. Main courses $7.50–$17 lunch, $17–$35 dinner. Children's menu $3.25–$4.25. AE, CB, DC, DISC, MC, V. Daily 11:30am–4pm and 5–11pm. STEAK/SEAFOOD.

Original Toulouse-Lautrec lithographs on the walls and knotty pine furniture and paneling mark The Tavern as a restaurant with unusual ambience. In the front dining room, nightly piano entertainment is followed by a four-piece ensemble—guests are welcome to take a turn around the floor between courses. The adjoining garden room, with luxuriant tropical foliage, is a quieter choice. Service in both rooms is impeccable.

The lunch menu features London broil au jus, seafood crepes Louis, Welsh rarebit, and a variety of sandwiches and salads. Dinners are more elaborate: Choose from slow-roasted prime rib, wood-grilled filet mignon, blackened or broiled salmon or swordfish, or half a roast duck or chicken. All entrees come with The Tavern's own wood-oven hearth bread.

MODERATE

Anthony's. 1919 E. Boulder St. ☎ **719/471-3654.** Reservations recommended for groups of five or more. Main courses $6–$10 lunch, $9–$18 dinner. AE, DISC, MC, V. Mon–Fri 11am–2pm; Tues–Thurs 5–9pm, Fri–Sat 5–10pm, Sun 5–9pm. ITALIAN.

Situated in a quiet east-side neighborhood, Anthony's offers a tranquil escape from a hectic day. In summer, dine on the outdoor patio; in winter, stay warm by the blazing fire. All pastas, from manicotti to fettuccine, are homemade. Regulars often choose chicken or veal parmigiana or saltimbocca alla Romana. Dinners include soup or salad, garlic bread, and sorbet; a plate of linguine accompanies meat dishes. The vintage bar serves Dorro (an Italian dessert liqueur) as a perfect conclusion to a hearty Italian meal.

Edelweiss Restaurant. 34 E. Ramona Ave. ☎ **719/633-2220.** Reservations recommended. Main courses $5–$7.75 lunch, $8.75–$18.25 dinner. AE, DC, DISC, MC, V. Mon–Fri 11:30am–2pm; Sun–Thurs 5–9pm, Fri–Sat 5–9:30pm. Located southwest of I-25, a block west of Nevada Ave. GERMAN.

The Edelweiss—housed in an impressive stone building with red trim, a big indoor fireplace, and an outdoor patio—underscores its Bavarian atmosphere with strolling folk musicians on weekends. It offers a hearty menu of Jägerschnitzel, Wiener schnitzel, sauerbraten, bratwurst, and other old-country specials, as well as New York strip steak, fresh fish, and chicken. The fruit strudels are excellent.

Giuseppe's Old Depot Restaurant. 10 S. Sierra Madre St. ☎ **719/635-3111.** Menu items $5–$20. AE, CB, DC, DISC, MC, V. Sun–Thurs 11am–10pm, Fri–Sat 11am–midnight. ITALIAN/AMERICAN.

Giuseppe's is lodged in a restored Denver & Rio Grande train station, with glass ticket windows lining the walls; a garden room has been added. The same menu is served all day, offering a wide variety of choices. Spaghetti, lasagna, and stone-baked pizza are house specialties, while American dishes include baby-back ribs, prime rib, and fried chicken.

The Hungry Farmer. 575 Garden of the Gods Rd. ☎ **719/598-7622.** Main courses $5–$12 lunch, $11–$19 dinner. AE, CB, DC, DISC, MC, V. Mon–Fri 11am–2pm and 5–9pm, Sat 4–10pm, Sun 11:30am–9pm. AMERICAN.

Locally famous for its generous portions and slow-cooked prime rib, this restaurant has a somewhat unusual kind of farm atmosphere, with bales of hay, stained-glass windows, and chandeliers. There's a large selection of steak, chicken, seafood, and ribs, and all dinners include a bottomless bucket of soup, vegetable du jour, salad, potato, and hot homemade oatmeal muffins and cinnamon rolls. Children get their own menu.

Phantom Canyon Brewing Co. 2 E. Pikes Peak Ave. ☎ **719/635-2800.** Main courses $5.25–$7.50 lunch, $9–$17 dinner. AE, CB, DC, DISC, MC, V. Mon–Thurs 11am–10pm, Fri–Sat 11am–2am, Sun 9am–10pm. URBAN COMFORT CUISINE.

This popular—and consequently busy and noisy—brewpub is located in the Cheyenne Building, home to the Chicago Rock Island & Pacific Railroad from 1902 to 1909. On any given day, ten of Phantom Canyon's specialty beers are on tap, including their homemade root beer. Their signature beer is the Phantom, a traditional pale ale; others include an amber ale, a light ale called Queen's Blonde, and Zebulon's Peated Porter.

The dining room is large and wide open, with ceiling fans, hardwood floors, and walls of windows facing two streets. Greenery abounds under a large skylight, and the large brewing vats are visible in one corner. Guests are seated at booths and tables. The lunch menu features several wood-fired pizzas, hearty salads, half-pound beef or buffalo burgers, fish-and-chips, shepherd's pie, and several pasta dishes. The dinner menu is varied, with unusual choices such as charbroiled garlic chicken breast with three-grain rice and honey-beer mustard; porcini-crusted salmon fillet with risotto and sweet corn sauce; and the more publike charbroiled New York strip with horseradish whipped potatoes, beer-battered onion rings, and stilton butter. The menu changes periodically. On the second floor is a billiard hall with its own menu of pizza, calzones, salad, and appetizers. See also "Colorado Springs After Dark," below.

The Ritz Grill. 15 S. Tejon St. ☎ **719/635-8484.** Main courses $6–$10 brunch and lunch, $8–$22 dinner. AE, MC, V. Mon–Sat 11am–2am, Sun 9:30am–2am. NEW AMERICAN.

This lively restaurant-lounge, with a large central bar, is where it's at for many of the city's young professionals. The decor is art deco, and the service fast and friendly. The varied, trendy menu offers such specialties as the Ritz veggie pizza, with fresh spinach, sun-dried tomatoes, bell peppers, onions, mushrooms, pesto, and three cheeses; and Southwest pasta—rock shrimp and chicken in a roasted red-pepper sauce, served with angel-hair pasta and topped with jack cheese. There's also a mesquite-grilled filet mignon, a variety of fish and chicken dishes, and salads and sandwiches. Sunday brunch favorites include traditional-style bacon and eggs, eggs Benedict, omelets, waffles, and a breakfast burrito of scrambled eggs, onions, bell peppers, jalapeños, and bacon, rolled up in a flour tortilla and smothered with green chiles and cheddar cheese. See also "Colorado Springs After Dark," below.

INEXPENSIVE

Adam's Mountain Cafe. 110 Cañon Ave., Manitou Springs. ☎ **719/685-1430.** Breakfast and lunch $3–$7, dinner $6–$12. MC, V. Daily 8am–3pm, Tues–Sat 5–9pm. CONTEMPORARY AMERICAN/NATURAL FOODS.

This cafe has a country French–Victorian setting, with exposed brick and stone, antique tables and chairs, fresh flowers, and original watercolors. The menu includes grilled items and fresh fish, although the restaurant made a name for itself with its vegetarian offerings made with the freshest ingredients. Many entrees are prepared in a decidedly Mediterranean style, such as goat cheese crostini—hazelnut-encrusted goat cheese served on semolina toast with grilled roma tomatoes, aged balsamic vinegar, and olive oil. Dinner options include a grilled filet of California white sea bass over saffron-scented tiger shrimp risotto with roasted red pepper and tomato broth.

Breakfast specialties include orange-almond French toast, made with whole-wheat-sunflower bread in an orange-cinnamon egg batter, served with sliced almonds; and a longtime favorite: the P. W. Busboy Special, consisting of two whole-grain pancakes, two scrambled eggs, and slices of fresh fruit. The syrup of choice here is Grade A pure Vermont maple, served by the ounce. Lunch offerings include sandwiches, soups, salads, fresh pasta, and Southwestern plates.

Dutch Kitchen. 1025 Manitou Ave., Manitou Springs. ☎ **719/685-9962.** Lunch $4–$6, dinner $5.50–$7.25. Sat–Thurs 11:30am–3:30pm and 4:30–8pm. Closed Thurs in spring and fall. Closed Dec–Feb. AMERICAN.

Good homemade food served in a casual, friendly atmosphere is what you'll find at this relatively small restaurant, which has been owned and operated by the Flynn family since 1959. The corned beef, pastrami, and ham sandwiches have been popular since the restaurant opened, and if you're there in summer be sure to try the fresh rhubarb pie. Other house specialties include buttermilk pie and homemade soups.

Judge Baldwin's Brewing Company. In the Antlers Adam's Mark Hotel, 4 S. Cascade Ave. ☎ **719/473-5600.** Main courses $6–$10. AE, CB, DC, DISC, MC, V. Sun–Thurs 11am–11pm, Fri–Sat 11am–midnight. AMERICAN.

Judge Baldwin's, like many good brew pubs, takes just as much pride in its food as it does in its hand-crafted beer. The great-tasting burgers are made from a half pound of fresh ground beef, charbroiled to order, served open-face with your choice of cheese, and accompanied by steak fries. Also popular is the English-style beer-battered fish-and-chips, served with homemade coleslaw, steak fries, and toasted pecan tartar sauce. The menu lists a variety of soups, salads, and sandwiches. Those opting for munchies and one of Judge Baldwin's fine beers might enjoy a huge pile of beer-battered onion rings, sliced thick and served with buttermilk-ranch dressing; or the El Grande Nachos: a platter of red, yellow, and blue corn tortilla chips, topped with jalapeños, guacamole, salsa, cheddar and jack cheese, sour cream, and black olives. You can see the beer vats and other beer-making equipment as you sample the brewmeister's latest efforts. Like most brew pubs, Judge Baldwin's is busy and a bit noisy. See also "Colorado Springs After Dark," below.

Michelle's. 122 N. Tejon St. ☎ **719/633-5089.** Reservations not accepted. Breakfast $2.50–$5, lunch and dinner $4–$7. AE, CB, DC, DISC, MC, V. Mon–Thurs 9am–11pm, Fri–Sat 9am–midnight, Sun 10am–11pm. AMERICAN/GREEK/SOUTHWESTERN.

The menu is eclectic, but it's amazing how many different dishes Michelle's prepares well—and at such reasonable prices. Since it opened in 1952, this restaurant has been known for its excellent handmade chocolates, fresh-churned ice cream, and

Greek specialties such as gyros and spanakopita. But it also has good burgers, crois-sant sandwiches, a half-dozen different salads, numerous omelets, and a delicious breakfast burrito. A three-page ice-cream menu includes everything from a single scoop of vanilla to the "Believe It or Not Sundae" featured in *Life* magazine in Novem-ber 1959; it weighs 42 pounds and includes every flavor of ice cream Michelle's makes.

There's also a **Michelle's** in the Citadel Shopping Center, at East Platte Avenue and North Academy Boulevard (☎ **719/597-9932**).

5 Attractions

Most of the attractions of the Pikes Peak region can be placed in two general cate-gories: natural, such as Pikes Peak, Garden of the Gods, and Cave of the Winds, and historic and educational, including the Air Force Academy, Olympic Training Center, museums, historic homes, and art galleries. There are also the gambling houses of Cripple Creek.

If you have just arrived in Colorado from a sea-level area, you might want to sched-ule any mountain excursions, such as the cog railway to the top of Pikes Peak, for the end of your stay; this will give your body time to adapt to the lower oxygen level at these higher elevations. See also "Health, Safety & Insurance," in chapter 2.

Suggested Itineraries

If You Have 1 Day

Begin your day early by visiting the Garden of the Gods, a unique geological site fea-turing red sandstone pillars, then go on to the Cave of the Winds, an underground cavern. Afterward, head downtown to the Colorado Springs Pioneers Museum for an overview of the history of the region. After lunch, tour the Air Force Academy, and if time remains, visit the Pro Rodeo Hall of Fame.

If You Have 2 Days

Spend your first day as suggested above. Begin Day 2 with a 1-hour tour of the Olympic Training Center, followed by stops at Ghost Town and Van Briggle Art Pot-tery. After lunch, visit Old Colorado City, McAllister House, the Fine Arts Center, and the Museum of the American Numismatic Association.

If You Have 3 Days

Spend your first 2 days as suggested above. On Day 3, head to Manitou Springs for a self-guided mineral-springs historical walking tour; information is available at the vis-itor center. Then go to Miramont Castle and the Manitou Cliff Dwellings. Check out the Manitou Springs shops and galleries, enjoy lunch, and then hop aboard the cog railway for a trip to the top of Pikes Peak. If time remains, stop at the Pikes Peak Auto Hill Climb Museum.

THE TOP ATTRACTIONS

United States Air Force Academy. Off I-25 exit 156B. ☎ **719/333-8723.** www.usafa.af.mil. Free admission. Summer daily 9am–6pm; winter daily 9am–5pm; additional hours for special events.

Colorado Springs' pride and joy got its start in 1954, when Congress authorized the establishment of a U.S. Air Force Academy and chose this 18,000-acre site from among 400 prospective locations. The first class of cadets enrolled in 1959, and each year since, about 4,000 cadets have enrolled for the 4 years of rigorous training required to become Air Force officers.

The academy is situated 12 miles north of downtown; enter at the North Gate, off I-25 exit 156B. Soon after entering the grounds, at the intersection of North Gate Boulevard and Stadium Boulevard, you'll see an impressive outdoor B-52 bomber display. Where North Gate Boulevard becomes Academy Drive (in another mile or so), look to your left to see the Cadet Field House, where basketball and ice hockey games are played (see "Spectator Sports," below), and the Parade Ground, where cadets can sometimes be spotted marching.

Academy Drive soon curves to the left. Six miles from the North Gate, signs mark the turnoff to the Barry Goldwater Air Force Academy Visitor Center. Open daily, it offers a variety of exhibits and films on the academy's history and cadet life, extensive literature and self-guided tour maps, and the latest information and schedules on academy activities. There's also a large gift shop and coffee shop.

A short trail from the visitor center leads to the Cadet Chapel. Its 17 gleaming aluminum spires soar 150 feet skyward, and within the building are separate chapels for the major Western faiths as well as an "all-faiths" room. The public can visit Monday through Saturday from 9am to 5pm and Sunday from 2 to 5pm; Sunday services at 9 and 11am are also open to the public. The chapel is closed for 5 days around graduation and during special events.

Also within easy walking distance of the visitor center are the Academy Planetarium, a classroom for astronomy, physics, and navigation classes that offers periodic free public programs; Arnold Hall, the social center that houses historical exhibits, a cafeteria, and a theater featuring a variety of public shows and lectures; and Harmon Hall, the administration building, where prospective cadets can obtain admission information.

After leaving the visitor center, continue south, then east, on Academy Drive to Stadium Boulevard, where you will see Falcon Stadium on your right. Turn right on Stadium Boulevard and follow it out to South Gate Boulevard, which leaves the academy grounds at I-25 exit 150B. En route, you'll pass the Thunderbird Airmanship Overlook, where you might be lucky enough to see cadets parachuting, soaring, and practicing their takeoffs and landings in U.S. Air Force Thunderbirds.

For specific information about the academy, write Visitor Services Division, Directorate of Public Affairs, 2304 Cadet Dr., Suite 318, U.S. Air Force Academy, CO 80840.

✪ **Garden of the Gods.** 1805 N. 30th St., I-25 exit 146. ☎ **719/634-6666.** www. gardenofgods.com. Free admission. Park, May–Oct daily 5am–11pm; Nov–Apr daily 5am–9pm. Visitor Center, Jun–Aug daily 8am–8pm; Sept–May 9am–5pm. Take Garden of the Gods Rd. west from I-25 exit 146 and turn south on 30th St.

One of the West's unique geological sites, the Garden of the Gods is a beautiful giant rock garden composed of spectacular red sandstone formations sculpted by rain and wind over millions of years. Located where several life zones and ecosystems converge, the city-run park harbors a variety of plant and animal communities. The oldest survivors are the ancient, twisted junipers, some 1,000 years old. The strangest animals are the honey ants, which gorge themselves on honey in the summer and fall, thus becoming living honey pots to feed their colonies during winter hibernation.

Hiking maps for the 1,300-acre park are available at the **Visitor Center,** which also offers exhibits on the history, geology, plants, and wildlife of the park; a cafeteria; and other conveniences. A 12-minute multimedia theater presentation—*How Did Those Red Rocks Get There?*—is a fast-paced exploration of the geologic history of the area

Colorado Springs Attractions

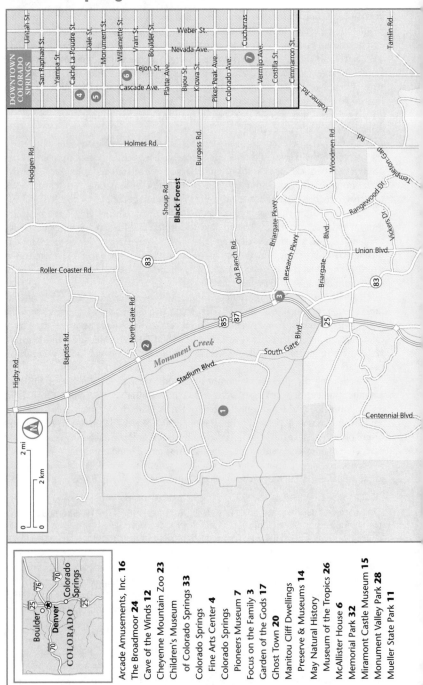

Arcade Amusements, Inc. **16**
The Broadmoor **24**
Cave of the Winds **12**
Cheyenne Mountain Zoo **23**
Children's Museum
   of Colorado Springs **33**
Colorado Springs
   Fine Arts Center **4**
Colorado Springs
   Pioneers Museum **7**
Focus on the Family **3**
Garden of the Gods **17**
Ghost Town **20**
Manitou Cliff Dwellings
   Preserve & Museums **14**
May Natural History
   Museum of the Tropics **26**
McAllister House **6**
Memorial Park **32**
Miramont Castle Museum **15**
Monument Valley Park **28**
Mueller State Park **11**

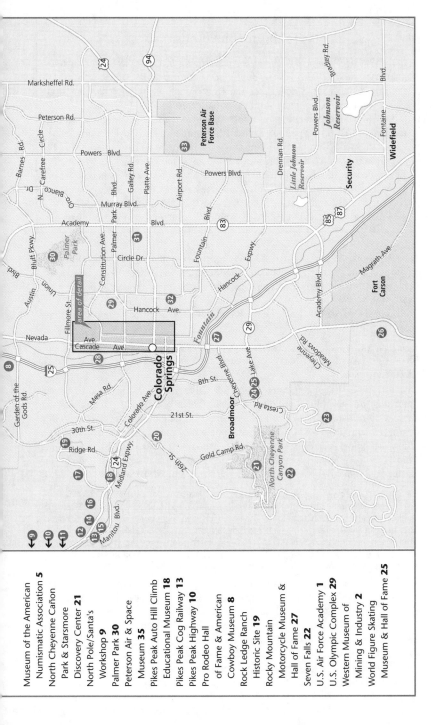

Museum of the American Numismatic Association **5**

North Cheyenne Cañon Park & Starsmore Discovery Center **21**

North Pole/Santa's Workshop **9**

Palmer Park **30**

Peterson Air & Space Museum **35**

Pikes Peak Auto Hill Climb Educational Museum **18**

Pikes Peak Cog Railway **13**

Pikes Peak Highway **10**

Pro Rodeo Hall of Fame & American Cowboy Museum **8**

Rock Ledge Ranch Historic Site **19**

Rocky Mountain Motorcycle Museum & Hall of Fame **27**

Seven Falls **22**

U.S. Air Force Academy **1**

U.S. Olympic Complex **29**

Western Museum of Mining & Industry **2**

World Figure Skating Museum & Hall of Fame **25**

Fit for the Gods

In 1859, large numbers of pioneers were arriving in Colorado hoping to find gold (their motto: "Pikes Peak or Bust"); many of these pioneers established communities along what is now called the Front Range, including Colorado City, which was later incorporated within Colorado Springs.

Legend has it that certain pioneers who explored the remarkable sandstone formations in the area wanted to establish a beer garden there. However, one Rufus Cable objected: "Beer Garden! Why this is a fit place for a Garden of the Gods!"

Fortunately for posterity, the area was bought some 20 years later by Charles Elliott Perkins (head of the Burlington Railroad) and kept in its natural state. Upon Perkins's death in 1907, his heirs gave the remarkable area to Colorado Springs on the condition that it be preserved as a park and open to the public. The park was dedicated in 1909 and is now a Registered National Landmark.

($2 for adults, $1 for children 12 and under). In summer, park naturalists lead 45-minute walks through the park and conduct afternoon interpretive programs. You may spot technical rock climbers on some of the park spires (they are required to register at the Visitor Center).

Also in the park is the **Rock Ledge Ranch Historic Site** (see "More Attractions," below).

Focus on the Family. 8685 Explorer Dr. ☎ **719/531-3328.** Free admission. Summer Mon–Sat 9am–5pm; winter Mon–Fri 9am–5pm, Sat 9am–4pm. Take I-25 exit 151 east to Explorer Dr.

The attractive Welcome Center contains a large bookstore, interactive displays describing the background and purpose of this Christian ministry, and a theater that shows a 20-minute video narrated by Dr. James C. Dobson, founder of Focus on the Family. Downstairs is a Kids Korner with a play area, plus a soda fountain the entire family can enjoy. A cafeteria upstairs serves breakfast from 8:30 to 10am and lunch from 11am to 1:45pm. A free 45-minute guided tour of the campus describes the outreach of the ministry both in the United States and around the world.

✪ **Pikes Peak Cog Railway.** 515 Ruxton Ave., Manitou Springs. ☎ **719/685-5401.** www.cograilway.com. E-mail: cogtrain@iex.net . Admission $23.50–$24.50 adults, $12–12.50 children under 12 (but children under 3 held on an adult's lap are free). June–Aug, 8 departures daily; in late April and Sept–Oct, 2 to 6 departures daily. Definite late Apr–Oct departures from Manitou Springs at 9:20am and 1:20pm. Reservations required (they can be made online). Take I-25 exit 141 west on U.S. 24 for 4 miles, turn onto Manitou Ave. west and go 1½ miles to Ruxton Ave., and turn left and go about half a mile.

For those who enjoy rail travel, spectacular scenery, and the thrill of mountain climbing without all the work, this is the trip to take. The first passenger train climbed Pikes Peak on June 30, 1891, and diesel slowly replaced steam power between 1939 and 1955. Four custom-built Swiss twin-unit rail cars, each seating 216 passengers, were put into service in 1989. The 9-mile route, with grades up to 25%, takes 75 minutes to reach the top of 14,110-foot Pikes Peak, and the round-trip requires 3 hours and 10 minutes (including a 40-minute stopover at the top).

The journey is exciting from the start, but passengers really begin to "ooh" and "aah" when the track leaves the forest, creeping above timberline at about 11,500 feet. The view from the summit takes in Denver, 75 miles north; New Mexico's Sangre de

Cristo range, 100 miles south; the Cripple Creek mining district, on the mountain's western flank; wave after wave of Rocky Mountain subranges to the west; and the seemingly endless sea of Great Plains to the east. The Summit House at the top of Pikes Peak has a restaurant and gift shop.

Take a jacket or sweater—it can be cold and windy on top, even on warm summer days. This trip is not recommended if you have cardiac or respiratory problems. Even those in good health may feel faint or light-headed.

Pikes Peak Highway. Off U.S. 24 at Cascade. ☎ **800/318-9505** or 719/385-PEAK. www. pikespeakcolorado.com. Admission $10 per person over age 16 or $35 per car. May–Oct daily 7am–7pm; the rest of the year, daily 9am–3pm, weather permitting. Take I-25 exit 141 west on U.S. 24 about 10 miles.

There is perhaps no view in Colorado to equal the 360° panorama from the 14,110-foot summit of Pikes Peak. Whether you go by cog railway (see above) or private vehicle, the ascent is a spectacular and exciting experience, although not for those with heart or breathing problems or a fear of heights. This 19-mile toll highway (paved for 7 miles, all-weather gravel thereafter) starts at 7,400 feet, some 4 miles west of Manitou Springs. There are numerous photo stops as you head up the mountain, and deer, mountain sheep, and other animals can often be seen on the slopes, especially above timberline (around 11,500 feet). This 156-curve road is the site of the annual July Fourth Pikes Peak Auto Hill Climb, the Pikes Peak Marathon footrace in August, and the New Year's Eve climb and fireworks show.

✪ **Colorado Springs Pioneers Museum.** 215 S. Tejon St. ☎ **719/385-5990.** www. cspm.org. E-mail: mmayberry@ci.colospgs.co.us. Free admission, donations accepted. Tues–Sat 10am–5pm, plus May–Oct Sun 1–5pm. Take I-25 exit 141 east to Tejon St. and turn right for 2 blocks.

Housed in the former El Paso County Courthouse, which was built in 1903 and is now listed on the National Register of Historic Places, this museum is an excellent place to begin your visit to Colorado Springs. Exhibits depict the community's rich history, including its beginning as a fashionable resort, the railroad and mining eras, and its growth and development into the 20th century. There's also the Victorian home of writer Helen Hunt Jackson, an exhibit on the city's dental, medical, and pharmaceutical industry, plus turn-of-the-century toys, quilts, and clothing.

You can ride an Otis birdcage elevator (more than 80 years old) to the restored original courtroom, where several *Perry Mason* television episodes were filmed. A recent renovation uncovered gold and silver images of goddesses, painted on the courtroom walls as a protest when the country was changing from a gold to silver monetary standard. Other murals depict three periods in the history of the Pikes Peak region, each represented by 12 panels.

Changing exhibit areas house traveling shows such as quilts, historic photographs, aviation, American Indian culture, and art pottery. The museum has hosted a wide range of events, including lectures on the American cowboy, antique auto shows, jazz concerts, and Hispanic celebrations. There's also a historic reference library and archives for public use.

United States Olympic Complex. 1 Olympic Plaza, corner of Boulder St. (entrance) and Union Blvd. ☎ **719/578-4618** for visitor center, 719/578-4644 for tour and events hot line. Tour reservations required for groups of 10 or more. Free admission. Complex open daily 9am–5pm. Take I-25 exit 143.

This 36-acre site in the middle of Colorado Springs houses a sophisticated training center for about a third of the 45 U.S. Olympic sports, providing a training ground for some 13,000 athletes of all ages each year. Free guided tours, which are available daily, begin with a film depicting the U.S. Olympic effort. A gift shop next to the visitor center sells Olympic-logo merchandise; the proceeds help support athlete training programs.

The complex includes the **Olympic Sports Center I,** with five gymnasiums and a weight-training room; **Sports Center II,** which accommodates 14 different sports; the **Indoor Shooting Center,** the largest indoor shooting facility in the Western Hemisphere, with areas for rifle and pistol shooting, rapid-fire and women's sport pistol bays, running target rifle ranges, and air rifle and pistol fire points; and the **Aquatics Center,** which contains a 50-by-25-meter pool with two movable bulkheads, ten 50-meter and twenty 25-meter lanes, and more than 800,000 gallons of water. One mile south of the Olympic Complex, in Memorial Park (see "Parks & Zoos," below) off Union Boulevard, is the **7-Eleven Velodrome,** with a banked track for bicycle and roller speed skating. Olympic figure skaters train at the **World Arena,** located southwest of downtown.

MORE ATTRACTIONS
ARCHITECTURAL HIGHLIGHTS

The Broadmoor. Lake Circle, at Lake Ave. ☎ **719/634-7711.** www.broadmoor.com. Free admission. Daily year-round.

This famous Italian Renaissance–style resort hotel has been a Colorado Springs landmark since it was built by Spencer Penrose in 1918. (See "Accommodations," above.)

Miramont Castle Museum. 9 Capitol Hill Ave., Manitou Springs. ☎ **719/685-1011.** www.pikes-peak.com/Castle. Admission $4.50 adults, $3.50 seniors 60 and over, $1 children 6–11, free for children under 6. Memorial Day–Labor Day Tues–Sun 10am–5pm; Apr–Memorial Day and Labor Day to mid-Dec Tues–Sun 11am–4pm; rest of year, Tues–Sun noon–3pm. Located just off Ruxton Ave., en route from Manitou Ave. to the Pikes Peak Cog Railway.

Built into a hillside by a wealthy French priest as a private home in 1895 and converted by the Sisters of Mercy into a sanatorium in 1907, this unique Victorian mansion has always aroused curiosity. At least nine identifiable architectural styles are incorporated into the structure, which has four stories, 28 rooms, 14,000 square feet of floor space, and 2-foot-thick stone walls. One room is a miniatures museum, and a separate building outside the castle houses a model-railroad museum. In summer, light meals and tea are served from 11am to 4pm in the Queen's Parlour.

HISTORIC BUILDINGS

McAllister House. 423 N. Cascade Ave. (at St. Vrain St.). ☎ **719/635-7925.** www. oldcolo.com/hist/mcallister. Admission $4 adults, $3 seniors and students, $1 children 6–12, free for children under 6. Summer Wed–Sat 10am–4pm, Sun noon–4pm; winter Thurs–Sat 10am–4pm. Take I-25 exit 141 east to Cascade Ave., then left for about 6 blocks.

This Gothic cottage, listed on the National Register of Historic Places, was built in 1873. The builder, an army major named Henry McAllister, decided to construct the house with brick when he learned that the local wind was so strong it had blown a train off the tracks nearby. The house has many original furnishings, including three marble fireplaces. It is now owned by the Colonial Dames of America, whose knowledgeable volunteers lead guided tours. Tea is served on Friday afternoons in the summer and on certain holidays ($8 for tea and tour), and croquet is available on summer Sundays.

Rock Ledge Ranch Historic Site. Gateway Rd., Garden of the Gods. ☎ **719/578-6777.** www.colorado-springs.com/parksrec/places/rlrintro.htm. Admission $5 adults, $3 seniors and students (13–18), $1 children 6–12, free for children under 6. June–Labor Day Wed–Sun 10am–5pm; Labor Day–Dec 25, Sat 10am–4pm, Sun noon–4pm. Closed Jan–May. Take I-25 exit 146, then follow signs west to Garden of the Gods.

Visitors can explore the history of three different pioneer eras at this living-history farm at the east entrance to Garden of the Gods park. Listed on the National Register of Historic Places, the ranch presents the rigors of the homestead era at the 1860s Galloway Homestead, the agricultural difficulties of the working-ranch era at the 1880s Chambers Farm and Blacksmith Shop, and the more sophisticated estate period at the 1907 Orchard House. Special events, which take place frequently, include an old-fashioned Fourth of July celebration, an 1860s vintage baseball game in late summer, a Victorian Halloween party, and holiday celebrations from Thanksgiving through Christmas. The General Store has a wide selection of historic reproductions, books, and gift items, and the proceeds help with preservation and restoration of the ranch.

HISTORIC NEIGHBORHOODS

Manitou Springs, which is centered around Manitou Avenue off U.S. 24 West, is actually a separate town with its own government and is one of the country's largest National Historic Districts. Legend has it that Utes named the springs Manitou, their word for "Great Spirit," because they believed that the Great Spirit had breathed into the waters to create the natural effervescence of the springs. Pikes Peak soars above the town nestled at its base.

Today, the community offers visitors a chance to step back to a slower and quieter time, surrounded by numerous lovely and elegant Victorian buildings, many of which now house delightful shops, galleries, restaurants, and lodgings. Manitou Springs is also home to many fine artists and artisans, any number of whom you might spot painting or sketching at various points about town. A small group of sculptors began the Manitou Art Project in 1992, whereby over 20 sculptures were installed in various locations downtown and in the parks, creating a large sculpture garden for all to enjoy. The works, which stay on display for a year, are for sale, with 25% of the proceeds used to purchase permanent sculpture for the city. Five pieces have been purchased to date.

Visitors are encouraged to take the self-guided tour of the nine mineral springs of Manitou that have been restored. Pick up the easy-to-carry *Manitou Springs Complete Visitor's Guide,* which contains a map and descriptions to help you find each spring. It's available at the Chamber of Commerce at 354 Manitou Ave. (☎ **800/642-2567** or 719/685-5089), which is open daily.

Old Colorado City, Colorado Avenue between 21st and 31st streets, was founded in 1859, before Colorado Springs itself. The town boomed in the 1880s after General Palmer's railroad came through. Tunnels led from the respectable side of town to this saloon and red-light district so that the city fathers could carouse without being seen coming or going, or so the legend goes. Today this historic district has an interesting assortment of shops, galleries, and restaurants.

MUSEUMS & GALLERIES

Colorado Springs Fine Arts Center. 30 W. Dale St. (west of N. Cascade Ave.). ☎ **719/ 634-5581.** Admission to galleries and museum $4 adults; $2 seniors, students and children 6–16; free for children under 6. Free for everyone Sat 10am–5pm. Separate admission for performing arts events. Galleries and museum, Mon–Sat 9am–5pm, Sun 1–5pm. Open the 1st Thurs of every month until 8pm. Closed federal holidays. Take I-25 exit 143 east to Cascade St., turn right to Dale St., and then turn right again.

Georgia O'Keeffe, John James Audubon, John Singer Sargent, Charles Russell, Albert Bierstadt, Nicolai Fechin, and other famed painters and sculptors are represented in the center's permanent collection, which also includes a world-class collection of

American Indian and Hispanic works. Opened in 1936, the center also houses a 450-seat performing arts theater, a 32,000-volume art research library, the Bemis Art School offering visual arts and drama classes, a tactile gallery for those who are visually impaired, and a delightful sculpture garden. Changing exhibits in two galleries showcase local collections as well as touring international exhibits. Designed by renowned Santa Fe architect John Gaw Meem, the art deco–style building reflects Southwestern mission and Pueblo influences.

Ghost Town. 400 S. 21st St. ☎ **719/634-0696.** www.pikes-peak.com/ghosttown. E-mail: history@ghosttownmuseum.com. Admission $4.50 adults, $2.50 children 6–16, free for children under 6. Memorial Day–Labor Day Mon–Sat 9am–6pm, Sun noon–6pm; Labor Day–Memorial Day Mon–Sat 10am–5pm, Sun noon–5pm. Just west of I-25 exit 141, on U.S. 24 at 21st St.

Comprised of authentic 19th-century buildings relocated from other parts of Colorado, this "town" is sheltered from the elements in Old Colorado City. There's a sheriff's office, jail, saloon, general store, livery stable, blacksmith shop, rooming house, and assay office. Animated frontier characters tell stories of the Old West, while a shooting gallery, antique arcade machines, and nickelodeons provide additional entertainment.

Manitou Cliff Dwellings Preserve & Museums. U.S. 24, Manitou Springs. ☎ **800/ 354-9971** or 719/685-5242. www.cliffdwellingsmuseum.com. Admission $7 adults, $6 seniors, $5 children 7–11, free for children under 7. June–Aug daily 9am–8pm; May and Sept daily 9am–6pm; Oct–Apr daily 9am–5pm. Closed Thanksgiving and Dec 25. Take I-25 exit 141, go west on U.S. 24 about 5 miles.

The cliff dwelling ruins here are real, although originally they were located elsewhere. In the early 1900s, archaeologists, who saw such dwellings being plundered by treasure hunters, dismantled some of the ancient buildings, gathered together artifacts found there, and hauled them away. Some of them may now be seen in this relocated 12th-century village, built by archaeologists in Phantom Cliff Canyon around 1900. American Indian dancers perform during the summer.

May Natural History Museum of the Tropics. 710 Rock Creek Canyon Rd. ☎ **719/ 576-0450.** Admission $4.50 adults, $3.50 seniors, $2.50 children. Price includes admission to the Museum of Space Exploration. May–Sept daily 9am–7pm. Take Colo. 115 and drive southwest out of Colorado Springs for 9 miles; watch for signs and the Hercules Beetle of the West Indies that mark the turnoff to the museum.

Here you'll find one of the world's best public collections of giant insects and other tropical invertebrates. James F. W. May (1884–1956) spent more than half a century exploring the world's jungles while compiling his illustrious collection, which has now grown to more than 100,000 invertebrates—about 8,000 of which are on display at any given time. The specimens are irreplaceable, since many came from areas that are now so politically unstable that no one is willing or able to explore the backcountry to collect them again. Exhibits change periodically.

The **Museum of Space Exploration** opened on the grounds in 1996. Here you can take a pictorial trip through the history of space exploration, beginning with man's first attempts to fly and continuing up to the most recent photos of Venus from the Mariner Space Craft. On display are hundreds of official NASA photographs, plus models of early aircraft, World War II planes, and space craft. Take time to view one or more of the NASA space films, which include the first moon landing.

Museum of the American Numismatic Association. 818 N. Cascade Ave. ☎ **719/ 632-2646.** www.money.org. Free admission, but donations are welcome. Mon–Fri 9am–4pm, Sat 10am–4pm. Take I-25 exit 143 east to Cascade Ave., then turn right for about 6 blocks.

The largest collection of its kind west of the Smithsonian Institution, this museum consists of eight galleries of coins, tokens, medals, and paper money from around the world. There's also a collectors' library, a gallery for the visually impaired, and an authentication department.

Peterson Air & Space Museum. Peterson Air Force Base main gate, off U.S. 24. ☎ **719/ 556-4915.** Free admission. Tues–Sat 8:30am–4:30pm. Closed holidays and occasionally during military exercises. Take I-25 exit 141, then follow U.S. 24 east about 7½ miles.

Through its exhibits this museum traces the history of Peterson Air Force Base, NORAD, the Air Defense Command, and Air Force Space Command. Of special interest are 17 historic aircraft, including P-47 Thunderbolt and P-40 Warhawk fighters from World War II, plus four missiles and jets from the Korean War to the present. To mark the 50th anniversary of the USAF, a Memorial Grove of 58 conifer trees honoring the USAF Medal of Honor recipients was planted. There's also a small gift shop here.

Pikes Peak Auto Hill Climb Educational Museum. 135 Manitou Ave., Manitou Springs. ☎ **719/685-4400.** www.ppihc.com. Admission $5 adults, $3 seniors, $2 children 6–12. Mid-June to mid-July, daily 9am–7pm; rest of year, daily 9am–5pm. Winter hours vary; call ahead. Take I-25 exit 141 west 4 miles on U.S. 24 to Manitou Ave., then east 1 block.

Commemorating the nation's second-oldest auto race (the oldest is the Indianapolis 500), this museum displays nearly a century of memorabilia and historic photos, plus almost thirty complete race cars and motorcycles from the 1920s to today. Racing legends, including Mario Andretti, Parnelli Jones, and Al and Bobby Unser, have competed in the annual July Fourth race—156 turns on a gravel highway to the summit of Pikes Peak, 14,110 feet above sea level. The gift shop carries race souvenirs.

Pro Rodeo Hall of Fame & American Cowboy Museum. 101 Pro Rodeo Dr. (off Rockrimmon Blvd.). ☎ **719/528-4764.** www.prorodeo.com. Admission $6 adults, $3 children 6–12, free for children under 6. Daily 9am–5pm. Closed New Year's Eve and Day, Easter, Thanksgiving, and Dec 25. Just off I-25 exit 147.

The development of rodeo, from its origins in early ranch work to major professional sport, is featured in two multimedia presentations. Heritage Hall showcases both historic and modern cowboy and rodeo gear and clothing, and rodeo greats are honored in the Hall of Champions. Each inductee is described through photos, gear, personal memorabilia, and trophies. Changing exhibits of western art are featured throughout the museum, and outside you can see a replica rodeo arena, live rodeo animals, and a sculpture garden.

Rocky Mountain Motorcycle Museum & Hall of Fame. 308 E. Arvada St. ☎ **719/ 633-6329** or 719/487-8005. www.pro-promotions.com. Free admission, but donations welcome. Mon–Sat 10am–7pm.

Housed in the space adjoining southern Colorado's oldest and largest custom motorcycle shop, this museum has more than 75 classic motorcycles on display. Many are in superb condition—either original or restored—and others are in various states of disrepair awaiting their turn. Motorcycle memorabilia, photos, art, and sculpture fill the space between the machines. There are a number of classic Harley-Davidsons, and one entire room is set aside for Indians, including the oldest cycle in the museum—a 1913 Indian Twin. The gift shop carries original art, books, novelties, and T-shirts. The museum was scheduled to move to a new location on N. Nevada Ave. in late 2000; at press time, details were unavailable. Call the Convention and Visitors Bureau (☎ 719/635-7506) for current information.

⊙ **Western Museum of Mining & Industry.** Gleneagle Dr., at I-25 exit 156A. ☎ **719/ 488-0880.** www.wmmi.org. E-mail: admin@wmmi.org. Admission $6 adults, $5 seniors 60 and older and students 13–17, $3 children 5–12, free for children under 5. Mon–Sat 9am–4pm, plus June–Sept Sun noon–4pm. The 27-acre site is located just east of the north gate of the U.S. Air Force Academy.

Historic hard-rock mining machinery and other equipment from Cripple Creek and other turn-of-the-century Colorado gold camps form the basis of this museum's 3,000-plus-item collection. Visitors can see an operating Corliss steam engine with a 17-ton flywheel, a life-size underground mine reconstruction, and an exhibit on mining town life showing how early western miners and their families lived. You can also pan for gold—there's a wheelchair-accessible trough—and view a 23-minute video presentation on life in the early mining camps. The second Saturday of every month brings hands-on family activities with themes such as life in a mining town, minerals in everyday products, and recycled art. Guided tours are available, with times varying seasonally; call for information.

World Figure Skating Museum & Hall of Fame. 20 First St. ☎ **719/635-5200.** www. worldskatingmuseum.org. Admission $3 adults, $2 seniors and children 6–12, free for children under 6. June–Aug Mon–Sat 10am–4pm; Sept–May Mon–Fri and the first Sat of each month 10am–4pm. Closed holidays. Take I-25 exit 138 west on Lake Ave.; just before The Broadmoor, turn right onto First St.

This is the only museum of its kind in the world, exhibiting 1,200 years of ice skates—from early skates of carved bone to highly decorated cast-iron examples and finally the steel blades of today. There are also skating costumes, medals, and other memorabilia, changing exhibits, films, a library, and a gift shop. A gallery displays skating-related paintings, including works by the 17th-century Dutch artist Pieter Brueghel and Americans Winslow Homer and Andy Warhol. The museum is recognized by the International Skating Union, the international governing body, as the repository for the history and official records of figure skating. Here also are the U.S. national, regional, sectional, and international trophies.

NATURAL ATTRACTIONS

Cave of the Winds. U.S. 24, Manitou Springs. ☎ **719/685-5444.** www.caveofthewinds. com. Admission $15 adults, $8 children 6–15, free for children under 6. May–Labor Day daily 9am–9pm; Labor Day–Apr daily 10am–5pm. Adventure Tours depart every 15 minutes; in summer, Lantern Tours ($18 adult, $9 children 6–15, not recommended for those under 6) are conducted 4 times daily and Explorer Tours ($80 per person, children 13 to 17 must be accompanied by parent or guardian, under 13 not permitted) 3 times daily; other times by reservation. Visitors with heart conditions, visual impairment, or other physical limitations are advised not to take the Lantern Tour and may not take the Explorer Tour. Take I-25 exit 141, go 6 miles west on U.S. 24.

Discovered by two boys on a church outing in 1880, this impressive underground cavern has offered public tours for well over a century. The 40-minute Discovery Tour takes visitors along a well-lit three-quarter-mile passageway through 20 subterranean chambers, complete with classic stalagmites, stalactites, crystal flowers, and limestone canopies. In the Adventure Room, modern lighting techniques return visitors to an era when spelunking was done by candle and lantern. The 1¼-hour Lantern Tour follows unpaved and unlighted passageways and corridors, is rather strenuous with some stooping required in areas with low ceilings, and might muddy your shoes but not your clothes. There's also a physically demanding 4-hour Explorer Tour that's guaranteed to get participants dirty: Armed only with flashlights and helmets, adventurers slither and scramble through remote tunnels.

Impressions

The air is so refined that you can live without much lungs.
—Shane Leslie, *American Wonderland* (1936)

Cave of the Winds also offers outdoor laser shows nightly during the summer at 9pm ($6 adults, $3 children 6 to 15, free for children under 6).

Seven Falls. At the end of S. Cheyenne Canyon Rd. ☎ **719/632-0765.** www.sevenfalls. com. Admission $7 adults, $4 children 6–15, free for children under 6. May–Jun and mid-Aug to Sept daily 8am–10:15pm; July to mid-Aug daily 8am–11:15pm; Oct–Mar 9am–4pm. Take I-25 exit 141, head west on U.S. 24, turn south on 21st St. for about 3 miles, turn west on Cheyenne Blvd., and then left onto S. Cheyenne Canyon Rd.

A spectacular 1-mile drive through a box canyon takes you between the Pillars of Hercules, where the canyon narrows to just 42 feet, ending at these cascading falls. Seven separate waterfalls dance down a granite cliff, illuminated each summer evening by colored lights; an elevator takes visitors to the Eagle Nest viewing platform. A mile-long trail atop the plateau passes the grave of 19th-century author Helen Hunt Jackson (*Ramona*) and ends at a panoramic view of Colorado Springs.

PARKS & ZOOS

✪ **Cheyenne Mountain Zoo.** 4250 Cheyenne Mountain Zoo Rd., above The Broadmoor. ☎ **719/633-9925.** www.cmzoo.org. Admission $8.50 adults, $7.50 seniors 65 and over, $5 children 3–11, free for children under 3. Summer daily 9am–6pm and until 8pm Tues; rest of year, daily 9am–5pm. Take I-25 exit 140A, then head south on Colo. 115 to Lake Ave., which you follow west to Cheyenne Mountain Zoo Rd.; watch for a sign.

Located on the lower slopes of Cheyenne Mountain at 6,800 feet above sea level, this medium-sized zoological park claims to be the country's only mountain zoo. Animals, many in "natural" environments, include lions, black leopards, red pandas, elephants, hippos, monkeys, giraffes, reptiles, snakes, and lots of birds. Rocky cliffs have been created for the mountain goats; there's a pebbled beach for penguins and an animal contact area for children. The zoo is home to more than 50 endangered species, including the Siberian tiger, Amur leopard, and black rhinoceros. The zoo's giraffes are the most prolific captive herd in the world, producing four live births in 1999; visitors can actually feed the long-necked beasts.

There's also a colorful antique carousel (1926), as well as a tram that makes a full loop of the zoo in about 15 minutes (it operates from Memorial Day to Labor Day, and you can ride all day for $1; it's both stroller and handicapped accessible). Strollers, double strollers, wheelchairs, and wagons are available for rent at Thundergod Gift and Snack Shop.

Memorial Park. 1605 E. Pikes Peak Ave. (between Hancock Ave. and Union Blvd.). ☎ **719/ 385-5940.** Free admission. Daily year-round.

One of the largest parks in the city, Memorial is home to the Mark "Pa" Sertich Ice Center and the Aquatics and Fitness Center, as well as the famed 7-Eleven Velodrome, which is used for world-class bicycling events. Other facilities include baseball/softball fields, volleyball courts, tennis courts, a bicycle criterium, and jogging trails. At Prospect Lake on the south side of the park, you can fish, swim, and rent paddleboats (about $8 an hour). The park also hosts a terrific fireworks display on Independence Day. See the sections on ice skating, swimming, and tennis under "Outdoor Activities," below.

Monument Valley Park. 170 W. Cache La Poudre Blvd. ☎ **719/385-5940.** Free admission. Daily year-round.

This long, slender park follows Monument Creek through downtown Colorado Springs. At its south end are formal zinnia, begonia, and rose gardens, and in the middle are demonstration gardens of the Horticultural Art Society. Facilities include softball/baseball fields, a swimming pool (open daily in summer; $4 adults, $2.50 children), volleyball and tennis courts, children's playgrounds, picnic shelters, and two trails—the 4¼-mile Monument Creek Trail for walkers, runners, and cyclists, and the 1-mile Monument Valley Fitness Trail at the north end of the park, beside Bodington Field.

✪ **Mueller State Park.** P.O. Box 39, Divide, CO 80814. ☎ **719/687-2366.** www.coloradoparks.org. Admission $4 per vehicle. Take U.S. 24 west from Colorado Springs to Divide (25 miles), then go 3½ miles south on Colo. 67.

Somewhat like a junior version of Rocky Mountain National Park, Mueller has 12,000 acres of prime scenic beauty along the west slope of Pikes Peak. There are 75 miles of trails, designated for hikers, horseback riders, and mountain bikers, with opportunities to observe elk, bighorn sheep, black bear, and the park's other wildlife. The best times to spot wildlife are spring and fall, just after sunrise and just before sunset. In the summer, rangers lead hikes and offer campfire programs in an 80-seat amphitheater. See also "Camping," under "Accommodations," above.

North Cheyenne Cañon Park and Starsmore Discovery Center. 2120 S. Cheyenne Cañon Rd. (west of 21st St.). ☎ **719/578-6146.** Free admission. Park, May–Oct daily 5am–11pm; Nov–Apr daily 5am–9pm. Starsmore Discovery Center, mid-June to mid-Aug daily 9am–9pm; mid-Aug to Labor Day daily 9am–5pm, Labor Day–early June Wed–Sat 10am–4pm, Sun noon–4pm. Helen Hunt Falls Visitor Center, May Sat–Sun 9am–5pm, Jun–Sept daily 9am–5pm; Sept–Oct Sat–Sun 10am–4pm; closed Nov–April.

Entirely within the city limits of Colorado Springs, this city park includes North Cheyenne Creek, which drops 1,800 feet over the course of 5 miles in a series of cascades and waterfalls. The park contains picnic areas and hiking trails; the visitor center at the foot of Helen Hunt Falls has exhibits on history, geology, flora, and fauna. The Starsmore Discovery Center, at the entrance to the park, has maps, information, and interactive exhibits for both kids and adults, including audiovisual programs and a climbing wall where you can learn about rock climbing.

Palmer Park. Maizeland Rd. off Academy Blvd. ☎ **719/385-5940.** Free admission. Daily year-round.

Deeded to the city in 1899 by Colorado Springs founder Gen. William Jackson Palmer, this 722-acre preserve offers hiking, biking, and horseback riding opportunities across a mesa overlooking the city. It boasts a variety of minerals (including quartz, topaz, jasper, and tourmaline), rich vegetation (including a yucca preservation area), and considerable wildlife. The Edna Mae Bennet Nature Trail is a self-guided excursion, and there are numerous other trails. Other facilities include 12 separate picnic areas, softball/baseball fields, and volleyball courts.

ESPECIALLY FOR KIDS

In addition to the listings below, children will probably enjoy the **Cheyenne Mountain Zoo, May Natural History Museum,** and **Ghost Town,** described above.

Arcade Amusements, Inc. 930 Block Manitou Ave., Manitou Springs. ☎ **719/685-9815.** Free admission; arcade games range from 1¢ to 75¢. First weekend in May–Labor Day daily 10am–midnight. In winter, open on nice weekends 11am–6pm; call first.

Among the West's oldest and largest amusement arcades, this game complex just might be considered a hands-on arcade museum as well as a fun place for kids of all ages. Some 250 machines range from original working penny pinball machines to modern video games, skee-ball, and 12-player horse racing.

Children's Museum of Colorado Springs. Upper level of Citadel Mall next to JCPenney, 750 Citadel Dr. ☎ **719/574-0077.** Admission $3 children 2 and up, $1 adults, free for children 1 and under. Mon–Sat 10am–5pm, Sun noon–5pm. Closed major holidays.

Come to this museum to "discover the art and science of being a kid." Children can crawl through a model of the human heart, explore an "inside-out" house that demonstrates the inner workings of a modern home, and play in front of a screen that reflects colorful whirling shadows of dancing visitors. The nonprofit art and science museum offers many more hands-on activities, special programs on Saturday, a gift shop, a toddler's room with a Little Tykes computer, and birthday parties by arrangement.

North Pole/Santa's Workshop. At the foot of Pikes Peak Hwy. off U.S. 24, 5 miles west of Manitou Springs. ☎ **719/684-9432.** www.santas-colo.com. Admission $11.50 ages 2–59, $4.95 seniors 60 and over, free for children under 2. Mid-May to May 31, Fri–Tues 9:30am–6pm; June–Aug daily 9:30am–6pm; Sept–Dec 24 (weather permitting), Fri–Tues 10am–5pm. Closed Dec 25 to mid-May. Take I-25 exit 141, go west on U.S. 24 about 10 miles.

Santa's workshop is busy from mid-May right up until Christmas Eve. Not only can kids visit shops where elves have some early Christmas gifts for sale, but they can also see Santa himself and whisper their requests in his ear. This 26-acre village features numerous rides; including a miniature train, a Ferris wheel, and a replica of the *Enterprise* space shuttle; as well as magic shows and musical entertainment, snack shops, and an ice-cream parlor.

ORGANIZED TOURS

Half- and full-day bus tours of Colorado Springs, Pikes Peak, the Air Force Academy, and other nearby attractions are offered by **Pikes Peak Tours/Gray Line,** 3704 W. Colorado Ave. (☎ **800/345-8197** or 719/633-1181). From May through October, a variety of other tours are offered, including an excursion to Royal Gorge and white-water rafting trips. Prices range from $30 to $70 per person.

Prearranged group walking tours are available from **Talk of the Town,** 1313 Sunset Rd. (☎ **719/633-2724**); they also publish a book of walking tours, *Trips on Twos,* available at local bookstores.

A free downtown **Walking Tour** brochure, with a map and descriptions of more than 30 historic buildings, is available at the Colorado Springs Convention and Visitors Bureau, as well as at local businesses.

Another free brochure, titled *Old Colorado City,* not only shows the location of more than a dozen historic buildings, but also lists shops, galleries, and other businesses.

During the summer months, the **Town Trolley** provides tours and transportation through Manitou Springs and into part of Garden of the Gods (see "Getting Around," earlier in this chapter).

Visitors to Manitou Springs should stop at the **Manitou Springs Chamber of Commerce,** 354 Manitou Avenue (☎ **800/642-2567** or 719/685-5089), to pick up a free copy of the *Manitou Springs Complete Visitor's Guide,* which includes a self-guided walking-tour map to Mineral Springs, as well as information on where to find a variety of outdoor sculptures. See "Historic Neighborhoods," above.

6 Outdoor Activities

For information on the city's parks and programs, contact the **Colorado Springs Parks and Recreation Department** (☎ 719/385-5940). Most of the state and federal agencies concerned with outdoor recreation are headquartered in Denver. There are branch offices in Colorado Springs for **Colorado State Parks,** 2128 N. Weber St. (☎ 719/471-0900); the **Colorado Division of Wildlife,** 2126 N. Weber St. (☎ 719/227-5200, or 719/227-5201 for a 24-hour recorded information line); and the **U.S. Forest Service,** Pikes Peak Ranger District of the Pike National Forest, 601 S. Weber St. (☎ 719/636-1602).

You can get hunting and fishing licenses at many sporting-goods stores, as well as at the Colorado Division of Wildlife office listed above.

AERIAL SPORTS   The **Black Forest Soaring Society,** 24566 David Johnson Loop, Elbert, CO 80106 (☎ 877/931-SOAR or 303/648-3623), some 30 miles northeast of the Springs, offers glider rides, rentals, and instruction. Rides cost about $75, with rentals running $15 per hour (to those with gliding licenses) and instruction running $24 an hour. A one-day mini-course of the first three beginners' flying lessons is also offered for $150. Advance reservations are required.

Those wanting to rise above it all in a hot-air balloon can contact several commercial ballooning companies, including **High But Dry Balloons,** P.O. Box 49006, Colorado Springs, CO 80949 (☎ 719/260-0011), for tours, champagne flights, and weddings. Sunrise flights are scheduled daily year-round, weather permitting. Cost depends on the number of passengers, locations, and type of flight. Generally, flights last 2 or 3 hours, with a minimum of 1 hour. On Labor Day weekend, the **Colorado Springs Balloon Classic** sees more than 100 hot-air balloons launched from the city's Memorial Park. Admission is free (☎ 719/471-4833; www.balloonclassic.com).

BICYCLING   Aside from the 4¼-mile loop trail around Monument Valley Park (see "Parks & Zoos" under "Attractions," above), there are numerous other urban trails for bikers. You can get information at the city's Visitor Information Center, 104 S. Cascade Ave. (☎ 719/635-1632).

For guided tours and rentals, contact **Challenge Unlimited** (see "Mountain Biking," below).

FISHING   Most serious Colorado Springs anglers drive south 40 miles to the Arkansas River or west to the Rocky Mountain streams and lakes, such as those found in Eleven Mile State Park and Spinney Mountain State Park on the South Platte River west of Florissant. Bass, catfish, walleye pike, and panfish are found in the streams of eastern Colorado; trout is the preferred sport fish of the mountain regions.

Angler's Covey, 917 W. Colorado Ave. (☎ 800/753-4746 or 719/471-2984), is a specialty fly-fishing shop and a good source of general fishing information for southern Colorado. It offers guided half- and full-day trips ($150 to $300 for one to three persons), as well as state fishing licenses, rentals, flies, tackle, and so forth. Another good source for licenses, advice, and equipment is **Gart Sports,** 106 N. Tejon St. (☎ 719/473-3143).

GOLF   Public courses include the **Patty Jewett Golf Course,** 900 E. Española St. (☎ 719/385-6950); **Pine Creek Golf Club,** 9850 Divot Trail (☎ 719/594-9999); and **Valley Hi Golf Course,** 610 S. Chelton Rd. (☎ 719/385-6917). Nonresident greens fees range from $24 to $32 for 18 holes (not including a cart).

The finest golf courses in the Springs are private. Guests of The Broadmoor hotel can enjoy the 54-hole **Broadmoor Golf Club** (☎ 719/577-5790).

Impressions

Could one live in constant view of these grand mountains without being elevated by them into a lofty plane of thought and purpose?
                    —General William J. Palmer, founder of Colorado Springs (1871)

HIKING   Opportunities abound in municipal parks (see "Parks & Zoos," under "Attractions," above) and Pike National Forest, which borders Colorado Springs to the west. The U.S. Forest Service district office can provide maps and general information (see addresses and phone numbers, above).

Especially popular are the 7½-mile **Waldo Canyon Trail,** with its trailhead just east of Cascade Avenue off U.S. 24; the 10-mile **Mount Manitou Trail,** starting in Ruxton Canyon above the hydroelectric plant; and the 12-mile **Barr Trail** to the summit of Pikes Peak. **Mueller State Park** (☎ **719/687-2366**), 3½ miles south of Divide en route to Cripple Creek, has 75 miles of hiking and backpacking paths. See "Parks & Zoos" under "Attractions," above.

HORSEBACK RIDING   The **Academy Riding Stables,** 4 El Paso Blvd., near the Garden of the Gods (☎ **719/633-5667**), offers guided trail rides for children and adults by reservation ($25 to $40).

HUNTING   Opportunities for hunters abound in the plains east of Colorado Springs (especially for hunting waterfowl) and in the Rockies west of the city (for hunting deer, bear, and even cougar). For information and licenses, consult the Colorado Division of Wildlife (see address and phone number, above).

ICE SKATING   The **Mark "Pa" Sertich Ice Center** at Memorial Park (☎ **719/385-5983**) is open daily, offering prearranged instruction and rentals. In 1995, the U.S. Olympic Complex opened the **Colorado Springs World Arena Ice Hall,** located at 3185 Venetucci Blvd. (☎ **719/477-2100;** www.worldarena.com), with public sessions daily (admission $1 to $4). To get there, take I-25 exit 138, go west on Circle Drive to Venetucci Boulevard, and south to the arena.

MOUNTAIN BIKING   There are abundant mountain-biking opportunities in the Colorado Springs area; contact the U.S. Forest Service for details (see address and phone number, above). From May through early October, **Challenge Unlimited,** 204 S. 24th St. (☎ **800/798-5954** or 719/633-6399; www.bikithikit.com), hosts fully equipped, guided rides for every level of experience. Your guide on the 19-mile ride down the Pikes Peak Highway, from the summit at 14,110 feet to the toll gate at 7,000 feet, presents an interpretation of the nature, history, and beauty of the mountain. To participate, you must be 10 years or older; advance reservations are advised. Rates are $68 to $89 for a 5-hour trip. Challenge Unlimited also rents bikes ($18 for 3 hours; $26 for full day), so you can explore the area on your own.

RIVER RAFTING   Colorado Springs is 40 miles from the Arkansas River near Cañon City, and there are several licensed white-water outfitters who tackle the Royal Gorge. **Echo Canyon River Expeditions,** 45000 U.S. 50 West, Cañon City, CO 81212 (☎ **800/748-2953** or 719/275-3154; www.echocanyonrafting.com), offers half-day to 3-day trips on "mild to wild" stretches of river. The company uses state-of-the-art equipment, including self-bailing rafts. Costs range from $33 to $325. **Arkansas River Tours,** P.O. Box 337, Cotopaxi, CO 81223 (☎ **800/321-4352** or 719/942-4362; www.arkansasrivertours.com), offers white-water trips of lengths varying from a quarter of a day to all day for about $17 to $80, and 2-day trips for about

$180. For trips on the Arkansas ranging from gentle to exciting, try **Adventure Quest Expeditions,** P.O. Box 283, Cañon City, CO 81215 (☎ **888/448-7238** or 719/ 269-9807; www.coloradovacation.com/rafting/quest). Trips last a half or full day and cost from $30 to $85; multi-day packages are also offered. Another renowned Arkansas River rafting company is **Wilderness Aware,** P.O. Box 1550, Buena Vista, CO 81211 (☎ **800/462-7238** or 719/395-2112; www.inaraft.com). Half-day to five-day trips are available, ranging from $31 to $495. All rates are per person.

SWIMMING   Among the many attractions at the city-run Memorial Park (see "Parks & Zoos" above) is the pool at the **Aquatics and Fitness Center,** 270 Union Blvd. (☎719/385-5984). Admission is $5.25 for adults, $3.75 for children. Call for seasonal hours. You can also swim at Memorial Park's **Prospect Lake,** open daily in summer from 10am to 5pm ($3.50 adults, $2.75 children).

TENNIS   Many city parks have tennis courts, including **Memorial Park** (see "Parks & Zoos," above). Contact the Colorado Springs Parks and Recreation Department (☎ **719/385-5940**). Use of city courts is free.

7 Spectator Sports

The **Air Force Academy Falcons** football team dominates the sports scene here, although there are also competitive baseball, basketball, hockey, and soccer teams. Call for schedules and ticket information (☎ **800/666-USAF** or 719/472-1895).

AUTO RACING   The **Pikes Peak International Hill Climb** (☎ **719/685-4400;** www.ppihc.com), known as the "Race to the Clouds," is held annually on July 4. An international field of drivers (which always seems to include at least one member of the famous Unser racing family) negotiates the winding, hairpin turns of the final 12.4 miles of the Pikes Peak Highway to the top of the 14,110-foot mountain. For information, contact the Pikes Peak Auto Hill Climb Educational Museum (see "Museums & Galleries" under "Attractions," above).

   NASCAR and Indy Racing make annual stops at **Pikes Peak International Raceway,** 16650 Midway Ranch Rd., Fountain, CO 80817 (☎ **888/306-RACE** or 719/ 382-RACE; www.ppir.com) located 15 miles south of Colorado Springs, exit 124 off I-25. The track held its inaugural season in 1997, with a capacity crowd of 40,000 fans in the grandstand. Event tickets usually range from $45 to $65 for a weekend pass, or about $25 for a single day. There are also motorcycle races, driving schools, and occasional concerts at the facility.

BASEBALL   The **Colorado Springs Sky Sox** of the Pacific Coast League, the AAA farm team for the Colorado Rockies, play a full 144-game season, with 72 home games at Sky Sox Stadium, 4385 Tutt Blvd., off Barnes Road east of Powers Boulevard (☎ **719/597-3000;** www.skysox.com). The season begins the second week of April and runs through Labor Day. Games are played afternoons and evenings. Tickets cost $7 for adults, $6 for children 2 to 12 and seniors 60 and over for reserved seating; $4.75and $4.25 respectively for upper reserved seats; and $4 for general admission. Call the stadium or check the newspaper sports pages for schedule information.

GREYHOUND RACING   Dog racing takes place from April through September at **Rocky Mountain Greyhound Park,** 3701 N. Nevada Ave. (☎ **719/632-1391;** www.rmgp.com), with both evening and weekend races. There is also full horse simulcasting from around the country and a $12.95 prime rib buffet on Friday and Saturday evenings.

HOCKEY   In addition to Air Force Academy Hockey (see above), the **World Arena,** 3185 Venetucci Blvd.(☎ **719/477-2100;** www.worldarena.com) is home to the Colorado College Tigers and the Colorado Gold Kings of the West Coast Hockey League. The Tigers season runs from October to March and the Gold Kings play October through April. Tickets are available by phone (☎ **719/576-2626**) and online.

RODEO   The **Pikes Peak or Bust Rodeo,** held annually (since 1941) in early August, is a major stop on the Professional Rodeo Cowboys Association circuit. Its purse of more than $150,000 makes it the 2nd largest rodeo in Colorado (after Denver's National Western Stock Show), and 19th largest in North America. Events are held at Penrose Stadium, 1045 W. Rio Grande Ave. off Fountain Creek Boulevard (☎ **719/635-3547**). Various events around the city, including a parade and a street breakfast, mark rodeo week.

8 Shopping

Five principal areas attract shoppers in Colorado Springs. The Manitou Springs and Old Colorado City neighborhoods are excellent places to browse for art, jewelry, arts and crafts, books, and other specialty items. The Citadel and Chapel Hills malls combine major department stores with a variety of fashionable boutiques. Downtown Colorado Springs, of course, also has numerous fine shops.

SHOPPING A TO Z
ANTIQUES

Antique Emporium at Manitou Springs. 719 Manitou Ave., Manitou Springs. ☎ **719/685-9195.**

The shop's 4,000 square feet of floor space provides ample room for displaying its collection of antique furniture, china, glassware, books, collectibles, and primitives. Consignments are welcome.

Nevada Avenue Antiques. 405 S. Nevada Ave. ☎ **719/473-3351.**

This is Colorado Springs' oldest multidealer mall. With 7,000 square feet filled with antiques, there should be something to satisfy everyone.

The Villagers. 2514 W. Colorado Ave., Old Colorado City. ☎ **719/632-1400.**

Here you will find a diverse array of quality antiques and collectibles. The shop is run by volunteers, and all proceeds go to Cheyenne Village, a community of adults with developmental disabilities.

ART GALLERIES

Business of Art Center. 513 Manitou Ave., Manitou Springs. ☎ **719/685-1861.**

Primarily an educational facility to help artists learn the business end of their profession, there are also workshops, classes, and lectures, plus numerous artists' studios (open for viewing by visitors), three exhibition galleries, and a gift shop. Featured are renowned Colorado artists and juried exhibits of regional art. The shop offers a varied selection of regional artwork including prints, photographs, jewelry, sculpture, ceramics, wearable art, hand-blown glass, and carved wood objects. Theater, music, and dance performances are occasionally staged (donation requested).

Colorado Springs Art Guild/Gallery. 1700 E. Platte Ave. (in the lower suite of the First United bank). ☎ **719/630-1611.**

A showcase for local artists, the guild has promoted fine arts in the Colorado Springs area since the 1940s. The CSAG sponsors ongoing juried shows and classes, with a major juried exhibition annually. It also sponsors workshops and demonstrations by leading artists in the region.

Flute Player Gallery. 2511 W. Colorado Ave., Old Colorado City. ☎ **719/632-7702.**

This gallery offers contemporary and traditional American Indian silver and turquoise jewelry, Pueblo pottery, Navajo weavings, and Hopi kachina dolls.

Michael Garman's Gallery. 2418 W. Colorado Ave., Old Colorado City. ☎ **800/731-3908** or 719/471-9391. www.michaelgarman.com.

This gallery serves as a showcase for Garman's sculptures and casts depicting urban and western life, plus "Magic Town," a large model of an old-time inner city, with sculptures and holographic actors. Admission to Magic Town is $3 for adults, $2 for children 7 to 12, and free for children under 7.

BOOKS

Barnes & Noble Booksellers. 795 Citadel Dr. E. (on the edge of Citadel Mall). ☎ **719/637-8282.**

Looking for the latest best-seller to read on the flight back home? You'll find it here, at a discount, along with a good selection of regional titles and just about every other subject imaginable. Attached to the store is a Starbucks Coffee. There's another Barnes & Noble near the Air Force Academy, at 1565 Briargate Blvd. (☎ **719/266-9960**).

Book Sleuth. 2501 W. Colorado Ave. #105, Old Colorado City. ☎ **719/632-2727.**

For all your mystery needs, visit this bookstore. In addition to a wide selection of mystery novels, there are numerous puzzles and games to choose from.

Borders. 110 Briargate Blvd. (in Chapel Hills Mall). ☎ **719/266-1600.**

Like others in this well-respected national bookstore chain, this Borders stocks a wide range of books, including regional titles and all the latest bestsellers. It also sells maps and has an attached cafe.

Chinook Bookshop. 210 N. Tejon St. ☎ **800/999-1195** or 719/635-1195. www.chinookbook.com.

Open since 1962, this is a gem of a bookstore, with 75,000 titles, including an extensive western Americana collection. An entire room is devoted to maps and globes, and the Children's Room offers kids a large, sunny area with a two-story playhouse and a carpeted and cushioned reading platform.

CRAFTS

Candle Shoppe. 2421½ W. Colorado Ave., Old Colorado City. ☎ **719/633-4856.**

Candles in all shapes, scents, and sizes are offered in this unique shop. Among the 25,000 candles for sale here are a 20-pound wax grizzly bear and religious and historic figures that are much too beautiful to burn.

Van Briggle Art Pottery. 600 S. 21st St., Old Colorado City. ☎ **719/633-7729.** www.vanbriggle.com.

Founded in 1900 by Artus Van Briggle, who applied Chinese matte glaze to Rocky Mountain clays and imaginative art-nouveau shapes, this is one of the oldest active art potteries in the United States. Today artisans demonstrate their craft, from "throwing on the wheel" to glazing and firing. Free tours are available, and finished works are sold in the showroom.

FASHION

Rags 'n Riches. 2526 W. Colorado Ave., Old Colorado City. ☎ **719/634-7299.**

This ladies' clothing boutique, an Old Colorado City fixture for 30 years, sells new clothing, jewelry, and accessories. The apparel selection is unique, ranging from casual tops to lacy wedding dresses, as well as the latest fashions and wearable art.

GIFTS & SOUVENIRS

Gourmand. 2530A W. Colorado Ave., Old Colorado City. ☎ **719/578-1386.**

Gourmet food made in Colorado is the forte here, from salsas to chokecherry jelly. You'll also find fun knickknacks, dishware, hand-painted glassware, cookbooks, and kitchen gift items. Don't forget that Colorado specialty—chocolate moose droppings (chocolate-covered almonds)!

Kris Kringle Ltd. 30 S. Sierra Madre St. ☎ **719/633-1210.**

This is the place to come for Christmas year-round. The shop is stuffed with doll-houses, miniatures, and Yuletide decorations of all kinds.

Penguin & Friends. 742 Manitou Ave., Manitou Springs. ☎ **719/685-0700.**

This unusual shop sells souvenirs of the Pikes Peak region, Christmas items, American Indian crafts, angels and other collectibles, and—of course—penguins.

Simpich Character Dolls. 2413 W. Colorado Ave., Old Colorado City. ☎ **719/636-3272.** www.simpich.com.

These exquisite handmade dolls are the creation of Bob and Jan Simpich, who made their first dolls in 1952 as Christmas gifts for their parents. Friends would see the dolls and ask about buying them—and the business just sort of grew from there. Today, there are numerous dolls representing characters from literature, the Victorian era, and early American life, as well as creations ranging from the whimsical—such as leprechauns and elves—to the historical (an Abraham Lincoln bust).

JEWELRY

All That Glitters. 2518 W. Colorado Ave., Old Colorado City. ☎ **719/475-7160.** www.allthatglitters.net.

This well-established Colorado Springs jeweler is known for beautiful custom gold work and one-of-a-kind designer jewelry.

Manitou Jack's Jewelry & Gifts. 814 Manitou Ave., Manitou Springs. ☎ **719/685-5004.**

Black Hills gold, 10- and 14-karat, is the specialty here. There's also an extensive collection of American Indian jewelry, pottery, sand paintings, and other art. The shop will create custom jewelry and make repairs.

Megel's Jewelers Ltd. 12 E. Pikes Peak Ave. ☎ **719/632-2552.**

A downtown institution since 1949, this well-respected shop offers full-service jewelry and watch repair, plus a large selection of diamonds and gems.

MALLS & SHOPPING CENTERS

Chapel Hills Mall. 1710 Briargate Blvd. (N. Academy Blvd., at I-25 exit 150A). ☎ **719/594-0111.**

Foley's, Sears, Mervyn's, JC Penney, Dillard's, and Kmart are among the 135-plus stores at this mall, which also houses an ice-skating arena, two movie theaters, and about two dozen food outlets.

The Citadel. 750 Citadel Dr. E. (N. Academy Blvd. at E. Platte Ave.). ☎ **719/591-2900.** www.shopthecitadel.com.

This is southern Colorado's largest regional shopping mall, with Dillard's, Foley's, JCPenney, Mervyn's, and more than 170 specialty shops and restaurants.

SPORTING GOODS

Leading sporting-goods dealers in the city include **Grand West Outfitters,** 3250 N. Academy Blvd. (☎ **719/596-3031**), which sells and rents camping gear, and also sells outdoor clothing, bikes, hiking and climbing gear, and winter sports equipment. A good source for fishing as well as camping and winter sports equipment is **Gart Sports,** 106 N. Tejon St. (☎ **719/473-3143**).

WINE & LIQUOR

Cheers Liquor Mart. 1105 N. Circle Dr. ☎ **719/574-2244.**

This liquor supermarket has a huge selection of beer and wine, including Colorado wines, at good prices.

Coal Train Wine & Liquors. 330 W. Uintah St. ☎ **719/475-9700.**

Located on the north edge of downtown, this liquor store offers a good selection, personal service, and reasonable prices.

Pikes Peak Vineyards. 3901 Janitell Rd. (I-25 exit 138). ☎ **719/576-0075.**

This small, award-winning winery produces 8 to 10 moderately priced red, white, and blush wines. Tours and tastings are offered by appointment. **The Winery** (☎ **719/538-8848**), a continental fine dining restaurant featuring fresh seafood, steaks, lamb, and duck, opened at the site in summer 1998. It is open for dinner Tuesday through Saturday with dinner entrees ranging from $17 to $25.

9 Colorado Springs After Dark

The Colorado Springs entertainment scene is spread throughout the metropolitan area. Pikes Peak Center, the Colorado Springs Fine Arts Center, City Auditorium, Colorado College, and the various facilities at the U.S. Air Force Academy are all outstanding venues for the performing arts. The city also supports dozens of cinemas, nightclubs, bars, and other after-dark attractions. Downtown is the major nightlife hub, but Old Colorado City and Manitou Springs also have their fair share of interesting drinking and entertainment establishments.

Current weekly entertainment schedules can be found in the Friday *Gazette Telegraph.* Also look at the listings in *Springs* magazine and *The Independent,* free entertainment tabloids. Or call the city's weekly events line at ☎ **719/635-1723.**

Tickets for nearly all major entertainment and sporting events can be obtained from **Ticketmaster** (☎ **719/520-9090**).

THE CLUB & MUSIC SCENE

Cowboys. 3910 Palmer Park Blvd. ☎ **719/596-2152.**

Two-steppers and country-and-western music lovers flock to this east-side club, which boasts the largest dance floor in the area. It's open Wednesday to Sunday, and dance lessons are available.

Poor Richard's Restaurant. 324½ N. Tejon St. ☎ **719/632-7721.**

An eclectic variety of performers appear at this Bohemian landmark 1 or 2 nights a week, presenting everything from acoustic folk to Celtic melodies to jazz to bluegrass. The menu includes pizza and sandwiches, as well as beer and wine.

Rum Bay. 20 N. Tejon St. ☎ **719/634-3522.**

Located in the renovated Woolworth Building downtown, the lively Rum Bay is a massive nightclub sporting a wall full of rum bottles and a tropical theme. Disc jockeys spin records for two dance floors; there's also a piano bar featuring dueling players Wednesday through Saturday. (Monday is karaoke night.) The kitchen serves American and Caribbean standards for lunch and dinner daily. There's also a game room with pool, video games, and foosball.

The Underground. 130 E. Kiowa St. (at Nevada Ave.). ☎ **719/633-0590.**

This popular hangout attracts a diverse crowd, from college students and other young people to baby boomers and retirees. Patrons come to dance or just listen to the equally eclectic music (live or recorded), which ranges from rock to jazz to reggae, with some occasional folk.

THE BAR SCENE

Golden Bee. Lower level entrance of The Broadmoor International Center, Lake Circle. ☎ **719/634-7711.**

An opulent English pub was disassembled, shipped from Great Britain, and reassembled piece by piece to create this delightful drinking establishment. You can have imported Bass Ale by the yard if you choose, while enjoying a beef-and-kidney pie or other English specialties. Evenings bring a ragtime pianist to enliven the atmosphere.

Hide 'n' Seek. 512 W. Colorado Ave. ☎ **719/634-9303.**

The Hide 'n' Seek, which opened in 1972, is one of the oldest and largest gay bars in the West. It has five bars with country-western and other themes, dance areas with DJ music most nights, and a restaurant.

Judge Baldwin's Brewing Company. In the Antlers Adam's Mark Hotel, 4 S. Cascade Ave. ☎ **719/473-5600.**

This popular and busy restaurant—the Springs' first microbrewery—is also a good spot to stop and sample the local brews, including a lager, amber ale, and nut brown ale. On any given day, ten of their brews are on tap. See also "Dining," above.

MacKenzie's Chop House. 128 S. Tejon St. ☎ **719/635-3536.**

MacKenzie's specializes in martinis—shaken not stirred—with over forty on the menu. The luxurious cigar lounge in back has a fragrant walk-in humidor, with cigars ranging in price from $7 to $30. The extensive wine list includes American, French, Italian, and South African choices. See also "Dining," above.

Meadow Muffins. 2432 W. Colorado Ave., in Old Colorado City. ☎ **719/633-0583.** www.meadowmuffins.com.

A boisterous barroom packed to the gills with movie memorabilia and assorted knicknacks ranging from two buckboard wagons (hung from the ceiling near the front door) to a five-ton cannon to buffalo and moose heads, Meadow Muffins certainly doesn't lack personality. It features DJs or live musicians five nights a week and karaoke every other Tuesday. There's a good menu with wings, onion rings, sandwiches, and other bar fare—the specialty burgers include "The Jiffy," a slab of beef covered with peanut butter. On most days, there's great food and drink specials, with happy hour from 4pm to 7pm Wednesday to Monday and 4pm until closing time on Saturdays. There are also pool tables, a pair of big-screen TVs, and arcade games.

Phantom Canyon Brewing Co. 2 E. Pikes Peak Ave. ☎ **719/635-2800.**

This popular brew pub generally has 10 of their specialty beers on tap as well as home-made root beer. A billiard hall is located on the second floor. See also "Dining," above.

Ritz Grill. 15 S. Tejon St. ☎ **719/635-8484.**

Especially popular with young professionals after work and the chic clique later in the evening, this noisy restaurant-lounge, with a large central bar, brings an art-deco feel to downtown Colorado Springs. Stop by on the weekends for live rock. See also "Dining," above.

THE PERFORMING ARTS

Among the major venues for performing arts in Colorado Springs is the 8,000-seat **Colorado Springs World Arena,** 3185 Venetucci Blvd., at I-25 exit 138 (☎ **719/477-2100**). The area's newest entertainment center, it presents big-name country and rock concerts and a wide variety of sporting events. Other major facilities include the handsome **Pikes Peak Center,** 190 S. Cascade Ave. (☎ **719/520-7453** for general information, or 719/520-7469 for the ticket office; www.pikespeakcenter.org), a 2,000-seat concert hall in the heart of downtown that has been acclaimed for its outstanding acoustics. The city's symphony orchestra and dance theater call the Pikes Peak Center home, and top-flight touring entertainers, Broadway musicals, and symphony orchestras make appearances here as well. The **Colorado Springs Fine Arts Center,** 30 W. Dale St. (☎ **719/634-5581** for general information, or 719/634-5583 for the box office), is a historic facility (see "Museums & Galleries" in "Attractions," above) that includes a children's theater program, a repertory theater company, dance programs and concerts, and classic films. Recent productions have included *Annie* and *Oklahoma.* At the historic **City Auditorium,** 221 E. Kiowa St. (☎ **719/578-6652**), you can often attend a trade show or concert, or drop in at the Lon Chaney Theatre, with its resident Star Bar Players (see below).

CLASSICAL MUSIC & OPERA

Colorado Opera Festival. 219 W. Colorado Ave., suite 108. ☎ **719/473-0073.** www.colo-opera.org.

Each summer, a variety of classical operas is staged at the Pikes Peak Center. Original-language productions with English supertitles feature nationally known opera singers. Call for schedule and prices.

Colorado Springs Symphony Orchestra. 619 N. Cascade Ave. ☎ **719/633-6698,** or 719/520-7469 for ticket information. www.cssymphony.org. Tickets $8–$42.

This fine professional orchestra annually performs about a dozen classical concerts, as well as youth, pops, chamber, holiday, and free summer concerts. Most performances are held at the Pikes Peak Center. Tchaikovsky's *The Nutcracker* is performed over Thanksgiving weekend to kick off the holidays, and there's a New Year's Eve celebration with entertainment ranging from Viennese waltzes to Broadway musicals as a finale to the season.

THEATER & DANCE

BlueBards, Arnold Hall Theater, U.S. Air Force Academy. ☎ **719/333-4497.** www.usafa.af.mil/wing/clubs/bluebards.

The Air Force Academy's cadet theater group performs to appreciative townspeople and visitors as well as fellow cadets.

Colorado Springs Dance Theatre. 7 E. Bijou St., Suite 209. ☎ **719/630-7434.** www. csdance.org. Tickets $15–$50, with discounts for students and seniors.

This nonprofit organization presents dance companies from around the world in a September-to-May season at Pikes Peak Center, Colorado College's Armstrong Hall, and other venues. Notable productions have included Mikhail Baryshnikov, Alvin Ailey Repertory Ensemble, Ballet Folklorico of Mexico, and other traditional, modern, ethnic, and jazz dance programs. Each year three to five performances are scheduled, and there are often master classes, lectures, and other programs coinciding with the performances.

Rocky Mountain Cloggers. 806 Cardinal St. ☎ **719/392-4791.**

The eight members of this national exhibition clog-dance team perform some three dozen shows in the Colorado Springs area each year. Call for a current schedule.

Star Bar Players. Lon Chaney Theatre, City Auditorium, 221 E. Kiowa St. ☎ **719/ 573-7411.**

Each year, this resident theater company presents several full-length plays, ranging from Greek comedies to modern murder mysteries, plus children's and other productions.

DINNER THEATERS

Flying W Ranch. 3330 Chuckwagon Rd. ☎ **800/232-FLYW** or 719/598-4000. www. flyingw.com. Reservations strongly recommended. Chuck-wagon dinners, $15.50 adults, $7.50 children 8 and under; winter steak house, $20–$21 adults, $7.50 children 8 and under.

This working cattle and horse ranch just north of the Garden of the Gods treats visitors to a western village of more than a dozen restored buildings and a mine train. There are also demonstrations of Navajo weaving and horse-shoeing. A western stage show features bunkhouse comedy, cowboy balladry, and foot-stompin' fiddle, mandolin, and guitar music. From mid-May through September the town opens each afternoon at 4:30pm; a chuck-wagon dinner is served ranch style at 7:15pm and the show begins at 8:30pm. The winter steak house is open October to December and March to May on Friday and Saturday evenings, with seatings at 5 and 8pm, and a western stage show at each seating.

Iron Springs Chateau Melodrama. 444 Ruxton Ave., Manitou Springs. ☎ **719/ 685-5104** or 719/685-5572. www.pikes-peak.com/Theatre. Reservations required. Tickets, dinner, and show, $21.50 adults, $20.50 seniors, $12.50 children; show only, $1150 adults, $11seniors, $7.50 children.

Located near the foot of the Pikes Peak Cog Railway, this popular comedy/drama dinner theater urges patrons to boo the villain and cheer the hero. Past productions have included *Farther North to Laughter or Buck of the Yukon, Part Two,* and *When the Halibut Start Running or Don't Slam the Door on Davy Jones' Locker.* A family-style dinner offers oven-baked chicken and barbecued ribs, mashed potatoes, green beans almondine, pineapple coleslaw, and buttermilk biscuits, with free seconds. The show is followed by a sing-along intermission and a vaudeville-style olio show. Iron Springs Chateau is open Tuesday through Saturday in summer, Friday and Saturday in winter, with dinner served between 6 and 7pm (you should arrive before 7pm); the show starts at 8:30pm.

10　Side Trips to Florissant Fossil Beds National Monument & Cripple Creek

FLORISSANT FOSSIL BEDS NATIONAL MONUMENT

Approximately 35 miles west of Colorado Springs on U.S. 24 is the small village of Florissant, which means "flowering" in French. It couldn't be more aptly named—every spring its hillsides are virtually ablaze with wildflowers. And just 2 miles south is one of the most spectacular, yet relatively unknown, fossil deposits in the world, Florissant Fossil Beds National Monument (from Florissant, follow the signs along Teller County Road 1).

The fossils in this 6,000-acre National Park Service property are preserved in the rocks of ancient Lake Florissant, which existed 34 million years ago. Volcanic eruptions spanning half a million years trapped plants and animals under layers of ash and dust; the creatures were fossilized as the sediment settled and became shale.

The detailed impressions, first discovered in 1871, offer the most extensive record of its kind in the world today. Thousands of specimens have been removed by scientists, including 1,100 separate species of insects. Dragonflies, beetles, and ants; more fossil butterflies than anywhere else in the world; plus spiders, fish, some mammals and birds are all perfectly preserved from 34 million years ago. Leaves from willows, maples, and hickories; extinct relatives of birches, elms, and beeches; and needles of pines and sequoias are also plentiful. These fossil plants, very different from those living in the area today, show how the climate has changed over the centuries.

Mud flows also buried forests during this long period of time, petrifying the trees where they stood. Nature trails pass petrified tree stumps; one sequoia stump is 10 feet in diameter and 11 feet high. There's a display of carbonized fossils at the visitor center, which also offers interpretive programs. An added attraction within the monument is the homestead of Adeline Hornbek, who pioneered the area with her children in 1878. The national monument also has some 14 miles of hiking trails.

Nearby, about a half mile north of the monument, there's superb fishing for German browns and cutthroats at Spinney Mountain Reservoir.

Admission to the monument is $2 per person, up to a maximum of $4 per family, making a visit here an incredibly affordable outing. It's open from 8am to 7pm daily from June to September; during the rest of the year, 8am to 4:30pm daily. It's closed New Year's Day, Thanksgiving, and Christmas. Contact Florissant Fossil Beds National Monument, P.O. Box 185, Florissant, CO 80816 (☎ 719/748-3253; www.nps.gov/flfo), for further information.

CRIPPLE CREEK

This old mining town on the southwestern flank of Pikes Peak was known as the world's greatest gold camp after the precious metal was first discovered here in 1890. During its heyday at the turn of the 20th century, Cripple Creek (elevation 9,494 feet) had a stock exchange, two opera houses, five daily newspapers, 16 churches, 19 schools, and 73 saloons, plus an elaborate streetcar system and a railroad depot that saw 18 arrivals and departures a day. By the time mining ceased in 1961, more than $800 million worth of ore had been taken from the surrounding hills.

Today, Cripple Creek has several dozen limited-stakes gambling casinos, most lining Bennett Avenue, cashing in not only on the lure of gambling but also on the nostalgia for the gambling houses that were once prominent throughout the Old West. Although gamblers must be at least 21 years old, some casinos offer special children's

Famous Native Sons

Lowell Thomas (journalist, author, lecturer, radio newscaster) began his career working as a paper boy for the Victor *Record*.

Jack Dempsey lived in Cripple Creek for a time, working as a miner by day and training as a boxer by night.

Groucho Marx delivered groceries for a while in Cripple Creek.

Bernard Baruch (financier) worked briefly as a telegraph operator in Cripple Creek.

areas, along with other family activities. Among the more interesting of the many casinos in town is the **Imperial Casino Hotel,** located at the corner of Third and Bennett (☎ **800/235-2922** or 719/689-7777; www.cripple-creek.co.us). Built in 1896 following a disastrous fire that razed most of the city, the fully renovated Imperial offers Victorian accommodations in a handsome historic building, a casino, and several restaurants and bars. The best-known bar is the Red Rooster, so called because of its international collection of roosters.

One of the town's unique attractions is a herd of wild donkeys, descendants of the miners' runaways, that roam freely through the hills and into the streets. The year's biggest celebration, **Donkey Derby Days** in late June, culminates with a donkey race.

Although gambling takes place year-round, many of the historic attractions are open in summer only, or have limited winter hours. Among those you'll want to check out is the **Mollie Kathleen Gold Mine,** one mile north of Cripple Creek on Colo. 67 (☎ **719/689-2466;** www.goldminetours.com), which offers visitors a rare chance to join hard-rock miners on a 1,000-foot underground descent into a genuine gold mine and take home an actual gold-ore specimen as a souvenir. The mine is open from 9am to 5pm daily year-round. The **Cripple Creek District Museum,** at the east end of Bennett Avenue (☎ **719/689-2634**), includes three historic buildings that are packed with turn-of-the-century relics, including mining and railroad memorabilia. There's a gold-ore exhibit, Victorian fashions and furniture, exhibits on local wildlife, historic photos, a fully restored Victorian-era flat, and an assay office where fire-testing of local ores took place. The museum is open daily from Memorial Day through September, and weekend afternoons the rest of the year.

The **Cripple Creek & Victor Narrow Gauge Railroad Co.,** at the Midland Terminal Depot, east end of Bennett Avenue (☎ **719/689-2640**), takes visitors on a 4-mile narrated tour past abandoned mines and over a reconstructed trestle to the ghost town of Anaconda. A 15-ton "iron horse" steam locomotive pulls the train out of the station approximately every 45 minutes beginning at 10am, from Memorial Day through early October.

Cripple Creek is located 45 miles west of Colorado Springs via U.S. 24 west and Colo. 67 south. For additional information, contact the **Cripple Creek Chamber of Commerce,** P.O. Box 650, Cripple Creek, CO 80813 (☎ **877/858-GOLD** or 719/689-2169). A good Internet resource is www.cripple-creek.com.

NEARBY SCENIC DRIVES

When you leave Cripple Creek, two drives of particular beauty offer alternatives to Colo. 67. Neither is paved and both are narrow and winding, but both are usually acceptable for everyday vehicles under dry conditions. Each is roughly 30 miles long but requires about 90 minutes to negotiate. First, take Colo. 67 south out of Cripple Creek for 6 miles to the historic mining town of **Victor,** a delightful and picturesque town that is worth a visit.

The **Gold Camp Road** leads east from Victor to Colorado Springs via the North Cheyenne Cañon. Teddy Roosevelt said that this trip up the old Short Line Railroad bed had "scenery that bankrupts the English language." The **Phantom Canyon Road** leads south from Victor to Florence, following another old narrow-gauge railroad bed known as the Gold Belt Line. A number of ghost towns and fossil areas mark this route.

11 A Side Trip to Royal Gorge

From Colorado Springs, it's an easy day trip to the breathtaking **Royal Gorge** and **Royal Gorge Frontier Town & Railway.** From the Springs, head southwest on Colo. 115 for about 33 miles, turn west for about 12 miles on U.S. 50 to Cañon City (about 45 miles altogether), and then south to the Royal Gorge.

The Royal Gorge, one of the most impressive natural attractions in the state, lies 8 miles west of Cañon City off U.S. 50, at the head of the Arkansas River valley.

This narrow canyon, 1,053 feet deep, was cut through solid granite by 3 million years of water and wind erosion. When Zebulon Pike saw the gorge in 1806, he predicted that man would never conquer it. But by 1877 the Denver & Rio Grande Railroad had laid a route through the canyon and it soon became a major tourist attraction.

The gorge is spanned by what is said to be the world's highest suspension bridge and an aerial tramway, built for no other reason than to thrill tourists. The quarter-mile-long bridge was constructed in 1929, suspended from two 300-ton cables, and reinforced in 1983. An incline railway, believed to be the world's steepest, was completed in 1931; it plunges from the rim of the gorge 1,550 feet to the floor at a 45° angle, giving passengers the view from the bottom as well as the top. Added in 1969, the 35-passenger tram provides views of the gorge and the bridge from a height of 1,178 feet above the Arkansas River.

Owned by Cañon City, the park also includes a 260-seat multimedia theater (where visitors can see a video presentation on the area's history and construction of the bridge), miniature railway, trolley, old-fashioned carousel, various children's attractions, restaurants, gift shops, and herds of tame mule deer. Live entertainment and a variety of special events are presented throughout the year.

The park is open year-round, daily from 8:30am to dusk. Admission—$14 for adults, $12 for children 4 to 11, free for children under 4—includes crossing the bridge and all other park attractions. For information, contact **Royal Gorge Bridge,** P.O. Box 549, Cañon City, CO 81215 (☎ **888/333-5597** or 719/275-7507; www. royalgorgebridge.com).

An interesting way to view the canyon is from the **Royal Gorge Route Railroad,** 401 Water St. (south of U.S. 50 on 3rd St.), Cañon City, CO 81212 (☎ **888/RAILS-4U** or 303/569-2403; www.royalgorgeroute.com). The train takes passengers on a 24-mile trip through the canyon that lasts two hours. From mid-May to early October, the train departs daily at 9am, noon, and 3pm; the rest of the year, there are trips departing at noon on Saturdays and Sundays only. Tickets cost $24.50 adult, $16.50 children 3 to 12, and free for children under 3 who sit on a guardian's lap.

To see this beautiful gorge looking up from the river, while also enjoying some thrills, consider a raft trip. Rates for adults run $80 to $90 for a full-day trip, including lunch;

a half-day trip is about $50. Most Royal Gorge raft trips include rough white-water stretches of the river, but those preferring calmer sections should inquire about such excursions with local rafting companies. Major outfitters include **Arkansas River Tours** (☎ 800/321-4352), **Echo Canyon River Expeditions** (☎ 800/748-2953), and **Wilderness Aware** (☎ 800/462-7238 or 719/395-2112). See also "River Rafting" under "Outdoor Activities," earlier in this chapter.

OTHER AREA ATTRACTIONS

Cañon City was a popular setting for making films during the industry's early days, and it was a special favorite of silent screen actor Tom Mix, who reputedly worked as a cowboy in the area before becoming a film star. The drowning death of a prominent actress temporarily discouraged film companies from coming here, but the area's beautiful scenery and Old West heritage lured the industry back in the late 1950s with the creation of Buckskin Joe, a western theme park and movie set where dozens of films have been shot, including *How the West Was Won, True Grit,* and *Cat Ballou.*

While movies are rarely shot here nowadays, **Buckskin Joe Frontier Town & Railway** (☎ 719/275-5149; www.buckskinjoes.com), located about 8 miles west of Cañon City on U.S. 50, remains a popular tourist attraction. The authentic-looking Old West town was created from genuine 19th-century buildings relocated from across the state. Visitors can watch gunfights, pan for gold, see a magic show, ride horseback (or in a horse-drawn trolley), and wander through a western maze. **The Scenic Railway** (☎ 719/275-5485) offers a 30-minute trip through rugged Royal Gorge country, where you're likely to see deer and other wildlife, to the rim of the Royal Gorge for a panoramic view of the canyon and bridge.

Frontier Town is open from May through September. Hours from Memorial Day to Labor Day are 9am to 6pm; call for hours at other times. The railway runs from March through December. Hours from Memorial Day to Labor Day are 8am to 8pm; call for hours at other times. Combination admission tickets, which include the Scenic Railway, horse-drawn trolley, and all the attractions and entertainment in Frontier Town, are $13 for adults, $11 for children 4 to 11, and free for children under 4. Separate tickets are also available.

Other Cañon City attractions include the **Colorado Territorial Prison Museum,** 201 N. First St. (☎ 719/269-3015; www.prisonmuseum.org). Housed in the state's former women's prison, just outside the walls of the original territorial prison that opened in 1871, the museum contains an actual gas chamber, historic photos of life behind bars, weapons confiscated from inmates, the last hangman's noose used legally in the state, a simulation of a lethal injection system, a simulation of the "Old Gray Mare" (a cruel apparatus used to punish misbehaving prisoners), and other artifacts and exhibits showing what prison life was like in the Old West and even into more modern times. There's also a gift shop selling arts and crafts made by inmates housed at a medium-security prison next door. The museum is open May through September, daily from 8:30am to 6pm; October through April, Friday through Sunday from 10am to 5pm. Admission is $5 for adults, $4 for seniors, $3 for children 6 to 12, and free for children 5 and under.

The **Cañon City Municipal Museum,** 612 Royal Gorge Blvd. (☎ 719/276-5279), displays American Indian artifacts, guns, gems, minerals, wild game trophies, historic photos, old dolls, pioneer household items, and other memorabilia. Behind the main museum building you'll find the renovated and authentically furnished 1860 log cabin built by Anson Rudd, local blacksmith and first warden of the Colorado Territorial Prison, plus the Rudd family's three-story stone house built in 1881, which contains a collection of Victorian furniture and western artifacts. The museum is open from early May through Labor Day, Tuesday through Sunday; the rest of the year, Tuesday through Saturday. Hours are 10am to 4pm. It's closed Christmas Eve plus all state and federal holidays. Admission is $1.50 for adults, $1 for children 6 to 12, and free for children 5 and under.

Another attraction that will fascinate kids of all ages is **Dinosaur Depot,** 330 Royal Gorge Blvd. (☎ **800/987-6379** or 719/269-7150; www.dinosaurdepot.com). Created jointly by Cañon City, the Bureau of Land Management, and the Denver Museum of Nature and Science, the featured exhibit here is the dinosaur lab, where experts are working to remove a stegosaurus skeleton from rock that has encased it for the last 150 million years. There are several other interpretive dinosaur exhibits, including fossilized bones that visitors can hold in their hands, as well as a gift shop. Dinosaur Depot also arranges tours of the internationally-renowned **Garden Park Fossil Area** just north of town, which is the source of many of the museum's exhibits. The museum is open daily, 9am to 5pm from June to September; and from 10am to 4pm Tuesday to Saturday during the rest of the year. Admission is $3 for adults, $1 for children ages 4 to 12, and free for children under 4. Tours of the Garden Park Fossil Area must be arranged in advance and cost $5 for adults, $2.50 for children 4 to 12, and free for children under 4. These tours are only available on Friday, Saturday, and Sunday.

There are several mid-priced lodging options in Cañon City, including the **Best Western Royal Gorge Motel,** 1925 Fremont Dr., Cañon City, CO 81212 (☎ **800/231-7317** or 719/275-3377) with double room rates ranging from $65 to $99; and **Cañon Inn,** 3075 E. U.S. 50, Cañon City, CO 81212 (☎ **800/525-7727** or 719/275-8676; www.canoninn.com), which features six indoor hot tubs, with rooms priced from $65 to $100 double. The **Barquero Restaurant** at the Cañon Inn (see address and phone number, above) features Mexican and American food (most entrees under $10) for dinner, opening at 5:30pm nightly. Another good dining option is **Merlino's Belvedere,** 1330 Elm Ave., Cañon City, CO 81212 (☎ **719/275-5558** or 800/625-2526; www.belvedererestaurant.com), which specializes in gourmet Italian and American cuisine and seafood (dinner main courses run from $8 to $21) and is open daily.

For more information on where to stay and eat, a walking tour of historic downtown Cañon City, and details on scenic drives and other attractions, contact the **Cañon City Chamber of Commerce,** 403 Royal Gorge Blvd., Cañon City, CO 81215 (☎ **800/ 876-7922** or 719/275-2331; www.canoncitychamber.com).

Appendix: Denver, Boulder & Colorado Springs in Depth

1 History 101

To explore Colorado today is to step into its past, from its dinosaur graveyards and impressive stone and clay cities of the Ancestral Puebloan people (also called the Anasazi), to reminders of the Wild West of Bat Masterson and Doc Holliday and elegant Victorian mansions. The history of Colorado is a testimony to the human ability to adapt and flourish in a difficult environment, and this land of high mountains and limited water continues to challenge its inhabitants today.

The earliest people in Colorado are believed to have been nomadic hunters who arrived some 12,000 to 20,000 years ago via the Bering Strait, following the tracks of the now-extinct woolly mammoth and bison. Then, about 2,000 years ago, the people we call the Ancestral Puebloans arrived, living in shallow caves in the Four Corners area, where the borders of Colorado, Utah, Arizona, and New Mexico meet.

These hunters gradually learned farming and basket making; then pottery making and the construction of pit houses—basically large underground pots. Eventually they built complex villages, such as can be seen at Mesa Verde National Park. For some unknown reason, possibly drought, they deserted the area around the end of the 13th century, probably moving southward into present-day New Mexico and Arizona.

Although the Ancestral Puebloans were gone by the time the Spanish conquistadors arrived in the mid–16th century, in their place were two major nomadic cultures: the mountain dwellers of the west, primarily Ute; and the plains tribes of the east, principally Arapaho, Cheyenne, and Comanche.

Spanish colonists, having established settlements at Santa Fe, Taos, and other upper Rio Grande locations in the 16th and 17th centuries, didn't immediately find southern Colorado attractive for colonization. Not only was there a lack of financial and military support from the Spanish crown, but the freedom-loving, sometimes fierce Comanche and Ute also made it clear that they would rather be left alone.

Nevertheless, Spain still held title to southern and western Colorado in 1803, when U.S. President Thomas Jefferson paid $15 million for the vast Louisiana Territory, which included the lion's share of modern Colorado. Two years later the Lewis and Clark expedition passed by, but the first official exploration by the U.S. government occurred

Dateline

- **12,000 B.C.** First inhabitants include Folsom Man.
- **3000 B.C.** Prehistoric farming communities appear.
- **A.D. 1000** Ancestral Puebloan cliff-dweller culture peaks in Four Corners region.
- **Late 1500s** Spanish explore upper Rio Grande Valley, colonize Santa Fe and Taos, New Mexico, and make forays into what is now southern Colorado.
- **1803** The Louisiana Purchase includes most of modern Colorado.
- **1805** The Lewis and Clark expedition sights the Rocky Mountains.
- **1806–07** Capt. Zebulon Pike leads first U.S. expedition into the Colorado Rockies.
- **1822** William Becknell establishes the Santa Fe Trail.
- **1842–44** Lieutenant John C. Frémont and Kit Carson explore Colorado and American West.
- **1848** Treaty of Guadalupe Hidalgo ends Mexican War, adds American Southwest to the United States.
- **1858** Gold discovered in modern Denver.
- **1859** General William Larimer founds Denver. Major gold strikes in nearby Rockies.
- **1861** Colorado Territory proclaimed.
- **1862** Colorado cavalry wins major Civil War battle at Glorietta Pass, New Mexico. Homestead Act is passed.
- **1863–68** Ute tribe obtains treaties guaranteeing 16 million acres of western Colorado land.
- **1864** Hundreds of Cheyenne killed in Sand Creek Massacre. University of Denver becomes Colorado's first

continues

when Jefferson sent Capt. Zebulon Pike to the territory. Pikes Peak, Colorado's landmark mountain and a op tourist attraction near Colorado Springs, was named for the explorer.

As the West began to open up in the 1820s, the Santa Fe Trail was established, cutting through Colorado's southeast corner. Much of eastern Colorado, including what would become Denver, Boulder, and Colorado Springs, was then part of the Kansas Territory. It was populated almost exclusively by plains tribes until 1858, when gold-seekers discovered flakes of the precious metal near the junction of Cherry Creek and the South Platte, and the city of Denver was established, named for Kansas governor James Denver.

The Cherry Creek strike was literally a flash in the gold-seeker's pan, but two strikes in the mountains just west of Denver in early 1859 were more significant: one at Clear Creek, near what would become Idaho Springs, and another in a quartz vein at Gregory Gulch, which led to the founding of Central City. The race to Colorado's gold fields had begun.

Abraham Lincoln was elected president of the United States in November 1860, and Congress created the Colorado Territory 3 months later. The new territory absorbed neighboring sections from Utah, Nebraska, and New Mexico to form the boundaries that comprise the state today. Lincoln's Homestead Act of 1862 brought much of the public domain into private ownership and led to the plotting of Front Range townships, starting with Denver in 1861.

Controlling the American Indian peoples was a priority of the territorial government. A treaty negotiated in 1851 had guaranteed the entire Pikes Peak region to the nomadic plains tribes, but that had been made moot by the arrival of settlers in the late 1850s. The Fort Wise Treaty of 1861 exchanged the Pikes Peak territory for 5 million fertile acres of Arkansas Valley land, north of modern La Junta. But when the Arapaho and Cheyenne continued to roam their old hunting grounds, conflict became inevitable. Frequent rumors and rare instances of hostility against settlers led the Colorado cavalry to attack a peaceful settlement of Indians—who were flying Old Glory and a white flag—on November 29, 1864. More than 150 Cheyenne and Arapaho, two-thirds of them women and children, were killed in what has become known as the Sand Creek Massacre.

Vowing revenge, the Cheyenne and Arapaho launched a campaign to drive whites from their ancient hunting grounds. Their biggest triumph was the destruction of the northeast Colorado town of Julesburg in 1865, but the cavalry, bolstered by returning Civil War veterans, managed to force the two tribes onto reservations in Indian Territory in what is now Oklahoma—a barren area that whites thought they would never want.

Also in 1865, a smelter was built in Black Hawk, just west of Denver, setting the stage for the large-scale spread of mining throughout Colorado in years to come. When the first transcontinental railroad was completed in 1869, the Union Pacific went through Cheyenne, Wyoming, 100 miles north of Denver, but 4 years later the line was linked to Denver by the Kansas City–Denver Railroad.

Colorado politicians had begun pressing for statehood during the Civil War, but it wasn't until August 1, 1876, that Colorado became the 38th state. Because this occurred less than a month after the 100th birthday of the United States, Colorado became known as the Centennial State.

The state's new constitution gave the vote to blacks, but not to women, despite the strong efforts of the Colorado Women's Suffrage Association. In 1893, women finally succeeded in winning the vote, 3 years after Wyoming became the first state to offer universal suffrage.

At the time of statehood, most of Colorado's vast western region was still occupied by some 3,500 mountain and plateau dwellers of a half-dozen Ute tribes. Unlike the plains tribes, their early relations with white explorers and settlers had been peaceful. Chief Ouray, leader of the Uncompahgre Utes, had negotiated treaties in 1863 and 1868 that guaranteed them 16 million acres—most of western Colorado. In 1873, Ouray agreed to sell the United States one-fourth of that acreage in the mineral-rich San Juan Mountains in exchange for hunting rights and $25,000 in annuities.

But a mining boom that began in 1878 led to a flurry of intrusions into Ute territory and stirred up a "Utes Must Go!" sentiment. Two years later the Utes were forced onto small reserves in southwestern Colorado and Utah, and their lands opened to white settlement in 1882.

institution of higher education.

- **1870** Kansas City–Denver rail line completed. Agricultural commune of Greeley established by Nathan Meeker. Colorado State University opens in Fort Collins.
- **1871** General William Palmer founds Colorado Springs.
- **1876** Colorado becomes 38th state.
- **1877** University of Colorado opens in Boulder.
- **1878** Little Pittsburg silver strike launches Leadville mining boom, Colorado's greatest.
- **1879** Milk Creek Massacre by Ute warriors leads to tribe's removal to reservations.
- **1890** Sherman Silver Purchase Act boosts price of silver. Gold discovered at Cripple Creek, leading to state's biggest gold rush.
- **1893** Women win right to vote. Silver industry collapses following repeal of Sherman Silver Purchase Act.
- **1901–07** President Theodore Roosevelt sets aside 16 million acres of national forest land in Colorado.
- **1906** U.S. Mint built in Denver.
- **1913** Wolf Creek Pass highway is first to cross Continental Divide in Colorado.
- **1915** Rocky Mountain National Park established.
- **1934** Direct Denver–San Francisco rail travel begins. Taylor Grazing Act ends homesteading.
- **1941–45** World War II establishes Colorado as military center.
- **1947** Aspen's first chairlift begins operation.

continues

- **1948–58** Uranium "rush" sweeps western slope.
- **1955** Environmentalists prevent construction of Echo Park Dam in Dinosaur National Monument.
- **1967** Colorado legalizes medically necessary abortions.
- **1988** Senator Gary Hart, a front-runner for the Democratic presidential nomination, withdraws from race after a scandal.
- **1992** Colorado voters approve a controversial state constitutional amendment barring any measures to protect homosexuals from discrimination.
- **1993** Denver becomes 15th U.S. city with three major professional sports teams by adding the Rockies, a new major-league baseball franchise.
- **1995** The $4.2-billion state-of-the-art Denver International Airport and $2.16-million Coors Field baseball stadium open. Denver goes sports-crazy with its fourth major professional sports team, the Avalanche, a member of the National Hockey League.
- **1996** The U.S. Supreme Court strikes down Colorado's 1992 constitutional amendment, stating that it could prevent homosexuals from enjoying basic constitutional rights granted to all Americans.
- **1996** The Avalanche win the Stanley Cup, giving Colorado its first championship in any major league.
- **1997** Weather wreaks havoc across the state. First, a summer rainstorm turns a small creek that runs through Fort Collins into a roaring river. Then, in late October, a 24-hour blizzard, the worst October storm in Denver since 1923, virtually

continues

Colorado's real mining boom began on April 28, 1878, when August Rische and George Hook hit a vein of silver carbonate 27 feet deep on Fryer Hill in Leadville. Perhaps the strike wouldn't have caused such excitement had not Rische and Hook, 8 days earlier, traded one-third interest in whatever they found for a basket of groceries from storekeeper Horace Tabor, the mayor of Leadville and a sharp businessman. Tabor was well acquainted with the Colorado "law of apex," which said that if an ore-bearing vein surfaced on a man's claim, he could follow it wherever it led, even out of his claim and through the claims of others.

Tabor, a legend in Colorado, typifies the rags-to-riches success story of a common working-class man. A native of Vermont, he mortgaged his Kansas homestead in 1859 and moved west to the mountains, where he was a postmaster and storekeeper in several towns before moving to Leadville. He was 46 when the silver strike was made. By age 50, he was the state's richest man and its Republican lieutenant governor. His love affair with and marriage to Elizabeth "Baby Doe" McCourt, a young divorcée for whom he left his wife, Augusta, was a national scandal that became the subject of numerous books and even an opera.

Although the silver market collapsed in 1893, gold was there to take its place. In the fall of 1890, a cowboy named Bob Womack found gold in Cripple Creek, on the southwestern slope of Pikes Peak, west of Colorado Springs. He sold his claim to Winfield Scott Stratton, a carpenter and amateur geologist, and Stratton's mine earned a tidy profit of $6 million by 1899, when he sold it to an English company for another $11 million. Cripple Creek turned out to be the richest gold field ever discovered, ultimately producing $500 million in gold.

Unlike the flamboyant Tabor, Stratton was an introvert and a neurotic. His fortune was twice the size of Tabor's, and it grew daily as the deflation of silver's value boosted that of gold. But he invested most of it back in Cripple Creek, searching for a fabulous mother lode that he never found. By the early 1900s, the price of gold, like silver, began to be driven down by overproduction.

Another turning point for Colorado occurred just after the beginning of the 20th century. Theodore Roosevelt had visited the state in September 1900 as the Republican vice-presidential nominee. Soon after he acceded to the presidency in September 1901 (following the assassination of President McKinley), he began to declare large chunks of the Rockies as forest reserves. By 1907, when an act of Congress forbade the president from creating any new reserves by proclamation, nearly one-fourth of Colorado was national forest land—16 million acres in 18 forests. Another project that reached fruition during the Roosevelt administration was the establishment in 1906 of Mesa Verde National Park, in the state's southwest corner.

Tourism grew hand-in-hand with the setting aside of public lands. Easterners had been visiting Colorado since the 1870s, when General William J. Palmer founded a Colorado Springs resort and made the mountains accessible via his Denver & Rio Grande Railroad.

Estes Park, northwest of Boulder, was among the first resort towns to emerge in the 20th century, spurred by a visit in 1903 by Freelan Stanley. With his brother Francis, Freelan had invented the Stanley Steamer, a steam-powered automobile, in Boston in 1899. Freelan Stanley shipped one of his steamers to Denver and drove the 40 miles to Estes Park in less than 2 hours, a remarkable speed for the day. Finding the climate conducive to his recovery from tuberculosis, he returned in 1907 with a dozen Stanley Steamers and established a shuttle service from Denver to Estes Park. Two years later he built the luxurious Stanley Hotel, still a hilltop landmark today.

- shuts down Interstate 25 from Wyoming to New Mexico and strands thousands at Denver International Airport.
- **1997** Gary Lee Davis, convicted of the 1986 abduction and murder of a Colorado farm wife, is executed by lethal injection, the state's first execution in 30 years.
- **1998** The Denver Broncos win the Super Bowl, defeating the Green Bay Packers. The stunning victory saves the Broncos the indignity of becoming the first team to lose five Super Bowls.
- **1999** The Broncos win the Super Bowl again, this time defeating the Atlanta Falcons.
- **1999** The worst school shooting in United States history takes place in suburban Denver inside Columbine high school, with 13 killed.
- **2000** Colorado ski resorts reported that the 1999–2000 season was the worst in history due to poor snowfall and potential skiers' fears about Y2K problems.

Stanley developed a friendship with Enos Mills, a young innkeeper whose property was more a workshop for students of wildlife than a business. A devotee of conservationist John Muir, Mills believed tourists should spend their Colorado vacations in the natural environment, camping and hiking. As Mills gained national stature as a nature writer, photographer, and lecturer, he urged that the national forest land around Longs Peak, outside Estes Park, be designated a national park. In January 1915, the 400-square-mile Rocky Mountain National Park was created by President Woodrow Wilson, and today it is one of America's leading tourist attractions, with more than 3 million visitors each year.

The 1920s saw the growth of highways and the completion of the Moffat Tunnel, a 6.2-mile passageway beneath the Continental Divide that in 1934

Impressions

I spent a night in a silver mine. I dined with the men down there . . . .
Poems every one of them. A complete democracy underground. I find people less rough and coarse in such places. There is no chance for roughness. The revolver is their book of etiquette.

—Oscar Wilde, quoted in the *Morning Herald* (1882)

led to the long-sought direct Denver–San Francisco rail connection. Of more tragic note was the worst flood in Colorado history. The city of Pueblo, south of Colorado Springs, was devastated when the Arkansas River overflowed its banks on June 1, 1921; 100 people were killed, and the damage exceeded $16 million. The Great Depression of the 1930s was a difficult time for many Coloradans, but it had positive consequences. The federal government raised the price of gold from $20 to $35 an ounce, reviving Cripple Creek and other stagnant mining towns.

World War II and the subsequent Cold War were responsible for many of the defense installations that are now an integral part of the Colorado economy, particularly in the Colorado Springs area. The war also indirectly caused the other single greatest boon to Colorado's late-20th-century economy: the ski industry. Soldiers in the 10th Mountain Division, on leave from Camp Hale before heading off to fight in Europe, often crossed Independence Pass to relax in the lower altitude and milder climate of the 19th-century silver-mining village of Aspen. They tested their skiing skills, which they would need in the Italian Alps, against the slopes of Ajax Mountain.

In 1945, Walter and Elizabeth Paepcke—he the founder of the Container Corporation of America, she an ardent conservationist—moved to Aspen and established the Aspen Company as a property investment firm. Skiing was already popular in New England and the Midwest, but had few devotees in the Rockies. Paepcke bought a 3-mile chairlift, the longest and fastest in the world at the time, and had it ready for operation by January 1947. Soon, Easterners and Europeans were flocking to Aspen—and the rest is ski history.

The war also resulted in the overnight creation of what became at the time Colorado's 10th largest city—Amache, located in the southeastern part of the state. Immediately after the bombing of Pearl Harbor, the U.S. government began rounding up Americans of Japanese ancestry and putting them in internment camps, supposedly because the U.S. government feared they would side with the Japanese government against the United States. Although there was a great deal of prejudice against those of Japanese ancestry throughout the United States at the time, Colorado Governor Ralph Carr came to their defense, stating, "They are loyal Americans, sharing only race with the enemy." He welcomed them to the state and authorized the Amache Relocation Center, which at its peak had a population of more than 7,500. Amache was much like other Colorado towns of the time, with a school, post office, hospital, and even its own government, although its residents did not have the freedom to travel.

Colorado continued its steady growth in the 1950s, aided by tourism and the federal government. The $200-million U.S. Air Force Academy, authorized by Congress in 1954 and opened to cadets in 1958, is Colorado Springs's top tourist attraction today. There was a brief oil boom in the 1970s, followed by increasing high-tech development and even more tourism. Colorado made national news in 1967 when it became the first state to legalize abortions, allowing medically necessary abortions with unanimous approval of a panel of three doctors.

Weapons plants, which had seemed like a good idea when they were constructed during World War II, began to haunt Denver and the state in the 1970s and 1980s. Rocky Mountain Arsenal, originally built to produce chemical weapons, was found to be creating hazardous conditions at home by contaminating the land with deadly chemicals. A massive cleanup was begun in the early 1980s, and by the 1990s the arsenal was well on its way to accomplishing its goal of converting the 27-square-mile site into a national wildlife refuge.

The story of Rocky Flats, a postwar nuclear weapons facility spurred on by the Cold War, is not so happy. Massive efforts to figure out what to do about contamination caused by nuclear waste have been largely unsuccessful. Although state and federal officials announced early in 1996 that they had reached agreement on the means of removing some 14 tons of plutonium, their immediate plan calls for keeping it in Denver until at least the year 2010, and Department of Energy officials don't know what they'll do with it then. In the meantime, plans are under way to build storage containers that will safely hold the plutonium for up to 50 years.

In 1992, Colorado voters approved a controversial state constitutional amendment that would bar any legal measure that specifically protected homosexuals. The amendment would have nullified existing gay-rights ordinances in Denver, Boulder, and elsewhere. Enforcement was postponed pending judicial review, and in the meantime, gay-rights activists urged tourists to boycott Colorado. (Tourism did decline somewhat, although many Colorado ski resorts posted record seasons.) Then, in May 1996, the U.S. Supreme Court struck down the measure in a 6-to-3 vote, saying that, if enforced, it would have denied homosexuals constitutional protection from discrimination in housing, employment, and public accommodations.

On April 20, 1999, in a suburb of Denver, two students shook the city, state, and nation when they went on a shooting spree through Columbine high school. They killed 13 students before turning their guns on themselves in the worst school shooting in the nation's history.

As the state enters the 21st century, attention has turned to controlling population growth. With a growth rate of nearly twice the national average, both residents and government leaders question how this unabated influx of outsiders can continue without causing serious harm to the state's air, water, and general quality of life.

2 Denver, Boulder & Colorado Springs Today

Today, Colorado's major cities retain much of the casual atmosphere that has made them popular through the years, both with tourists and transplants. Many of those moving to Colorado's cities are fleeing the pollution, crime, and crowding of the East and West coasts, and some native and long-term Coloradans have begun to complain that these newcomers are bringing with them the very problems they sought to escape.

There is also a growing effort in Colorado to limit, or at least control, tourism. For instance, in 1995, just as the ski season was winding down, town officials in the skier's mecca of Vail reached an agreement with resort management to limit the number of skiers on the mountain and alleviate other aspects of overcrowding in the village. The word now from Vail and other high-profile Colorado tourist destinations is that visitors will be given incentives, such as discounts, to visit at off-peak times. Ski area officials have not ruled out the prospect of turning away skiers after a set number of passes have been sold.

Several years ago, Colorado voters approved a measure that effectively eliminated state funding for tourism promotion. That resulted in the creation of the Colorado Tourism Authority, funded by the tourism industry, but debate continues over whether or not state government should take a more active role. Those in the tourism industry who run small businesses or are located away from the major attractions say they have been hurt by the lack of state promotion, whereas others insist that government assistance for one specific industry is inappropriate and argue that the tourism industry is doing very well on its own—too well in some areas.

One particular problem is the increasingly popular Rocky Mountain National Park, which is not only attracting increasing numbers of out-of-state visitors, but also becoming a popular day trip for residents of the fast-growing Front Range cities of Denver, Boulder, Colorado Springs, and Fort Collins. During the summer park roads are packed and parking lots full to overflowing, and in autumn, during the elk-rutting season, hundreds of people make their way to the Moraine Park and Horseshoe Park areas each evening. National park officials say that motor vehicle noise is starting to have a negative effect on the experience, and disappointed visitors are asking where they can go to find serenity. A limited shuttle system has been put into effect in one of the busier areas of the park, and park officials have begun studying ways to expand public transportation in the park, possibly by creating parking areas outside the park where day visitors could leave their vehicles and hop a shuttle.

3 Colorado's Natural Landscape

First-time visitors to Colorado's Front Range are often awed by the looming wall of the Rocky Mountains, which come into sight a good 100 miles away, soon after you cross the border from Kansas. East of the Rockies, a 5,000-foot peak is considered high—yet Colorado has 1,143 mountains above 10,000 feet, including 53 over 14,000 feet! Mount Elbert, which is southwest of Leadville, is the highest of all at 14,433 feet.

The Rockies were formed some 65 million years ago by pressures that forced hard Precambrian rock to break through the earth's surface and push layers of earlier rock up on end. Millions of years of erosion then eliminated the soft surface material, producing the magnificent Rockies of calendar fame.

An almost perfect rectangle, Colorado measures some 385 miles east to west, and 275 miles north to south. The ridge of the Continental Divide zigzags more or less through the center of the 104,247-square-mile state, eighth largest in the nation.

You can visualize Colorado's basic topography by dividing the state into vertical thirds: The eastern part is plains; the midsection is high mountains; and the western third is mesa.

That's a broad simplification, of course. The central Rockies, though they cover six times the mountain area of Switzerland, are not a single vast highland but are composed of a series of high ranges running roughly north to south. East of the Continental Divide, the primary river systems are the South Platte, Arkansas, and Rio Grande, all flowing toward the Gulf of Mexico. The westward-flowing Colorado River system dominates the western part of the state, with tributary networks including the Gunnison, Dolores, and Yampa-Green rivers. In most cases, these rivers are not broad bodies of water such as the Ohio or Columbia, but streams, heavy with spring and summer snowmelt, that are reduced to mere trickles during much of the year by the demands of farm and ranch irrigation. Besides agricultural use, these rivers provide necessary water to wildlife and offer wonderful opportunities for rafting, fishing, swimming, water-skiing, and sailboarding.

The forested mountains are essential in that they retain precious water for the lowlands. Eleven national forests comprise 15 million acres of land, with an additional 8 million acres controlled by the Bureau of Land Management, also open for public recreation. Another half-million acres are within national parks, monuments, and recreation areas under the administration of the National Park Service. In addition to all this, the state operates more than 40 state parks, including about 10 within an hour's drive of Denver, Boulder, or Colorado Springs.

Colorado's name, Spanish for "red," derives from the state's red soil and rocks. Some of the sandstone agglomerates have become attractions in their own right, such as Red Rocks Amphitheatre west of Denver and the startling Garden of the Gods in Colorado Springs.

Of Colorado's almost 4 million people, some 80% live along the Front Range, the I-25 corridor, where the plains meet the mountains. Denver, the state capital, has a population of about half a million, with almost 2 million in the metropolitan area. Colorado Springs has the second largest population, with almost 400,000 residents, followed by Pueblo (99,000) and Boulder (84,000).

4 Recommended Books & Videos

Those planning vacations in Denver, Boulder, and Colorado Springs and the nearby mountains can turn to a number of sources for background on the state and its major cities. A good place to start is the short, easy-to-read *Colorado: A History* (New York: W. W. Norton, 1984), by Marshall Sprague. Those who enjoy long novels will want to get their hands on a copy of James Michener's 1,000-page *Centennial* (New York: Random House, 1974). For in-depth information on Denver, try Thomas J. Noel's *Denver: Rocky Mountain Gold* (Tulsa: Continental Heritage Press, 1980); and those interested in finding wildlife, even in the cities, will likely be successful with some help from the *Colorado Wildlife Viewing Guide* (Helena, Mont.: Falcon, 1992), by Mary Taylor Gray.

An excellent video introduction to the state is *Explore Colorado,* a 55-minute video tour that touches on most of the state's scenic and historic highlights. Those planning to visit Colorado Springs will enjoy *Pikes Peak Country;* and the video *Rocky Mountain National Park* gives potential visitors a glimpse of that park's wondrous scenery before they leave home. Videos, in both VHS and PAL formats, can be obtained from **Interpark,** 1540 E. MacArthur St., Cortez, CO 81321 (☎ **800/687-5967** or 970/565-7453; www.petroglyphtrail.com).

Index

See also Accommodations and Restaurant indexes, below.

General Index

Restaurant Indexes

FROMMER'S® COMPLETE TRAVEL GUIDES

Alaska
Amsterdam
Arizona
Atlanta
Australia
Austria
Bahamas
Barcelona, Madrid &
  Seville
Beijing
Belgium, Holland &
  Luxembourg
Bermuda
Boston
British Columbia & the
  Canadian Rockies
Budapest & the Best of
  Hungary
California
Canada
Cancún, Cozumel &
  the Yucatán
Cape Cod, Nantucket &
  Martha's Vineyard
Caribbean
Caribbean Cruises & Ports
  of Call
Caribbean Ports of Call
Carolinas & Georgia
Chicago
China
Colorado
Costa Rica
Denmark
Denver, Boulder & Colorado
  Springs
England
Europe

European Cruises & Ports
  of Call
Florida
France
Germany
Greece
Greek Islands
Hawaii
Hong Kong
Honolulu, Waikiki & Oahu
Ireland
Israel
Italy
Jamaica
Japan
Las Vegas
London
Los Angeles
Maryland & Delaware
Maui
Mexico
Montana & Wyoming
Montréal & Québec City
Munich & the Bavarian
  Alps
Nashville & Memphis
Nepal
New England
New Mexico
New Orleans
New York City
New Zealand
Nova Scotia, New Brunswick
  & Prince Edward Island
Oregon
Paris
Philadelphia & the
  Amish Country

Portugal
Prague & the Best of the
  Czech Republic
Provence & the Riviera
Puerto Rico
Rome
San Antonio & Austin
San Diego
San Francisco
Santa Fe, Taos & Albuquerque
Scandinavia
Scotland
Seattle & Portland
Shanghai
Singapore & Malaysia
South Africa
Southeast Asia
South Florida
South Pacific
Spain
Sweden
Switzerland
Thailand
Tokyo
Toronto
Tuscany & Umbria
USA
Utah
Vancouver & Victoria
Vermont, New Hampshire
  & Maine
Vienna & the Danube Valley
Virgin Islands
Virginia
Walt Disney World &
  Orlando
Washington, D.C.
Washington State

FROMMER'S® DOLLAR-A-DAY GUIDES

Australia from $50 a Day
California from $60 a Day
Caribbean from $70 a Day
England from $70 a Day
Europe from $70 a Day

Florida from $70 a Day
Hawaii from $70 a Day
Ireland from $60 a Day
Italy from $70 a Day
London from $85 a Day

New York from $80 a Day
Paris from $80 a Day
San Francisco from $60 a Day
Washington, D.C.,
  from $70 a Day

FROMMER'S® PORTABLE GUIDES

Acapulco, Ixtapa &
  Zihuatanejo
Alaska Cruises & Ports of Call
Bahamas
Baja & Los Cabos
Berlin
California Wine Country
Charleston & Savannah
Chicago
Dublin

Hawaii: The Big Island
Las Vegas
London
Los Angeles
Maine Coast
Maui
Miami
New Orleans
New York City
Paris

Puerto Vallarta, Manzanillo
  & Guadalajara
San Diego
San Francisco
Sydney
Tampa & St. Petersburg
Venice
Washington, D.C.

FROMMER'S® NATIONAL PARK GUIDES

Family Vacations in the
  National Parks
Grand Canyon

National Parks of the
  American West
Rocky Mountain

Yellowstone & Grand Teton
Yosemite & Sequoia/
  Kings Canyon
Zion & Bryce Canyon

FROMMER'S® MEMORABLE WALKS

Chicago
London

New York
Paris

San Francisco
Washington, D.C.

FROMMER'S® GREAT OUTDOOR GUIDES

New England
Northern California

Southern California & Baja
Southern New England

Washington & Oregon

FROMMER'S® BORN TO SHOP GUIDES

Born to Shop: France
Born to Shop: Italy

Born to Shop: London
Born to Shop: New York

Born to Shop: Paris

FROMMER'S® IRREVERENT GUIDES

Amsterdam
Boston
Chicago
Las Vegas

London
Los Angeles
Manhattan
New Orleans

Paris
San Francisco
Seattle & Portland
Vancouver

Walt Disney World
Washington, D.C.

FROMMER'S® BEST-LOVED DRIVING TOURS

America
Britain
California

Florida
France
Germany

Ireland
Italy
New England

Scotland
Spain
Western Europe

THE UNOFFICIAL GUIDES®

Bed & Breakfasts in
  California
Bed & Breakfasts in
  New England
Bed & Breakfasts in
  the Northwest
Bed & Breakfasts in
  Southeast
Beyond Disney
Branson, Missouri

California with Kids
Chicago
Cruises
Disneyland
Florida with Kids
Golf Vacations in the
  Eastern U.S.
The Great Smoky &
  Blue Ridge
  Mountains

Inside Disney
Hawaii
Las Vegas
London
Miami & the Keys
Mini Las Vegas
Mini-Mickey
New Orleans
New York City
Paris

San Francisco
Skiing in the West
Southeast with Kids
Walt Disney World
Walt Disney World
  for Grown-ups
Walt Disney World
  for Kids
Washington, D.C.

SPECIAL-INTEREST TITLES

Frommer's Britain's Best Bed & Breakfasts and
  Country Inns
Frommer's Britain's Best Bike Rides
The Civil War Trust's Official Guide
  to the Civil War Discovery Trail
Frommer's Caribbean Hideaways
Frommer's Adventure Guide to Central America
Frommer's Adventure Guide to South America
Frommer's Adventure Guide to Southeast Asia
Frommer's Food Lover's Companion to France
Frommer's Gay & Lesbian Europe
Frommer's Exploring America by RV
Hanging Out in Europe

Israel Past & Present
Mad Monks' Guide to California
Mad Monks' Guide to New York City
Frommer's The Moon
Frommer's New York City with Kids
The New York Times' Unforgettable
  Weekends
Places Rated Almanac
Retirement Places Rated
Frommer's Road Atlas Britain
Frommer's Road Atlas Europe
Frommer's Washington, D.C., with Kids
Frommer's What the Airlines Never Tell You